Being Different

ENCOUNTERS OF GOD'S GRACE AND LIFE LESSONS
FROM MY 40-YEAR MODERN WILDERNESS JOURNEY

MoDee

CONTENTS

DEDICATION

I dedicate this book to God Almighty, who saved me through the Lord Jesus Christ. Knowing God through the help of His Holy Spirit has been the best thing I could ever have been gifted. My life has been a rollercoaster. Sometimes I was not sure how I was ever going to make it through the day (if I did at all), and just when I think *This is it*, He shows up strong and mighty.

You formed me in my mother's womb and set me apart for Your glory. Otherwise, when life has happened, I would not have been able to make it through, let alone have "victory stories" to share with the world. I will forever praise You—my Redeemer, Guide, and deepest Love.

I am forever grateful to God for the family He placed me in. The love I have and enjoy from my parents is comparable to none from any other human being. They taught me to know God for me, to grow into and "always be me," and to be respectful of others. They have stood by me irrespective of the circumstances. As I reflect on these past forty years, I realise that to have such loving parents, who sacrifice all within their reach to give me (and our siblings) a great head start in life and who always lead by example, is a rare gift and a huge blessing from God. My dad's love for me was evident and incomparable to anything a human can provide—I will cherish his memory as long as I live.

Dad and Mum, you both have truly been the leg-ends upon which I stand and always rise tall. Thank you for everything from the depths of my being.

I also thank God for my siblings. I will always respect the memory of my two older brothers, Táíwò and Kẹ́hìndé.

Although your time on earth was brief, you made a huge impression on our parents, and the benefits of which I (and siblings) have enjoyed. Your birthday is fondly remembered because you both were special. Someday, we will meet at God's side, where I know you both are.

To my three living and younger brothers, *I always thank God for each of your lives and families. Although we are often miles apart, I take each of you everywhere I go, trusting in the love that we have for one another. You make it fun to be your sister, the only one with this rare honour and privilege. I certainly wouldn't trade any of you for anything in the whole wide world!*

Lastly, I will cherish the memories of my maternal and paternal grandparents. The stories of your lives are ones of heroism, dedication, perseverance, wisdom, justice, and love for both your family and the people you came in contact with. Your legacy lives on.

My immediate family

Mum with twin brothers

INTRODUCTION

"Where do I start?" That is perhaps the most common thought of every writer, especially when the story is about you. How much to say without boring the audience can be a difficult balance to attain, but the cost of saying nothing far outweighs the risk of saying "too much." So here I am, finally.

Previous opportunities for sharing snippets of some stories in this book with varying groups of people across all ages over the years have contributed to the conviction to write them down. This is not because I have the most stories to tell or the most precarious experiences, but because of the lessons I have drawn from them—I have found that to be the point of interest to listeners. So, this book is an opportunity to share with you too, lessons drawn from my life experiences—the good, the bad, and the not-so-pretty. And this is probably the juncture to mention that the unfathomable depths of Christ's love, peace, and grace, are also at the core of the stories being shared.

One of the common sayings that I remember challenging, as a debater at primary age, was "Experience is the best teacher." My recollection of the key point in my debate argument was that though the statement might be true, it is not entirely true in the light of how it is often interpreted. Most people assume one can only effectively learn when the experience is personal. Yet, how often have you seen the same person make the same mistake over and over again? Why have their experiences not taught them to do things differently? Whereas the body of knowledge in the world today is a build-up of experiences from various people throughout history—meaning, we are all capable of learning from other people's experiences. After many years of accumulated experiences, I still hold that viewpoint because it has proven beneficial.

Though I have made several mistakes of my own along the way, there are many more I might have made had I not learnt a few things from others—through observation, reading articles or books on their experience, etc. These people, too numerous to mention and relevant in various areas of life, have been the leg-ends on which I have stood, and still stand. It therefore feels right to share my experiences and, perhaps, contribute to the improvement of some other person's life.

My love for problem solving was awakened about age six. I recall returning home from school and feeling very miserable. Normally after school, I had the choice of doing my homework, having a nap, or going out to play—in whatever order I chose, alongside lunch, in the four or so hours between getting back from school and about 7:00 p.m., dinner time (when it would be getting dark outside). I knew to do my homework first because my dad didn't quite tolerate playing when I still had schoolwork to do that probably needed turning in the next day. It was a "work first and play later" kind of principle. The only allowed reasons for not completing homework before playing were that the day was either a Friday and I would make time to do it over the weekend or I was struggling with it and needed support. With the latter, I had to attempt it by myself so as to identify the area you needed help with. Otherwise, it was not a good reason. My misery that day therefore stemmed from having mathematics homework, which included a lot of complex equations where BODMAS principle was needed. I took a look at the assignment and was miserable, not knowing where to start. Nothing my mum did could console me, so we left things until my dad got back from work. Seeing me miserable and finding out that I had barely eaten or even played that day, he enquired on what the issue was. My response, "Math is hard," took him so aback that he dropped his work bag and decided to eat nothing himself until we got to the bottom of that comment. I recall quite vividly the following conversation between us:

Dad: Where did you hear that?

Me: My classmates said that math is hard.

Dad What?! Go bring your homework and the counters.

(I got my math exercise book out of the school bag and reached up onto the shelf for my counters, a set of orange coloured thin plastic pieces that could be fitted together to make different shapes. Dad took a look at the homework, put the exercise book aside, and got me to pour out the counter pieces on the centre table in the living room.)

Dad: What is two times two?

Me: Four

Dad: That's right, but use the counters to show me how you arrived at that answer.

(I took two pieces out, then another two, and merged them together to depict two multiplied by two. Then I counted each piece—one, two, three, four.)

Me: Two times two equals four.

(Dad made me use the counters for various equations he called out until I started to get into it, and my countenance lifted. This was fun, I thought.)

Dad: Now let's look at your homework."

(Not surprising, the scenarios we went through were similar to what was on paper. So, using the counters, I started to go through the questions mostly on my own, while my dad sat and watched, until I completed the homework.)

Dad: How was that?

Me: Easy

Dad: So, next time you are given a problem that you have never seen, just break it down to known elements and start to solve each piece at a time. If there is still any part you don't know, find someone who does. There is no problem on earth that doesn't have a solution. If you don't know it, find somebody who does. All you need to do is ask. What do you think of math now?

Me: It is easy!

That experience taught me never to feel silly asking questions of others (even those outside my family) and to be comfortable with the idea that someone out there knows something that I don't. In fact, what became silly to me was not knowing something and pretending that one did for whatever reason, or choosing ignorance over self-esteem. My parents were never embarrassed to admit that they learnt something from what we shared about what we had been taught in school that day at the dining table. Therefore, I have never had the mentality that anyone is too young for me to learn from. I gained from my parents the knowledge that you can learn from everyone. Dad often said, "Everyone is good for at least one thing. Even if it's to be an example of what you shouldn't be or do." The experience also taught me never to withhold knowledge or belittle anyone who asks me a question. The principle is the same—as someone knows something I don't, I also know something someone else doesn't. By sharing what I know, I make another's life easier, as it will likely give them the ammunition required to face a challenge or solve a problem troubling them. To me, it takes as much humility to ask a question as it does to share knowledge—especially when you see another struggling and, without them asking, you offer your knowledge to help.

My passion for sharing my knowledge was further etched in my soul when, during a school activity, I heard someone say that "the grave is the richest place on earth." Later, asking my dad what the statement meant, he explained that many intelligent, creative, and diversely skilled people are dead—hence, in the grave. However, many have died without reaching their full potential or even discovering what they were born to be. Remembering my mum's motto, "I will pass through this world but once," I made a solemn vow to myself. I vowed to ensure that anything I know is shared with at least one other person. This was the first time that I grasped the concept of death. The reality that it was every living person's lot to live once—here today and gone tomorrow—couldn't have been any clearer, and it was truly a humbling reality even at my young age.

Yes, I will exit this earth someday (by death or rapture), but at least one living person will have gained the knowledge I have and be in the position to pass it on. This is not based on an assumption that there is something I know at any given time that someone else on the planet doesn't know at that same time; there are over seven billion of us, for heaven's sake! It is based on a sense of responsibility and strong motivation to ensure that "flowing knowledge" must never stop in my court.

Therefore, as you journey with me through my past four decades, I hope you will find at least one thing that speaks to you. I hope you will learn something that helps you put what you might be facing in a better context, and imbues in you the confidence to stand tall in times of adversity and to live life to your full potential while you are "going through." More importantly, I hope you find Christ for yourself—if you haven't already—and commit to living according to His wisdom; the quality of your life will only be the better for it.

Enjoy the read!

THINK ON THIS...

Do you think of yourself as a legend? Well, you ought to and should actively desire to be one. Put another way, each generation ought to pave the way for the next, even if it is just to put structures in place to help them easily overcome the challenges faced in yours if they have to face the same challenges at all. Thus, each individual and collection of people in a generation should be the 'leg-ends' upon which the next generation can stand taller. Therefore, I encourage you to start doing something (at whatever level or scale), if not done already, to bring about progression in your family, community, and sphere of contact for the benefit of the next generation(s).

THE MAKING OF ME

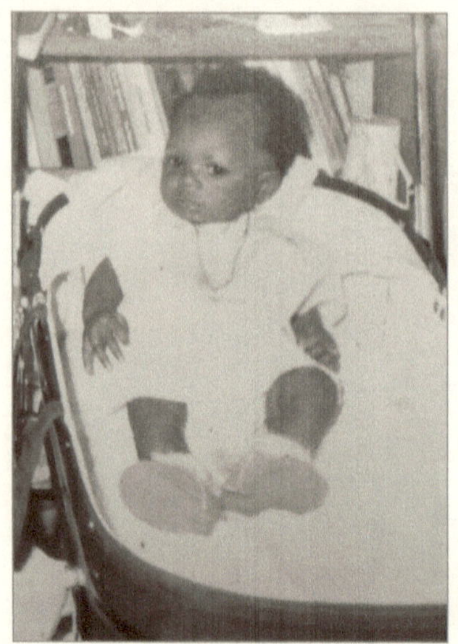

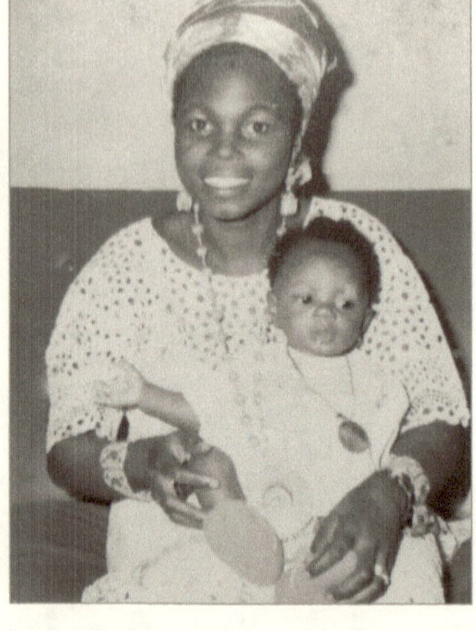

Baby me   Baby me with mum

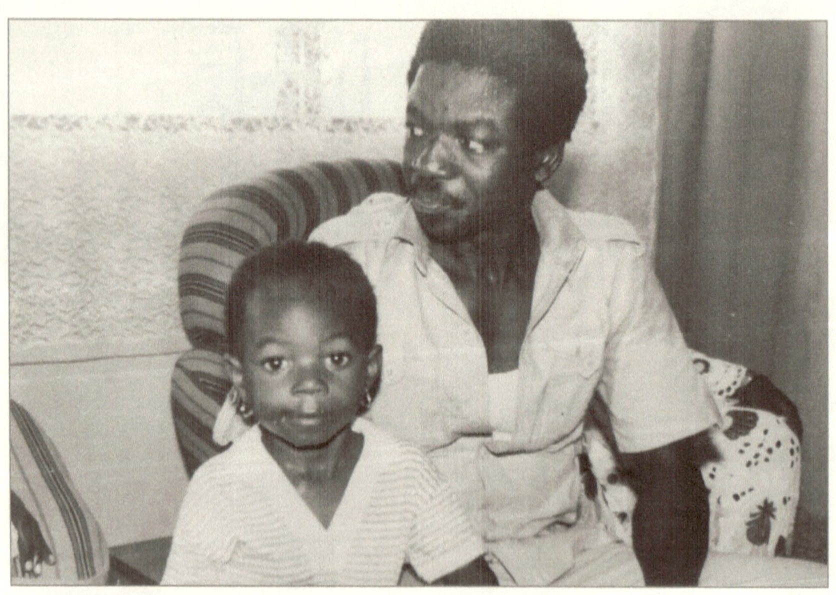

Young me with dad

IN THE BEGINNING

It was about 5:00 a.m. on a "Nigerian-cold" harmattan morning in January 1979, when I had my first taste of life. What might have been a cry for help for being pushed out of my comfort zone (in Mum's belly) was a welcomed sound of joy to my parents, a young couple who were still going through a very traumatic incident at the time. I was born exactly two weeks before the first anniversary of the passing of my identical twin brothers, Táíwò and Kẹ́hìndé, who were said to have died due to what remains a mysterious illness that started in the dead of night. A sudden spike in their temperatures, and both passed on the same day. My mum was said to have been in a coma for some weeks and could not return to the city of Lagos, where they had lived with the boys. They had been visiting Oǹdó for a paternal uncle's wedding, some days after which the boys passed. So, my conception was bittersweet, as they were grateful to conceive again but were still grieving the death of their twin boys. They were also dealing with the stress of moving to a new town, having relocated to Àkúrẹ́ following the incident. Though my birth brought my parents much joy, being born with and suffering the effects of iron anaemia for many years did not do much to help them take comfort or quickly recover from their earlier loss. Talk about having an eventful start to life!

In the *Yorùbá* culture (an African tribe predominantly based in the western part of Nigeria), it is customary for parents not to reveal a child's name to anyone until the Naming Ceremony held on the eighth day of the child's birth, or seven calendar days later. But because the same culture has certain names given to children born under various circumstances, I had two names that were applicable and would have been expected to be included in my given names by anyone who knew the circumstances of my birth. The first was for being a single child born immediately after twins or multiple births. The other was for being the first female grandchild born to a family where the grandmother was deceased. Although both parents had lost their mothers at a young age, there were many granddaughters already born on my maternal side, but I was the first in my dad's family. But only these two default names made it to my birth certificate, as my parents saw no further need to give me more names. I was mostly called by the second name, having refused to be called by the first from as early as I could understand the traditional epithet that went with it, which I despised.

My mum often tells of the various unique things they noticed about me quite early on and how they had to learn pretty quickly that I was different—and really, that all children are different. In the first few weeks, they observed my acute sense of smell and sensitivity to my environment. For example, when I was just a few weeks old, a time when a baby's vision is believed not to be very clear, my mum was confused by my incessant cries every night and how nothing offered seemed to pacify me. Disturbed by the cries but being more experienced, an elderly lady living next door told her that she had observed the cries only happened on nights that my dad was not home—nights he had to be away for work. She told my mum to try covering me in a piece of my dad's worn clothes when next he travelled for work, as I might be sensitive to his smell. My mum took the advice (thankfully), and it worked like magic. I was back to sleeping perfectly, and so was everyone else. So, my eyesight might not have been fully developed enough to recognise those around me, but I already knew what each one smelt like! And the cries were a recognition that someone, obviously dear and loved, was not around—that was not cool by me.

My extreme attachment to my dad was to be revealed in other ways as the years went by. I was the child that some would describe as "gum-body" (a Nigerian slang used to describe a person who sticks close to you like gum to the skin; they follow you everywhere). This closeness, however, did not deter my dad from disciplining me. If anything, I probably received the most smacking compared to my siblings, as I was very stubborn and Dad just could not tolerate indiscipline from anyone. He would usually say that the reason for the discipline and ensuring I turned out right was because he loved me, and that was true. My mum often said, "The day I gave birth to you, I knew I had a second wife," that is, someone else with whom she had to share her husband's attention and affection. My dad never put me in a position where I second-guessed his love for me. We could disagree over a misbehaviour and I would get some flogging, but the next minute, we are eating, playing, gardening, or doing some other activity together. We also enjoyed watching movies together, although never on a school night. He always happily acted as my shield from "scary" or "bloody" scenes—covering my ears and eyes or having me duck behind him if needed, then letting me know when it was safe to carry on watching.

My dad's discipline (and my mum's) always came with an explanation of what we did wrong, a walk-through of what we were thinking and why we did what we did, and helpfully, suggestions of what would have been the right action to take in the situation we were in so that next time we would be able to think differently and independently whilst arriving at the right course of action. With time, we also learnt that we were better off (punishment-wise) reporting ourselves to our parents than allowing them to find out what we did. Interestingly, they did not appreciate or pat us on the back for snitching or telling on siblings. We were taught to look out for one another, but it was each person's responsibility to own and come forward with what they did wrong themselves. So, life in the family was approached mostly from a principle perspective. "What principles govern a thinking?" is what my parents taught—not just what action to take per scenario. My dad being an engineer by trade and my mum, a teacher, might have helped with this approach to raising kids. But I also feel that having a child like me—stubborn, inquisitive, very observant, mischievous, and quite a "deep thinker"—meant my parents had to develop a parenting approach that allowed me to flourish as an individual (which was an important element in our upbringing), whilst communicating essential values of societal living. For example, it was okay to explore and seek to understand how electricity works, but doing so had to be within the confines of safety and respect for oneself and others. Although an injury might be self-inflicted or a result of negligence, it didn't change the fact that the whole family would still be impacted by the aftermath in some form.

My mum often said, "When most kids' first words included things like 'Daddy', 'Mummy', 'no', 'yes', etc., yours was 'why?'." So, they knew quite early on that I couldn't be raised in the conventional Nigerian way at the time, in which children were not necessarily heard or were told "because I said so" when they queried the reason behind something. I was the type of child who wanted to know the "why" of things, not just the "what." Also important was that the "why" had to make sense to my rather young, but logical mind. I was known to keep challenging any reasoning until the entire story "made sense." Being a primary school teacher at the time, Mum understood the importance of identifying each child's characteristics and helping them become the best of themselves. So, on several occasions, she would point out my strengths and weaknesses. While she encouraged improving on weaknesses, especially the ones with damaging effects like anger propelled by my swift reflex, she acknowledged that no one would ever be perfect. Hence, she encouraged focusing on strengths and working on weaknesses to either eliminate them where possible or have them at a manageable level (i.e., where they do not overshadow one's strengths or become damaging to oneself or others).

At age seven, when we found out that my mum was pregnant, I was so excited about the news and prospect of having a younger sister that I practically monitored its development in Mum's belly every day. Using the knowledge from my "Thread & Needle" sewing class, I made a little girl's dress from one of my mum's old outfits. It was designed and stitched all with my hand and received with gratitude by my mum. When the baby was born, my gross disappointment could not have been more evident the moment I saw him, realising it was a boy. I don't think that I said much to anyone or even touched him for many days after he was brought home. Although I recall my parents trying to help me through that phase, my disappointment overshadowed much of what was said. Then one day, I walked into the bedroom where he had been sleeping but had awoken and started crying. Mum was busy in the kitchen while my other two brothers were outside playing. So, I made a move to go call my mum, but his cry tugged so deeply at my heart that the moment I turned to look at him, I remember accepting that this little person was my brother, and he needed my help. Suddenly, all of the disappointment faded, and I became content with the thought of being the only girl. I picked him up and was walking towards the living room when my mum must have heard his voice and came dashing out of the kitchen. Surprised to find the baby in my hands, she showed me how to rock him, gave me his bottle of food, and showed me how to feed him. I watched him keenly as he ate and was amazed by his size, fitting into my arms, yet realised that he was a full human being—one that was already showing unique characteristics.

From that moment on, my sense of responsibility towards him as a sibling was awakened; I loved him and had the desire to look out for him, as I did the others. I started to enjoy feeding him and helping him learn new things—like holding his feeding bottle by himself, sitting upright, and so on. My parents couldn't have been more grateful for this change of attitude because they understood the weight of it in my world. I was known to be very protective of my siblings, and as my mum recounts, I never let anyone else discipline them (including my parents) or speak wrongly about them. At least, not in my presence.

With his birth, I started to understand and relish my position as the first child and the "only girl;" the former signalled responsibility, while the latter was about entitlement. It was a thing of pride to describe myself as the only girl (surprisingly)—the only girl my parents were capable of having if the situation demanded a more authoritative tone (imagine that!). Needless to say, my brothers, especially my immediate, knew it was not a good idea to challenge my position as the "first" child (makes me wonder sometimes how Esau in the Bible gave up his right as firstborn in exchange for porridge—not judging, just wondering). My first-child syndrome was more evident whenever Dad was away for work. It felt like someone needed to "step into his shoes," and I was the rightful heir to this imaginary throne!

Most of my help was with the baby; learning to sterilise the bottles, make the baby food, ensure it was at the right temperature, and feed him when he got hungry. When Mum was busy in the afternoons, I often laid him on a mat outside of the house so I could play while keeping an eye on him. But when he woke, my playtime would be over—and I didn't mind. With no washing machine or disposable nappies available, Mum had to hand wash an all-white collection of cloth nappies (plus our clothes), so I helped with little things like our school socks, vests, and underwear. Sometimes, she got up at 5:00 a.m. to get things done—have breakfast ready in good time for us to shower, eat, and be at school before 7:30 a.m. so that we were not late for the assembly. As a result, I got up too. I was never a deep or long sleeper anyway, so her mere whisper of my name was enough to get me up. But when Dad was around, it was easier because he took on any of the chores that Mum wasn't doing; often getting us ready (shower, dressing up, and breakfast) and dropping us off at school.

Their sharing of chores was something I assumed to be normal until I started to mix with other kids at my boarding school and later university, realising it wasn't commonplace in Nigeria for men to look after children or even cook. But my dad was an excellent cook! There were certain meals that he was better at and always obliged our demand for him to cook. When Mum was on a profession-related course at the University of Ife and was away for several days every couple of weeks, we never had any inclination that something would have been done better if she had been around. Despite having to cope with ever-active kids running around the house. Being older now, I find it incredible and take huge lessons from their ability to balance both family and career development, and to support each other through each phase.

Despite their busy schedules, I do not recall a time when my parents missed any of our school activities; at least one of them was present. Thinking back, I alone was a handful. From nursery to primary age, I was involved in all sorts of competitions, both at school and later at the state level. Athletics and singing were like the equilibrium constant K in my life. I always took part in any event. Add on other sporting activities like skipping races, high jumps, long jumps, march pasts, school debates, writing competitions, and school (music or cultural) plays. Phew!!! Honestly, I wonder how my parents made it all possible for me, let alone my brothers, with each of us encouraged to find and develop into our own, and without any of us feeling neglected.

OUR FAMILY VALUES

Although we were raised as individuals—in that it was perceived as near taboo to compare our abilities as siblings—certain similarities in our personalities and principles guided our upbringing. In terms of personality, we were all athletic and full of mischief, although I think my brothers learnt the latter from me, being the first and often, the ringleader. My brothers and I ran everywhere possible; we were always involved in sports at school and organised races with other kids on our street (back when neighbours looked out for one another and kids played freely).

A bizarre similarity we had, which was observed by my dad, was that we never took afternoon naps even though it was planned into our daily routines. Dad noticed that whenever we slept in the afternoon, it was because we were either sick or hungry. Who sleeps when they are very hungry, huh? Well, it wasn't until my late teens that I observed this to be true with me. I wasn't a foodie, so I often skipped meals, living mainly on snacks and fruits. But when I became really hungry, I found that sleeping helped me regain some energy, such that when I woke, I had some strength to either cook or find somewhere to eat.

Storytelling, the use of proverbs, and sarcasm were also the order of the day in our home. With my dad especially, sarcasm came so naturally to him that you need to pay good attention to his words to fully understand the joke. While he always made us laugh, there was often a lesson or two embedded within the sarcastic moment that needed drawing out. With my mum, it wasn't so frequent, but when she was having such a moment, it was always impactful. One incident of such that I vividly recall occurred when I was asking her for something that we had both agreed was needed. So, she told me that she would get this as soon as they had the money for it. But I kept pestering her to get a commitment to a more immediate timeline, knowing that my parents always did whatever they said.

As I kept on with the justifications for a "now-solution," she stopped and very calmly said to me, "Okay, why don't we wait till nightfall? At midnight," Mum continued, "we will both put on balaclavas, scale the fence to our neighbour's house, and steal theirs. Will that be OK?"

That was so not the response I expected and thinking she was being serious, I worriedly asked why she would want us to steal from the neighbours. "Isn't stealing supposed to be wrong?"

Mum replied, "Well, since you refused to be content with the fact that we cannot afford it now then the only way I can give it to you is to steal it."

With that, the penny dropped. Mum was being sarcastic about the scenario but serious at the same time!

MORAL –

Prioritise your needs and wants. There are things you think are needed now and may cause some form of "death" if not acquired immediately. But if you take a closer look at the reason for it, you find that the acquisition is not time-bound and you will survive without it. It also pays to wait as long as is necessary to get (the best quality available) what is needed and to be content with what you have or can afford whilst you wait.

My parents made it abundantly clear, in every way they could, that it was OK that we were individually different. This, they said, made family (life) and the world more "colourful". We were encouraged to learn from others, but the desire to become like a so-and-so person was never our orientation. Knowing who we are and being true to ourselves was something they repeated over and over again. What we were taught was to "strive to be a better version of yourself," recognise that there is always room for improvement no matter your age, and be comfortable with those characteristics that make you unique or different from others (and vice versa). They emphasised that everyone goes through a *journey* in life, and we don't know what journeys other people have been on to get to where they are nor what lies in store for them in the future. So, it's a waste of time and effort to be striving to become someone else—when you can focus that energy on your path to becoming the best you!

Celebrating birthdays was also a big thing in our house. The buzz started days before the actual date, when Dad came in with crates of soft drinks featuring Coke, Fanta and my personal favourite, Vimto, whilst Mum asked what meal we wanted to eat that day, so she could get the ingredients ready. Better still if our birthday fell on a school day; we were sure to have a new outfit to put on as that was the only day pupils were allowed to not wear the school uniform. I could barely sleep the night before my birthday out of excitement for the unveiling of all that was packed into each hour of that day. Then, when the morning arrived, we always woke to the sweet sound of music coming from my dad's favourite vinyl record player. No matter how early we woke up, Dad was always up before us and would have a particular "Happy Birthday" song by Ebenezer Obey already playing. Though he did this for everyone's birthday, hearing that tune early in the morning was never old—I looked forward to it each year.

If our birthday fell on a Saturday or national holiday, we might even be treated to a family dance-off or sing-along "karaoke" to our favourite soundtrack from any artiste in Dad's collection, and he had a wide range. His collection included artists from various genres and across continents, such as pure Entertainers, like King Sunny Adé, Sir Shina Peters, Michael Jackson, Whitney Houston, Yvonne Chaka Chaka, and Brenda Fassie; political or civil rights artists, like Fẹlá Aníkúlápò-Kútì, Orlando Ọwòh, Sonny Okosun, Bob Marley, and Miriam Makeba; gospel artistes, like the Handel Messiah Choir, Ebenezer Obey, Evangelist Níyì Adédòkun, and The Atáyérọ Voices; comedy artistes, like Bàbá Sàlá and Adẹ̀rùpọkò; and numerous others, like Christy Essien-Igbokwe, Fúnmi Adams, Victor Ọláìyá, Bongos Ikwue, Barry White, Lionel Richie, Marvin Gaye, and so on.

Music was woven into the fabric of our home. To me, it is one of those pleasures God gifted man to allow us a taste of what it means to have the entire universe working together in harmony—"Heaven" right here on planet Earth. Unfortunately, the mostly studio-produced sound of today's music seems like a loss or deterioration of the purity of quality music and the artistry involved in putting together a piece using a variety of instruments (no offence intended). Nevertheless, I still tap my feet and sing along with any decent sound.

I am probably the most musically involved in the family—singing in choirs, taking part in music competitions, occasionally dabbling in song-writing, and doing more than "the sway" dance step to every song. The blend of melodious voices is truly "music to my ears," and the sound of each instrument, especially the drums, playing together in harmony transports me out of this world. I would go into cathedrals just to hear the sound of the organ reverberating through the entire room as the choir sang a hymn. Reliving this particular feeling is one of the reasons I love church weddings, especially in an Anglican church. My dad's love for musical variety grew on me, and since it so happened that I could hold a note on my own, I sang unashamedly everywhere and anywhere.

THE VALUE
OF GIVING

Over many years, I saw my parents taking in young adults from relations, church groups, or friends' families as an act of support for their education or career development. Dad was one of the leaders in the Anglican Youth Fellowship (AYF) at the time and working in one of the Oǹdó State ministries allowed him to support many of the young people in his care with jobs or apprentice opportunities that came his way. On the other hand, Mum, being a teacher in state-owned primary schools, was often in contact with less-privileged children and struggling families, most of whom she helped out with paying their school fees to avoid the kids' education being stopped and providing meals or clothing to the children (and their families) as she was opportune.

One of the most outrageous moves my parents made in seeking to help young people was with two notorious boys—both in their twenties then—who lived in the neighbourhood. On an occasion, they scaled our small fence in the dead of night to steal one of the four brand-new tyres my dad got fixed on his car that day. I heard the thud of their bare feet when they jumped over but not knowing what the strange sound was, I quietly got up from my bed, crept up to my dad's room, and told my parents what I had heard. By the time my parents woke up, understood what I was saying, and Dad switched on the outside lights, the thieves had managed to remove one tyre. Upon being seen, they scaled the fence again and ran off with the tyre.

Some days later, my parents found out that those boys were the culprits, so my dad paid them a casual visit. Understanding a bit more of their background and whatever else he learnt when he went to their home, my dad later invited them to our house for a meal, armed with work placement application forms for them. Following the meal, he had a chat with them both; one of them took the opportunity while the other didn't. A few weeks later, the one who applied got called for training while the other decided to move out of the neighbourhood.

Some months later, dad and I were standing at our gate when a police officer walking down the street started to head towards us. When he got to my dad, the officer prostrated (a cultural form of greeting for an elder) before my dad, except that he lay flat on his belly not caring about onlookers, full of gratitude. When he rose, lo and behold, I saw it was one of the "troublesome" boys, now turned policeman. Although I believe my dad was standing at the gate at that time to welcome him home, knowing he was due to return that day, his manner of expressing his gratitude completely caught my dad off guard. He spoke of how tough and rigorous the training process was. The young man also spoke of his determination to become a better person, having spoken to my dad and realising that there was someone who saw 'good' in him. The combination of these was his motivation for completing the process, and having also passed the exams, he was now a police officer!

The remarkable transformation was one of my most memorable and one that changed my views about people. I asked my dad why he had invited them over to the house and what he saw when he initially visited the two boys. His response—he gained the understanding that they didn't know better and had never been given an opportunity to prove themselves otherwise. Everyone classed them as notorious and kept away from them, but no one attempted to speak directly to them. He also saw that their mother was well-advanced in years, without the physical ability to correct their shenanigans, and desperately needed help. Being a youth leader, my dad chose to forgive their wrong and give them the opportunity he knew of rather than demand justice. Last I heard, after several years, the young man remained a respectable police officer in the state. Nothing however was heard again of the other.

Dad and Mum were not and have never suggested that they were the wealthiest parents around but they have been known to always look out for what they can give. Be it a room in the house, some vegetables from the garden, poultry produce, childcare for a Mum attending evening classes, helpful information, etc.—if they could help a journey to a better future in some form, they were signed up to it without thinking twice. As kids, this was something we had to learn; it wasn't always by nature! I can still see the picture of my mum walking into our room, ever so often, with a bag in hand. She would have asked weeks before for us to put stuff (clothes, shoes, books, toys, etc.) that we could part with in there for her to give to kids in her school or to charity. They had to be things we could still wear; otherwise, she'd bin them. If she was not satisfied with the content, assuming we "remembered" to put anything there in the first place, she came into the room with the bag with one purpose only—to "raid" our wardrobes. She would pick out those clothes that we hadn't worn in some time. I don't mean the ones we were tired of wearing, but the ones we were probably reserving for a "special" outing. Sometimes, we had to present a case for why we would need or "miss" that thing we had not used for some time. Soon enough, we learnt to freely offer what we had and to only offer what was good enough for us. And if I loved something or found it relevant, I had to ensure I used it (because Mum was watching—lol).

MORAL —

Just because someone is less privileged does not mean that they should be treated less human!

Life is all about opportunities. You are blessed to have things given to you but don't take them for granted. Should you ever find yourself in an undesirable position, don't let anything weigh you down. Life is in phases and everything is "but for a moment." Pick yourself up and keep pressing in towards your goal.

THINK ON THIS...

To parents; the proof that you love a child is not in how much stuff you can give them but in the values that you teach them. The word 'discipline' has been so demonised in modern society that we miss the opportunity it provides to 'train' a child (Hebrews 12:5–11, Proverbs 13:24). Things will fade away one day, and so will you, but what tools have you given your child to enable them to remain standing in the face of challenges which life will no doubt hurl at them and to know how to treat others with respect? The equation that demonstrates true love for a child is Affection + Discipline; one without the other creates an imbalance which often results in the various dysfunctions observed in our societies today.

THE VALUE OF EDUCATION

Education—in the broad sense of the word—was equally woven into the fabric of our family. If one stayed around my parents long enough (and I'm talking hours), one would come away either having learnt something new or being clear that they had impacted some knowledge. They believed every association should be improving oneself and the other party in some shape or form. Although I could summarise my dad's views as "Education is a privilege," and my mum's as "Education is a right," the one consistent element was the importance of being educated about life or a subject matter of choice.

My dad often said, "Opportunity does come around, but only those who are prepared get to take it!" Spoken like a true Boy Scout! His experience of losing his Mum—who was their main breadwinner—when he was about six years old led him to drop out of school to look after his aged father and younger brother, whilst not losing hope that he would become educated somehow and help his family become independent, which he did.

Dad often mentioned how there are more opportunities in our time than when he was growing up, and how he felt some people preferred to wallow in self-pity than dust their backsides and get up to do something about it. He once told me how after dropping out of school, he walked past his former primary class, looking on at his mates, and that day made up his mind to give his children and anyone around him a much better chance at life than what he had been dealt. He did not feel sorry for himself but had the mind to push himself to ensure that he still made something good out of his life, formal education or not. This was why he was always on the lookout for those who needed help and what opportunity there was that he could help them get. And for us, his children, he always emphasised that our opportunity and true inheritance was our education! To Dad, sending us to school was to give us the very thing that had been taken from him. Then, sending us to a private school was to give us the best of what he didn't get and of what was available then (very humbling, I think).

Although it was not always convenient for them, especially when as civil servants they could be owed several months of salary, my parents prioritised our education above all else by ensuring our fees were paid well in advance. Being opportune to attend the state governor's Christmas party every year at the state government house, and having everything I needed, I must have somewhat assumed that the civil service paid much. But over time and as they became more open about their finances, I realised that the only reason we didn't quite experience lack was because of their conscientious financial planning and prioritisation of what was absolutely necessary above other pleasures of life. For example, rent and school fees were the topmost priority, with food and transportation costs (theirs to work and ours to school) coming next. All else were subject to the availability of funds, which explained why we couldn't afford to travel out of the country on holidays, for example. That said, I don't ever recollect feeling "less" than my classmates, who had stories of their holiday experiences in other countries. Aside from being raised to always be content, I also always had a "holiday story" to tell. Dad made sure we either went to visit relatives living in some other part of Nigeria or went on an adventure trip to at least one tourist site during the break. Dad was a fast driver, and I loved the thrill of riding in his car. He was also very knowledgeable about political affairs around the world, as well as the people and cultures in Nigeria. Add that to my mum's understanding of science and nature, and we had an explosive, never-boring travel time. To me, the time spent on the road was as much a part of the holiday as was the people or sites we were visiting because of the *fun-unlimited* and the new knowledge acquired, usually of some place or thing encountered during the trip.

Personally, these adventures developed in me a love for sightseeing, travelling, and learning about different cultures. Such was the love I developed for tourism that I chose it as the research area for my first-degree dissertation. This was (and still is) important to me especially as Nigeria started to neglect tourism, turning its attention to only the oil and gas industry. Finding out that some of the sites from my childhood were a shadow of what they were in the 1980s brought me great pain. Some were in ruins and others were completely forgotten. Therefore, choosing tourism as a research topic was an initial endeavour to rediscover what things needed to be in place to revive Nigeria's tourism industry.

MORAL —

Tip for parents; a "good holiday" does not always have to involve travelling outside your country of residence. Each nation, region, city, or state has something beautiful about it. Find out what these are and explore them with your children. Aside from saving money to invest in what matters most, it also helps kids to know more about where they live and to have a heart for their environment beyond what they can get to what they can give.

THINK ON THIS...

Education is the right of every child, and to be enlightened is a necessity of any human society. Therefore, it is responsible for parents, governments, teachers, and leaders of all forms and at all levels, to work to protect and prevent the erosion of such values in their societies. This is not an advocacy for the supremacy of one form of education over another, rather it is a submission that all societies should be open to every form of progressive 'thinking' across the world—providing the necessary structures that facilitate easy access to such by everyone who seeks to take advantage of them, without discriminating. The world is a 'global village', making it easy to learn and easily benefit from our diversity.

OUR ANIMAL FARM-ILY

Our family would not be complete without a mention of the many animals, fish, and birds that formed part of our daily lives. We had no more than a few fish in the aquarium and some small birds in a cage to feed, until one day an aunt gifted me with a chicken for my birthday (don't laugh!). As it was my gift, it was my decision what to do with it, and not able to think of one immediately, my parents built it a cage placed in the back garden.

Then one afternoon while we ate, we started hearing noises coming from the chicken's cage. Having had the chicken for a few weeks and never heard it make such noises, I leapt off the table after my dad to check what was happening to it. Upon opening its cage, the chicken moved to the other side, revealing an egg it had just laid—it was still very warm to the touch. "What!" I exclaimed, swiftly followed by a barrage of questions for my dad—"How did that happen?"; "Is that where eggs come from?"; and so on. Taking the egg from him, I rushed inside to show the rest of the family.

To our utmost surprise the following day, the chicken started to make the same noises around the same time as the previous day. So, I dashed out again and behold, there was another egg. Dad then suggested that we save the eggs until there were six, so we could enjoy a boiled egg each, together as a family. True to form on day three, the same thing happened…and on every day thereafter. The timing of her laying became so predictable that my brothers and I started to take turns on who would pick up the egg that day—the beauty of it being that the chicken laid it close to the cage door, and always stepped away when anyone approached.

My dad later brought a vet to check the chicken's health and provide better insight into what was happening. Then we found out that this was a *layer*, and that there were different types of chicken—each had different maturity rates and could be bred for varying reasons. A few weeks after that, my dad got someone to build a shelter over another area at the back. A few days later, he turned up after work with some chicks—a mix of broilers and layers. And so began our poultry farming experience with everything being learnt on the job. Soon, our annual intake of poultry expanded to include four-week-old turkeys, raised to maturity by Christmas for us to eat; gift to our family, friends, and relatives; and sell. Then came the rabbits, though these were not bred for food. Then, fast-forward six years, and goats joined the gang.

As I took a personal liking to caring for the animals, far more than cooking or even eating, my chores were naturally centred on their upkeep. It demanded a lot of effort, which did not seem as rewarding as my sports activities, but I kept at it because I loved learning about and from the animals. Over the years, I realised that whilst sports taught me discipline, self-awareness, and strategy, looking after our "animal family" honed my observation and nurturing abilities. It also taught me patience and how to persevere (think training goats), commitment to what I believe in or enjoy, and the importance of paying attention to details—because each animal came with intricacies that, if ignored, could have deadly outcomes. This wasn't just about knowing when to feed them, change their water, or clean out their houses. It was about understanding their instincts and unique characteristics, even down to those of individual animals. Who knew that animals could have personalities too!

A "PLANNER" IS BORN

My life started to get "serious" about age eight when I was preparing for the National Common Entrance Examinations to secondary school, which were the following year. School was becoming more than the place for learning new things or participating in enjoyable activities; it was starting to influence my ideologies and shape my thoughts for the future. From the exposure to current affairs or the socio-political and cultural landscapes of Nigeria to the study involved in preparing my viewpoints on varying debate topics and defending them in front of other pupils and teachers, I started to discover the things that made me tick. Inspired by the little globe in our living room, and possibly the fact that most of my class teachers were not native Nigerians, I started to see myself as a *global citizen*—one who had something to give to the world, not just my country of origin. When plugged in, the globe glowed in different colours making the countries of the world and their major cities more luminous. I would often toss it around to familiarise myself with yet another continent or country, thinking about what it might be like when I visited it.

I recollect being past the level of "opinion formulation" to having a view on more topics than most kids my age cared to think about. My logical reasoning seemed complex, and questions became less tolerable by those who didn't know me well, especially the older ones as I asked more and more questions before being convinced about a matter. Yet, it seemed like the more I knew, the more I wondered "the point of it all." I started to ask myself questions like *"Am I on earth just to grow up, work like my parents, go to church, have kids and travel the world?"*; *"What was the ultimate purpose for human beings?"*; and *"Why am I here?"*

Although important, the question of *"What do I want to become?"* seemed less daunting. I guess it felt easier to tackle because of my parents' assured support of whatever I chose to become. From a very young age, my mum helped to highlight the likely professions that my natural strengths played to, and both parents helped to walk through the pros and cons of any profession I could dream up. So, although I might have been way ahead of what was required at that age, planning the type of schools that I wanted to attend up to university seemed fairly easy. I had already outlined "the dream" to my parents—secondary had to be a Federal Government school (which were the best group of unity schools in Nigeria), and university was going to be the University of Lagos (Unilag) in Lagos State. By this time, I had been to the University of Ife (later renamed Obafemi Awolowo University in the now Osun State) for my mum's teachers' training graduation, and to Unilag for my cousin's graduation. For whatever reason or observation, I decided that Unilag was going to be the place for my undergraduate studies.

My plan was up to university because my dad had often mentioned his plans to sponsor each one of us to that level—emphasising that by his calculation, we would all be graduates before his retirement if each one focused on their studies and progressed to the next class when due. He had personally faced setbacks in civil service, where despite his professional experience, people with university degrees were often promoted ahead of him. Also, the Nigerian Society of Engineers had constantly denied him membership because he didn't have a university degree in engineering. They gave no attention to his technical City and Guild qualifications and decades of electrical engineering experience, including working in the Governor's Office where he led most of the electrification projects that put the majority of the rural areas in Oǹdó State on the National Energy Grid. Having accepted this as "his fate," Dad was determined to not have his children experience the same. He wasn't too hung up on what we wanted to study or become, but emphasised the need for us to obtain the best formally recognised qualification or university degree in our chosen field, to open up our minds to thinking differently, and to remove potential stumbling blocks in our future career development.

By age nine and year 5, I had weighed the pros and cons of some "potential" professions of interest like it was a requirement for secondary school. One by one they came off the table as they either involved a type of risk I didn't think was for me, or succeeding in them would involve some compromises that might blur the lines between integrity and injustice—two things that started to become important to me. For example, being a lawyer had the least physical risk of those considered and was my top preference—that was until I saw a movie which had a female lawyer appointed by the state to defend a known criminal. It was an appointment she didn't seem to have a choice other than to accept, and being a sound lawyer who knew how to argue a case with a track record of being successful at it, she won the case. Oh, how that infuriated me! It was injustice, and I realised that I detested that feeling very much. Asking my dad why the lady had to take on the case even though she knew the man had committed the crime, he explained that the state was obliged to appoint the accused a defending lawyer if they could not afford one. Worse, the lawyer cannot easily refuse such appointments and has to do everything possible to defend their client. He further explained that because the court only goes by "evidence" or what can be proven, then such a case where there was insufficient evidence against the accused could be won. With that explanation, I remember feeling so disappointed that my "chosen" profession involved such compromises. Not wanting to ever be in that position, it became a no-no profession for me. Of course, this is not an assumption that all our "learned colleagues" out there always make such compromises.

With the sciences seeming like the only viable option, I decided on becoming a pharmacologist. I would make drugs to cure my dad who often had severe asthmatic attacks, especially at night. His inhaler seemed hardly helpful so he would either lie on the living room floor reeling in pain, or step outside the house battling to get some air. He always went away from the rooms and made efforts to be quiet, so as not to wake up anyone. Except, I always awoke being a light sleeper and quite sensitive to him and his pain, as I often felt it when he had such troubles. I would creep up behind him and silently "sit with him" through it, although safely from the shadows—because if he saw me, he would attempt to get me back to bed (if he still had some energy). Otherwise, he waited it out until he could speak and we both went back to sleep—often barely feeling okay but concerned for me being awake.

Although I suffered from malaria much more frequently than others in the family, the pain of being hospitalised, taking injections, and being fed via intravenous drips for a few days every couple of months was nothing compared to the pain I felt whenever I witnessed my dad's asthma attacks. Seeing him in so much pain and being unable to do anything about it made me detest sickness. Therefore, I perceived that the only way to "get back" at sickness and help alleviate my dad's pain was to get the education that would help me develop a cure for him and everyone else who might be in his shoes. There was just one concern—pharmacology required taking predominantly science subjects, which my mum had often advised against, as a route for me. Stressing, as always, that the choice was mine, her advice often included statements, like "Going for purely science courses will not give room to your arty side, so find something that incorporates drawing"; or "Though you have the brains for science, your emotions might not be able to handle the journey, because you get distressed by sickness." About the latter, she was right, as I was known to cry at the sight of blood from even a tiny wound, or if I saw a stranger in pain with no one to help. But my young mind seemed resolute on pharmacology being the course to study at university. That settled, I was now set to move on to the next level.

Of the handful of acquaintances that I had, there were two boys that I was best friends with—one of them being Mike, who lived about two streets away from mine. While preparing for our secondary school National Common Entrance Examinations, we spent a lot of the school hours together, running from 8:00 a.m. to 6:00 p.m., which included after-school lessons that started about 2:00 p.m. As best friends, I also wanted to be in the same secondary school with him, which meant I had to attend a mixed boarding school. Since I only wanted a Federal Government secondary school, the closest—Federal Government College, Ìdóàní in Oǹdó State—naturally became my first and main school of choice. Therefore, this choice was what

I told my parents, who were to complete the form on my behalf. The ensuing conversation, however, became the first time, and probably one of the rare occasions, that I can remember my parents advising and asking me to make a decision based on my gender! They had observed that I had no female friends, so my dad was genuinely concerned that if I went to a mixed secondary school, I would end up with only male friends—thereby, likely "missing out" on a thing or two about being "a lady," which they as parents might not be equipped to teach me. However, I am sure that they (nor I, in fact) did not realise how deeply etched this "tomboy" personality trait was in me.

After much discussion on the appropriate school of choice, I eventually agreed to their plan, simply because the concept of learning something about the womenfolk sounded intriguing and, more importantly, did not change my dream of attending a Federal Government College (FGC). Mike and I could always catch up during the holidays and would have even more fun stories to tell each other since we would be in different schools. Upon our agreement, my parents completed the forms specifying my choices as Federal Government Girls College, Àkúrẹ́, which was in the same city where we lived, and Federal Government Girls College, Ṣágámù in Ògùn State, which was located in a different state but still within the western Yorùbá-speaking region of Nigeria, making it familiar. So, to my young mind, my pivotal reason for going to a Federal Government Girls College (FGGC), aside from being educated, henceforth became *to know more about women and being a lady.* Whilst this may sound silly, to me it seemed an important "education" to obtain when I got into the school because it underpinned the justification used for the school choices made.

MORAL —

Parents, be mindful of how you present the ideas that help convince a child of an action that you want them to take, especially kids who are goal-driven. The effects could last a lifetime!

THE START OF SOMETHING NEW

Though my final year in primary school seemed to go by very quickly—between studying and sitting several examinations, school activities, and our growing animal farm—I had a vivid encounter towards the end of that period that completely interrupted and changed my life forever. While I was preparing for the next phase of life, Heaven seemed to have paid attention to my innermost, but unvoiced, questions around the meaning and purpose of life. I just felt that there had to be more to life and a reason for being here; otherwise, "the cycle"—go to school, have friends, grow up to work, have children, then eventually die—seemed futile.

I had read *My Book of Bible Stories* and went to Sunday school at church, so I was familiar with the name *Jesus* but didn't quite get what it was all about. Church for us was in Oǹdó at St. Mary's Anglican Church, so we travelled there every Sunday from Àkúrẹ́. It was only about a forty-minute drive, and it gave us, especially my parents, the opportunity to see relatives—the main being my paternal granddad, who was the only surviving grandparent we had. Although he was well advanced in age, he often walked to the church by himself, and we came back to his home after the church service. I loved the music at church, but that was it. I did not like most of the rules around attendance, as I couldn't understand the *whys*, nor did I like the "hanging around" after, when we had to wait for my parents to finish their various meetings. So, at the time, the only thing that made sense as to why we needed to travel that far every week was to spend time with my paternal granddad, *Baba,* as he was fondly called.

Therefore, there was truly nothing mentally, physically, spiritually, academically, and all the "–ally" speaking, that could have prepared me for the encounter I had. Having dreams was something I had grown accustomed to by this time; it happened nearly every time I shut my eyes. My dreams were made up of random pictures, often horrific, that seemed to want to convey a message, usually too complex for me to describe to my parents, let alone understand. They were probably the reason I didn't like sleeping, and when I did sleep, it wasn't deep or for more than six hours at a time. Unlike my brothers who could fall asleep within seconds, I needed a bit more "conjuring" to do so and would wake up at the slightest change in the atmosphere—light, temperature, or sound. The only sleep routine that I knew was one of "late to bed and early to rise." So, it was quite a profound experience for me to have a dream so pleasant that I did not want to wake up. It was a dream like none other!

That day, I slept and dreamt that I was sleeping. In the dream, I was asleep on the right side of my mum's king-sized bed that was in the room I shared with my brothers. My normal bed was the top of the bunk bed, which was the only other bed in the room. The left side of the bed was towards the wall, so I was sleeping on the right side, which was my mum's side of the bed and had a direct view of the bedroom door that led into the passage. The light was on in the room, but I was awoken, in the dream, by the rays of a much stronger light that seemed to be coming down the passage through the curtains at the bedroom door and straight into my eyes. Curious as to the source of that light, I sat upright and was leaning forward, when I realised the light was coming towards me. While sitting still in the bed, the glow grew stronger, warmer, and brighter than anything I had ever seen, yet it was not blinding. Within seconds, I saw Him walk through the doors and stop at the foot of the bed. The moment I saw His face, I knew who He was. I instantly leapt off the bed and knelt at His feet—willingly and in awe of His beautiful presence. Kneeling, the only words I could utter were, "Jesus, my Lord. What do you want me to do?" Then with His arms stretched out and a warm smile, He started to speak to me. Looking up at Him, I noticed the red scars in the middle of both His palms, and that the light seemed to be oozing from His core—radiating through His eyes and springing out from His body right through His garment, like unending joyous floods of life. Now and again as He spoke, I would rest my head on His feet, completely engulfed by His light and mesmerised by how welcoming it was. His voice was calm and gentle, yet every word He spoke reverberated within my bones to the depths of my very soul but in a surprisingly enjoyable way, such that I did not want it to end. To this day, I have felt absolutely nothing like it and do not think I will ever be able to accurately describe that feeling.

I woke up from the dream, but this time I was seeing only the light coming from the bulb in the room. Staring at the spot where He stood in the dream, I felt again the inexplicable joy of being in His presence and knew beyond any iota of doubt that this was an encounter to remember… not just another one of my dreams. He had given me an assignment that needed to be done before He revealed more of what He had for me to do. It was a task that was perfectly appropriate for my age, but I didn't do it then, because I slipped back into my natural form and reasoned it away. My biggest concern, then, was how to tell my parents that I had met Jesus in person. At that time, I had never heard a teaching about such happening, certainly not at church nor in my Bible story books. How was it, too, that I knew exactly who He was? Especially since it was our first meeting and He looked nothing like the pictures in my storybooks or the paintings of Him that I had come across. Hence, I kept the entire experience to myself. However, its imprint on my mind was so strong that it started to drive a hunger for more than the "religious" exposure I had. I knew there was more to life, but I decided to explore exactly what that meant for me.

THINK ON THIS...

God loves you unconditionally; nothing you can do to make Him love you more or less than He already has by sending Jesus to bridge the gap between us and Him. Through Jesus, God expressed the intensity, immensity, and infinite nature of His love for us, and for this, we ought to be grateful. Accepting His love is what makes the difference in how much you 'enjoy' Him and can extend that love to others.

FAR AWAY FROM HOME

Come January 1989, students were resuming the new academic year, and people like me were doing so in a different school. I was moving up to year 7, commonly referred to as Junior Secondary School year 1 (JSS 1) in Nigeria. It was, however, not an exciting time for me because I didn't receive an admission letter from either of my chosen Federal Government schools, although I had passed the exams according to the results released. Instead, I was admitted to St. Helen's Unity Secondary School in Oǹdó town where Baba lived. I had grudgingly sat the exams for State Unity Schools because my parents wanted a fallback in case I didn't get into an FGGC. The only thing the two types of schools had in common for me was that they were both boarding schools. But still, I did not want to attend a State Unity school simply because they were not run by the Federal Government. To my mind, attending them did not align with my ideology to "always go for the best." The Federal Government ran the best secondary schools at the time, so for one who always saw herself as a global citizen, my carefully thought-out plan, albeit childish, for becoming internationally acclaimed involved gaining my education (secondary and university) at an institution with a national reputation, as a stepping stone for undertaking a profession with an opportunity to play on an international stage. So, although St. Helen's was one of the best State-run secondary schools in Oǹdó State at the time, it just didn't fit into my plans…and for this reason, I became very miserable. Therefore, I pleaded with my parents to let me stay at home and re-sit the Federal School exams for the following year's intake. But they refused on the premise that it was better to resume at St. Helen's, so I could be learning new things, pending when the next exams are to be sat. So, I did.

Although my closest maternal first cousin was a senior at St. Helen's, and my parents visited every Sunday on their return route to Àkúrẹ́ with the hope that it would help me settle into the school better, the misery of deviation from my plan had the better of me. I was seldom in class, spending most days in the school's clinic, bedridden and fed mostly via intravenous drips, even on my tenth birthday. My health was so bad that the school's principal was alerted of my condition—a constantly sick student whose test results did not reveal what was wrong with her, and all they were doing was keeping me alive via drips. This, and the fact that I always cried asking to see my dad, caused the principal to allow for frequent visits from my parents. Although seeing my parents always brought some relief, it was short-lived because of this misery—I just didn't feel like I was where I ought to be.

One day towards the end of January 1989, my parents came to visit. It was a weekday and they were accompanied by the principal to the school's clinic where I was. Much of the conversation that I remember was a casual mention by my dad that they had received an admission letter from an FGGC in Owerri, which was a surprise considering it wasn't one of my choices. I had been a "specimen" of the then Minister of Education's experiment to shuffle some students to Federal schools outside their cultural region, as was done for the National Youth Service Corps (NYSC). Dad continued trying to explain that the postal system often took about three months to get letters by standard post from one end of the country to another, east to west in this case, and that was probably why my admission letter was not received in time for the January resumption. Well, the mere mention of "FGGC" jolted me up from the sickbed, and without thinking, I yanked off the intravenous drip, got off the bed, and motioned "Let's go" to my parents. I remember the principal remarking on the sudden regain of my strength and enthusiasm, and being greatly surprised by my reaction, exclaimed "So your sickness has been about the type of school all this while!"

It took some minutes of my parents' attempt to calm me down before I realised that they, especially my dad, were expressing their objection and decision not to accept the offer because the school was located in Imo State—in the eastern and Igbo-speaking region of Nigeria. They were uncomfortable with the idea of sending me, a ten-year-old who was constantly sick, to a boarding school in a faraway location where they didn't know anyone. But whilst they were getting hung up on the location, my only interest was in it being a Federal Government school—and that was all that mattered. Finally succumbing to my determination evidenced by a sudden recovery, we struck an agreement for me to wait a few days to allow for the preparation of the necessary paperwork for my discharge from the school. In the two or so days that passed, I never returned to the school clinic and went to the classroom for one of the few times since school resumption, knowing that they were going to be my last in that school. Some of my classmates were meeting me for the first time, so I was introducing myself and saying 'goodbye' to them at the same time. In my last days there, I also visited the school dining hall for record purposes and gave out all my remaining 'provisions' (dry foods and snacks) to other boarders.

On the morning of my departure, I could barely contain my excitement while waiting for my parents' arrival. They headed to the administration block to sign the necessary documents while I waited by the car. They said something about being surprised that I had spent less than ₦2 (two naira) out of the ₦20 pocket money they had deposited for my upkeep upon resumption. For someone who didn't eat school meals and had leftover provisions, this was more a testament to my sustenance by drips as opposed to actual food in that period. For me, however, all that seemingly lost time quickly became the past as we rode home. My mind was now set on resuming in the type of school I wanted to attend; my plans were back on track!

My return home was busy with us gathering all of the necessary registration documents requested by the Federal school, including detailed medical assessment reports and x-rays. About a week later, approximately mid-February, my parents and I were in a commercial "public" transport headed to Owerri. We caught the transport at first light so we could arrive during school hours, in time to meet the administrative staff for my registration and acceptance into the school. Apparently, my dad was still very worried about letting me attend a boarding school this far away from home. He had only been comfortable with St. Helen's or the Federal school choices we had because they were within easy reach and located in the western region, where we were familiar with the predominant local language and culture. To him, this would make settling in a lot easier on a ten-year-old. He worried that if I didn't settle in easily, what happened during my time at St. Helen's could repeat itself, only this time they would be too far away to quickly respond or see me. Discussing his concerns with my grandfather, Mum told of how Baba had reminded Dad of my goal-oriented traits and persistence with anything I believed in. He, therefore, encouraged my dad to let me go, since it was my dream and choice to attend this Federal Government school despite the location and to trust that it would be enough to help me adjust as required. So, we were on the eight-hour journey, travelling by road, which was the only means of travel between the western and eastern sides of the country at that time. I was filled with excitement, though without any inclination of what lay ahead.

YETUNDE GOES TO SCHOOL

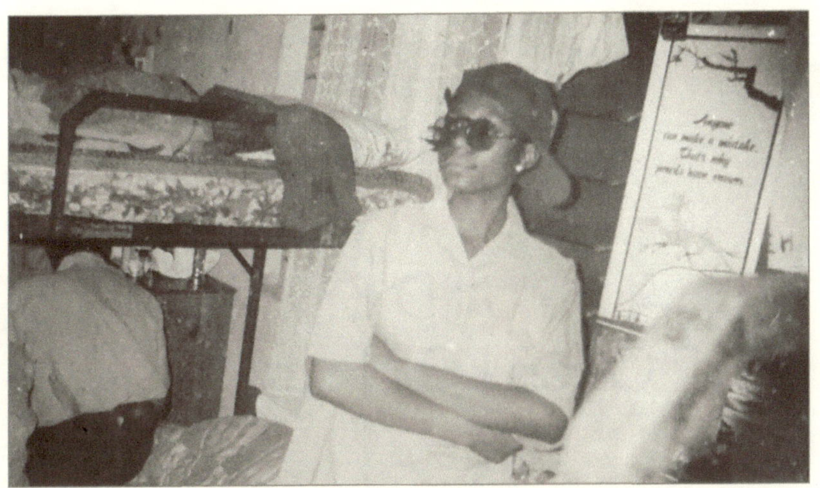

In the senior school uniform

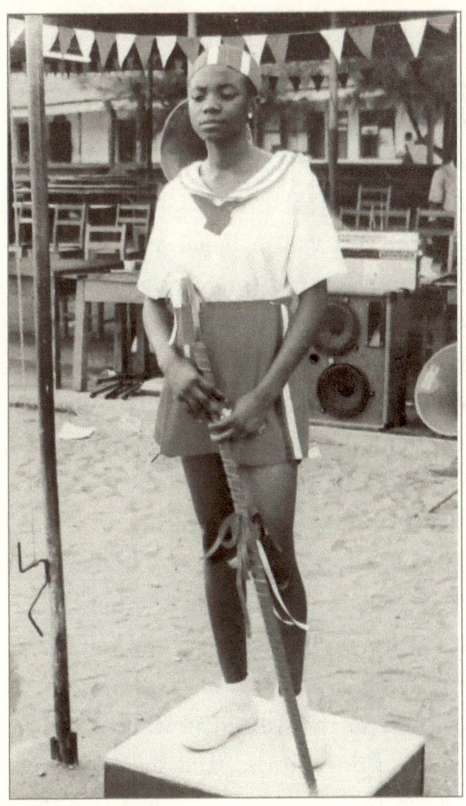

On sports day – Red house march past uniform

A GUIDE IN A FOREIGN LAND

My parents and I arrived at Federal Government Girl's College, Owerri in the early afternoon and got directed from one block to another for my registration. I was one of the last batch of students to resume. Registration included the school uniforms and all recommended textbooks for each subject, as the cost was included in the school fees—which were subsidised by the Federal Government. Supply of books was one of the perks of attending such a school then—the hassle of searching for textbooks or turning up without the right ones, which could be very disruptive to learning, was removed for the individual student. The school uniforms consisted of Class Wear (for attending lessons—shirt on pinafore for juniors or skirts for seniors), the Outing Uniform (used on Sundays or special school events), and the Day Wear (worn at every other time in between). All uniforms were in the school's blue-and-white colour tones. Upon completing my registration, I waved "goodbye" to my parents and off I went with my 'buddy'—student told to show me around for the rest of the day.

My tour began immediately with her pointing out the Form 1 dining hall, which was closest to the Administration "Admin" Block. Then we passed through a set of dormitories, and she explained that the student dorms were organised by the school year, just like the dining halls, and that each year was referred to as Form 1, Form 2, ... to Form 6; elsewhere known as years 7 to 12. Forms 1 to 3 were the Junior Secondary School (JSS 1-3) classes while Forms 4 to 6 were the Senior Secondary School (SSS 1-3) classes. Although the school operated on a first-name basis, anyone in a set that was at least two years ahead of one's own must be referred to as *Senior*. They could also send one on errands of their choosing or mete out 'punishments' for whatever reason they deemed fit, and one must oblige. For a Form 1 student like myself, this meant anyone from Form 3 and above— and that soon felt like practically the whole school! This was the first point of culture shock for me; contrary to my upbringing as the first child—one to lead—here, I was at the very bottom of the ladder.

Upon getting to the Form 1 dorm, she took me to the hall prefect, who although a Form 6 student was a resident in the Form 1 dormitory. It was said that the situating of some school prefects within the junior dorms was to protect the junior girls, but my experience in the first two years of that dormitory style was that these seniors were more of the "enemy within" than protectors. I was allocated a top bunk bed in the 'first apartment' (dorm room), which had at least ten bunks. As this was the closest apartment to the dorm's entrance, we often were easier targets for seniors, who came from other dorms looking for junior girls to send on errands.

Soon the school bell rang, and my guide came to fetch me—the bell was for dinner; being a weekday, everyone had to exit the dorms to go to their respective dining hall and then to their classroom for the 'night prep'. Having not attended any lessons yet, the night prep was my opportunity to get a desk in the temporary class I was assigned to. I had been told earlier by the administration staff that there were six arms in each form, ranging from U to Z. Although I was assigned to the Y arm, I was to join W for lessons until further notice. So, I went into the Form 1W classroom for the night prep; getting to know other girls and immediately standing out, not just for starting school more than a month after the others, but for being a Yorùbá girl with a predominantly Ghanaian accent in a class where 99 percent of the girls were Ibos. Needless to say, it was a relief to go back to the dorm that night and settle into bed after a quick bucket bath. Soon the bell rang for lights out and I fell asleep. Though it had been a very long day, I recall going to bed pleased that I was finally in the type of boarding school that I wanted.

The next day started early. Having been used to rising at about 5:30 a.m. when Mum called my name, I woke up automatically at that time and was dressed before most girls got up. Thankfully, my parents had trained us to always be prepared in good time for the day. Mum, especially, taught us that when in a group or full-house setting, we should take a shower before going to bed and endeavour to rise before everyone else so we could have a quick wash and be set for the day. That way, she taught, if chaos were to arise later from many people needing the bathroom at the same time or there was a water shortage, then we would have escaped such (for the day, at least). This was exactly what happened in the dorm day after day, but for six years I hardly ever got caught out in the mayhem because of this singular discipline instilled in me!

MORAL –

Parents, your children may look like they aren't listening to you. But if you keep teaching what is good for them, consistently without smothering, then you can rest assured that when they are alone, they will hear your voice guiding them to do what is right. Leading by example with evident results is the best way to pass on knowledge to a child.

That next morning, during classes, I received a note asking me to report to the Admin Block because my parents were there to see me. Upon getting there, I remember asking in a fairly firm tone, "What are you still doing around?" followed by, "I thought you would be on your way back to Àkúrẹ́ by now." I will never forget the surprised expression that cut across my mum's face as I spoke those words. Dad was still attempting to explain that they wanted to check on me to be sure I was fine before they returned home considering the experience at St. Helen's, when Mum turned to him, saying, "Let's go; she is obviously fine and settled in." Then Dad handed me a piece of paper, which had a teacher's name on it. They had run into Auntie Jane while waiting, and Dad knew her somehow. So, he told her about me and asked if she could look out for me. This, I believe, was God's way of assuring my dad that His plans were ahead of ours and He would look after me, which gave him peace of mind. We said another round of goodbyes, and off they went, while I dashed back to the Form 1 classroom block for my lessons. A few days later, I found Auntie Jane, who happened to be one of my teachers. Upon introducing myself, she greeted me warmly. Subsequently, she started to truly look out for me, becoming my official 'guardian' throughout my time at the school.

THINK ON THIS...

Get to know people for who they are and relate with them as such, rather than by popular opinions or prejudices that do not reflect who God has created them to be. Everyone deserves the 'benefit of doubt', irrespective of their skin colour (it works both ways), social status, religious background, nationality, ethnicity, or any other differences we choose to observe—some of which the individual had no control over. We all feel pain and we all bleed 'red' so being human is all that should matter. This is especially important for a Christian to make a habit of because it is the example Jesus laid down for us, and the work He did even in our own lives—accepting us as sons and daughters of God when we did nothing to deserve that privilege.

A RUDE
AWAKENING

A few weeks after resumption at Federal Government Girl's College, Owerri, it was time for Form Order Tests! No one had told me that every term—and there were three in a year—the school conducted two Form Order Tests, each lasting a week. In the chosen week, all six forms underwent a test based on what had been covered so far on every subject an individual was undertaking. Each test accounted for 20 percent of the term assessment, such that the final term exams accounted for 60 percent. Then when the Form Order Test results were in, the school principal announced the names of the girls in the last three and the first three positions in each arm; going from Form 1 to Form 6 at the school assembly, which took place every Tuesday and Thursday. That was six arms per Form so there was hardly any other agenda covered on such assembly days.

These first Form Order tests must have occurred about three weeks after I resumed and about a week into my move to Form 1Y from "W-arm"—and for some subjects, the teachers were different. Hence I was still trying to catch up on more than a month of missed lessons and settling into the new class when the tests began. I tagged along, not fully understanding the gravity of what was happening. Therefore, on the day of the first Form Order Test results announcement, I was completely oblivious as to what that school assembly was about. At the time, the Assembly Ground was an open space in the middle of a block called the Quadrangle. The principal and some staff sat on the Assembly Grounds stage, whilst the students and all else sat on benches facing the stage under beautiful almond fruit trees.

It was like any other Assembly Day to me when the principal stood up to make the announcements. Then in quick succession starting from Form 1U, she called out the names of the last three positions first, followed by the first three. Getting to Form 1Y, I heard my name in the eighteenth position, meaning I was top of the last three in a class of twenty girls, but still had no idea about what just happened. On and on she went until she called out the results for the last class, Form 6Z. Shortly after the assembly ended, Auntie Jane came to find me where the Form 1 girls sat having heard my name. My countenance changed as she explained to me what had happened. I became inconsolably sad in the moment it dawned that I had been bottom of the class! Though I often relied on my "pictorial" memory and a little brushing up on notes taken to sit exams, being at the bottom of my class was unfamiliar territory. She tried consoling me by explaining that the tests were based on about eight weeks of lessons when I had only been in the school for a few weeks and still settling in. Nevertheless, I recall being weighed down by this incident until that first Sunday in March when my dad came to visit.

Visiting Days were the first Sunday of each month in a school term. So, on March 5, 1989, Dad came to visit me for the first time, and I was very excited to see him. Parents or guardians waited at the stands in the school's mini-stadium while a message was sent to their daughter to meet them there. When another student found me and said, "Your dad is looking for you," Usain Bolt could not have outrun me with the way I ran to the mini-stadium (lol). Seeing him, I leapt on Dad with so much joy and force that he staggered backwards a little bit. On such days, parents were allowed to visit with cooked meals and provisions, and to spend time with their children or ward up to 6:00 p.m. Knowing the distance from which Dad had come and not expecting to see my parents that soon, I was too overjoyed to notice that he had nothing on him. Being his first experience of this, he came with only cash for me to add to my 'pocket money', which was more than enough for me. As we spoke, he told me Auntie Jane had called to inform him of my

Form Order test results. I will never forget how he encouraged me that day. Whilst he wasn't OK with my being at the bottom of the class, Dad told me that he completely understood that I was still settling into the school and that it no doubt impacted my academic performance. Therefore, he was proud that I even made it so far without any incidents that could have resulted in him being called back sooner to come pick me up. Dad reminded me that he believed in my abilities and encouraged me to stay focused on why I was in the school, which was predominantly to learn. "*When you learn, you will do well in any test or exam because you know what you are answering, and are not just studying to pass alone.*" Sticking in my brain like glue, those words shaped my approach to life ever since.

Saying "goodbye" to my dad that day was one of the hardest things for me. But in that moment, I grew a heart muscle that has helped me through life's journeys to this day. It was right then that I realised I would be doing life without my parents always being present. Therefore, I needed to "toughen up" to face whatever may come my way whilst remembering that I would always have my parents' support and love no matter where I go. Although Dad came to visit every first Sunday in each term until the end of my Form 3 (year 9), it was after this first visit that I started to grow into my own.

THINK ON THIS...

In our supposedly modern society, the family unit has been derogated to a mere collection of (happy) individuals under the same roof. What a fallacy! Then we wonder why the sense of 'individualism' is on the increase, with fewer people caring about others or the impact of their actions on the wider society. Our society today has nearly lost the sense of what it means to live with the consciousness that "life isn't just about you!" Whilst we all are created with unique abilities, the intention is for such to be used in a societal context—that is, primarily for the benefit of others around you. It is why the culture of self-aggrandisement has done nothing more than tear down the fabrics of what makes a good society and given room to previously unimaginable atrocities being committed. So, this one is for leaders in various capacities—let your examples, policies, and celebrated ways of life be those that encourage families to stay together and foster societal unity. A salute to single parents, mostly mothers, who are doing a great job raising their children to be good citizens. But, much better is a home where the father is 'present'—in every sense of that word. Having local authorities or charities take responsibility for displaced children is good, but isn't it much better when neighbours look out for one another and communities come together to prevent the decay of each family unit? Let's create environments where each person in our societies can thrive. Hopefully, seeing clearly (with hindsight), we can agree that the answer to what our world needs is certainly not an individualistic approach to societal living.

HERE TO
SURVIVE

My life in FGGC Owerri soon became routine. As with my primary school days, I took on running and other field sports as well as joined the music group for my assigned school 'house'—Red House. So every term, I was busy with schoolwork and at least one other extracurricular activity. As the years went by, different landmark events took place—some of which are told here, but there were three things I recall as having the most influence on my determination to "survive" in the school or any "new" place and on hindsight, my mental and overall wellbeing.

One, had to devise a means of escaping the clawing jaws of the Form 6 girls, whose dorm was across a field from the Form 1 dorm. It was either that or be consumed. They were often outside their dorm's main entrance, like hawks seeking a junior girl to "devour." Whereas, the steps leading into the Form 1 dorm were as high as those leading to my maternal grandparent's home in Ọǹdó town! They were steep and wide, and formed the perfect opportunity for a senior to 'swoop down' on an unsuspecting junior girl before the youngling can make it into the safety of the dorm. Being an athlete, although of fragile frame and rather small stature, I mastered the art of playing deaf to their calls as I came around the corner and getting up those steps so quickly as to disappear out of sight in split seconds before they could recognise who it was that so valiantly disobeyed their calls. The only times I fell prey were either when they came into the dorm to take several of us to their dorm on a Saturday to help them clean and run other errands, or when I was on punishment by one of the resident prefects, which often involved them sending us to the Form 6 dorm for them to do with us as they pleased. And yes, it was as bad as that sounds! We even christened their dorm *Kurmin Rukiki,* meaning "the land of no return," drawn from the book, *An African Night's Entertainment* by Cyprian Ekwensi.

Being in the school at age ten when the average age for my set was twelve years old, made me one of the youngest students in the entire school. So, to the likes of me, the Form 6 girls looked like giants—they were grown women! Good thing, they also perceived me as a weakling, often overlooking my disguised rude comments and attitude with comments such as "You, what can you do? Please get out of here."—which was music to my ears. And even when my behaviour was recognised as stubbornness, the punishments were "bearable" when compared to those of my mates who attempted same. I had recognised pretty early on that the game was one of *survival of the fittest* and my *fit* was not in physical strength but in the power of my mind, which was often underestimated. Some people would have been offended by that but not yours truly—I learnt to take full advantage of this. To me, it was the perfect cover for studying people and having the tools necessary to always stand in the best possible position should things go awry. This is in no way seeking to manipulate others but in learning to turn their presumptuous behaviours and underestimation of my capabilities, to my advantage.

The second was in the fact that I always took ill to Malaria in particular, at least once every term for six years! The illnesses often couldn't be managed with drugs alone so I was admitted into the school Sick Bay and placed on intravenous drips for about two days followed by several injections before I could get back on my feet. This was so frequent, that the school nurses became familiar with my face. They conducted several tests, changed my diet to eliminate beans especially, ordered that I be given hot water for baths every morning, and tried all sorts of combos of available medications, yet it always seemed a puzzle as to why I took ill so frequently. Discounting iron anaemia, my blood group and genotype seemed perfect on paper so the root cause was never uncovered. Often in the pain, I would remember my dad's encouraging words about not letting anaemia, sickness, or anything ever stop me from pressing on towards my goals. That always gave me a little extra boost to "push through" another day until I was well enough to stand on my two feet again. But the experience taught me to be more resilient, to be more empathetic towards sick people, and never to be quick in attributing any form of illness to myself—even so-called "simple headache."

The third was a direct result of my quest to know more about being a lady. Considering I had no sisters or girlfriends at primary school, I later realised that being in a girls-only boarding school tainted my view of the female species more than it did teaching me to become one. It over-exposed me to what I thought summarised the "world of women," though not totally inaccurate, skewed my perceptions for a long time as they were based on attitudes of maturing women—ladies who were equally growing into their own persons. At the time, what I observed were the manipulative behaviours, forming of cliques based on possessions rather than intelligence, backbiting, malice, unnecessary competition with others resulting in jealousy and envy, dishonesties, meanness, excessive focus of conversations on boys, and so many other things that I detested. So, I made deliberate efforts not to get into any cliques and to be independent in my way of thinking. As the years went by, I grew more and more dislike for women and could hardly see what good there was about being a lady.

My despise for anything related to women was heightened when I started menstruating at fourteen years old and in Form 5 (year 11). That first period was excruciatingly painful and so heavy that I thought I was going to die—there are no words to describe the intensity of the pain. Thankfully, a classmate loaned me some pads and taught me how to use them, but I still ended up staining my clothes every day for more than a week. Many nights, I would stay in the kneeling position just to get an uninterrupted five or so minutes of pain-free sleep. To top it up, when I returned home for the term holidays and Mum discovered that I had started my periods, she gave me the most detailed sex education talk I have ever heard. Now, most African parents shy away from such conversations but not my mum. Being a teacher, a science one at that, she minced no words! It was so detailed, it felt like the potential repercussion of extramarital sex—that is, falling pregnant—was a woman's punishment and burden to bear alone. To my mind, the agent for this inequality was the menstrual cycle. So, I hated it even more.

Although having my period compelled me to associate with some realities of being a woman, against my deepest wishes, I found it difficult to describe myself as one—often rationalising it as "I may look like a woman but I was certainly nothing like them." To my mind, being a woman was synonymous with being malicious, jealous, given to temperaments, etc., and that was not how I saw "me" or planned for "me" to become. Unconsciously, I developed a self-righteous attitude; one that made me think I was better in character than most of the school girls and womenfolk in general. I also became insensitive to other people's feelings, especially those of women, as I often considered them exaggerated and manipulative, and was often abrasive in how I communicated. But thanks to 'life', a new light would be slowly shed on my then myopic views.

THE QUESTION OF AN AFTERLIFE

Back in Form 2, the year 1990, my dad did not come on the Visiting Day in February. Normally, he would arrive on the Saturday preceding the visiting day to collect my shopping list and chat a little while before he went into town to buy the items requested and then, stay the night in a hotel. On the Sunday earmarked for Visiting Day, he would come before 10:00 a.m. to drop off the purchased provisions, give me some pocket money, and travel back home from there. Often, I was one of the first girls to be visited in school each month. Hence, I was disappointed when I waited both on Saturday and Sunday for my dad, but he didn't show up.

The following Sunday night, February 11 to be precise, I had a dream. In the dream, Baba came to visit me in school. Surprised to see him come alone, I asked after my dad. Baba joked about not knowing why my dad didn't come to visit the week before and apologised on his behalf. After chatting for a while, he handed me some provisions which he got me and we said our 'goodbyes'. As he took his leave, I saw him join an endless line of really happy people, all robed in white, and singing joyfully as they walked on. The farther away from me that he walked, his clothes shone brighter— turning white—yet he seemed to be walking into an even brighter light. There was an innumerable number of people before him and more started to join in behind him, as they all walked on into the clouds. While watching all these unfold, my dad's car appeared on the horizon, driving right past Baba and heading towards me so I waited at the school gate where I had been meeting with Baba. When my dad got out of the car, I asked why he didn't pick up Baba as he drove past and pointed towards the crowd for him to see Baba still walking on. Dad turned around but couldn't see anything and started trying to convince me that there was no way Baba could have come to Owerri all by himself. With my eyes still fixated on Baba, he suddenly faded into the light and I woke up. It was one of the most beautiful things I had seen, and although that was exciting, the reality of what I dreamt slowly dawned on me—Baba was dead! I began to weep.

I cried the entire walk to class that Monday morning. When a classmate asked what the matter was, I told her my grandad had passed. She laughed because I mentioned that I saw it in a dream (forgetting that she wasn't family and would know nothing about the peculiarity of my dreams). She told a few others and they mocked calling me *Josephine,* akin to Joseph in the Bible who was known for his dreams and interpretation of dreams. The next day, I received an EMS Speedpost from my dad. It contained a letter dated February 5, 1990, explaining that Baba had taken ill, hence he couldn't come for the Visiting Day the Sunday before. I instinctively knew it must have been a serious incident, for my dad to send a letter without cash or postal order (to convert to cash) by Speedpost so I could receive it within a week—as opposed to the one or more months it took for standard posts. Therefore, the letter did nothing but confirm the dream I had. So, I cried some more.

At term end when both my parents picked me up from the Ọ̀rẹ̀ drop off point for *Ekene dili Chukwu* coach transport to Lagos—organised for our school girls, which I often joined though stopping along the way— they initially told me Baba was feeling better, when I asked after him, not wanting to cause me pain. Then I told them of my dream and conviction that he was dead. At that, they told how he had started recovering from the illness before that fateful Sunday of February 11, when things took a turn for the worst. Sensing that might be his last day, my dad was said to have sent for the church priest so Baba could be given the Holy Communion at home. Although an unusual request, the priest obliged apparently because he also sensed what was going to happen. Following the Communion, they relayed how Baba called them into his room individually to pray for them and say "goodbye" before breathing his last. I was expecting to cry when Baba's death was confirmed but instead, hearing the account brought me an unusual peace. Seeing as my dream occurred the same night, I felt so loved to have had an opportunity to also say "goodbye" to him and more importantly, catch a glimpse of where he was going.

Before this experience, I had no idea what happened to human beings after they died. It all seemed pointless that life could end suddenly and just be no more. So, at the time, my deepest and silent quest was to understand the meaning of life. But hearing the account of Baba's final hours and remembering how joyful he was singing hymns alongside other happy people, in my dream, started to incline my young mind to thinking that there is likely more to life (as we know it) than just the hundred-or-so years that an individual can hope to live here. And that it was possible for this 'afterlife' to be a beautiful experience, with the key likely in what Baba believed in—that is, Christianity. My follow-on quest then became, "How do I ensure being in the same beautiful place that I saw Baba taken to?" Believe it or not, I was unsure of how to go about this despite being "raised" in church and having had a personal encounter with Jesus. So, I started to read anything I could find and interact with others with different "ways of worship" in a bid to find some answers.

Through the years, I found people's thoughts on the 'afterlife' differed as much as their approach to gaining eternal peace. Not surprisingly, some didn't believe in the concept at all; believing that when you are dead, you are dead, and that is where it all ends. Others were unsure, while those who believed there to be something had often different descriptions of this *never-ending land;* call it Heaven or Paradise or Nirvana, I cared little for the name. Despite the confusing findings, it was difficult to so easily dismiss what I had seen in that dream. Although I was only eleven years old at the time, my experience of Baba's death set a strong and unshakeable example of a "good way" to die. Therefore, I did with it what I knew best—that is, to formulate a "goal" as to how I would want to "check out" of this realm when I grew old enough. My longing then became obtaining the "how to" ensure that when I am ready to depart this life, I would die peacefully like Baba—blessing the next generations—and be smiling all the way into the afterlife.

THINK ON THIS...

All men and women have the gift of *Time*. It is the one resource that we all have an equal amount of irrespective of nationality, skin tone, gender, belief, social status, or any other differences that the human society creates. The use of Calendars can be deceptive in making you think that 'time' is passing when in actual fact, you are the one passing (to put it bluntly). Time doesn't age but we do! Each day you draw breath, you equally draw closer to your grave—not to be grim, but to inspire wisdom in the same light as King David's prayer in Psalm 90:12 for God to "teach us to number our days, that we may apply our hearts unto wisdom." Therefore, I encourage you to invest your time wisely.

GIRLS OF
PREY

In 1991, at the start of my Form 3, the Federal Government announced a change in the school year system. The year was going to start running from September to August as opposed to from January to December. This meant that schools across the country had to cover in just two terms, January to June, what would have been covered in three terms in order to align with the new system. This change however had the most impact on those who were in Forms 3 (JSS 3) and 6 (SSS 3) being the ones sitting national examinations that year. These examinations were crucial in that they determined if we could move up to the Senior Secondary School (SSS 1) for students sitting the JSS-3 exams, like myself, or could gain a university admission for those in SSS-3 as success in their examinations was a requirement. So, having the year's syllabi cramped into six months had huge implications for both the schools and their students. To manage this, my school decided to give the Forms 3 and 6 girls only a week's break during the Easter holidays between the two terms after which we resumed what was known as the "Extension Period" to allow us to cover our syllabi before the exams in May and June.

Although my set girls were regarded as 'seniors' of sort because the Form 1 students had to call us that, with just us and the Form 6 students in school, we were the only juniors and the easy prey to answer to their every beck and call. The school arranged for Form 3 students to stay in a converted arm of the Quadrangle, while the Form 6 students stayed in their dorm, *Kurmin Rukiki*. The two dorms were deliberately a distance apart, as were our classroom blocks, in an attempt to avoid altercations between the two sets. But this wasn't as effective because the Quadrangle was on the way to the dining halls and other shared school amenities, like the tap area for 'fetching' water, laundry room for ironing, and 'Tuck Shop' for purchasing snacks.

To make matters worse, the current school prefects were Form 6 students. At meal times, they would first inform their classmates of food being ready at the dining hall before ringing the school bell to alert us of the same, by which time they would have raided our dining hall, leaving very little food to be shared amongst the over one hundred of us in Form 3. Therefore, most of us went hungry for many days; living on scraps left behind, our provisions, or whatever one could afford to buy from the Tuck Shop. It was tough enough having to deal with longer school hours, the frustration of only seeing our families for one week in what was then leading up to five or six months, the pressure of sitting national exams that were set on a full syllabus which we had to learn in a condensed period, and general boarding life. Layering on this practice by the Form 6 girls, not surprisingly, increased the tensions between the two sets and set the scenes for what came next.

One faithful afternoon, I went to the taps with some classmates to fetch water. It was at a time of day we had observed the taps were often quiet— with no Form 6 girls lurking around, and my set girls were few so no queues. On the way back, we noticed the kitchen ladies setting up the tables for dinner and were completely surprised that it happened that early, as it was more than an hour before the time we would normally have heard the bell ring for food. Hastening back to the Quadrangle, we alerted our other set girls so that everyone could get some food, for once, before it all got raided by the Form 6 girls. But one of the girls, who had an appetite for "trouble-making," had an even better idea! She decided to rally up some others, seeing as this presented the perfect opportunity for a showdown.

The meal that evening was *moin-moin* (Nigerian bean pudding) with *ogi* (white-coloured custard made from corn). Although it wasn't a favourite of mine, I joined the herd of girls who were now heading to the dining halls. We split ourselves between the Forms 3 and 6 dining halls and carted away most, if not all of the food pots on the tables, taking them to our dormitory. Upon getting to the Quadrangle, those who wanted the meal had their fill, and we (intentionally) littered the remainder all over the quarters in the middle and open area of the Quadrangle. By the time the Form 6 girls got to the dining halls before ringing the bell, in their usual practice, they were met with empty tables.

Realising that we must have gotten there first, they stormed down to our dorm and were visibly livid to find that we not only took their food but had wasted it by decorating the Quadrangle lawns with it. Unlike them, we were used to going hungry because of their practice, so this comeback of ours was a major blow for them. To fully understand their predicament, imagine that you are starving but the only meal available is lying in front of you mingled with sand. (Is it mean if I still relish the feeling of seeing the look on their faces? LOL!!!) It was a real-life application of Newton's third law of motion, which says *"Action and reaction are equal but opposite in direction."* Anyway, a fight broke out! The school matrons and eventually the vice principal of administration had to be called in to broker some peace. That day, we achieved one thing—justice! The Form 6 girls got a taste of what it meant to study on empty stomachs and thereafter, started to treat us with a little more respect. Did we envisage how the events would turn out? Certainly not! But taking the opportunity that presented, as best as we knew how, certainly paid off.

THINK ON THIS...

Age, gender, skin tone, educational achievements, social class, etc. may give individuals an advantage in our societies but please know, that none of them is a determinant of intelligence or wisdom, and certainly not who you are. What you become or the level of success you can attain in life is dependent on what you set your mind on to achieve and how much you are willing to put into it. No one can enforce a *"you are"* until you have declared, by words and actions, that *"I am"*.

Special note to fellow citizens of nations that were/are subjected to slavery of any kind or, are under some form of dictatorial leadership, might I encourage you with two words—emancipate yourself. The real battle and consequently, the victory is first won in our minds. Let us FREE ourselves from any mental limitations—consciously or unconsciously introduced by these dehumanising circumstances—to feed our minds with information that empowers us to create better narratives for our future generations. Let us ride on the backs of these terrible circumstances, with strength and by joining forces, to rebuild our societies without violence or retaliation—turning experiences of dysfunctional pasts into tales of strong national heritages that we have so long desired!

MY FIRST LOVE

When we finished our JSS-3 exams, at the end of 'extension period', we returned home for a proper holiday—the results would determine if one could move to the next class, SSS-1 or Form 4. While home, I caught up with my best friend, Mike, and we had lots and lots of things to talk about. In the three years since leaving primary school, we mainly exchanged letters; hence, we relished this opportunity for many face-to-face interactions. Since the rest of the country was still on school time, both our parents enrolled us in a lesson school that had been set up by our mathematics teacher in primary school. So, we were together most of the day—at lesson school or in one of our homes after lessons, every weekday.

One day when Mike was at my house, I must have been so engrossed in our conversation that I didn't notice when my mum and brothers returned home. Mum came to the living room where we sat to ask if I had entertained Mike with anything since he came. I hastily responded saying that I had offered but he didn't want anything, and that quite frankly, he was "no visitor" so should be free to ask if he did. Mum looked at me, smiled, and went back to whatever she was doing in the kitchen. But I knew that look! It spelled, YOU ARE IN TROUBLE. It was customary in our home to leave individuals alone with their visitors, unless you knew the visitor too or were invited into their conversation. So, though my mum and brothers left us alone, I strongly suspected that the "topic" was not over.

Surprisingly, Mum said nothing when I came back from walking Mike part of the way to his house. In fact, she said nothing to me at all. Instead, she told what happened to my dad, who in turn said nothing to me that day. The next morning as they were getting into the car, heading to work, Dad looked at me and said in a very calm but firm tone, "I do not want to see any boy visiting you in my house again." Then he got into the car, and they drove off. It took me a moment to comprehend what had happened. Rarely had my parents ever given directives without asking our input, but I knew not to disobey this one however distraught it made me. I walked back into the house and cried.

Later that morning when I had managed to pull myself together, I went to Mike's house. Normally, I would take my strides with gusto but not this time. As I walked down, the weight of the rather difficult message I had for him bore heavily on my mind so I became anxious. Arriving at Mike's house, he opened the door and was happily welcoming me in when I told him that I had something important to tell him. Before he could ask, I said with a very straight face, "Please do not come to my house again." Taken aback, he asked why. All I could muster was, "Because my dad said so." Feeling the tears welling up, as I could hear the shock and pain in his voice, I immediately turned my back and walked away. Picking up the pace, I broke into a run and headed back home. To this day, I still number that moment as one of the most difficult in my life! At the time, and apart from my immediate family, Mike was the most important person to me. Therefore, seeing his reaction to the news dealt a further blow to my heart. So I kept running, perhaps it could numb some of the pain I was feeling.

On getting home and for several days after, I remained physically in pain. So, I decided to ask my mum for some explanation of what happened—knowing that for some reason, Mike's visit that day met with her disapproval. Mum explained that she noticed from the way we were interacting that we likely had feelings for each other, more than friends should. Therefore, she had to tell my dad what she suspected, and they both felt that I was too young, at age twelve, to have a boyfriend hence the decision to stop us from spending any more time together. They agreed for Dad to have that conversation with me, due to our closeness, but it ended up being more of an 'order' than a discussion. Although I argued that Mike and I were just friends and her intuition must have been wrong this time, the pain I was feeling suggested otherwise. In exploring with her why I felt so much hurt, I realised for the first time that I was not only very fond of Mike as a long-time friend but probably loved him as Mum suspected. With this realisation, I felt even worse. I had just told the one person I enjoyed spending time with, the likely first object of my love, and my best friend that we couldn't see each other again—without any explanation for why. Neither could I tell him how I truly felt, being now aware, lest it destroy whatever might be left of our friendship. Therefore, the only logical action left was for me to "shut down" my feelings so that the pain, at least, could go away. And to emotionally shut down, I did.

Mike and I continued to write to each other in school, but the timing was too far apart due to postal delays to count for any meaningful communication. It wasn't until the completion of our SSS-3 (year 12) that Mike summoned the courage to attempt to see me again. Unfortunately, I was out of town visiting relatives in Lagos. On my return home, Mum gave me the package that he had left for me. In it were a birthday card for my sixteenth birthday, a heart-shaped luminescent green keyring, and some other little gifts. The card read "To the one I love," and had in it a handwritten note informing me that he was leaving for the United States of America (USA), where he planned to attend university, in a few days. By the time I was reading his message, it was too late to act. Oh, how pained (again) I was realising that Mike had felt the same way about me all along. Mike and I were never to see or speak again for several years—leaving me with many "what ifs"—that is, until...

FINDING MY VOICE

As of September 1991, I resumed school in Form 4 (SSS 1). Now a bona fide senior, my school uniform changed from the navy blue pinafore to a skirt—both were worn with a short-sleeve sky blue shirt. Though still of a small frame, being aged twelve, the school uniform was a visual indicator of my 'seniority' thereby reducing the chances of being mistaken as a Form 1 (JSS 1) student. Now, I could only be sent on errands by the Form 6 girls, which in itself was liberating, but much better was the fact that that rarely happened since the school had changed the dormitory system to be by "house" colour, not class "form." This meant that each senior girl could be allocated a lower bunk space while the junior girls got the top bunk. In this structure, it was technically expected that the junior girl would attend to that senior's needs, while the senior was to protect their junior girl from maltreatment by other seniors. Compared to our time when juniors were at the mercy of any senior girl that laid eyes on them, this turned out a better approach to protecting the younger ones from the harsh realities of boarding whilst allowing for healthier bonds to develop among students across class forms—the sisterhood.

My assigned junior top-bunk girl was small-statured like me, kind, and soft-spoken. We worked so well together that I retained her through to my Form 6—my SSS-3 (year 12) and her JSS-3 (year 9). Oftentimes, I went with her to the taps to avoid her being in endless queues and being 'chanced' by others, as I had experienced. In our room, I also made it clear to the other *seniors* that she was not to be sent on errands without my permission thereby protecting her from being 'preyed' upon even in my absence. Somehow, I felt the need to protect this young girl's innocence and gentleness from being "corrupted" by the dark sides of boarding life— and with this, I realised that my protective instincts extended beyond my brothers to anyone I considered younger or more vulnerable than myself. It was the first time, as I recall, that I made a conscious decision to give another person the opportunities or luxuries that I never got—a trait I always admired in my dad.

Over time, I became more vocal about any perceived injustice towards me or anyone else. I was OK being 'direct' in addressing issues and gave little care to the size or emotions of whoever was caught in the line of my fire. These actions earned me the nickname *Voltron* amongst classmates, mostly alluding to the tone of my voice and aura projected when in defence mode. Soon, the littlest things always rubbed me the wrong way and would rapidly be followed by an outburst of anger. This, my parents noticed so they started to have deep conversations with me about it. Since becoming a senior, Dad had stopped visiting me in school hence their opportunities for these inter- actions were limited to the holidays—they ceased each one to understand my viewpoints and offer advice.

In our conversations, we found that the biggest root causes for the out- bursts were my growing awareness of the socio-political environment and loathe of the inequalities in Nigeria. I was especially troubled by the eth- nic divides and the Federal and State Governments' attitudes towards the populace. For example; civil servants like both my parents were increasingly owed several months of their salaries, which facilitated the increasing foot- hold of societal decadence; those with means using their wealth as a tool to oppress others considered to be less privileged; the ever-reducing funding of public schools making access to good education difficult; decaying infra- structures including the roads which I had to frequently travel, and many more. Essentially, I was angry at the system.

To these, Mum's thoughts were often for me to show more gratitude. As one attending a Federal school and had half of her school fees paid, she helped to see how I was more a beneficiary of that system. My response, however, was that although I was grateful for being able to attend the type of school I desired and having part of my fees paid in that process, I still found it difficult to ignore other kids my age who were unable to access the same quality of education—some of which were in the public school where she taught. Interestingly, my views in this regard were more towards hers—that *"Education is every child's right, not a privilege."* Hence, my concerns were for the increasing educational gap constituting a form of injustice. But I later learnt that she was teaching me how to be grateful for the opportunities and things I have, though life as a whole may not yet be perfect.

Also worthy of note was how I felt towards the prevalent stories told in school of the 1967 Nigerian Civil War, involving the Republic of Biafra. It often felt like I was being unjustly held responsible for losses the Igbos experienced as they fought for Biafra—being a Yorùbá indigene, the ethnic group said to have caused the republic's major downfall. As a minority in the school, such stories were not helpful to my daily existence. With our school situated on one of the battlegrounds, lines were inked into the school anthem to remind of that war although with a positive outlook of a 'unity' school like ours being born from it. Every Tuesday and Thursday at the Assembly Grounds, I sang the anthem, along with other students and teachers:

Nigeria we all make thee a promise
To serve thee with strength of hand and brain
To build and not break down
Bury quarrels in the ground
So that those who died may not have gone in vain

As much as I genuinely believed and wanted to do what I could to make possible those words, drawn from the second stanza, my everyday school reality did not inspire the need to strive towards "bury[ing] quarrels," for example. To my mind then, the best solution to the ethnic tensions seemed to be to divide Nigeria and let every region become a sovereign state—just as they were before Lord Frederick Lugard, the British colonial administrator, decided to merge the once independent Northern, Southern, Western, and Eastern regions into one. Moreover, every other Nigerian seemed to reason this way, so I thought *Why not?* But Dad would caution otherwise. His words were that such separations are often not devoid of war. Having personally experienced the Civil War, he did not wish any form of war on anyone. Therefore, he advocated for me to learn to be calm when expressing my views and always toe the line of peace in my dealings with others. Invaluable lessons that will take some years to sink in.

THINK ON THIS...

My first rule for solving a problem is recognising that there is one. Being true to yourself about an issue's existence is the most important ingredient to finding a solution or healing from past hurts. As long as the issue remains covered or you act precious around it, the problem will linger. Yes, God knows all things but He still asks us to confess our sins and to share one another's burdens because in doing so, we are opened up for light to flood any darkness and the solution-process kick-started. Also important to be mindful of who you open up to—can be a professional, parent, or trusted friend who has the ability to help or to find another trusted someone who can. However, to not acknowledge there is a problem or being unwilling to seek help and talk about it, does one more harm than good.

THE CLOAK OF DILIGENCE

At the start of Form 5 (SSS 2), each student had to choose the subjects they would undertake that year and consequently, in Form 6 (SSS 3)—the final year of secondary school. We had been exposed to all subjects offered in Form 4, with the only choice allowed then being the Nigerian languages. Now, every subject was optional except mathematics and the English language. There were guiding rules, such as the chosen subjects had to include at least one science subject and one Nigerian language. This was a crucial decision because it shaped the subjects one would also undertake in Form 6 and, importantly, those for which the West African Examination Council (WAEC) exams can be sat—one of the prerequisites for university course choices. Still going with my plan from primary school to study pharmacology at university; my subject choices were a no-brainer! My core selections were the science subjects of physics, chemistry, biology, and further (advanced) mathematics. Although I had thoroughly enjoyed literature in Form 4, I recall not choosing it because, in my eagerness, I started to read books on the reading list during the holidays. Shakespeare turned out an easier read, as my highly graphic mind struggled to cope in just the first chapter of *The Beautyful Ones Are Not Yet Born*—the author, Ayi Kwei Armah, was so detailed in describing events, it made my skin crawl. So, my additional subjects became Yorùbá language, which I was now really enjoying the study of, and home management.

Two terms into Form 5, it became apparent to my parents that there was a problem. Before this, my general performance was "average" so I got the same "pep talk" from my dad every term when he received my school report sheet. He often went on about how I had the capability to attain much better scores if only I exerted myself just a little. But I never quite saw the need to do that when I seemed to do "just fine" in the exams by attending classes alone. However, this term, the conversation with my parents was very different. They observed a decline in my scores for chemistry, such that I was on the borderline of failing, if not failed in the second term. Therefore, they enquired to know what was happening in school.

I revealed to them that I had been skipping my chemistry classes since the first term because I felt bullied by the teacher. She did an attendance roll call each lesson but had difficulty pronouncing my surname, being Igbo, and I might have corrected her pronunciation during the very first lesson. Remembering my "rude self" back then, I probably didn't answer "Present" when she called my name in the next couple of lessons, by which time I expected her to have learnt to pronounce my surname correctly. Taking an offence or exception to my behaviour, she started to pick on me in the course of the lesson to answer questions posed to the class and would deliberately make a mockery of my surname as she called me out. So, I started to skip her classes. After the lessons, I will borrow the handwritten notes of any classmate taking the subject and willing to release them for a few hours to enable me to copy the notes—with the hope that they were paying full attention and had put down the right things. Therefore, my poor results were a reflection of having not attended any of her classes in the second term and having to sit exams based on what I could understand by myself from the copied notes and textbooks.

Although upset that I did not bring this to their attention in good time, my parents decided to focus on the solution going forward. I intended to continue "winging" it, with the hope that she wouldn't be my chemistry teacher in Form 6 and that I might be able to recover the lost year before sitting the WAEC exams in preparation for university. But after much deliberation with my parents, who felt leaving things until Form 6 to resolve was too high of a risk compared to the alternative, I agreed to drop chemistry as a subject. This was a major blow to my dreams! It would mean also dropping physics and further mathematics subjects, and the end to the plans to study pharmacology—a long-term desire and thought route to finding cures to the major ailments that had plagued me and my loved ones for so many years. Working together with my parents, we decided for me to take on economics, geography, and government as replacements, moving me from "pure science" courses to the social sciences. The more important next step, of course, was for the school authority to allow me to make these changes. Therefore, Dad decided to accompany me to school, one last time, upon resumption of the third term in Form 5.

On the first day of school, Dad and I paid the vice principal (VP) of academics a visit to table my parents' concerns and our proposed subject changes. As expected, the VP of Academics initially objected to having so many changes that late in the year, but with my dad's persistence, she decided to investigate my claims and historical performance before deciding on what was acceptable. Meantime, she told me to start attending classes for the new three subjects being proposed as well as the three to be dropped—to ensure adequate cover for me, whenever the school made the final decision—while Dad stuck around in Owerri for what might have been about three or four days before she gave us her verdict.

On the day she told us her decision, the VP mentioned that my chemistry teacher in Form 4 had vouched for my behaviour when he was queried. He was also said to have been surprised to hear of my poor performance in Form 5, which helped the VP of Academics ascertain my claims that being bullied by the Form 5 teacher had a direct impact on my studies. When asked, Dad insisted that they had no interest in pursuing disciplinary charges against the teacher, but the focus was on obtaining a solution that allowed me to switch to the subjects we proposed. The VP, therefore, decided to approve the proposed changes on one condition only—that I would pass all three new subjects at the first Form Order Test that term. If I were to fail any of them, then I would have to revert to the initial "pure science" courses and find a way to recover the lost time before needing to sit the WAEC exams. With that agreement, Dad encouraged me to seize the opportunity with both hands (figuratively speaking). The ball was now in my court, and as he often reminded us, *Every man is the architect of his own future.* This was my future at stake, and I had just one goal—to pass the next Form Order Tests.

The first Form Order Tests often occurred a few weeks into a new term and each Form Order Test was designed to include any of the topics that have been covered in that subject up to the week before the tests. So, it was usually difficult to get anyone to loan out their class notes during that period—and with this being the third term, it was even more difficult getting notes because the tests will include everything taught since the start of the year. Therefore, I identified girls who kept good notes since the first term for each of my three new subjects and started making irresistible deals with them. The deals included giving them my share of any school meal of their choosing in exchange for some hours to copy their notes—most of which was those hours they would be asleep, and the dorm lights could be turned on, meaning between the hours of 10:00 p.m. and 5:00 a.m. My aim was simply to have sufficient notes covering the first two terms missed, in each subject, before the declared test week so, the sacrifices of food and sleep were my means to a crucial end. I spent many nights sitting on the concrete room floor copying notes so that I wouldn't fall asleep—my natural inability to sleep for long hours came in very handy during this period. I also learnt to assimilate information as I copied the notes because the chances of getting time to revise them before the tests were very slim, considering this was happening in conjunction with attending normal classes for about nine subjects and preparing for tests on all of them. All this I did day after day for several weeks, with just the one goal on my mind.

On the day of the Form Order Test results announcement, the closer the principal got to my class, Form 5Y, the farther back on the assembly line I moved. Up until this time, I had never invested so much time or emotion into my schoolwork but now, I had a lot at stake. I became incredibly nervous and so visibly shaken that I had to move to the very back of the line so I could crouch down with my hands wrapped tightly around my stomach. Then I heard the principal's voice saying, "Here are the results for Form 5Y." As before, she started with the last three positions. By this time, we had about thirty girls in my class. When she got done and my name was not called, I stood up heaving a huge sigh of relief. Of course, it didn't mean that I hadn't failed any of the all-important three subjects because the results were based on consolidated score averages, but it gave me the hope needed to survive this moment and to wait till the class teacher handed out the individual results per subject.

Now slowly starting to make my way back to the line, the principal was calling the names of the first three positions in our class. I was half-heartedly paying attention because we all knew the usual names that came up in those positions. For the first position, she said that there was a tie and called out one of the known names, immediately followed by my name. It took me, and my classmates too, a split second to realise what had just happened. As if on cue, most of the class girls erupted in shouts and hand claps, which caused the principal to pause a little before she continued with the results for Form 5Z. I was completely in shock for the rest of that assembly. One moment, I was recovering from nervous shakes; the next, my name was being called as top in my class. What?! I felt elated but didn't know how to fully express it. This was certainly proof that I had passed the three new subjects—the goal had been met. Phew!

Rather than head to our classroom after the assembly with my classmates, I went straight to the office of the VP of Academics. Seeing me, she commended my efforts and determination, and wasted no time in rubber stamping the forms confirming a change in my subjects. I later learnt that Auntie Jane called my dad to inform him of the great news, and the VP of Academics did the same to confirm the school's approval of my subject changes.

Following this experience, my parents didn't need to give me any more "pep talks," as this showed me that they had been right all along about what they believed to be my academic ability. I never did exert myself with that much intensity again, but neither have I performed "averagely" ever since. The events helped to change my perception of my abilities from "just fine" to "above average." More importantly, it ingrained in me the mindset my parents always talked about, which is true of every individual:

You can achieve anything you set your mind on to do, and that
The only person capable of stopping you, is you!

The rest of that term and into Form 6, I was in "cruise mode" having discovered more about how I learn. I remember coming third position in the very last Form Order Tests that we sat in the school, and reflecting on how much my perception of my abilities had significantly changed in the space of one year. I thought, this is the same 'me' who came last three in the very first Form Order Tests sat in Form 1 and had my view unconsciously tainted into believing that there were certain girls I couldn't do better than academically hence, there was no need to step out of my comfort zone. But out of this seemingly dire situation, came the realisation that I wasn't born to be subpar to anyone.

MORAL –

The point is never to compete with others, but to strive to be a better version of yourself each time and to make a habit of taking stock (introspection). That way, you can identify what has improved and what needs doing or improving to get you closer to achieving your goals. Just as an athlete runs a race, it is important to keep your eyes on the finish line, so that you may run your personal race with endurance and finish with gusto.

THINK ON THIS...

Knowing your grace helps you focus on your race! Too many people are jealous of other people's achievements, or trying to copy another while completely ignoring their God-given purpose. Each person is uniquely created by God Who has deposited in them what they need to succeed and be fulfilled in their lifetime—that is 'your grace'. Therefore, know your grace or find your place so you can run that race with diligence. That way, you can focus on being a better version of yourself each time rather than trying to be like someone else or becoming frustrated when you don't seem to be getting their kind of result. It is admirable to be able to learn from others' qualities that can help improve you, but the aim shouldn't be to copy them so you can become their shadow—in which way, you live a life becoming a second best when you were created to be unique and the only one of you that there can be.

MY
REBIRTH

Now in Form 6 (SSS 3 or year 12), all focus was on preparing for the WAEC aka Senior Secondary School Certificate Exams (SSCE) which occurred during May and June. Life in school was generally uneventful until one fateful Sunday evening, the 15th of May, when I was hanging out with two roommates in a "corner" they shared. Esther, who was in my set, was clearing out her things in preparation for her departure from school having sat for most of her exams and had only a few subjects left—a time when I was yet to sit any of mine. The other roomie was Tiffany, a Form 4 girl infamous for her "stubbornness" but was one of the few juniors I was friends with and fond of because we had fairly similar characters. I was lying on Tiffany's bed while discussing 'life' and plans after school with Esther when suddenly I started gasping for air like one who was having an asthma attack; except I had never had such. Struggling to breathe, my last recollection was hearing Esther ask Tiffany to get me some water, and I completely passed out. Everything became pitch black. I seemed to be falling into what seemed like a space that had no end. It was so dark I couldn't even see my own hands or feet, just knew I was falling…and it was very scary.

Those in the dorm room thought I had fainted; hence, another roommate in our set was said to have performed cardiopulmonary resuscitation (CPR) on me, but when I wasn't responding, they called for the house matron and school nurse. They even moved me to Esther's bed, which was closer to a window in the hope of getting more ventilation but still couldn't revive me. Then suddenly, they said, I started talking, still very much unconscious, about things that were deeply spiritual; like calling out names of girls who were demon-possessed and exposing some of their activities—all of which was surprising to me because I didn't believe in such at the time, let alone be one to speak of them in the nature they recounted. It seemed that I said so many things that no one present at the scene felt comfortable sharing them at all, even with me. News of the incident spread quickly, causing pandemonium across the school, rousing fear in some and anger in others, and sending drones of girls gravitating towards our room to see what was happening. Therefore, they decided to send out all the junior girls and lock the doors to preserve some sanity in the room, while the seniors, the matron, and the nurse continued their efforts to bring me back to consciousness. They said that after talking for a while, I fell silent and seemed "dead" again, so CPR was again administered. The whole saga lasted a couple of hours.

On the other side of my consciousness, I was still falling into the pitch-black space wondering if it was ever going to end. Then, I felt a hand reach out to grab me and throw me upwards with so much force that it thrust me into a very bright light in a split second. It was in the same moment of the quick glimpse of light and feeling calm that I woke up. Oblivious to all that had taken place while I was unconscious, I looked around to confirm that I was still in school and wondered why so many concerned eyes were staring back at me. The overwhelming feeling I had, though, was one of 'good emptiness'; like I had been poured out and nothing was left inside me; like a vessel that had just undergone some thorough cleaning—utterly empty but clean! Rather than conjure fear, considering what I had just been through, the feeling was of an indescribable peace and a calm deep within my core. I knew something deep down in me had changed, and somehow knew, with incredible clarity, what I needed to do next—to seek God so that He could fill me up with the 'right' stuff. But I was unsure of where to start, so I turned to Amy for help.

Prior to this encounter, it had been a couple of years since I regularly attended Sunday services in school. Each year, I grew more defiant than the last because most of the teachings then were rules, "the dos and don'ts," that made the life of a Christian seem like a "stuck-up" life. I also based my understanding of Christianity on my observed behaviour of the girls who professed to be Christians. Though my growing dislike for women folk did not help, I mostly found it difficult to reconcile the 'inviting feeling' I felt in Jesus' presence (in my childhood dream) with the often unfriendly and seg-regating attitudes of most professed Christians I knew. The dream engulfed me in a peaceful and joyful calm, while being with Christians often made a chore out of being happy, so I avoided the gatherings.

Once, at about age eleven or twelve, a classmate had to literally drag me out of the dormitory to see an outdoor screening of the movie, *Pilgrim's Progress*, organised for students by some missionaries. For various reasons, including "scary scenes," I didn't quite enjoy the movie hence ended up not paying it much attention. However, I vividly recall that as we were leaving the grounds when it ended, I heard an audible voice say to me, "*Lo, I am with you always, even to the end of the age.*" I initially spun around to double check if the movie crew still had their speakers on or if it had come from anyone nearby, but it wasn't either case. The voice reverberated through me such that I couldn't be mistaken about who it was. He was the same Person who spoke with me in the dream; it was Jesus. I kept those words to myself, and it wasn't until after this encounter in 1994 that I found out these words were in Matthew 28:20 (NKJV). It was the first direct promise in God's Word that I heard and took hold of personally—even to this day.

Therefore, following this encounter and knowing with absolute clarity that God was the 'what' I needed, I turned to Amy because of her faith and personality—often friendly, generous, and very calm. Unable to describe what I experienced whilst being unconscious and still slightly perplexed by the brief I got from those around me, I asked Amy, "What do I need to do to become a Christian?" Seeing the state that I was in, she asked if she could spend the night with me, which proved invaluable. Amy explained that she felt the need to come over from her apartment block to my room when she heard through the news spread that I was at the centre of all the commo-tion. Although the room doors were later reopened, most room girls did not return to sleep there that night. There were empty bunks all over, so to have a familiar face stay the night with me was a blessing. That night, Amy pointed me to Romans 10:9, 10 and following the simple steps in those two verses, I confessed Jesus as my personal Lord and Saviour. At that moment, I too became a Christian. And with much peace in my heart, I went to bed.

The next morning, I started discovering the extent of the previous night's events. I got cheeky glances, pointing fingers, angry looks, boos, and open jests, to name a few, from the moment I stepped out of my room in Red house—the farthest of all dormitories, same block nicknamed *Kurmin Rukiki* in my Form 1 days—all the way to the newest dining hall at the other end. Even Tiffany refused to speak to me, and I don't recollect her ever doing so until I left the school, which hurt in itself. Amy, thankfully, decided to walk with me that Monday, although I still felt hugely embarrassed and pained by the unwanted attention. To make things worse, I started sitting my WAEC exams that week so had to make that walk often. Notably, I passed out about halfway through the mathematics paper due to a build-up of trauma from all of the mockery I experienced that week. By the time I woke up, in the school Sick Bay, it was evening and the exams were long ended. Being a national exam, my script must have been submitted where I stopped. So, it was a miracle in itself that I passed my mathematics exam and all subjects sat during that period.

One evening that week, Amy told me of the Holy Spirit—the One who makes God's presence real to us and can help me on my journey as a Christian. Prior, the most I knew of the Holy Spirit was that He is the third Person of the Trinity and that He came on the apostles on Pentecost Sunday. So, my fairly religious and orthodox mind (wrongly) assumed that Pentecost Sunday was the only day anyone could receive the baptism of the Holy Spirit. Thankfully, this was the next Sunday—May 22, 1994. (I don't want to imagine how long I might have waited before discovering that the gift of the Holy Spirit could be received immediately upon the acceptance of Jesus.) As one parched and in desperate need of help, I prayed earnestly that week, as best as I could, for one thing only—the baptism of the Holy Spirit.

On Pentecost Sunday, I went to the church service for the first time knowing why I was going and full of expectations from God. At the service, which was held in the evening, I prayed as hard as I could but 'felt' nothing.

I was expecting the Holy Spirit to fill me in a *spectacular* way. So, on our way back, I was lamenting to Amy that despite all my prayers to God, He didn't seem to have heard because I felt nothing throughout the service. Amy, who had sat next to me in the service, was surprised by my complaint and told how she heard me praying in another tongue—the only known 'evidence' of receiving the Holy Spirit at the time (we know better now). I argued that this could not be true because I was the one praying, and I prayed in English, and could even hear myself in English. But she stood her ground, confident that I had received the Holy Spirit. The next morning, Monday, May 23, I felt the urge to pray before getting ready for school. As I did, I heard myself speaking in other tongues. I was elated! To me, this was *my evidence* that God had heard my prayers after all. I believe and now know that it was Him who helped me through the remaining period in school, giving me the strength to carry on with my exams amidst the aftermath of that fateful event which led to my new birth in Christ—a journey that has continued to be transformational ever since.

As the weeks went by, news of that fateful event continued to spread around school, making more girls aware of what happened. So, every day, I got even more intense stares and constant ridiculing for the things said whilst unconscious, even though I was still largely at a loss for all that transpired that night. This was my first introduction to being a Christian—daily taking a "walk of shame." However, I was confident of the change that had occurred in me and the peace now deep within, both of which I wouldn't wish never happened nor be apologetic about. So, I decided to hold my head up every day, blanking out the jests and embarrassing noises as I walked, and keep my focus on June, when I would finish my exams and leave school. Upon completing my exams, I was incredibly glad to see the end of this phase. I woke up early on the morn of my departure to get ready, packed up my belongings, and waved a "final" goodbye to Owerri as the public transport left the town borders. I signed off in the true fashion of boarding students—I came, I saw much, and certainly, I conquered!

THINK ON THIS...

Facing adversity is not an indication of failure—it is only 'natural' for life to hurl stones at you. But, when you are able to see the storm through God's eyes and hide under His shadow, you will be able to face the challenges from a position of peace, and strength, and with the mentality of a victor.

MY GAP
YEAR

Preparing for Uni

My confirmation

ANSWERING "THE CALL"

Mid-year 1994, I was home with my family. The typical next step in my education would be to prepare for university. But being fifteen years old, which is a year under the minimum university age at the time, Dad asked me to stay home—to learn to cook some basic meals, at the least, and be somewhat capable of looking after myself when I got into university. This meant delaying my Joint Admissions Matriculation Board (JAMB) exams until the following year, for university resumption in September 1995.

Whilst home, I told my family nothing of the 'drama' that ensued in my last days of school, besides that I was now a Christian, which sounded strange at first seeing as I was raised one. But I knew there was a difference in the way I wanted to lead life now, having accepted Jesus as my Lord and Saviour, compared to when I attended church out of habit. The latter approach amounted to *religion*, but the former opened a way to have a *relationship* with God.

Before making that decision, I would say things like "I love the person of Jesus (because of my early encounter), but I do not like His representatives." This mindset probably explains why I struggled with the concept of being a 'born again Christian' for a long time until that encounter in May 1994. The experience made me realise that though people will behave as humans do, it doesn't change the fact that God is God, and that in Jesus Christ, He made a way for us all to have a personal relationship with Him. To emphasise the point, it dawned that my now being a Christian meant that I was a member of the "body of Christ," bringing with me all of my imperfections—meaning it is God Who knows where each person is at and by surrendering to His will, He can take each from one stage of their relationship with Him to the next. Hence, we all are on a spiritual growth journey and our behaviours, at a point in time, are not necessarily the full reflection of the God-Person in me/you.

Therefore, as my parents often taught, I ought to focus on "my race," in as much as I ought to learn from others who are doing "that thing" better. These moments of reflection helped me better appreciate my parents and the upbringing we had. I even started appreciating the prayers my mum always prayed for us every night. She would come round to our room when we slept, lay hands on each person, and pray over us. Perhaps, it was those prayers that God heard and He "snatched" me out of that dark pit I was falling into and set me on the right path. I often wondered what my life might have looked like if I had left boarding school and proceeded to university without ever knowing Christ and the peace He brings—I shudder at how horrid that life would be. Yes, I'm still a work in progress, but thankfully, I became aware of the Truth by which to measure my life.

MORAL —

People are not perfect but that doesn't detract from who God is—it is erroneous to project human image on God. And as much as God has "corporate" guidance for His church, His relationship with humanity is ultimately with individuals, because He alone knows where each is at on their journey and how to get them to the final destination. So, be prepared to find different 'characters' of people in any church—we are all God's work in progress.

In terms of actions, I knew that my next bold step was to tell my parents of the dream where I first encountered Jesus—back when I was in primary school. I told them of the task He gave me and how I had reasoned it away, but now felt strongly that this was the next action God required of me. It had remained at the back of my mind all these years, especially the aspect where He mentioned that doing this was a pre-step to getting further revelation of what I was to do. The assignment was to cover both sides of our bedroom door with plain white paper. From their facial expressions, I could tell that it didn't make much sense to them, but they gave me their permission to do it anyway and provided the necessary materials to do so. So, I did it—taping white paper all over the bedroom door, which still felt embarrassing despite being an act contained within the family. It might have been overlooked if I was eight, but as I was fifteen, not even my brothers could hide their laughter at the ridiculousness of it all. Nonetheless, they gave their support, in our fashion as a family, by not tearing it all down.

I'm not sure how long the paper covering was left up there. What I recollect vividly was that sometime within the very week that I had put it up, I had another dream that has also stayed with me. In that dream, I was playing a game with kids my age, when a young man called me out of the group and told me that he had a message for me. On stepping aside, he introduced himself as an angel and said that his message was from God. Asking what the message was, he told me that it was in the book of Ephesians 3 verse 8 and that God's promise was in verse 16—if I walked in that purpose. I tried to enquire a bit more from him stating that I wasn't familiar with any of the verses he mentioned because I had just started reading the Bible for myself. Having started from Genesis, I was nowhere close to the New Testament. His response, however, was all the message he was asked to give me, and in due course, more would be revealed.

Waking up from the dream, I opened my Bible, the King James translation, and read Ephesians 3, but was completely clueless as to what it all meant. The only word that resonated in some way was "teach"—an ability I had recognised in myself and enjoyed doing, much so that my personal logo (a cross between sunrise and sunset, with flying birds) had a tagline that said, *"KINBOBO...thÔt the world to follow!"* Reading the bible passage, I realised that God had already deposited the ability to teach in me; I just needed to discover and channel it into activities that He directs. Therefore, my search changed from wanting to know the meaning of my life—as I had now found that—to understanding these verses in the book of Ephesians that are to shape my purpose and essence of life going forward so that I might align myself accordingly. My prevailing thought then was that it had taken me seven years to have this information; I wouldn't have lost so much time if only I had just done what was asked years before, but God in His mercy did not change His mind despite my lack of obedience. I didn't want to waste any more time, so my hunger grew for God's Word and I continued reading the Bible all by myself. It would take more than a decade before I got the first real understanding of what the verses meant and how they applied to me, and what an eye-opener that was.

From this point on, my real "school" began. I started to experience "life" in the real sense of the word. I had initially thought that to be able to "teach" others, I only needed to be familiar with God's Word, which although important, would have been insufficient. I realise now that God's approach has been to take me through life experiences that will enable me to better communicate His Person and the many graces He daily covers us with.

CALLED TO SERVE

The first thing that God started teaching me, in hindsight, was service to others, starting with my family and our animals (yeah, I said animals). This gap year would be the first time I was truly spending time with the family since I left for boarding school in 1989. With my two middle brothers also in boarding, I was mostly home with my youngest brother, who was still at primary school so, I did most of the chores. My daily chores included helping Mum out in the morning when they were getting ready for work and school, looking after the poultry animals, weeding the front lawn, and making sure there was sufficient water in the house at all times. The last two were pretty tough chores because our new family home was located in an area full of rocks and predominantly laterite soil.

There was no government-provided water supply to the area. Everyone in the community relied on the local spring for water. This spring was roughly a mile away from the house—the actual spot required a descent down a rather steep and muddy slope, which was a challenging climb because I would be ascending with a full bucket or 10-litre jerry can of water. I took ill the first week of having to do this having never carried any weight on my head, which was the only way to make it up that mud hill without toppling down or spilling most of the water collected. Soon, I figured out that the best time to go there was early in the morning when all of the kids were home getting ready for school—it was less busy and there would be little or no water spillage on the slope, making it less slippery to climb. Plus the spring was least disturbed, so I collected an exquisitely clean and refreshing water. Aside from the associated stress, the water from this spring is probably the best water I have ever drank.

It took eight trips to the spring every morning, to collect enough water for the family to use that day. Partway through my trips, my parents and brother would leave home for their day's activities thereby allowing me to refill whatever was used. When done with getting water, I fed the animals and then, moved to weeding the 'stubborn' grass that grew in our front lawn, because it kept growing back within days. Later, Dad advised that digging out their roots was the best way to curb their regrowth, which was no mean feat because of the laterite soil. I found that their roots went down several inches deep into the soil and were a string of nodes that had to be completely uprooted, or else they grew back within a few days. Getting to the bottom of this was a slow and painful process—took several weeks of doing a portion every day, and many blisters, to completely rid the entire front lawn of them. Weeding that lawn certainly tested my resolve—teaching me to keep at any task at hand, no matter the challenges faced.

With regards to the animals, although I had cared for them for years, the mix had changed slightly, so I had new things to learn. For example, we no longer had an aquarium with fish, or birds like canaries, or rabbits. But my parents had started a new approach to the poultry birds—made up of broilers, layers, cockerels, and turkeys. Rather than take on birds that were a few weeks old, Dad now got day-old chicks, which demanded a lot more attention than I envisaged; their room temperature had to be right; the room, water and food trays cleaned out daily to avoid them eating on worms or be infected; daily vitamins had to be administered; and most of all, I had to be very watchful so as not to step on them when going into their area. They were so tiny, there were lots of them, and they ran around like toddlers do. I thought I had good attention to detail, but they taught me a whole lot more.

Then, there were the goats. Often perceived to be "stubborn" animals, I initially did not understand why my parents were interested in rearing them.

Apparently, Dad had visited a friend who lived on the top floor of a building and had a goat named Akuya. Akuya was said to have been so disciplined that she never ventured downstairs. Intrigued, Dad bought her from his friend. Her level of discipline, ease of taking correction, and some other unique characteristics, were like nothing I had seen in my experience of looking after animals. When we corrected Akuya about anything, she took the lesson immediately and best of all, would pass it on to her kids, such that we didn't have to retrain any of them to do the same. For example, visitors to our home could never believe that we had 'free range' goats until they met Akuya and her clan because our compound was always clean, with no goat dung littering the area. I swept it once in the morning. And so, it would remain until the next day, even though the goats would have come out to 'play' first thing in the morning, come back home for lunch, and returned for the night at about 6:00 p.m. to get back into their home (the second flat of my parent's house). They kept to their routine, and we never had to worry about them returning home.

Akuya, particularly, had a standard of only eating food served from a plate, never the ground. I tested her many times, and not once did she ever budge (lol). Her most striking characteristic, however, was her doglike behaviour. When we called out Akuya's name, she came running from wherever she was and would bleat every couple of seconds to let you know she was coming. Then, if she noticed anyone heading towards our house, she would follow the person to our doorstep and wait for one of us to welcome them in before she turned back to go her way. This behaviour was mostly remarked on by those visiting for the first time because she could recognise faces, so those who visited more frequently were less watched closely, like a hawk. Oftentimes, when the goats came home for lunch, Akuya would stay with me for some time, while the others wandered all over the rocks, making personal contact by rubbing her soft hair on me. Hence, I made sure to have my lunch ready about that time and sit outside with her. We ate side by side and stayed a little while together before she went off again.

Therefore, to me (and my family too), Akuya was not only smart and neat; she was also a family member. I grew so fond of her that I cried when my mum sent a letter, in my first year of university, informing me that

Akuya had died of natural causes and was given a befitting burial. Some of my roommates had a good laugh when they found out that my tears were for a goat. I guess they could never understand the bond between a human being, a Nigerian at that, and a goat. Losing Akuya was like the passing of a close family member which felt even more painful because I wasn't there to "pay her my last respects."

Aside from the soft skills I was learning from looking after the animals, observing their individuality as well as common characteristics also started to teach me some things about God. Beginning with their dependence on us; to our ability to communicate with different species using various manners of human speech, yet achieve a common understanding of the conversation; to the innate nature of animals to respond to humans; and more. It started to baffle my mind about the structures God put in place—mostly documented in the book of Genesis—all of which we have the privilege to oversee.

I pondered some of the simple yet profound things in nature, appreciating God more just by considering the sheer detail that would have gone into creating each animal and plant I cared for. For example, goats have a gestation period of five months while it's typically nine months for humans, but both go through labour pains to bring forth their young. Or, that the difference between eating an egg and raising a chick lies in the hen incubating the egg for a couple of days—how does that make a yolk grow feathers? Then, think of plants grown on the same piece of land and exposed to the same environmental conditions, some become juicy fruits or tasty vegetables while others have incredibly bitter produce, yet each plant still has a distinct value. By pondering nature, I started to observe the "expressions" of God in everything around me and to understand that nothing in existence does so by coincidence—everything serves a unique purpose. But, what happens most often is that we never take time to find out what that purpose is hence, we misdirect or abuse that purpose.

Being surrounded by such profound things in nature, I equally started to wonder how anyone could comprehend the intricacies of each and still come to the conclusion that there is no God. Well, I still wonder at it all. To my mind, contrary to common myths, God and 'science' are not at loggerheads. I think that *science* is our discovery process of what God has already put in place. For example, human beings have existed for thousands upon thousands of years, but it wasn't until recently that we started knowing more about our DNA and how to use it to track relatives. Does that mean DNA just popped into existence when we discovered it? No! It just means that we are advancing in knowledge as God always intended us to, and as we do, we can take full advantage of the things He put in place for our enjoyment as well as for us to take care of. Science simply helps us catch up with the knowledge that was embedded in creation, thereby fulfilling the scripture in Proverbs 25:2, which says, *"It is the glory of God to conceal a thing: but the honour of kings is to search out a matter"* (KJV).

MORAL —

Let no one deceive you into thinking that you might offend God by seeking to know more about us and our planet. Nor should you think that "you have arrived" when you discover something no one else has so far, thereby thinking that you do not need God—there are yet more depths that we (humans) are yet to discover.

THINK ON THIS...

God is. He is Sovereign and the Supreme Lord of all creation—humans, angels, spirits, animals, plants, galaxies, and all things that exist; from the greatest to the smallest, and the seen to the unseen. He exists before all and in Him are all sustained. He just is! Therefore, our acceptance or denial of that fact can neither add nor remove anything from Him.

For example, the Earth will continue to orbit the Sun whether or not you understand 'the how' and gravitational force exists though invisible to our naked eyes—a denial does not stop it from pulling you down when you jump from a height. Long before science discovered these things, they existed and affected our lives, but our increasing knowledge of them enables us to take advantage of their benefits, as God ordained. Therefore, it is to your advantage to know and accept that there is a Power much higher than you, to Whose wisdom a billion of our brains put together cannot compare, but Who has made Himself known through the ages so you can relate with Him freely and enjoy the full capacity of who He has made you—His image and likeness. Rejecting Him doesn't detract from Him because He is and will forever be, but does you much disadvantage.

THE PERSON OF GOD

The more I read through the Bible, I started to understand that there was a "single story" being told—of the Person of God, which began to shape how I viewed and related with God. My understanding was shifting from God being some kind of grandmaster controlling all things or a punisher just waiting for us to err, to God being a person (don't mean human) with own characteristics. The core of His characteristics, which seemed to be the recurring theme, was that He is *Love* itself and is *Principled* in His approach to things. In the immediate, I could comprehend the latter having been raised by parents who used principles to guide their approach to "doing life". This helped develop my relationship with God, as Father, and to start debunking previously held opinions of God, including those suggesting that He was mysterious.

Two incidences that I recall tested and helped my further understanding of God in the early days, as a born-again Christian, involved an unplanned discussion with a long-term friend from primary school, and the other was with my youngest brother.

One day, I was at a nearby fuel station waiting in a long queue, following prolonged fuel scarcity, to purchase kerosene for the house. Steve was passing by and must have seen me, so he yelled out my name. Seeing who it was, I ran to him with much excitement having not seen each other since we left primary in 1988. We hugged and tried to catch up on the past six years. Then he invited me to a club, at which point I told him that I was now a Christian and didn't quite engage in such activities anymore—listening or dancing to 'worldly' music. Although the focus of this conversation was on "clubbing," my understanding of dancing itself was warped at the time as I thought being a Christian meant I wasn't supposed to dance publicly, despite having a flair for it. This was my first declaration of my faith to anyone outside my home or church, so I was completely taken aback when Steve replied (and I quote), "If MJ [referring to Michael Jackson] will be playing in hell, then I wouldn't mind going to hell." His response was a surprise because I hadn't considered that anyone would willingly choose 'hell', and certainly not because of what they assumed of another person. This discussion prompted me to write MJ a fan letter telling him why he needed Christ, if he wasn't a Christian already. Not to be presumptuous, I still consider his death in 2009 a huge loss to the craft.

I was an MJ fan, like most teenagers then, but had given up non-gospel music and dancing due to my perception of such music. When non-gospel tunes which I once loved popped into my head, I took time to rewrite the lyrics into gospel lines so I didn't feel guilty about singing them—such is what religiosity does to you! However, I now know that though it is important for me to constantly retrain my mind in the light of God's Word (Romans 12:1, 2), God will not disown or condemn me just for the style of music I listen to.

Steve went on to challenge me about how I could ascertain that God existed or if hell was even real. I remember my response then as clear as day; although I don't know how I formed those words, they expressed my limited knowledge of God, yet my full resolve about Him. My response was that each one of us only gets to live once, and then we die. But we will not know with absolute clarity whether God exists or not until we die, by which time it will be too late to change our minds. Hence, I will hedge my bet on the fact that God exists and that I need Him whichever way things play out. If I died only to find out that He doesn't exist and our spirits simply vaporise, then I wouldn't have lost anything because I would at least have lived based on good principles from the Bible here on Earth. However, if

I discovered upon death that God is, and everything written in the Bible is true, then all the gain is mine because I would have lived well here and then, proceed to enjoy eternal rest with Jesus in Heaven—just as He promised. So, I asked Steve what his choice would be because none of us knew how long we would have on planet Earth. We parted ways, and I recall the conversation stirring up deeper thoughts in me about what I believed and knew of God. It prompted me to strengthen my resolve in Him, by getting to know Him better. I did not see or hear from Steve again until 2010, sixteen years later, when we bumped into each other on Lewisham High Street in London. He also remembered this conversation and told me that he was now a Christian—to which I was overjoyed.

The second incident, involving my youngest brother, occurred at home. That day, I had picked him up from school, and on our way home, I sighted a roadside delicacy which I wanted to eat. Knowing that my parents would not approve, I knew that I had to buy and eat it before they got back from work, and that I couldn't share it with my brother because he might unwittingly tell them—as kids often do. So, I hatched a quick plan to use some cash from my weekly allowance and tell my brother that I was going down the road briefly to get something, which would have been true but not the whole truth. On getting into my wardrobe where I kept my funds, I realised that the only cash I had was what Mum gave me some days back to use as my church offering the coming Sunday. She had increased my weekly offering amount to ₦10 (ten naira), saying I was now an adult and should "graduate" from giving coins like I did as a child. Also, she gave me clean notes when it was for church offerings, as she believed in giving God the best of whatever one had.

Seeing that the 'offering' money was the only cash I had, I thought out a plan whereby I could replace the funds at a later date or give whatever was left on Sunday since what I needed was less than ₦10. The moment I took the offering bill out of my wardrobe and headed out of the room, my brother walked in singing *"Owó Jésù, ẹ má fi ra dòdò jẹ, ẹ má fi ra ẹpà;"* a Sunday School song which translates (and teaches) not to use monies intended for Jesus—as an offering— to buy fried plantain, groundnut, or other things. You can imagine how I felt! Immediately, I reprimanded him (imagine!) and demanded to know why he was singing that song. He replied, "I don't know, but the song is playing in my mind, so I am singing it." Then he continued singing as he walked around the room randomly and later went out like one who was sent for that purpose only.

My heart cut deep within me because, in the first place, all the plans I hatched were in my head…I did not voice any of it. Yet, the song my brother was singing described exactly what I was just about to do, so I knew this could only have been God trying to correct me. He knew my thoughts and was gracious enough to use a child to speak to me. This was the first time it dawned on me that from God's perspective, we could err just by thinking a thing. Also, I learnt that God can use anyone or anything to communicate His direction, although we each still have a choice to follow it or not. Thankfully, I took the correction and immediately lost my appetite for whatever it was, which also freed me from having to hide anything from my parents.

From that moment on, I was 'dead' certain that God is a person! He has a way of doing things and still speaks to us today. The issue is that we often don't pay close enough attention to what He is saying, perhaps because it comes in the simplest or gentlest forms. Even when we notice, we can dismiss it as mere coincidence and carry on down the wrong path. I am still improving my ability to recognise His workings and to listen for His voice daily, but I don't disregard the timing of events anymore—I've had too many of these types of experiences to brush things off as such. Now, I view them as an expression of God's grace toward me (and us all) because that is just how God operates.

MORAL —

As you increase in ability and earnings, you should also seek to increase in your generosity and in giving to God. It helps to make a plan of your giving so you can "give" Him your best, if just because He was the first to extend a hand of everlasting generosity towards you. Also, get to know the person of God. You will be amazed about how loving and gracious He is—simply inexhaustible!

THINK ON THIS...

I reiterate, *God is*. He is love—the true definition of the word. Everything He does is rooted in, and motivated by love. Thus, to see God's Will be done on Earth is to show love to one another and to all that He has put in our environment. So, I encourage you to learn to love like God. In particular, love is and must be the Church Culture because we have the Spirit of God Who helps us spread the love of God, that is already in our hearts, to others. (Romans 5:5)

LOVE

A poem incorporating 1 Corinthians 13:4–8 (in italics, NIV), expresses my thoughts on ways that the love of God can be demonstrated in our day-to-day lives. Written by me in 2020.

Love is patient, love is kind.
To love like God will often feel like you're losing your mind.
It does not envy, it does not boast, it is not proud.
A gift of love to another need not be said out loud.
It does not dishonour others, it is not self-seeking, it is not easily angered, it keeps no record of wrongs.
Love provides for what the other needs, and keeps giving until they know they belong.
Love does not delight in evil but rejoices with the truth.
It also feels and weeps for the pains of those counted uncouth.
It always protects, always trusts, always hopes, always perseveres.
Love always stands with you, whatever trouble so severe.
Love never fails.
And most definitely never ails.
But where there are prophecies, they will cease; where there are tongues, they will be stilled; where there is knowledge, it will pass away.
But the Source of all creation will never fade; God's love outworked in us each day, I pray.

HIDDEN SACRIFICES OF LOVE

After being home for some time and getting into the rhythm of my morning activities, I decided to take on some sports activity to keep me active in the hours before my family returned home around 4:00 p.m., which was also a good time to feed the animals their evening meal. Dad recommended going to the Oǹdó State sports stadium, as there were State-funded, coached sports that could be useful. I went there hoping to take up lawn tennis, but the coach did not so much as let me try out. He told me (and I will never forget this) that he "only trains champions" and that my wrists were already formed so they would not be flexible enough to be trained for championships—not that I have ever seen or heard of anyone from Oǹdó State in the major leagues nor did I ask to be trained for such.

Feeling dejected but not wanting to return home without seeing what else was available, I gravitated towards the indoor sports hall as there were lots of noises coming from that direction. On getting in, I saw a basketball team (Ebun Comets to be precise, the then Oǹdó State champions) in practice, so I decided to sit in the stands to watch. Suddenly, the coach popped up the stairs and asked why I was sitting down. "Can you not see what the others are doing? Come on, will you join them?" he said quite firmly. So, I got up and jogged up the stairs, then down, then up, then down, like the others. After that, we bounced balls around. It wasn't until the end of practice that I realised the newbies started that day and the coach assumed I was one of those that had come in for trials. I returned home happy in that I found something to do—a ball game that I enjoyed. So, I kept going back.

One day, something happened that I will never forget. My parents started having some financial difficulty due to their salaries not being paid for several months. Once again, they were open about it, especially as we had to start "managing" supplies so they could last longer. Although nothing had to be rationed yet, we were more mindful of consumption as they didn't know when next they would be paid—their habit of buying everything in bulk was sustaining us. The impact of this was quite minimal on me because I wasn't a foodie nor did I engage in any social activity that required major funding. Hence, Dad only had to give me about ₦150 to cover the weekly cost of my approximately twenty-five-minute 'taxi' ride to the sports stadium and a little extra in case of an unexpected expense—an accidental collision with an egg hawker was his typical example (lol). Also at this time, Dad's car had been parked for several weeks, because it needed major repairs which couldn't be afforded yet. So, we took taxis, the public form of transport, to wherever. His office was at the other end of town to where we lived, so he needed about one or two taxi changes to get there.

On this given day, Dad was going to work slightly late and was home until I completed my eight trips to fetch spring water. He would normally have left my allowance on the cabinet, but when I didn't see it there, I asked. Then he took out all the cash in his pocket. Counting it, the total came to roughly the ₦150 that I needed for the week. But Dad said that the cash was all that he had on him for his transport to work that week. Although insufficient to cover his transport costs, he had planned how to stretch it throughout the week with the hope that they would be paid in a few days for at least a month out of the several months they were owed. So, he asked if I didn't mind skipping basketball for that week, but I came up with reasons not to, partly thinking he was probably joking about that being all the cash he had. At that point, he said, "Why don't we split it then?" with a plan to give me the balance before the week ran out if they got paid. With that, he handed me half of the cash and went on his way.

I went in to shower and left the house about thirty minutes later. About halfway down the road, in a taxi, to the sports stadium, I noticed someone walking—it was my dad. Whhhaaaatttt!!! My eyes welled up as it suddenly dawned on me what was happening. He was walking to *Ọjà Ọba*, a stone's throw from the sports stadium, which would be one leg of his taxi trip. From there, he might be lucky to get a single taxi going to his work location, but he would most likely have to take two taxis before getting to work. There I was thinking he was joking earlier and sat pretty in a taxi, while my dad was having to walk!

I barely made it out of the taxi when I ran to a corner at the stadium and wept because of the pain I felt. I wept, not only for my selfish behaviour but also for how the Government treated dedicated civil servants like my parents, who did everything possible to continually give the best of themselves at all times, even when not being appreciated. Was anyone seeing the sacrifice he had to make to be at work that day? Or did they know the impact it was having on the affected families? My heart broke so much that I could barely concentrate on the game.

That day, I walked back home and continued walking for several other days thereafter—about an hour's walk each way. It was nearly two weeks after that Dad realised I hadn't asked for pocket money and wondered how I was getting to the sports stadium. I told him that I discovered I enjoyed walking, but never told him why I started doing so.

It was from this incident that I started to comprehend and truly appreciate the sacrifices my parents were making to provide for my siblings and me. Dad might not have often put into words how much he loved us, but his actions constantly revealed that we were unquestionably his number one priority. Today, there is absolutely nothing I have that is too much to give to my parents, although they hardly ever ask for anything. It taught me that family is very important.

THINK ON THIS...

It takes sperm to become a 'father', but only through many un-repayable labours and sacrifices of love does one become a 'dad'. The longing of a loving parent, towards a child, is an infinite well of goodness! Embrace your parents, no matter their other flaws. Let us be the child or society that encourages and celebrates those stepping up to the mark—biological parent or otherwise.

PRESENT DANGER

Close to the end of 1994, I stopped basketball sessions to start preparing for university—reading through the JAMB booklet to identify suitable courses, the subjects required, and the universities where each course was being offered, although I worked backwards from the latter because I was already set in my plan from primary to attend the University of Lagos. Besides doing this and my daily chores, most of my day was free, and soon enough, I became bored.

One day, I decided to go onto the set of a TV program—a quiz show in the Yorùbá language with a live audience, aired by the Oǹdó State Radiovision Corporation (OSRC). Although the station was located on the outskirts of town, it was a single taxi ride from our home, so my parents did not object to me going. I was by no means vast in the Yorùbá language but had become keen to learn, following a Yorùbá proverbs assignment in my Form 5 (SSS 2 or year 11). Not knowing what to expect, I arrived at the TV station at least an hour before the program started. Being a young person, I was looked after by the station staff, which led me to trust these adults but sadly, to a very costly end.

Normally, on the show, three questions were asked to contestants who had the opportunity to play, and anyone who correctly answered all of the questions posed to them went home with lots of prizes—products donated by local businesses to the program, in exchange for brand marketing. But it was within the moderator's discretion to gift any prize items to people who answered one or two questions correctly, as I recall. My thought was that the contestants were preselected, so I was only attending to see how live TV was conducted and to enjoy the program from an audience perspective rather than a TV screen. So, it was a rude shock when during the recording, I was called up as the next contestant, following the failure of the few people who arrived ahead of me to correctly answer their questions. Of course, I got none right, but the moderator decided he would give me a little prize for taking an interest and attending the show at my age. People clapped, I went back to my seat in the stands, and the cameras kept rolling till the one-hour slot was filled.

Having been promised a prize, I had to wait till the top scorers got theirs. Upon receiving mine, I headed out of the recording studio only to discover it had become pretty dark outside and I did not know where the stop was to get a taxi, so I went back into the station to ask directions of the staff. The moderator saw me as I came back in and asked what the matter was. Explaining my problem, he told me that he was getting ready to leave and would be passing by my area so he could drop me off. Taking the offer, he asked me to follow him—I did, thinking we were going straight to the car park. He led me through a maze of corridors at the station, some of which had the lights out as people had left for the day. Unbeknownst to me, he was leading me through areas where he knew no one would be at that time. Then without warning, as we came through a set of swinging doors, he grabbed and started to grope me, whilst keeping a hand over my mouth to stop me from screaming. With all the strength I had, I pushed him away and shouted. Just as he was coming back for me, someone appeared at the other end of the corridor and turned on the lights—a God save! Recognising him, the person asked if all was okay and started to chat with him, so the moderator had no choice but to start heading towards the car park. Not having any other choice to get out of that area, I still got into his car, but this time I was fully guarded, and he wouldn't dare lay a hand on me till I got out close to home.

I was still shaken by the time I got into the house, whereas my family were excited having seen me on TV. They asked about my experience on the set, but I couldn't say much more than "I was surprised to be on," as I was still trying to compute what had happened. Moreover, I knew that if I so much as breathed a word of what that man did to me, my dad would not only have been at the TV station the next day, but he would also have the guy's head rolling before leaving. Hence, I said nothing to save myself from reliving the experience and my dad from "murdering" someone on my account.

The incident, however, scarred me in ways that I did not fully understand at the time. All that I knew then was that I started to despise being a *woman* even more! Putting aside the things I had observed whilst at boarding school, this was the first time I despised a part of my own body—I hated my breasts and almost felt like they were no longer my own. Previously, my issues were with other *women*, but now, I hated being in my own skin and mentally started to detach from my body. To cope with the moment, I defaulted to what I knew to do best—take my mind off the present and focus on what lay ahead, which at this time was getting into the university. So, I faced my books.

In hindsight, I realise I should have told my parents. One, they would have believed me and taken necessary action to address the issue. Two, I would have had the opportunity to discuss how it made me feel so that the effects would get addressed as opposed to being swept away into the dark corners of my mind, where it was harming my emotions. And three, talking about it then would have helped me fully realise that what happened had nothing to do with me but had everything to do with the misconduct of a man who chose to take advantage of a vulnerable person rather than step into his God-given role of being a protector or defender.

It took more than fifteen years after this incident and an outpouring of God's lavished grace towards me through that time for me to realise the subsequent cycles of abuse that I tolerated or allowed to happen. Peeling back the layers helped reveal the fact that each incidence was traceable to this moment of repulsive behaviour and my naivety in thinking that not talking about it would make it go away! My road to healing started when it dawned on me that God loves me intensely, has never left me despite the circumstances, and can bring good out of a past that causes pain, shame, or any form of reproach. God showed me His Fatherhood in a way that broke me, and I opened up everything ever bottled up to Him, permitting Him to get into the crevices of my heart to bring healing—where I was able to appreciate and love every inch of my body. The healing process isn't finished, I know, but I am at least confident that I do not have to tolerate such behaviour anymore and that it is absolutely important to "speak up," even when the offence is not committed against me.

MORAL —

Through my healing process, I have realised the importance of teaching our boys and young men about the damaging impact of such behaviour on victims so that they are equipped with the knowledge and emotions required to choose not to perform or perpetuate such behaviour. This needs to be done from a woman's perspective! There is much support being provided to victims, most of whom are women, but this is not enough. The perpetrators, mostly men, also need to be provided educational and psychological support so that the root causes are addressed from a young age and they can grow up to be decent, emotionally stable, protective, and exemplary men in any society where they find themselves.

At the start of 1995, my parents enrolled me in a Lesson School run by my primary school math teacher to better prepare me for the upcoming JAMB exams. The exams were organised once a year for student admissions into a university, polytechnic, or any other tertiary institution in Nigeria, depending on the individual's score out of 400 points. Not only was my mind set on getting into a university, it was also set on one of the best and most competitive universities at the time. I was sixteen and could finally sit for the exams. Although as I recall, Dad still had to swear an affidavit when we were submitting the application forms to confirm that I would certainly be sixteen by the time I gained admission for the 1995-96 academic year.

At the Lesson School, I kept a fairly low profile because I knew the owner, and he had a direct line to my parents. I only interacted with a few people, and as always, the first person that I became close to was a dude. Ollie came to Àkúrẹ́ with his dad, who was on a short transfer from Lagos. His dad enrolled Ollie in the Lesson School to keep him busy while he was at work. Ollie and I got along very well because of his calm demeanour, which was a good match for my massively work-in-progress tough personality at the time. He was good-looking, so as I later found out, I was the envy of most of the other girls in the class who wanted to date him. I suspect he knew this but might not have been interested in dating anyone due to the temporality of his stay in Àkúrẹ́—hence, our mutual need for no more than casual friendship worked well.

One blessed day while I was waiting outside the classroom for the ongoing lesson session to end so I could get back in for my class, I got into a fight. (What?!! Yeah, thought you might wonder how—as did I after the events unfolded.) Normally during classes for subjects that we weren't taking, I would have been outside with Ollie chatting till the next one. But on this day, he was not around due to an illness. So, I was quietly waiting all by myself, when this hefty-looking girl and two others rocked up through the gates. I didn't recognise her face as one of the students in the class, so I did not remotely imagine she was coming to me until she got close and tapped me on the shoulder to catch my attention. Her first words were "I hear you are the girl who snatched my boyfriend." I looked on puzzled.

Knowing that I had no boyfriend and the only person that could be misconstrued as such was Ollie, I took a good look at her from head to toe and thought that there was no way she was Ollie's type, let alone girlfriend. So, having no words to say to her, I hissed and turned away. Without warning, she spun my lightweight body around, took hold of my t-shirt, and in one forceful pull, ripped it apart. My reflex kicked in. I took hold of whatever she was wearing and started to rip it before I could even think properly about the implications of my actions as a professed Christian. The overwhelming thought in my mind was "How dare she!" Her friends pounced on me and began to beat on me, but I wouldn't let go of the girl until Mr. Parker, the Lesson School owner, came to break it up. Here I was in a fight in which I didn't even know who I was fighting nor the person her quarrel was about, and more sickening for me was that this was over some boy!

Mr. Parker separated us and immediately identified that neither the girl nor her friends were students in his Lesson School. They were therefore dismissed and banned from returning to the premises. As for me, however, standing there half-naked with my bra still thankfully in place, he had more reprimanding words. He took me away from the scene, which now had a crowd gathered, to his apartment in the same compound, so I could change into one of his daughter's t-shirts. Of course, Mr. Parker called my dad after speaking with me and sent me home afterwards for the rest of the day. When my parents got back home from work, I told them the whole story, at which point I started to cry for the first time. It wasn't because my parents were disappointed but that I felt abused again, all within a short space of time—being in a physical fight where my breasts were on public display (in a bra did not make me feel any better) and for no just cause!

The next day, I returned the loaned t-shirt, having washed and dried it overnight as my parents made me. I was grateful I got off with only a warning from them. Ollie was back in school and did not stop teasing me about the fight, as one of the girls had told him of the incident before I arrived. He assured me that he had no girlfriend, which made the reason for the fight all the more mysterious. Until a few days later when another guy in the class walked up to me to apologise about the fight. The girl had seen me walking with him outside the Lesson School, some days earlier, and assumed we were dating, not knowing I only did so to collect a math textbook. The worst part, per his explanation, was that she was his ex-girlfriend! So, I was simply a target for directing all of her anger about their breakup—something I knew absolutely nothing about.

The incident did further damage to how I felt about women! A feeling that went even further south when I got into the university. I could not, and still cannot, fully comprehend why women fight one another over men when guys tend to settle such scores less violently. My only regret was allowing myself to be dragged into such a meaningless squabble, although my initial reaction was in self-defence.

THINK ON THIS...

Life is full of choices that we all have to make on a daily basis. I submit to you the need to practice "the pause," which allows you to draw breath before you decide which choice to make, especially in a tense situation. The most important thing isn't what people do to you but how you respond—which you can have absolute control over. So, practice repaying evil with good, if for nothing more than the fact that your actions have consequences irrespective of the trigger for them. The significance of those consequences can range from negligible to grave but, oftentimes, are never anticipated. Therefore, be mindful of your choices.

EVIL LURKING IN DAYLIGHT

I sat the JAMB exams and passed, with scores good enough to get into my desired university. So, the next phase of activities kicked in—preparing all required documentation for registration, one of which was my Senior Secondary School Certificate Examination (SSCE) results. Although I knew in principle that I had passed the exams, my secondary school was required to issue me a certified copy of the results as evidence of the subjects undertaken and my grade in each. This would normally have been posted to the student, but it was now May 1995, about a year from sitting the exams, and I had yet to receive mine. My parents decided that I should visit FGGC Owerri, to pick up my certificate to eliminate the risk of not having it to hand when required. So, on Wednesday, May 24, 1995, I was on the road to Owerri yet again.

I arrived in Owerri late in the evening and decided to still go to the school. Having been in boarding school all through my six years there, I had never really explored the town itself. Hence I went to the one place I was familiar with.

On getting into the school, I met one of the junior girls I was friends with in year 12 coming back from the night prep. This was a huge blessing, as I was still pondering where I needed to go to secure a bed for the night. Christine and I became friends through Tiffany. When we got the pleasantries out of the way, I told her what brought me back, and she immediately offered to share her bed with me. At that time of the night, and for an early rise the next day, no one would bat an eyelid even if they noticed someone who was not a current student at the school in the dorm with another student. But, "I am now a Christian," I told Christine, so I wanted to do things right. Hence, I persuaded her to go with me to the house mistress' home, which was right beside the Red House dorm, so I could obtain her permission to stay with my friend for one night only.

Auntie Maggie, as we called the house mistress, recognised me, having been involved in the Red House choir, drama, and other sports teams during my time there. Once I relayed my reason for being in school, that I was stranded and didn't know where to go in Owerri, and that Christine was willing for me to spend the night with her, Auntie Maggie did not hesitate to permit me to stay. With this, I went off with Christine and was even more pleasantly surprised when I found out that she had taken on my "corner" and still had one of my inspiring wallpapers on the wall. She intentionally kept that aspect quiet when we bumped into each other, as a surprise. We managed to catch up a little bit more before I fell asleep because it had been a long day.

I rose early the next morning, on Thursday, May 25, 1995, so that I could be ready before the bell rang for breakfast and everyone would have to vacate the dorm. I walked most of the way to the dining halls with Christine before parting ways to go to the Administration "Admin" Block, where I would commence the necessary process for obtaining the certified copy of my SSCE results. My plan for the day was simple—get in there; say hi to the aunties in the accounts department, especially the one who dutifully kept my pocket money accounts for several years; obtain the document; then head to the motor park to catch the bus back to Àkúrẹ́.

On getting to the Admin Block, everything seemed to be going according to plan until it was time to pick up the one thing that brought me all this way. I was informed that due to the riot that occurred during the school Send-forth for my set girls (which I wouldn't venture writing about), we each had to pay a certain amount of money towards repair of the damages before the certified SSCE result could be released. This was why it was never put in the post! Although not exactly the best approach, this was technically the only remaining "power" the school had over us, hence they wielded it to their advantage.

More alarming was the amount that was apportioned, which was more than ₦1000 per person. Although the funds on me could cover the amount, because Dad had given me some extra in case of an eventuality, what remained would be insufficient for my return fare home to Àkúrẹ̀. Therefore, I needed to borrow more money from someone. The school bursar was the closest person I could think of for that purpose, so I asked him for help. He obliged because he knew my dad well enough to trust that his money would be refunded once I got back home.

As the "good girl" that I was trying to be, I thought it was not right for me to borrow money in my dad's name and not inform him at least before committing him to the debt. So, I thought to give him a quick call first. Unfortunately, the school's telephone lines were down following a storm some days before. The closest and most assured location to find a working telephone line was at the Nigerian Telecommunications Limited (NITEL) building on Okigwe Road, which was only a few minutes' drive from the school. There, I could use a pay phone to call my dad at his office to let him know what I was about to do. So, I kept my small overnight bag with an auntie in the accounts department, having explained what I was going to do, and set out for NITEL with only my purse in hand.

The Admin Block was at one end of a long stretch of road that separated the classroom area from the dorms and led to the school's second gate, which in turn led to Okigwe Road. By this time, the students were back from breakfast and classes were in full swing, so I needed to be quick to avoid a late start and arrival in Àkúrẹ̀. Walking briskly as one on a mission, I got to the second gate in a few minutes then, walked down the shorter road, before running across a three-lane dual carriageway (or divided highway) to catch a short taxi ride to NITEL. I could even see the tip of the building's mast in the distance, so I could have walked but the fact that it would take much longer and time was of the essence—or so I thought!

Shortly after I got to the right side of the dual carriageway, I saw a taxi and hailed it. It was the old five-seater Peugeot 504, which was commonly used for town taxi rides then. When it came close, I yelled "NITEL," and it came to a stop for me to get in. There was room for one more passenger at the back, so I hopped in. Although it was a bit of a squeeze with three adults already sitting there, I took no note of anything as they made some room for my tiny body to fit in. The moment I shut the door, the driver started to move while I did a bit of wriggling to settle into the corner a bit more comfortably.

Just as I sat back, I heard a quiet voice in my right ear say, "Pay the driver the fare now." This was strange in that it was the norm, not a rule, to pay taxi fares when you were approaching your stop. There was also no one to my right, as I had my head leaning against the door for comfort. To my mind, NITEL was about a five-minute ride, so I didn't see the need to pay a few seconds after getting in. Because of the clarity of those words, however, I sensed this was a nudge from God—I was getting more familiar with this approach of His. So, I asked the driver how much my fare was, and he replied, "Ten naira." A bit pricey, I thought, but didn't want to argue because the instruction was to pay the fare. I reached into my purse and took out one of the brand new bills Dad had given me. Leaning forward with a stretched ten-naira note in hand, I said to the driver, "Please take your money," but he did not respond. So, I sat back.

Then, I heard the Voice say again, "Pay the driver now," in a fairly firm tone. Again, I reached out and lightly tapped the driver's shoulder with the ten naira note, thinking maybe he did not hear me the first time. With that, he turned around and gave me the most evil look I have ever seen on a grown man's face. Then he just turned forward to continue driving without uttering a word.

Completely surprised by his reaction, I said, "Do you not want your money?

OK, I will keep it then," I continued.

Thinking I had managed to upset the driver in less than a minute of being in the car, I wiggled my bum to sit back, but there was just this unrest in my spirit that compelled me to lean forward again and do the same thing. I tapped him on the shoulder with my hands and shoved the ten naira note in his face. When he turned to look at me this time, it was with devilishly rolling eyes and a long hiss. Again, he looked away saying nothing, so I became agitated and said, "Stop the car now please, I would like to get off here."

At this statement, the lady who sat in the front passenger seat spun around and started to shout at me. "Keep quiet! Keep quiet!!" she said. Then she went on saying things like, "Why are you distracting the driver?"; "Didn't you say you are going to NITEL?"; "Why not wait till you get there before paying"; and so on.

As calmly as possible, I said, "Madam, please tell the driver to take his money now."

"Well, he is not going to take it, so stop disturbing him," she replied.

"OK, tell him to stop the car, because I want to get down here."

"No, he will not! You said you were going to NITEL, so to NITEL you will go."

"Well, I have changed my mind. I would like to get down here, so tell him to stop the car."

The lady turned away, saying things in Igbo language which I didn't understand. Then I noticed the driver push down on the accelerator and make a move to change to the middle lane. I fell back into my sitting position at the sudden change in speed. It occurred to me that three grown men were sitting in the back and none of them uttered a single word in those moments of heated conversation between the woman and I, or the exchange with the driver. Putting two and two together, my brain finally connected the dots as I realised that I was being kidnapped.

In that same moment of realisation, I heard a voice as clear as day say to me "You will have to jump out of the car." Whaaatttt!!! "That cannot be God," I thought. It must be my mind playing back all those things I read in the James Hardley Chase novels or saw in Bond movies. So, in this moment when I sensed danger, I could not help but think it was the consumption of those action series that was messing with my brain on the logical cause of the action. But as that was all that came to mind, I opened the door to check the distance between the car floor and the road.

Just then, the woman spun around again with her full body turned towards me. Putting her hands through both sides of her chair, she shut the door with her left and had her right hand firmly placed on my leg. "Do you want to kill yourself?"

My reply—"How is that important to you? Are you my mum?" Then I repeated the request, "Please tell the driver to stop the car now."

Her response—"I cannot do that."

Still holding the door firm, she released her grip on my leg. Then I realised that the man sitting next to me had a tight grip on the side of my blouse as a way of holding me down. I looked at his hands and looked up into his face; he was of a very dark skin tone. As our eyes met, he looked away, still not letting go of my blouse and not uttering any sound.

By this time, I could see the NITEL building a little clearer ahead, but the driver was not making any move to get back into the slow lane, which is what one would expect of a taxi planning to drop off a passenger. Right then, I felt weak and powerless, thinking "Lord, is this my end?" I fell quiet, absolutely lost on what to do next. After a few moments of my being quiet, the woman let go of the door and turned to sit back in her seat. A few seconds later, I felt the man's grip on my left side relax a tiny bit.

As if on cue, I heard the voice again like a bang in my head saying, "Jump!" This time, I knew it was God speaking. Without thinking, I opened the door and threw my full weight forward simultaneously. As my body hit the ground, the world went dark, but it only lasted a few seconds as I was jolted to reality when the back tyres of the car ran over my knees, pressing them hard against the heated surface of the coal-tarred road.

Realising that I was still alive, I looked around and saw people's feet and my purse a few inches away from the reach of my hands. So, I crawled forward to pick it up and was slowly starting to get up, when I noticed the woman getting out of the car and the driver coming round to where I was lying. They had stopped perhaps to pick up my body, I thought. She was cursing as she came towards me, but before she got close, I felt strength in my legs, got up, and started to run like I had never run before. As I ran, I noticed that a vehicle had stopped behind the taxi, either to drop off or pick up someone. I recall thinking God must have stopped that vehicle, otherwise, it would have run over me and I likely would not have survived that crash. I kept running, not minding oncoming traffic or anything else. Getting back to safety was the only thing on my mind…and that meant getting back to school!

I kept running and running and running. I ran through the second gate at such speed that the gateman could not stop me. I heard his voice in the distant background shouting, "Stop. Get back here!" but I just couldn't put the brakes on. I ran the whole length of the long road inside the school, taking the turn near the principal's office to the Admin Block. Then, I saw one of the aunties from the Accounts department coming from the opposite direction so I ran to her. The last thing I remembered was her catching me and saying, "What happened? You are bleeding all over." As I looked down to see both of my legs covered in blood, I fainted. The time would have been about 11:00 a.m.

At about 4:00 p.m., I was woken by the voice of a nurse calling my name. As I opened my eyes, I realised that I was in the school's Sick Bay. It was a very familiar environment because I spent at least one week every term for six years laying on one of those beds and being fed via intravenous drips. The setting was hardly different this time, except both my knees were covered in bandages, and there was an excruciating pain all over my body. Every part ached, and my limbs felt so heavy I could barely lift them. The nurse was talking, but the only thing I could make out from everything being said was that I was wanted in the vice principal's office. Yep, the same woman and office I had been in during my Form 5 (SSS 2) when I needed permission to change some subjects.

"What could she want with me?" I asked.

The nurse replied, "You have visitors. They are in her office waiting for you."

Rather quickly, she mentioned that they had done a quick x-ray of my legs and found, thankfully, that I had no broken bones but pretty torn ligaments. I would be able to walk, but my full recovery might be slow. At that, she pulled a wheelchair close and helped me into it. Then she handed me my overnight bag, which had been brought there from the administration office, and was giving me instructions on how to change the bandages, etc.—all of which came as muffled sounds to me. I was wheeled into a hospital car for the drive up to the VP's office. It was upon arrival that some of the things the nurse had said about the impact of the injuries on my ability to walk started to "hit home." Standing up sent as many sharp pains through my nerves as it did when I sat down. So, the nursing staff had to wheel me into the VP's office and help me into a chair before leaving.

In the VP's office, I noticed two men sitting across her desk; one was clearly a police officer, the State's Divisional Police Officer (DPO), while the other was a police officer in plain clothes. After the VP introduced the two gentlemen, she mentioned that they had been waiting in her office since early afternoon for me to wake up to obtain my statement on what happened that morning. She went on to tell how my collapse in the arms of the lady from the accounts department had triggered several investigations, including who I was and what I was doing in the school. By so doing, they discovered that I had spent the night in the school. She commended my discipline for having obtained the appropriate permission to stay on the premises from the house mistress. This act, she said, was the reason the school was taking full responsibility for my care till I returned to my parents. In addition, they had issued my certified SSCE result at no further cost and placed it in my overnight bag, which I had left with one of the aunties. When she finished, she handed the conversation over to the police officers for their interrogation, although she remained in the room as the legal adult.

The DPO started by asking my name, then went on to things like what I was doing in Owerri, my journey into the town the previous day, the events of that morning prior to the accident, what took place in the car, and eventually how I ended up back in the school. At the end of the interrogation and "statement" taking, he mentioned that he wanted to check if I panicked unnecessarily or was reacting to any stories heard when I got into town. He said there had been a recent increase in kidnappings, especially on Okigwe Road which had several schools on its long stretch. After speaking with me, the officer understood that I had perceived real danger and took the best escape option available to me.

Then the DPO explained that he had been investigating the kidnapping spikes and found that a Cabal was behind the illicit activities. There were also corrupt police officers who helped to cover up the crimes. Therefore, he had set up a "tiger team," which were only known to him, and positioned them in plainclothes at strategic points along Okigwe Road. They were on orders to monitor kidnapping in particular and stationed in their directed posts at certain times of the day when the kidnappings were known to be rather prevalent—mainly school resumption, lunch, and closure hours.

So, in what I can now see and wholly attribute to God's precision, the DPO said that the other plainclothes officer in the room was stationed right at the spot where I jumped out. Therefore, the guy was at the scene of the incident and saw for himself what happened—that is, a young girl jumping out of a taxi, three men at the back running off when the taxi came to a stop, and an attempt by two adults to pick her up until she got up and started to run without looking back through what would be considered dangerous traffic. Seeing as it all looked suspicious, he moved in to arrest the two adults—a man and a woman—and took them to the police station for a statement. Of course, they denied any wrongdoing, claiming it was a normal taxi ride and the woman was just another passenger.

Not fully convinced by their statements, the DPO requested the man and woman be detained in police custody until my side of the story was heard. Hence, they were determined to wait until I woke up, to hear my story that same day, to enable them to decide whether to release those arrested or charge them with the crime for further investigations and prosecution. They found me by returning to the crime scene and asking about town if anyone had seen where the young girl ran to. Of course, the news had spread by that time, so from one eyewitness to another, they discovered I had run into FGGC Owerri.

The next step, therefore, was for me to identify the two people that had been arrested. When asked if I could remember their faces, I answered in the negative. I barely saw either of their faces before the atmosphere changed in the car. The DPO chose to parade them anyway, in case something about them triggered my memory—what a great idea that turned out to be!

The man was the first to be brought into the VP's office. They asked if I recognised him, and I said "No." Since the man wouldn't utter a word, the DPO asked the officer-in-charge to take him back to their police vehicle and bring in the woman. But as he was being led out of the office, the man looked back and gave me the very evil eye he had made in the car. I immediately called the DPO's attention to that fact, having described the driver's unusual rolling eyes during my statement. It was a big error on the man's part because that was the gesture that nailed him to the crime. Hence, he was immediately charged with a kidnapping offence and told that he would be detained, pending further investigations and a court hearing.

After the man was taken away, the woman was brought into the VP's office for me to identify. But when asked if I recognised her, my response again was "no." However, out of what seemed to be distress, she started to talk—she was innocent; she just happened to be a passerby, like other people, when I jumped out; since she was a mother, she had rushed to help me up when the police officer arrested her. I couldn't confirm or nullify anything she said because I didn't recognise her. Frankly, she spoke too many words for my mind to process past the excruciating pains I was feeling. In the process of talking, however, she made a comment, which I didn't even hear but the DPO picked up on. It was a comment that aligned with what I had previously described to him regarding what took place whilst I was still in the vehicle—which meant that she must have been present in the car for her to know about that. So, he questioned her further about it, but she covered up with some other story, which didn't make much sense. Hence, the DPO asked for the driver to be brought back into the VP's office.

In what were clever moves by the police, both had been kept apart since their arrest that morning, and their statements were taken independently at the police station, so neither knew what the other had said or not said. The moment he came back in, she positively identified him as the taxi driver, which begged the question, "How do you know that he is the taxi driver if you were not in the taxi?" Unbeknownst to her, I had also identified him as the driver. Then, she was asked, "If indeed you felt for the girl like a mother, why did you not ask the driver to stop when she got agitated about remaining in the vehicle?" Her responses from there on became disjointed and did nothing but increasingly connect her to the crime. If she had kept quiet, it might have been difficult to link her to him because I didn't recognise her. Based on her testimony, she was also charged with the offence, and both were taken out of the VP's office back to police detention. The time must have been about 7:00 p.m. because the night sky could be seen through the windows by the time this whole saga played out.

Now, it was just the DPO, the VP of Academics, and I left in the VP's office. The DPO told the VP what neither of us was expecting to hear. It was the last thing he wanted to get done before leaving the school premises—a strong recommendation that I be moved to a secure location that night and not be about town for the next couple of days, at least.

Whilst it would be helpful for the investigation if I remained local for some days should they have further questions about the incident, the DPO stated that it was best if no one involved in the process knew where I was, including himself. The news of my run into the school grounds was all over town, and the Cabal would now be aware that some of their agents had been arrested. Police officers who were involved could be threatened to give me up; hence, it was best if they were genuinely unaware of my whereabouts. The DPO added that my case was the first in which they had ever apprehended perpetrators, making it a high-profile police case that would not be handled lightly. Consequently, he expected the Cabal to unleash their fury as the police closed in on them, making me a prime target.

Although I would not be required to testify in court, being a minor, the DPO said that I was nonetheless at risk because my face was somewhat known to the "gang," who would definitely have their people scouting around to find me. If they did find me, I was not likely to survive the ordeal to follow! Therefore, they must be made to believe that I was either under police protection, so the focus was on the police, or that I had left town that same day, which could be anywhere in the vast country and too wide an area for them to invest in such a search.

The DPO reckoned that it would be a few days before the Cabal reduced their efforts to find me, hence the recommendation for me not to go anywhere under any circumstance, including a hospital, as we could never know who was working with them. He promised to send word to the VP when field reports indicated that the "temperature" had died down and it was safe for me to return home. With the VP also compromised, technically, the questions became "Where can I hide for some days whilst still having my wounds properly attended to?" and "Who will tell my parents what happened?" With that, the DPO left us.

Alone with the VP, she asked if there was anyone that I could think of staying with, pending the 'green light' from the DPO. I could think of no one but Auntie Jane. She was my guardian for the six years I was in the school and knew my parents, especially Dad, well enough to know how to break the news to them. So, the VP called her and some minutes later, she arrived to pick me up. The VP arranged for one of the school's drivers to drop us at Auntie Jane's house, one who didn't know what was going on and could not be compromised. Thankfully, she had instructed her housekeeper to prepare a room for me so I went to bed immediately I managed to get into the house.

The next morning, I was woken up by her youngest child who came into the room excitedly to meet "their visitor" on his way to (primary) school. There are no words to describe the intensity of the pain I felt when I attempted to sit up. I wanted to share in his excitement but could not, which started the flow of tears as I laid back down. I remember his cute little voice saying, as he held my hands, "Auntie, don't cry. You will be fine." The housekeeper came in to stop him from "disturbing" me and to get him to have breakfast before it was time for him to leave for school.

Once Auntie Jane and her son left the house, the housekeeper focused on me and did a great job looking after me that day and each day afterwards that I spent with them. She always made sure that I ate, although I did not have any appetite most of the time; regularly changed the wound dressings on both knees; washed me with a damp towel whilst sitting on a stool; and even cleaned up after me when I used the potty that was provided in my room as I could barely move a few steps before needing to sit. It was such a helpless and humbling situation for someone like me who was well-known to want to do everything for herself since I was a child. Most times, I lay on the bed either crying or asking God, *"Why did this have to happen to me?"* Sometimes, I even accused Him, saying; *"I've only been following You for a year* [at that time], *and this is how You reward me?"* In hindsight, I'm sure God understood my little knowledge of His Person because His response was to cover me with nothing but grace all through that period (the summation of my life, actually).

Every day, Auntie Jane's son came into the room in the morning before school and in the evenings when he returned. I do not recall a single thing that we ever talked about, but I looked forward to him getting home as he was always in an excited mood. This was one of the hardest times of my life, and this boy was God's little glimmer of light to me—a ray of sunshine that momentarily helped me forget the pain I was feeling. His energy was helpful in my recovery process as I started to push past the pain to oblige his request for me to move around, especially as the nurse had warned me not to stay in the same position all day. She suggested moving the legs in various positions every couple of hours to avoid the ligaments healing tightly in one direction, as that would mean I wouldn't be able to use the legs effectively for the rest of my life.

I'm not sure how long I eventually stayed at Auntie Jane's home, because day after day I looked forward to only two things—my conversation time with her son and her return home with news of when the DPO had signalled that it was OK for me to leave town. One day, the signal came. Early the next morning, I was taken to the motor park and had to disguise my pain as much as possible to avoid attracting other onlookers, which could in turn give me away. I don't remember who dropped me off, but I recall that they stayed with me until the commercial bus filled up and left the motor park. I heaved a sigh of relief as we left the town towards Onitsha, glad that I made it out alive. I have not been back to Owerri ever since.

I arrived home in Àkúrẹ́ late that afternoon, and Dad was waiting at the motor park to pick me up. Auntie Jane had called to inform him of my return. As I stepped through the doors of the house, leaning heavily on my dad to walk, my mum nearly passed out when she saw my knees in bandages. I could hear Dad saying to her, "You should be grateful to God that she is even here alive." Then Mum started asking, "What happened?" repeatedly.

From her reaction, I realised she thought the bus I was on had an accident. Almost immediately, it also occurred to me that Dad did not tell her a thing about what happened when he was informed by the school of the incident and my inability to return home until the "coast was clear," being a crucial witness in the resulting criminal investigation. I gave Dad the look that asked, "What did you tell Mum?"

He understood it to reply, "I told her that you ran into some friends from school and had decided to spend some time with them since you may not be seeing one another for some years to come."

I understood immediately what Dad had done. Knowing that my mum easily took things to heart and would worry every day about me, he told her that to protect her from panicking. Dad said that when the school informed him of the incident and that I was under some type of "witness protection" because it was not safe for me to leave Owerri immediately, at least not on my own, and they couldn't say when I would be able to come home, he knew he had two choices. One, he could relay the same message to my mum and set out for Owerri to pick me up. But this would undoubtedly send her into panic mode till we both returned. Or two, he could stay calm and trust that I would be safe with Auntie Jane until the DPO okayed my return home. Dad chose the second option, hence the cover story of me being with friends, which helped my mum sleep easier. Although she later mentioned that she started suspecting there was more to the story when I was away for several days without further contact—which was very unusual of me—but became relaxed when my dad showed no concerns about it. I understood then the difficult choice dad had, having to keep the true story to himself and mask his worst fears from my mum—the possibility that I may not make it back home. I could feel the pain he must have felt.

Rather than being glad to be back home and have my family look after me, however, I remember being quite despondent in the early days. I could hardly ignore the high-voltage pains that shot through my body as I had to change positions every few hours, or that were in my mind as I struggled to understand why God allowed this terrible incident to happen to me.

One day as I lay sulking on the living room chair, Dad sat down beside me to have a conversation that I will never forget—and one which changed my outlook on challenges till today. When he sat down, I expected him to endeavour to console or empathise with me as before, but this time he did none of that. He started by saying something about my need to focus on getting better rather than constantly asking God "Why me?"

"Well, it's happened to you so what do you want to do about it?" Then he asked, "By the way, why not you?"

I so was not expecting that! As this was my dad whom I knew would only be doing this for a reason borne out of love, I kept my gaze on him knowing he was going somewhere with that thought.

Then he continued, "Would you rather it was one of your brothers?"

"No," I said.

"OK. So, would you rather it was another student?" He asked again.

"No," I said.

As if to drive the point home, he asked, "So would you rather it happened to your enemy?"

I paused to give it some thought, but still replied "No."

Then he asked, "So who would you want it to happen to, if it had to happen to someone?"

"No one," I replied. "I wouldn't wish the experience and ensuing pain on even my worst enemy."

At that, he told me, "That is good. So, let's be grateful that you are alive and home, and that despite the car running over you, you have come free with no broken bones. From your story on what happened, it's evident that God was right there with you, watching over you."

Then Mum weighed in on the point, saying, "Who knows where you would be now if they had succeeded in kidnapping you?" At that, I realised the point that they were both making.

From then on, my attitude started to change. I didn't fully understand it all yet, but each day I focused more on gratitude and getting better than I did on the pain.

A few weeks after I returned home, we were watching the *Network News,* aired on the Nigerian Television Authority (NTA) and broadcast nationally at 9:00 p.m. It ran for one hour daily, and Dad hardly ever missed it. About this time, I had started sitting upright for more hours, rather than lying down, and was able to move a few steps unaided, although with a limp. Towards the end of this particular round, the newscaster read the headlines of the next news item and went on to say something like, "Following a recent lead and arrest of some members of a kidnapping ring in Imo State [where Owerri is the capital], the Nigerian Police have been able to trace many children that were kidnapped, rescued them, and brought them back home." Some were found subjected to slavery in neighbouring countries, others were traded for sex, and there was evidence that some had been killed.

While the anchor continued reading, they showed a picture of several hundred kids, most looking lean and in a really bad state. There were some parents there, looking frantically at the faces of the kids to see if theirs were among those rescued. As you might imagine, the scene was a little chaotic while the camera zoomed in on joyous faces lit up as they embraced a found child. My mind couldn't help but also feel sorry for the parents, who unfortunately might never have their children back!

I remember my dad turning to me to say, "Can you see how many children can go home and families that are now filled with joy because of what happened to you?" I certainly forgot the pain I was in and was very glad that other parents got to have their children back. Seeing the sheer number of kids that had been rescued from neighbouring countries where they had been subjected to various harsh treatments, filled me with untold gratitude and was exactly what I needed to completely reorient my viewpoint on what happened that day. The news anchor continued talking about how the police were continuing their investigation and were making more arrests.

Reminiscing over it all, my gratitude became not only to God but also to all the people He surrounded me with during the ordeal. I became respectful of the Nigerian Police, who had taken actions to mitigate the prevalent issue and chose to pursue justice for the innocent rather than allow themselves to be corrupted, despite the potential threats to them and their families as a result. It took a lot of courage on their part to stand for what was right and also protect my identity when I needed it the most. The Nigerian Police is probably one of the least respected government or law enforcement institutions in Nigeria by the populace, but I will never forget what those force members did for me.

Hearing the news of the other kids being rescued was so much of an encouragement to me that I started to actively count my blessings each day. Some days, I would ponder what might have happened to me had they succeeded. Being pretty strong-willed, bordering on stubborn at times, I was likely to have wound up dead, either by the hand of my captors or mine. I often stopped my imagination from going too deep, especially when I thought of those kids who were traded for sex having their innocence brutally snatched. I just could not fully imagine the state of their minds through the situations they found themselves in, and after they were rescued. They were the ones who had reasons to ask, "Why me?" Certainly not me! "Was I any better than any of those kids, especially those who did not make it out alive? No!!!"

Each day as I pondered, I became more and more grateful to God—most especially as I realised it was God who gave me the way of escape in that taxi. He knew the timing of everything around me to make sure that the very moment He asked me to jump, the vehicle behind stopped a few yards away, and a police officer was right at the spot to ensure the arrest of the perpetrators, thereby kick-starting a process that led to the rescue of other children. This was no coincidence; it was God at work! Year in and year out, I relive those moments and never have I stopped finding reasons to be grateful. With age, I am even more grateful that little me was the one God chose to use in His master plan to save other children from misery. So every year, on May 25, I have reflected and celebrated my new lease of life, as I appreciate even more the totality of what God did that day! And I wear my scars with pride.

THINK ON THIS...

Be thankful always! Take moments to celebrate you—your accomplishments and tough times too. Learn also to celebrate others. There is always a reason to be thankful; each day you live is one reason, at least, how much more each year that is added to your life. Cultivating the habit of gratitude will get you very far in life, and learning to be joyful or to laugh regularly is like taking a daily dose of medicine—it does great good for your spirit, body, and mind (Proverbs 17:22).

A STAGE CLOSES

It was about three months before I made a full recovery and started to walk again. I was thankful to have been able to recover fully and in time for university resumption. All through the period I was unable to walk, Dad did most of the required running around—shuttling between Lagos and Àkúrẹ́—to ensure I got a place in my preferred university. Although I passed my JAMB exams and scored above the initial cut-off marks, there were too many subscribers to business administration, which was my course of choice, so they changed the cut-off point as a means of reducing intakes. If Dad had not visited the university, assuming that I would just be sent an admission letter by the JAMB office, we would never have known this, and I might never have gotten a place at all. But because of his efforts, the University of Lagos offered me a course that was less subscribed—geography and planning in the environmental sciences faculty.

I wasn't entirely happy, initially, when Dad gave me the news that he had (temporarily) accepted the offer on my behalf as he prioritised getting into my university of choice over the specific course I wanted. His belief was simple—*being in a university environment opens up your mind to think differently, so it doesn't matter what course you are studying*. And to him, what I was offered still incorporated my core secondary school subjects;

hence, it couldn't be a complete opposite to the sort of things I was interested in. Mum's encouragement to cheer me up was from a different angle but nonetheless had the same intent as Dad's. Being a teacher and one who had studied us as individuals, Mum always recommended that I undertake a course that had elements of "drawing" in it. She believed in playing to one's strengths and was convinced that geography and planning would be a better course for me than the business administration I originally chose. Again, they wanted me to see that things working out this way was most likely for my good, although I might not yet see how. Gradually learning to "see beyond what presents on the surface," I accepted this and started to mentally prepare for university.

A few weeks after our confirmation of acceptance to the university, I received my university admission letter in the post directly from the JAMB office. This made it real—I was going to university and not just any, but the University of Lagos, which I had dreamed of attending since I was a little child. It also worked out well (for me, that is, at the time) that the Academic Staff Union of Universities (ASUU) had called a strike, which meant that the university's resumption and matriculation of new students had been pushed back from September to November. (Not a comment for or against strike actions, but that the timing of this turned out to be favourable to me, because I would barely have recovered from my injuries had resumption been in September.) The delay bought me some time to prepare, especially for being away from my family yet again in pursuit of my dreams.

Part of my preparation included making friends with a naturally reserved guy in the youth group at the Anglican church my family attends. He had recently graduated with a first-class in his degree, so was the ideal person for me to learn from. We became friends as he saw my appetite to learn what university life was like and how he managed to attain such prestigious grades in his five-year engineering program. These conversations were a timely blessing, as they helped me develop a university-oriented mindset and put my focus on what I wanted out of the experience. We hardly ever spoke for more than an hour at a time, but I gained so much knowledge from him each time we did. Towards the time of my departure for Lagos, he set me a challenge to attain a first-class degree on my course, as he did.

I took on the challenge, setting it as my academic goal, although not fully knowing all that it entailed to achieve, especially the concept of Cumulative Grade Point Average (CGPA).

My parents, on the other hand, focused their conversations on how to conduct myself at the university. I remember the core of Dad's advice being, *"Success in your education is the only passport that entitles you to remain on that campus,"* while Mum's addressed the morality of campus life. Mum said to me, *"Pass through the university and allow the university to pass through you. But whatever you do, remember the daughter of whom you are."*

It was also during this period that I remember Dad calling me into his room one evening to give me a talk that bore out his heart for us, his children, more than I had ever known. He started by congratulating me for making it to a stage where I was preparing to get into the university. Dad then told me how being driven to progress with my education was a strength. Seeing me take on responsibilities around the house, take the initiative to do things for others, and look out for my family, particularly my siblings, was a great joy for him and my mum. He, therefore, felt that I was emotionally mature enough to handle what he was about to say. Then Dad showed me a section in his wardrobe where he kept key documents, including those that identified him as a civil servant and his share certificates (this was back when they were in paper form). With that, he said, "I may not have been able to give you and your brothers the world, but the one opportunity I never got and have strived to give you all is a good education. And I promised to do so up to the university level. Therefore, if anything should ever happen to your mother and me, promise me that you will ensure that you and your brothers attain a university degree at the least."

This took me by surprise, as I was not expecting such a conversation with him, and one said with a deep sense of vulnerability. Dad must have noticed my shock, so he explained again why he felt the need to lay this responsibility on me. It wasn't just because I was the eldest child, but because of my demonstrated sense of responsibility and determination to succeed. He wanted me to start thinking of extending that determination to my brothers' success as well. Dad expressed his confidence in my ability to lead the family should he die. Hence, he wanted me to know this, as well as assure me that he had financially prepared the minimum required to help achieve this.

Then Dad added in a very firm tone, "I do not want my children forced to live with or depend on anyone to survive." Motioning to the house, "This belongs to me and will go to you all if I die. So, make sure that no matter what happens, no family member will take any of my children away from this house. And promise me that you will see to it that you all complete university, so each one can thereafter be independent enough to decide what they want to do with their lives."

To this, my response was "Yes, I promise."

I responded in the affirmative not because I suddenly felt empowered to step into my dad's shoes, but because I realised that this was important to him—a dream he had for his children—and I knew a little of what it meant to have dreams and pursue them. We often joked when he'd said in the past how he wanted us to have university degrees so we would not experience what he had to live with. But this moment was not one of such, so the least I could do was commit to honouring his dream. So, by saying "yes," I meant every word of that promise!

After the conversation, I went into our (the children's) room and let the tears flow. I cried mainly because that was the first time it occurred to me that my dad (and Mum) would not always be here—and that this could happen anytime. Reflecting on stories of both my parents losing their mums when they were rather young and the impact that had on them, I realised where my dad's mind was and his need to prepare me for such events in life. When one is young, most parents do not discuss their passing with their children except in cases of terminal illnesses. So, while the conversation took me by surprise, on reflection I really appreciated that Dad let me see what was most important to him concerning us. It scared me no doubt, but that pushed me to start looking out for my brothers in an even deeper way than I did before. I became interested in not just having them around to play games with, but in their success as young men in this life. This was the point I started to "carry my brothers in my loins." I had to do this so I could always have them with me and fight for their success as much as I did mine, especially as I was going away from home again and having physical distance between us seemed the likely path of my life. The conversation with Dad also caused me to start praying for both my parents, especially my dad. We were very close, and I could not imagine what it would feel like if he passed then. (I still didn't feel ready when he did.) Thus, my prayers asked God to please keep Dad alive so he could personally fulfil the dream he had for his children and be opportune to eat the fruit of his sacrifices for us. Thankfully, God answered those prayers.

MY LOVING DEVOTED. ACHIEVED. DISCIPLINED.

A poem for my dad. Written by me in June 2021.

Where is my shoulder to cry on?
The arm that cuddled, protected and always defended me
You taught me to be courageous and stand firm in times of adversity
You showed me what it means to be a person of integrity;
Standing up for what is true and just, even if I stand alone.

Where blows the wind in my sails?
The heart that poured out inexhaustible love and sacrifices for me
You were my wise sounding board and always encouraged my versatility
You exemplified the belief that there is no impossibility;
So long as I apply myself, I can be the best version of me that God made.

Where is the sound of my music?
The voice that encouraged, disciplined and rejoiced with me
You educated me in the ways of humanity and to take responsibility
You demonstrated that true leadership is founded on humility;
Service to others irrespective of how society may define them.

O! Where is my leg-end?
The hands that raised and continuously lifted me
You coached me in sports and helped me develop many
a natural ability
You practicalised the art of creativity, kindness and all manner of generosity;
Strong enough to inspire and celebrate the successes of others.

I look and see that fathers abound everywhere
Good fathers, though, are becoming hard to find
A great and sacrificial dad, like you, is a rare gem
So I know now that Heaven smiled on me when God made you mine
For in every way, you were the perfect dad for me!

Adieu mon Papa, Sai Gobe, Anyi g'afu, Sun re o
Good night dearest dad. O tun di igba kan na!

Dad

THE
GIRL
BECAME...

First year of Uni

First degree graduation – University of Lagos

A FROSH
AFFAIR

The ASUU body at the University of Lagos called off their strike at the end of October 1995—one of the first universities to do so—and registration for the new academic year was to commence immediately. So, a few days after the news broke, I packed my bags, ready to start this new adventure.

Dad and I set out early in the morning. As we stepped out of the commercial bus at Ọjọ́ta Motor Park in Lagos, I could feel the beginning of a new chapter in my life. Although I had visited my dad's family who lived in this metropolitan and most populous city in Africa several times during school holidays, the air about it brought on a different feeling this time. That day, I felt like a bona fide Lagos resident because in my bag was a document that entitled me to attend the university—an invitation of sorts to be part of the "big city community." Lagos would be home for now.

The first week of university resumption was busy with various registration requirements. As most processes were not digitised at the time, we went from building to building around campus to complete registration; from the Student Affairs offices to confirm my admission; to the Senate building to submit documentation, such as copies of my certified SSCE results and birth certificate; to the faculty and then department to register for courses; and to putting my name down for a bed space in the Mọremí Hall of Residence. It was so busy, I would often forget to eat until I got back to my uncle's (Dad's much older first cousin) Gbàgádà residence in the evening—where I stayed pending when I got an accommodation on campus. The sheer size of the campus and pure concrete-looking, high-rise structures also did their bit in intimidating a "Johnny-Just-Come" (JJC) like me. The distances on campus were so far apart I needed to ride a campus bus from the Main Gate to the Main Campus. City buses were not allowed on campus, and the campus buses were only permitted to get as far as the halls of residence situated closest to the lecture theatres and academic buildings. Then I walked to the building where I had to do the next registration for that day.

In the process of going from place to place for various registrations, I started to bump into the same people and soon began to make friends. We exchanged information to help one another with the process. When lectures began, the two people that became my first set of friends were Shane and Yvonne. Both were in for architecture, which was in the same environmental sciences faculty as my course. Naturally, I was much closer to Shane, so we often sat together when we were attending the same course in the faculty.

Yvonne, on the other hand, was very kind to me though we weren't so close. When it turned out that I wasn't going to be allocated a space in the halls of residence, she gave me hers for free. Most students who had accommodations in prime halls, like Moremí, because of its proximity to the faculties, either kept them for themselves or sold them at high prices to others in need of the space. Yvonne was not interested in either—most especially when her family home was in Lagos. The only condition she had was that on days she had to spend the night on campus, she would let me know ahead so I could make other arrangements on where to sleep. This was one of the first big favours God opened up for me because shuttling between my uncle's home and campus daily was stressful. To have someone give up a much sought-after space to me at no cost and after only a few weeks of meeting each other was a huge blessing.

The other big blessing I received throughout that first year was from my uncle's wife. Seeing as I wasn't a good cook and if left to myself, I would barely eat anything even when cooked for, she decided to make me a pot of stew (in Nigerian terms) every week. She got me a pot, which I would pick up on Sundays as she wanted to ensure that I had it empty by the time I came back that weekend. To her, this was to force me into consciously eating at least one good meal per day. What made this worthy of note was that she worked in Abuja and only came back to Lagos for the weekend. So in the few days she was back, she not only cooked for her husband and made sure there was enough food for him in the freezer; she also took time to make me food so that I could also have something good to eat during that week whilst on campus. This was an unexpected gesture and one for which I remain grateful.

Soon enough, lectures were in full swing, and I started to settle into university life. At the start, two things were paramount for me to work out—a study pattern and a Christian fellowship to attend while on campus. I was involved in the Youth Fellowship and Choir at the Anglican church in Àkúré, as a way of improving my relationship with God and people. Seeing how fast-paced campus life could be, I didn't want to be so distracted that I would lose the little that I knew of God. Shane was a Christian and had invited me a couple of times to join the fellowship he was attending, but I refused because I was looking for something "more Anglican." Believers' Loveworld (BLW) fellowship, which Shane attended, had a more Pentecostal feel, which I wasn't familiar with. Being born-again the way I came to Christ, I was after one thing only—a deep knowledge of this God that snatched me out of death and kept showering me with favour even when I did not know it, let alone deserve it. I wanted to know more about God's Person, as I could feel it within me that there was much, much more to know. I couldn't afford to attend a place where God's Word and Jesus were not the centre of the church's focus. So, my initial decision not to go with Shane to BLW was simply based on it being unfamiliar. To my mind, God found me and had been relating with me whilst I was in the Anglican church, so that must be where He was! How narrow-minded, incorrect, and immature that thinking was. And God was soon going to correct that.

Not having Shane in my particular department meant that we only saw each other during joint faculty courses, and occasionally in the evenings if he came to see me in "Holly-wood"—the hostel extension built into Mọremí Hall to accommodate more female students in the main campus area. It was built with wood, unlike the much older part of the Hall which was constructed of solid concrete, hence the funky nickname. My bed, inherited from Yvonne, was a top bunk situated in the first of about six apartments in that section. Each apartment had about four bunk beds intended to house only eight girls, but mine had about fourteen girls in it due to each person having at least one "squatter", of which I was one. This made conflicts inevitable, plus we had a particularly cantankerous roommate who easily turned to violence whenever she had a misunderstanding with anyone so I made a conscious decision to avoid getting into a confrontation with her, at all cost. Due to my past experiences, I wasn't interested in forming a close bond with a female anyway, so the display of violence further made me limit my interactions to the barest minimum.

Living in Mọremí Hall, hardly a day went by that there was no news of a fight turned violent. Ninety-five percent of them involved men—from a boyfriend or sugar-daddy being snatched by another girl, to babes "organizing" fellow students for rich and popular men in the society and not getting paid for their services (i.e., the connection of both), to the mere suspicion of a girl being close to their boyfriend (as I once suffered). What horrified me was that rather than talk through misunderstandings as civilised people, these women often chose to fight one another. Therefore, my other conscious decision was not to date any guy on campus, at least, not until I felt knowledgeable enough of the ins and outs of campus life and was ready to handle all the potential "drama" that could come with it. Plus, it felt like a bogus environment where I never really knew if I was "in love" or just fond of the person due to the constraints of campus. I realised many years later that my experiences at Mọremí Hall were the key reasons I subconsciously started to detach from any guy I found to be in a relationship with another woman—no matter how close we were before their relationship and even if the guy claimed that they weren't "serious" yet.

I "rolled" alone for some time, until I met Tosan and John, who were in my class. They had saved me a seat in the lecture theatre used for the philosophy class, taught by Professor Sophie Oluwole. Being a general studies (GST) course, the lecture theatre was often packed full of students from various faculties, so finding a seat was always a challenge. On this day, the course was immediately after another lecture which I had on the fourth floor of the Arts Block. By the time I made it downstairs to the philosophy class, the lecture theatre was swarming with people, so I started to make my way up the stairs searching row by row for a free seat. It was a cinema-style lecture theatre, so it was impossible to share a seat with another person. Getting close to the top, I had given up on the potential of finding a seat when Tosan beckoned to me.

He said, "You're in geography and planning class, right?"

I replied, "Yes."

He probably noticed my surprised look, so he explained that he and John had seen me in a few classes and noticed that I couldn't fight for a seat. So they decided to get me one. The catch, though, was that they also observed that I liked to take notes in class and hoped they could loan my notes after classes, which was fine by me. The deal benefitted all parties—taking notes was vital to my learning process hence, they were sure of getting good quality notes, while I could confidently stroll into classes knowing that Tosan or John would have a seat for me. This arrangement made us close, especially towards the end of year two when we all lived in the Gbàgádà area. Like so, I gained more friends.

THINK ON THIS...

God uses people to help people so, be kind to others. You don't have to be outgoing or be classed as "a people person" before you can relate kindly with others. And though it is not obligatory to make friends out of everyone you meet, you can be kind to them at least. Learn to lend a helping hand no matter how little, and show yourself friendly no matter the circumstance. We all need one another—be the one to repay kindness with kindness, and hurt with kindness still.

BUILDING BLOCKS
OF MY FAITH

At the turn of 1996, I fell ill with malaria. The stress of university life and the continuous exposure to unhygienic environments that were breeding grounds for mosquitoes had compromised my immune system. Fighting to stay focused on my education, I dragged myself to classes during the day but suffered severe fever in the night—high body temperatures with cold shivers.

During my gap year at home, I used a malaria medication, which was the only one that I didn't experience any side effects with. But I had forgotten to take it from the medicine cabinet back in Àkúrẹ́. Therefore, I started to go from pharmacy to pharmacy to find this particular malaria dose, but to no avail. As the days went by, my condition grew worse.

One day in class, Shane felt my body temperature and was alarmed, so he took me back to my room to have some rest. That evening, on his way to the BLW fellowship meeting, he decided to stop by my room briefly to see how I was faring. When he met me lying down, unable to move and still having a high temperature, he determined that I needed to go with him to the meeting. He said their program that day was entitled "Healing Hands," so it was the perfect opportunity to pray for me. Since he wouldn't take "no" for an answer, I mustered all the strength I had to get dressed and, with his help, made my way to the venue at the speed of a snail.

It had been raining that evening, so there were still light showers as we made our way down to the campus stadium where the group was meeting. Occasionally, I stopped to catch my breath, and if unlucky, the leaves "rained" down on me when the wind shook their trees, sending further cold shivers through my veins. By the time we got to the venue, they were rounding off the meeting, meaning we arrived nearly an hour after the meeting commenced at 8:00 p.m.

The group was gathered in a circle in the open field with their hands joined. Then, I noticed the person in the centre was a lady wearing trousers with no covering on her head. Oh! I immediately judged her, reluctantly joining the circle when two people separated their hands to allow Shane and me in. At that moment, I was glad we didn't arrive on time because I couldn't suppose that God was with them.

"How can He," I thought, "when they are being led by a woman who is not even appropriately dressed."

All the while she prayed, I had my eyes open, judging her and them all in contempt. I was OK with women wearing trousers but had never seen one leading a congregation, so I thought they must be wrong. I recall that not once in that moment did I think this was the same me that God saved from self-righteousness or the thinking that I was better than anyone else. I was so displeased with what I saw that the journey there started to feel like a waste of time.

While I was busy with negative thoughts about this lady, she led the congregation in saying "The Grace" together. Of course, I did not open my mouth to join in. "Sacrilege," I thought. As they finished, hands were coming unjoined, and people chatted with the next person. Suddenly, the woman motioned for everyone to stop what they were doing. Then she said that she had just felt a strong nudge from the Holy Spirit about someone present who still needed healing. The woman called for the person to step forward into the circle. Shane looked in my direction, but I immediately gave him a shrug, suggesting that I was certainly not stepping out. I just wanted to leave.

When a few moments passed without anyone stepping forward, the woman said that maybe she had heard wrong, so she decided to dismiss the group. As I turned to Shane for us to leave, her voice came up on top of everyone's again, saying that the Holy Spirit would not have them leave until the person stepped out. She said the feeling was so strong, that she couldn't dismiss it, so everyone should come back into the circle formation and wait. Then, the woman went on to describe the illness, saying "It occurs at regular intervals and has plagued you since you were young."

At this point, I knew she was referring to me. I had never told Shane about my history with malaria. "How could she know this?" I wondered.

While I pondered my next move, she went on to say, "God says He wants to break the hold of bondage because although it manifests as an illness, it is a spiritual attack on you."

That made me realise this was one of those moments when God was extending an undeserved hand of grace towards me, so I stepped forward. Embarrassed though I was, I recall thinking how God seemed to like bringing me out to the open, even though I prefer being in the background when in public. The way He worked with me was starting to be a pattern, and I couldn't help wondering if it was a result of my often mental debate of things or stubbornness.

Anyway, as I came to the middle of the circle, she asked for everyone to join her in praying for me. She laid hands on me, and in few words, prayed for that yoke of bondage to be broken and for God to restore health to me. We said "Amen." Then she brought the meeting to a final close, and Shane walked me back to my hall.

Although I could still feel some pains in my body, I wasn't the least bothered about that. I was more mesmerised by the ability of this barely five-foot-tall lady, who was wearing trousers and no hair covering, to hear God so clearly as to know what was happening with me and more than I knew myself, although we had never met. I knew that God speaks to people because I had personally experienced it, but I didn't know that anyone could hear Him clearly for another person nor that they could lay hands on another to ask God for the individual's healing.

That evening, I kept pondering on this experience because it showed me a different side of God. Despite my doubts, He orchestrated the circumstances in a way which made me realise that He was present at the meeting, and more importantly, that "He saw me!" Those realisations started to help me see that God isn't limited by my preconceived traditions or experiences and can use whomever or do whatever He chooses. *What matters is that we are willing to obey what He instructs, because only then do we experience the full results or good things that He is working out.* For example, if that lady did not act on the nudge she felt, the meeting would have ended and I might have missed my opportunity to be healed, especially as my mind was more on the surroundings than on God. With that conviction, I switched to admiration rather than contempt for this lady, because she seemed to know and have something of God that I desired.

That day, I decided that I would go back for their meeting the following week whether I got healed or not. I just wanted what (of God) this small-statured lady had. It was the sort of fellowship I had been seeking to join—one focused on God and the practicality of His Word. This encounter was the beginning of God chipping away at my "religiousness," and at the same time, helping me better understand that He loves me. That day was Wednesday, February 14, 1996.

The next morning, I woke up expecting to have to drag myself from the bed to get ready for lectures as was the case for the past few days. Instead, I arose with absolutely no pain or headache. The high body temperature was also gone, and I felt such energy that I hadn't felt in a very long time. I knew then that this had to be the result of the prayers that the lady pastor had prayed for me; the change that happened overnight was nothing short of a miracle. So, I couldn't wait to tell Shane and everyone else that God's Word is for real. My background knowledge of Christianity talked about healing or miracles like they only took place in the Bible, but here I was, experiencing it in 3D!

Thereafter, I became a Believer's Loveworld member, first joining the campus fellowship and then the choir. After some time, I started to attend Christ Embassy Church (CEC) on Sundays—the church to which the fellowship was affiliated. At CEC, I was exposed to God's Word in ways that I had never known before. As one who was already hungry to know more about God, I took every opportunity to sit under the teaching of the Word without ever losing my focus on this as what was most important to me. It felt like I just got born-again, again.

My hunger for God and passion for others to know Him the way I was discovering led me, one day, to stand up in front of my class, of over ninety people, and preach the gospel of Jesus Christ while we were waiting for a lecture to begin. I'm not sure where the boldness to do so came from, but I remember that my motivation was the desire for everyone to know this exciting Christian life too. It is a story of grace, not one of religion nor condemnation nor damnation as most people have experienced. This gospel was God demonstrating His love for each one of us by giving Jesus' life as ransom, no matter who we were and even when we didn't deserve it! Surprisingly, they listened to tiny little me!

About two years later, one of the student pastors in my class revealed to me that my preaching in our first semester of year one was the reason that he and some others filed to start an interdenominational Christian fellowship for the department. According to the student pastor, the Geography and Planning Students' Fellowship was the first of its kind, on the University of Lagos campus, receiving formal recognition by the department. Soon, other departmental fellowships began to spring up across the campus to preach the good news that Jesus brings to members of that department. Students came together to pray for their department and share challenges peculiar to them. Although I was involved in the departmental fellowship, I had no idea that I had anything to do with its initiation and cascade effect across campus. Therefore, hearing this was a humbling surprise and one for which I can never take credit. Only God could have set out to use that little action of mine to trigger a change across campus that unified Christians of different denominations and equally welcomed non-Christians by providing them with a space of no judgement. I wondered if there was a reason that God wanted me to know this. My guess has always been that it was to encourage me to keep playing my part no matter how insignificant it may initially seem.

MORAL —

Physically speaking, we may not understand, see in full, or ever hear of the results of our faith actions, but ours is to keep doing good and let God do His part of working it all out for good (Romans 8:28). Our part is to let the world know that God loves each and every one deeply, and that it's never too late to accept the free gift He gave us in Christ Jesus. God's love has no preferences—be it age, colour, gender, nationality, social status, denomination, or whatever else we use to create divides amongst ourselves today.

My first year on campus turned out to be one of my most foundational years of growth in Christ. CEC had several programs to help build our faith, and I attended as much as possible because no two meetings were the same, concerning worship, prayer, and the Word. One such meeting was an all-night Friday prayer service at the Indoor Sports Hall of the Lagos National Stadium. When the prayer session started, the person leading called out each prayer topic and asked the congregation to pray about that before saying the next. What amazed me was that while I was often done in about five minutes, he could go on for twenty or more minutes on each one. At some point, I looked up at him on the stage, and the leader was on his knees in tears as he prayed. It was a sight I had never seen before. So, I asked God, "What is that man telling You?" I was honestly surprised that he had so much to pray about on the topic that had been called. On and on this man went, praying deeply whilst I didn't know what words to say more than what I had just prayed.

Because I desired to know God like "these people" did, I prayed a simple prayer that night that changed my life. I told God, "Please help me pray with as much passion as that man has." The rest of the night, I tried to keep up with the prayers—conscious not to let myself feel discouraged. I was learning as much as I could.

Back to campus in the early hours of Saturday, I went to bed but couldn't sleep long because I am naturally a morning person. When I awoke, I intended to say a quick word of prayer as before and get to doing the chores planned for the day. What I recall was thanking God for the day and praying for family, friends, and the salvation of classmates, etc.—taking topics from the prayer meeting. While I do remember praying in other tongues, it was not until I finished that I understood what had happened.

My bunkmate, who had the lower bunk, said something along the lines of "Wow! So, you can pray like that? You have been praying for more than an hour and shaking the whole bed. By the way, when did you start speaking with a 'Janded' accent?"

Another roommate walking past said, "It must be that 'tongue' she was speaking in."

I realised what they were saying and was equally surprised at myself. *What could I have been praying about for more than one hour*, I thought! I had prayed in other tongues before, but never had I prayed for more than ten minutes at a time. But an hour! Immediately, my mind went to the solemn prayer I said at the all-night meeting. God had answered my prayer and must have impacted me with an ability that I didn't even know at the time—so much so that the way I spoke changed and my Muslim bunkmate took note of the change.

Since that day, I have never lacked words to pray—don't know how it happens. I am not suggesting that the length of time spent praying determines if God hears you or not—after all, my request was done solemnly in few words and God answered it—but that the Holy Spirit can use your vocal cords to pray if you yield them to Him.

God sees the heart, and He does respond to heartfelt prayers (James 5:16), especially when it is done for others.

Why don't you pause here for a moment and speak to God? He is a loving Father; One that hears to answer, to save, and to restore.

Father, I thank You for the opportunity to commune with You. You said that when we ask, we should believe that we have received, and we shall have that which we have asked of you (Mark 11:24). I thank you for hearing our prayers in Jesus' name, Amen.

It was from this time that I started to notice my desire to pray for others and an increase in God's revelation of things to me, mostly via dreams. Indeed, I have always had dreams, but having a clear understanding of them was a rare occurrence. However, when I started to spend time praying (communing with God not just talking or ranting about life, although there are times for such), I started noticing a difference in the type of dreams I had. They were more vivid, and more often than not, I understood them and often knew the exact action to take. I put it down to the Holy Spirit because more of my prayer time was in other tongues than in languages I understand. So, it was really God doing most of the praying within me.

Another observed impact on me of spending time being taught, studying God's Word, and praying was my understanding of the Trinity. I used to think that the Holy Spirit being the "Third Person" of the Trinity meant that "He is the least in the Godhead of three separate individuals." The day I clearly understood that He is fully God and is the Person in the Godhead who helps us experience the fullness of God, I remember laying on my bed, unable to utter words. I just cried.

"How could I have discounted the very One who is the breath in my lungs?" I thought. The same One who stepped into that taxi and gave me timely instructions on how to escape. *As a human being's body (for sensing) cannot be separated from the person of their spirit (real person) nor their soul (knowledge citadel), so can God—in whose image we are created—not be separated from His Person as the* Father, Son *(expressed in Jesus)*, and Holy Spirit. I cried, not because I felt condemned for not knowing, but for how I had limited myself in relating with God by not fully appreciating the fullness of His Person. Well, this new knowledge led me to write a song entitled "Holy Ghost". It was a fusion between genres and languages too, showing how much I started to value Him. It may not be the best-scored piece of music, but it is from my heart, is the first song I ever wrote from scratch, and remains the only full song I have written to date.

As if to solidify my understanding of this new-found love and revelation I was having about God, I heard a gospel song which gave me a clarity that still helps to shape how I relate with God today. It was a weekend morning, and I was heading out of Mọremí when I heard this music blasting from somewhere. Either from a room or a car parked outside, I could not ascertain. I initially didn't pay attention because it was customary for people to just play music loudly in Mọremí Hall. A few of the lyrics came through, and I realised it was Christian music. I had never heard anything like it before! I was more familiar with hymns and solemn sounds being related to gospel, so to hear an upbeat sound having such lyrics caught my attention. I stopped at a corner outside Mọremí to listen to it better. Then I heard lines suggesting that what we have with God is a spiritual love affair. It immediately struck a chord in my spirit, like I suddenly understood that what I was experiencing about God could be likened to being "in love."

More heart-warming was the understanding that He has loved me since the beginning of time but I was only just realising it now.

I later found out that the music was "Gonna Be a Lovely Day" by Kirk Franklin. From that moment, Kirk became one of my favourites—for helping me give expression to what I was feeling and making it sink deep into my spirit that what I was developing with God was a love relationship. I went in search of the album and listened to the tape uncountable times. Listening to Kirk's music (and many other spirit-filled artistes over the years) also restored my confidence in dancing—this time knowing full well that God gave me the ability to do so, and when I dance, He gets the glory.

Another outcome of the chain reaction that Kirk's lyrics started is my involvement with young people—often from ages eleven to twenty-five—which started while I was but a teenager myself. I realised that there might be others stuck in a "religious rut" like I was, thinking they would have to choose between expressing their artistic abilities and God if they ever became followers of Christ. There was, at the time, the misconstrued assumption that being a true Christian precluded one from being true to their innate abilities or any form of creativity—forgetting that the Creator of all things (God) is Himself the Giver of such gifts and put them in each one of us to make us unique, but more importantly, for us to use in glorifying Him.

Interacting with my classmates and other students over time made me realise that although I was one of the youngest (as always), I had a well-grounded background, which was more than most people got. First, I was opportune to have parents who made invaluable investments in me, which I mostly took for granted, but being at the university and needing to make critical decisions all by myself made me realise it. Second, being born-again and knowing Christ for myself was even a far more precious gift than I could have known to ask for. Thus, a drive arose in me to help young people, like myself and those coming behind, understand how enjoyable life can be when we awaken to the love of God poured out for us in Christ Jesus. So, whilst I noticed some Christians generally avoided interacting with "unbelievers," I was comfortable doing so—perhaps I might win some that way. The commission Jesus gave us as His disciples (as expressed in Matthew 28:16–20) was to go into the world and teach them what He commanded—through love! We were never sent to condemn others, but to love them and allow the Holy Spirit to do the necessary conviction work in them, just as I was seeing Him do in my life.

Remembering the dream where I was told of my purpose, I started to get some clarity on how this call to teach might be worked out in everyday life. So from that point in 1996, I became actively involved in youth work. In the over eighteen years of my involvement, I was never discouraged nor tired out by any challenge, which I put down to having God's grace for my race.

Over the years, I found that developing a good understanding of God and having a relationship with Him is the pillar that has held my life up until today. I have been to the lowest of lows and been battered by circumstances in life (some of which were brought on by my actions), yet I remain standing only because Christ is my central focus. Understanding that He loves me and how much more beautiful life is when I know Him have been some of the forces that keep drawing me back to Him.

By the end of my first year at the university, I had achieved the goal of finding a fellowship or church where I would be taught God's Word. And honestly, the more I knew God, the hungrier I got for Him because I just knew that there was more to experience. However, the time spent settling into Uni life and later figuring out how to balance keeping up with my academics and attending church programs, impacted my grades. At the end of that year, I had a 2.1 CGPA. Remembering my academic goal to achieve a first-class, I came up with a plan to help me get back on track in the second year. It involved having specific study days, at least three per week (Mondays, Tuesdays, and Thursdays), to refresh my memory and ensure a good understanding of topics taught in class that day or week, as well as work on any assignments. That way, I would only be consolidating that knowledge by doing reviews at exam time. I would also use the school's library for further studying and research, although this later turned out to be harder than I imagined.

Also by this time, I had heard of the Holy Spirit being described as an Excellent Spirit (Daniel 5:12; 6:3). My take on it was that I—the one in whom He lives—ought to express that excellence in anything I was involved in. With my academics being my main business on campus, as my parents advised, I felt it was important that I excel in them to truly display God's excellence. Perhaps if I could have close to a 5.0 GPA that year, I would be able to bring my CGPA close to the 4.5 requirement for a first class. And doing the same for each year afterwards would certainly see me finishing my four-year program with a first-class, as originally intended. So at the end of year one, this became the key goal I set out to achieve in the next year.

The break between years one and two was very short, a couple of weeks rather than months over the summer period. The then Vice-Chancellor mandated an extension of the standard year to enable all programs (on campus) to cover their course content, which was impacted by the earlier Academic Staff Union of Universities (ASUU) strike. Therefore, the University of Lagos was still in session when most universities across the nation were closed for the 1995-96 academic year. With the break being only a few weeks, I stayed back at Uni and only went to Gbàgádà at the weekends.

During the break, I fell ill with malaria, just months after my miraculous healing. So, rather than go searching for the malaria tablet, I made a personal decision to "flex" my spiritual muscles to help me learn how to apply God's Word in my personal life, especially in the area of health. I had been learning God's Word and hearing other people's testimonies, and I had come to believe that it works. This illness, therefore, was my first real opportunity to not just consume or learn, but to put the Word into practice—that is, to apply what was in the Bible to my daily and personal experiences. I was not dismissing the relevance of medical science. When I experienced the earlier healing, it seemed like another's faith and God's grace gave me that; now was my opportunity to own that by demonstrating my faith. I had been sick with malaria all of my life, but God had shown me it was possible to live free of it, so I was determined to say, "Enough!"

MORAL —

The devil will ALWAYS challenge what God has told you in an attempt to disprove it. Like Jesus during His recorded temptation (Matthew 4:1–11), take a stand on God's Word (not your abilities) in order to establish and fully enjoy what was provided by Jesus' death and resurrection.

To help me in this fight, I moved to Madam Tinubu Hall (MTH) where some other ladies from the fellowship were also staying during the short break. I had known them to be women of great faith who could also help me learn how to "superimpose" God's Word on my physical circumstances. They were my support system to help me stay the course until I won the fight, which would be evidenced by my restoration to full health. I told them my plans, and two ladies agreed to stand with me in praying God's Word until we got the desired result. The main Scripture that I remember using was Isaiah 53:5 (NKJV):

But He was wounded for our transgressions, He was bruised for our iniquities; The chastisement for our peace was upon Him, And by His stripes we are healed.

The other Scripture was Romans 8:11 (NLT):

The Spirit of God, who raised Jesus from the dead, lives in you. And just as God raised Christ Jesus from the dead, he will give life to your mortal bodies by this same Spirit living within you.

Paul wrote the text in Romans within the context of resurrection to assure the church that the resurrection at the end is a definite because the same Holy Spirit that made it possible for Jesus, lives in us. At this time of life, however, I confessed it in this context—being present in me, the Holy Spirit can work out that same life-giving power in the "here and now." Every moment of the day as my physical strength diminished in the normal fashion of how the sickness dealt with me, I prayed those verses and also confessed them (by speaking out loud) upon myself. Taking the Isaiah verse to mean that Jesus already paid the full price and there's provision in God's Word for my healing, I declared the words by inserting my name where I could to make it personal. It might have been written thousands of years ago but that doesn't mean it's lost its potency. My mentality as I proclaimed those words was that "Jesus' precarious death on the cross will not be in vain in my life." This view helped my faith, alongside knowing that two others were praying with me.

Daily we came up against challenges as my health seemed to be deteriorating rather quickly. By the second day, I had lost appetite, and any attempt to force food in me was immediately met with an eruption of that meal plus any other fluid I might have had in my system. By day three or four, I could not stand by myself or take more than a few steps forward, but I never stopped muttering those verses to ensure that my focus was not on the physical circumstance but more on God's Word, that which was promised and is possible. Thankfully, the ladies were there to help me cook and to clean me and any mess made.

Then one day, about a week into the ordeal, I woke up with a resolve not to bear the pains any longer. I hadn't slept or had a good meal for days, so I did not have the physical strength to say the verses out loud. Hence, I intensified my resolve to get well. That day, we decided that it had to end; it was going to be a "malaria showdown!" The ladies cooked a full pot of rice and served me a fresh plate each time I vomited the last. Being able to keep food in was the first sign we wanted to evidence the start of my recovery, so we were not going to give up trying. We must have been on my tenth plate of rice serving when a minute passed, then two, then five, thirty, sixty, and whoa, an hour without me throwing it all up. Realising this was it, we burst out in thanksgiving and excitement knowing that this fight had been won. I had beaten malaria a second time; and this time, by actively playing a part in achieving the result I wanted.

The battle with malaria taught me how to "stay in the fight" using God's Word, amongst other things, and the importance of being surrounded by people of faith and those who believe enough in what you are trying to achieve that they bear you up in times of weakness. I started to realise that "putting faith to work" is not as easy as it sounds; but like the Bible teaches, it always yields the results that God's Word promises, for God always honours His Word. Also, for a sickness I grew up having every three months, I learnt how to defeat it without landing in the hospital for several rounds of intravenous drips and injections before I got some sense of recovery. Aside from one other time, I have never been sick with anything malaria-related again.

THINK ON THIS...

Your faith is revealed in your words and actions, especially in those times when the wrong things seem to be happening although you are doing all the right things. I encourage you to keep speaking in accordance with God's Word because words are powerful—spoken long enough, they create your reality. That is not a myth! Everything in creation came into being by words so, all things have the ability to hear and respond to words. Thus, I encourage you to choose and use your words wisely.

DIGGING DEEPER ROOTS

The new academic year soon came around, and I was immediately faced with another situation to deal with. During the course registration period for the first semester, I was informed of the personal loss a friend had suffered and the likelihood that he would not return to campus soon. I knew that if he did not register for any course that semester, it would result in an automatic carryover for him—that is, a complete loss of the year. So, I took the initiative to register for him, with permission of the Head of Department (HOD) to sign and submit the course registration form on his behalf.

The process of sorting things out for him consumed much of my time so, even my registration completion was delayed till nearly the end of the registration period. Therefore, I missed out on the opportunity to be allocated a room on campus. This would mean shuttling between Gbàgádà and campus daily, again, which would in turn negatively impact my evening study plans and overall goal. Stressful as the prospects of what lay ahead were, I felt better to have been able to help a friend out when it mattered the most. I did these purely from the understanding of how God's love goes over and beyond for us, plus my value for the little friendship that we had, and an understanding of his circumstances.

Following course registration, I searched around to no avail for people who had school accommodation and wanted to sell the space to another. This was one way that students made additional income on campus, as the official cost was in the region of ₦100 (one hundred naira) but could be sold for hundreds and even thousands more depending on the hall. Although this was not officially allowed, it was an accepted practice among students. Just when I had resigned any hope of being housed on campus, I got the news that there was an accommodation with my name on it at the Queen Amina Hall.

"How is that possible?" I asked the person who gave me the news.

He explained that the then-new Vice-Chancellor (VC), the late Professor Jelili Omotola, had decided to reward students by giving free accommodation to those with the top five CGPA in each department. The list had been compiled, and he had only just approved the room allocations, hence the delay in us finding out that we were recipients of this generosity. To me, this could only have been God, especially when I found out that he sanctioned this for only those starting their second year—of which I was one. Coincidence? Hmmm…I still think not. By this, I felt that God was yet again showing me that He cared even about the "littlest" of things on my mind. Although "Amina" Hall wouldn't exactly have been my first choice of hostel as it was a long distance from Main Campus where all my lectures were, I was excited at the news. It was an accommodation on campus, it came free of charge, and it was not Mọremí Hall.

My time in Mọremí Hall was a bag of mixed experiences, and I had specifically prayed never to have to stay there again. Aside from the constant bickering and fights amongst the ladies, its location allowed for excessive exposure to various forms of sexual exploitation and other vices, compared to the other female hostels on campus. I often walked looking over my shoulders during my time there as you never know when something dangerous could happen.

One such incident occurred on a late afternoon as I walked back to Mọremí Hall from Madam Tinibu Hall, singing as I walked and feeling very cheerful. Two guys ran past me, one on the heels of the other, shooting as he chased after the guy ahead. Still being bright outside, I assumed a movie scene was being filmed and the bullets being fired were blanks. To avoid obstructing the scene, I stepped aside slightly to let the first guy through, then watched as the second breezed past me on the chase. I looked around for a while to find the cameras and saw nothing, so I walked on calmly to my room.

On getting to the room, a roomie asked if I was at Arts Block when two cult guys came running in that direction with guns blazing. To which I replied, "No, but I saw the two guys as they ran past me. They must have been filming a movie, though I didn't see the cameras rolling."

My roommate looked at me in utter disbelief at how completely oblivious I was to the real event that took place. Then she told me that she had just run into the room moments before I walked in and that there was chaos at Arts Block as people were running for cover from the straying bullets. She then said something like, "Your God must really be watching over you." It was only after hearing her words and seeing other people running into the hostel blocks in a panic that I realised what God had just saved me from. So many dangers come our way daily, and by this incident, God started to help me realise the "gazillions" of them that He shields me from without my knowledge or the ability to fully appreciate the depths of.

Although this incident was not directly related to Moremí Hall itself, the fact that Moremí was the only female hostel in Main Campus and these sorts of occurrences were prevalent there meant that the risk of being caught in the middle of cult activities was higher if I stayed at Moremí. Amid those vices, however, there were many daily experiences of kindness I enjoyed from others—fondly recall those of my choir leader, who was in her final year then, and the Moremí porter. The former is one of the gentlest and most kind-hearted women I have ever known, and one of the first to show me a side of "being female" that I admired. When I joined Believers' Loveworld and the choir, she took me under her wings to help me navigate campus life, especially when living in a hall such as ours. The porter, on the other hand, always made my face light up each time I passed by, no matter how many times in a day I did so. He had nicknamed me "Always-smiling," and though I knew he called some other girls the same thing, it still made me smile.

Whilst I missed those positives, being in Queen Amina Hall was a welcomed relief on several fronts. To start with, there were only four of us in the room, and the three other girls were easier to get along with than I had previously experienced. We had a balance of cultures in the room. There were two girls each from the Yorùbá and Igbo ethnic groups, and two each on both ends of the campus social life spectrum—that is, party-going and church-going. Yet, there was love and mutual respect for one another. Saturday mornings were our bonding days, when Eugene, an Igbo lady, made us pancakes before the three-hour-long lectures on population geography by Professor Adégbọlá. It was a very pleasant experience.

During this period, I noticed a significant maturity in my approach to life— spiritually, academically, emotionally, and relationally. God seemed to begin the process of lifting the bonnet of my life, ever so gently, to expose layers of attitudes, behaviours, knowledge, etc. that needed addressing. The first I recall Him starting with was the exposure of the *motives* behind what I do. Then, bringing me into the place of *intercession*. The concept of motives isn't one that we easily think about, but I vividly recall hearing God's whisper on countless occasions, asking or helping me identify the real reason I was doing something, even up to the clothes I wore.

Take, for example, something that is easily familiar—going to church. A motive-identifying question would be, "Why do I go to church?" It may sound silly to ask that, especially if you are a Christian, but let's go beneath the surface of what is the expected response or what most people think to understand it for you as an individual. Is it so you are seen to have attended that service, or is it to catch up with people you haven't seen in a while? Or could it be that it's because you like the music and feel welcome there? Or you are a worker and are on duty, so you have to go? Whilst those are good reasons, they should be fallouts of our interactions and not the main reason we attend a service.

I have found it good practice ever since to consciously check my "reasons why", not out of condemnation, but to ensure they are for the right (not selfish) reasons. This concept also applies to everything in life—work, family, friendships, associations, conversations, you name it.

The Bible admonishes us to be driven by love and to do all things because of Christ (2 Corinthians 5:14–15; Colossians 3:17). Pause now to ask yourself, "Why do I __________?" If you are not comfortable with your real reasons why, ask "How might I begin to change this for the better?" Ask the Holy

Spirit to help you out—maybe by identifying what sits deep down in your heart or teaching you how to start putting things right. Don't be judgemental of yourself. This is geared to help you continuously improve, and not be a tool for self-deprecation or self-aggrandizement for that matter.

In the area of intercession, this developed out of my second "Jesus encounter." God started to speak to and show me things to pray about for other people, myself, the church, and even nations. Interestingly, the first country God ever discussed with me was the United States of America, not Nigeria. The prayers He led me to pray for the church were similar to that which Jesus Himself prayed—that we may be one as He and the Father are one (John 17:20, 21). God spoke to me about the creation of denominations or factions within the church, and how that could impact our effectiveness in evangelising the world or our ability to point the world to the true Light that He is. To onlookers, these divisions do little to corroborate the gospel of Jesus. Yes, there may be differences in the understanding of certain parts of the Scripture, but should these lead to factions?

The core of the gospel to those yet to believe is that God loves them and calls them to repentance unto Himself, at whatever level they are. What need is there in that message for the number of denominations we have out there today? We may worship in different locations, languages, styles, and giftings, but our God is the same and we are all members of His body (1 Corinthians 12:12–31). Just as the thumb differs from the big toe in what it contributes or does in the body, it still has to stay 'in tune' with the other parts, otherwise, the whole body will end up in pain or discomfort. Therefore, let us—the church—make room for one another's giftings so that we, as a whole, may benefit from what each one contributes such that the world may see His love and unity outworked in us, and believe in Jesus Christ.

Over the years, being willing to intercede for others has taught me certain things:

- The core of God's heart is people. To intercede effectively, you must genuinely be interested in and love people. This helps you to see past their current situation to what God wants to do, can do, or is doing in that person's life. This is a continuous work the Holy Spirit does in your heart and helps you improve upon; you just need the first ingredient of being interested in seeing things work well for others.

- The Holy Spirit knows exactly what to pray for; all you need to do is yield your heart and vocal cords for His use. The more yielded you are, the more God shows you, and the even more, He changes your heart.

- God never does anything on earth without involving at least one other human being. Somebody somewhere has a revelation of that event and has the opportunity to either speak into it or let it be. God in His sovereignty still chooses to involve the frailness of human nature in His divine interventions on earth.

- God takes care of your business when you are involved in His business—loving people. However, this is no ticket to neglect to pray for yourself too. No one is infallible, so it is key to pray and take heed to your ways, at all times (1 Corinthians 10:12, 13).

Am I perfect in this yet? I reckon you know my answer by now. Absolutely not! In fact, I am probably not as dedicated to seeking God's intervention for others today as I was in my university days. I recall a time in 2016 when I specifically asked God not to show me things for a while. My dreams had become more violent, reflecting the state of humanity and revealing lots of clandestine activities around the world. They were not driven by the news, as you might think because I hardly had time for TV. I spent many nights woken up by these dreams and praying into them as the Holy Spirit enabled, not knowing who was involved or where but just praying in other tongues. A change in my work situation then meant that I was constantly travelling. Not having a good night's sleep started to take a toll on me physically and mentally, so I prayed for God to stop. And He did. Did I regret that request later? Yes, I did. Not because God condemned me, but because I had come to know deep down the importance of having people stand in the gap to lift others before God. Somehow, the busyness of life got to me and distracted me from what should be the higher priority—a reminder to always keep up the practice.

MORAL —

We always need the Holy Spirit to help us in our walk with Him. Whatever your gift or role in God's kingdom, never rely on your own strength or experience because they will eventually lead to fatigue. Keep your focus on the One who makes you able to do that which He has gifted or called you to do. That way, you never run out of fervour, because He alone can supply the grace that you need to consistently run your race (Isaiah 40:28–31, Zechariah 4:6, Hebrews 12:1–2).

AN ACADEMIC DISAPPOINTMENT

In every way, my sophomore year at the university was nothing like I ever had envisaged. While some of the lessons learnt were from easier-to-handle scenarios, others were not apparent until much time had passed. One of these was with my academics. At the start of the year, Tosan and I drew up a study plan to enable us to study together in the evenings for at least two hours, three days per week, covering mostly what we had been taught. Having the same courses, including electives, turned out helpful as we were able to bring each other up to speed in areas we may have missed. By this time, my friendship circle had grown to include Ryan and Jay—and together with John—all five of us became best of friends. Tosan was, however, the closest to me of the four boys because of our studying together. With no mobile phones or technology available, Tosan and I told each other our plans, such that I knew exactly where he was at any time as he did with me, even if we were not in the same location. This especially came about when one weekend at the start of our second semester, I made a last-minute decision to visit my maternal uncle, who lived at Ìkòyí, and did not return for several weeks afterwards.

Uncle Julius Akínsulírè was a renowned engineer who served Nigeria faithfully for most of his working life, upon returning from his studies abroad, in the National Electric Power Authority (NEPA). He was popularly referred to as "Prof" due to his papers and lifelong dedication to fighting for Nigeria to have a sustainable source of power, way before it became "a thing" around the world today.

While visiting him and his family that weekend, he noticed that something was up with me, although I didn't quite feel anything beyond a lack of appetite which I assumed to be normal. So, he cajoled me by asking me to join him on a drive to somewhere on the Island, which I obliged. Unknown to me, my uncle was driving to a hospital. There and then, some checks, including a blood test, were carried out. After less than an hour of waiting, the results showed that I had acute malaria, coupled with thrush, and was to be under strong medication. The combo of the medications made me very drowsy, with occasional hallucinations. I had to be supervised by my family, so I was not allowed to return to school. What was a last-minute decision to spend the weekend away turned out to be several weeks of being away from school, which as I later heard, caused some people to rumour my death.

To compound the scare, a close friend from Gbàgádà, with whom I often spent time discussing Scriptures, had come to campus looking for me, as he hadn't seen me for some weeks. Nathan and I met at a church choir rehearsal for a Christmas concert in 1996, and with my mind now opened towards various music genres, he caught my attention with his unique style of rap music. Thereafter, we became really good friends and met up frequently to exchange what we were learning about Christ and how to put that to use in our day-to-day lives. We were never afraid to dig deep or ask questions so we could find out what the Bible says about the topic, so I always enjoyed our interactions. I attribute my spiritual growth in some part to those discussions—he sharpened me (Proverbs 27:17). Tosan knew of Nathan, so when he came to campus looking for me, Tosan knew something was seriously wrong.

At this time, Tosan only knew my paternal uncle's place at Gbàgádà. When he checked there and was told that I was still at Uni, he became alarmed and feared the worst. I remember the whole class staring at me like they had seen a ghost the day I walked back into school; barely recovered, I was quite lean and frail. Tosan got up and grabbed me by both hands, hugging me so tightly I almost couldn't breathe. Following this, we made a pact to discuss our plans for the week, with daily updates on any changes, so that the other knew where to look if one of us went AWOL next time.

By this time, however, I had slowly started to realise that my goal to achieve a first-class CGPA that year was unlikely because nothing was going exactly to plan; I was playing catch-up rather than "staying ahead" as intended. But, nothing could have prepared me for the terrible blow that was dealt to my grades that semester.

I had registered for a five-unit elective course, run by the economics department, as a way to boost my CGPA. Tosan and a few other people in my class also subscribed to that elective. Soon it was time for end-of-semester exams, and after sitting for that one, I recall walking out of the exam hall smiling from ear to ear. I was expecting nothing less than an "A". Everything I had taught others and prepared for came out as exam questions, so my confidence was way beyond the rooftop.

Imagine my horror when the results were released and I scored zero—as in, zilch! Everyone I taught passed, so I wondered how I could have scored zero. Even if I had just written my name on the exam paper, I would at least have been given a score of one point, so I knew something must have gone horribly wrong and decided to raise a query with the economics department. When they got back to me, they said the examiner, who had been a visiting lecturer, told them that he did not see my exam paper, hence the score of zero. Of course, I escalated it to my department for them to formally mount pressure on this lecturer to find the paper I wrote. It led to a letter being written by my department to the HOD for economics, which I later heard ruffled some feathers on that side.

At the start of the new academic year, our third year, my HOD called me into his office, along with a senior lecturer in our department, for a meeting I will never forget. There they told me that the economics department had apologised for their visiting lecturer's loss of my exam paper and were taking action not to invite him to participate in their courses going forward. The downside was that I had to accept the score of zero awarded because there was nothing for them to re-mark and being an elective, I was not required to retake the exams. Then, my HOD said that I could decide to escalate further, and he would gladly take the case to the Senate for further investigation. However, the apologies from the economics depart-ment seemed to have been accompanied by subtle threats, which alluded to the fact that the guy was well connected on the Unilag campus and any further action could cause him to launch a personal vendetta against me. When I didn't show any signs of backing down because I felt this was a great injustice, my HOD and lecturer further advised that I take the hit for that one course so I didn't end up being victimised by those in the guy's network and whose courses I would likely be taking within the remainder of my two years on campus. They stated that this would likely be done under a guise that even I would not be able to trace back to this incident, and could end up costing me much more than I could ever bargain for, including the addition of extra years. At that, I decided to let go of the battle so I didn't get caught in an unending political tussle that would do nothing but further damage my grades. As if to console me, they mentioned that due to this incident, they were replacing the economics elective with an in-house departmental elective called "Economic Geography" so that no other student had to face what I had been put through.

Despite the challenges faced that year and all of my hard work, it came down to one thing—my CGPA at the end of the second year had fallen to a 2.2 level, even worse than where I had ended in the first year. The one course I had chosen to be a boost became my bane. I was going to spend my remaining two years working even harder just to attain and retain a 2.1 CGPA. And just like that, away like a fleeting bird flew my first-class dreams!

Whilst I appreciated that my predicament bore some kind of fruit for the greater good, I remember pondering, "Why?" By this time, I knew not to ask, "Why me?" but still couldn't reconcile why my academics had to take the hit for someone else's carelessness. My preference was for God to fight my battle, either for my script to be found or a special exam set for me to undertake since the visiting lecturer had admitted to losing my paper. But that was not the case. And it was in the process of accepting that there are things I would never understand and others that I would not be able to change that I learnt a few lessons—one or two, golden.

Prior to this incident, I always set goals according to MY plan for my future and relied on my efforts alone to achieve them. Whilst those are lofty things to do, this experience taught me that the achievement of my goals has always involved the participation of others—God and humans alike—I just never recognised it. Even when I became a Christian, the most I probably did was to tell God about my plans and ask Him to bless them. So, the first lesson I learnt was as King Solomon advised in Proverbs 3:5–6—to trust in God wholeheartedly and not in my own understanding. It was several decades later before I further learnt that, as a Christian, I ought to find out God's plans for me first so that I could set goals that were more aligned with those than what I thought was best for myself.

I also learnt how to pray for my exams (or any situation), asking God to never allow me to be a victim of other people's mistakes and to grant me favour with everyone who would be involved with me in whatever shape or form. Humans are prone to errors, but God never makes mistakes. Furthermore, He can take a completely hopeless situation and make something good out of it, if only we learn to give it to Him—better still, to involve Him in our decision-making process. Did God cause that lecturer to lose my paper?

No, I can confidently say that it was a human error.

However, rather than despairing about the implications of that error on my ultimate goal of achieving a first-class, which became completely hopeless because of the incident, I found an unusual peace when I finally learnt to "take it to the Lord in prayer"—as a famous hymn encourages. It highlighted to me that God was interested in my mental well-being and could help me find peace even in the most tumultuous of situations, as this would not have been my normal reaction to the issue had I not entrusted it all to God. I would have been so disturbed by it and lost focus, that I might not have even been able to pull myself out of the 2.2 CGPA that this landed me in. I prayed for God's help because I knew that only He could help me focus and get back to finishing Uni with a 2.1, at the least. And over the next two years, I watched God bring beauty out of these ashes.

This was the first incident that started to help me see that though things may not always turn out as we plan, it doesn't mean that God has forsaken us. Nor does it mean that nothing good can ever come out of a seemingly hopeless situation. Ultimately, God remains God in spite of my experiences—nothing diminishes His Person or abilities; all we need to do is *trust Him*. This experience turned out to be a pivotal one for me.

THINK ON THIS...

It is commonly said that "to err is human, to forgive divine." Each one of us has been forgiven much by God and by other people in our lifetime, so it makes sense to pay it forward. Most especially because forgiving others brings you emotional healing and relieves you of bitterness, which is a festering ground for all sorts of physical ailments. I urge you, therefore, to think properly before you ink that pain, hurt, or disappointment into your heart—it ain't healthy for your body nor your soul.

STEPPING UP TO THE PODIUM

Towards the end of the academic year, about May or June 1997, it was time for new departmental executives to be elected into the then Geography and Planning Students Association (GAPSA). A couple of my classmates asked if I wouldn't mind becoming the next treasurer. They had observed and believed me to be a person of integrity and financial discipline, and wanted me to handle the departmental association's funds. Their one request was that I ensure the department had an end-of-year party for students the coming year because for some reason, we hadn't had one in the two years we had been in the school although we all paid the departmental association fees each academic year. When I accepted the offer, they ran my campaign and ensured that I went unopposed, because everyone wanted a change and joined forces to elect one candidate behind which they put their votes. So without me lifting much of a finger, I was elected GAPSA Treasurer for the 1997-98 academic year, which was our third year.

Thus began my exposure to politics beyond just reading and debating about them. As demanded by the electorate, I set myself to satisfy one main goal—to ensure there was an end-of-year party held for students in the department. Simple as that goal may sound, I remember fighting hard against several opposing forces, some of whom wanted to undertake other unbeneficial projects or worse, to syphon the funds. It may not have been the most elaborate, but it was the first end-of-year GAPSA party for students to be held in years—for our set at least. Subsequently, I was voted as a Parliamentarian into the House of Representatives in the 1998-99 academic year—our final year—to represent our department at the Student Union Senate.

This political experience on campus was an unexpected fulfilment of my innate political inclinations. The entire experience, spanning two years, taught me several things which have informed the bulk of my current disposition towards politics in the larger society. I am no politician (yet) or political expert but to me, campus politics were a mirror of what happened in the larger society. Certain things that I learnt from the experience, which I adapt to various forms of leadership, are:

- *Christians should absolutely seek leadership opportunities and be involved in actively shaping the political landscape wherever they are. It is a myth that God and politics do not mix. All through the Bible you find several examples where God had to raise up men and women as leaders at a national level in order to bring about a change that benefitted everyone. By nature, human beings crave power. We all know that power corrupts absolutely. So, it takes a person who is service-minded and recognises that they will give an account of what they do to Someone more supreme than themselves to truly serve the people. While on earth, Jesus—the One in whose footsteps we walk—was known to do good wherever He went (Acts 10:38). So should we with whatever our hands find to do. Whether you have a title that recognises your leadership of others or not, have this mindset of "doing good." Today, the highest level of being entrusted with such opportunities is often in a political position. While others may covet such, a Christian ought to see it as an opportunity to serve and be an example of Proverbs 11:10.*

  I am not suggesting that only Christians know how to do right by the people, but bursting a myth that I have often heard in discussions. Plus having a belief system which caters to the common good helps you stay focused when the storms rage and in diverse "weathers" that politics is froth with. Lots of temptations and challenges arise so having a strong core based on beliefs and principles bigger than just you is a great advantage.

- *The sheer structure of how politics works, especially at national and international levels, makes it very easy to lose one's integrity. Hence, you must pay close attention to your ways at all times when in that position. It is not to suggest that it is impossible to be trustworthy while being involved in politics. You get so exposed to diverse conversations, manipulations, and characters that you could almost lose focus on who you are and the values you hold dear in the process. This is why most people steer clear of being involved, but that shouldn't be the case. Being aware of the potential pitfalls is good, but it shouldn't deter you from trying if you have a flair or desire to bring about positive change in society.*

  I recall several instances as a Parliamentarian when others approached me to support a motion they planned to put forward at the House of Representatives. While some were good ideas to move the student body forward, the majority were intended to either cause chaos or oppose a good idea for personal gains. There were occasions when no meaningful conclusions could be reached or laws passed because of the disruptions, and once the House was adjourned, the seemingly warring parties went off together to get drunk. This is sadly the reality, even at national levels. So, it takes a lot of courage not to allow oneself to become a pawn for those just "playing the game."

- *Ultimately, the populace (your constituency or electorate) owns the power that put you in that position. So, you must represent their interests and place them above your interests or gains—so long as those interests please God, are good for humanity, and do not decimate the environment. The hallmark of leadership is dedicated service to the people. Unfortunately, the average person on the street is unaware of this fact. Hence they allow career politicians to do whatever they like, rather than paying attention and voicing their opinion when it matters, especially during elections. If you are of voting age, never trade your power for anything or allow anyone to deceive you that your vote does not count because it does!*

  For example, when my classmates realised the power of their votes, they united to use them wisely. Many people said it was impossible for a Christian to be voted in, but when the electorate determined it was time for change, not only did a Christian become treasurer that year, but the financial secretary was also one. We knew that it wasn't just our goodwill that brought about the change. Rather, it was the exercise of the individual voting power that the electorate held. They backed us up all of the way, which in turn gave us good grounds to deliver their paramount request that year.

- *Choose your battles carefully. This is not a get-out-of-jail-free card to do nothing with the opportunity, but a recognition of the constraints present at a point in time and clear-headedly choosing the option where everyone wins. It is also not a ticket to chicken out or buckle in the face of adversity, but a reminder that some battles are worth reconsidering deeply to identify where the gains truly lie—and pursue that path. Oppositions or challenges can be good triggers to help identify the real goal that should be pursued.*

Towards the end of my third year in 1998, the Vice-Chancellor (VC) decided to move the geography and planning department out of the environmental sciences faculty into social sciences. He also changed the course name to "Geography" to enable him to create a new course called "Urban and Regional Planning" in the same faculty he moved us out of. Of course, this angered the students because we had spent three full academic years undertaking courses designed for the degree stipulated during our matriculation. The worst part was that the final year students who had fully completed their program were also affected—as he planned to issue their degree certificates as "Geography" and as a member of the social sciences faculty. The students turned to us, the executives, to refuse this action being affected on anyone who had completed two years on the program. I was then nominated as one of three executives to represent the matter to Student Affairs and before the school Senate, chaired by none other than the VC himself. Two of us were at the end of our third year, while the third guy was the GAPSA president who was rounding off his final year.

On the eve of the Senate meeting, we were summoned by the Dean of Student Affairs to meet him at the VC's office under the guise that he wanted to hear our reasons for not supporting the

VC's proposed changes and the demands made by the students. That evening, all three of us sat waiting outside the VC's office for several hours until about 7:00 or 8:00 p.m., when the Dean joined us. Just before we went into the VC's office, the Dean asked to have a quick word with us. Looking directly at the three of us, he decided to tell us a "secret" behind the move—and I will never forget his words. He informed us that this was mainly driven by an age-long feud between the VC and our HOD. He didn't want to see us get caught in the middle because it would not augur well for any of us. He said the VC had asked to speak with us in person and wanted him present, to declare us as being disruptive or inciting rebellion amongst students if we strongly opposed the planned move. This, he said, would attract an expulsion from campus, meaning that none of us would graduate and we would be made an example of, should anyone else be planning to do the same. Therefore, he gave us five minutes to discuss among ourselves and agree on what we were going to say when we stepped into the VC's office—by which point there would be no turning back.

Although feeling strong-armed, all three of us decided to back down on this occasion, especially the GAPSA president, who was now only days away from graduating. To maintain our stance on what felt right, we still put our concerns forward to the VC. However, our tone changed from demands to recommendations on what was best for the students. The key questions we had asked ourselves in those five minutes were "Would it matter in ten years, the faculty named on our certificates?" and "Was the fight worth losing our qualifications over?" Although the threatened repercussions of our request were not right, it was however not commensurate with the weight of any benefits that could be derived from getting the preferred outcome for the matter being tabled. So, we chose a softer approach, and thereby everyone got to graduate. Not all of the students were happy when the change was enforced, but only we three knew the true price that was at stake was that "happiness" to be pursued.

UNHOLY INDULGENCES

My third and final years at the university seemed to breeze by. Towards the end of my fourth year and the beginning of 1999, when I turned twenty, I started to think and make plans for life after Uni—the first being completing my National Youth Service Corps year, then getting into the business world. This was the period that most final-year students made similar plans, so one often heard comments like "to start work and take my share of the national cake," referring to making some money by working in the oil and gas industry, especially. However, my mind was in a largely different place. I remember responding to such comments by saying, "I would like to bake another cake so that others can have more to share from." This mindset was influenced predominantly by the gospel.

Although I knew that I had to start somewhere by learning from others in the business world, my long-term focus was on attaining a position where I could help businesses and nations solve complex problems, and also have enough knowledge to share with younger generations. Therefore, the first big question was, "Which dissertation topic will lend itself to my course, "Geography," while looking at a problem of national scale?" My focus was also towards a topic of interest that would truly be addressing a gap in society, not just something that was easy to write about. I shared this desire with my supervisor, who then made me think hard. After going through several proposals on topics of interest, we settled on the tourism industry—in particular, reviewing the importance of tourist infrastructures in the growth of the industry in Nigeria. And what a hard topic that turned out to be—barely any existing literature to go on, so I had to do tonnes of research work to get any meaningful data. Walking the streets of Lagos to collect surveys from directors and managers of related businesses—hotels, food sellers, art shops, etc.—for this dissertation exposed a non-streetwise twenty-year-old to various dangers, but I made it through in the end (thank God!). It prepared me at least for the level of research required for a master's program, which I undertook several years later.

The second big question was "Which industry will give me such an opportunity?" My conclusion was "Consulting". I decided to become a management consultant straightaway for two reasons:

- During my four-year study of "Geography," the department had mandated and chosen elective courses from across various faculties, over and above those mandated by the University for all students. I took courses in engineering, surveying, law, architecture, estate management, accounting, economics, philosophy, psychology, sociology, and marine biology, to name a few. So, it felt like I knew a thing or two about every other aspect of work-life and the only way to build on those principles was to get into a reputable and international consulting firm.

- A good consulting experience would adequately expose me to various industries using proven principles—both nationally and internationally—affording me an experience that was not limited by geographical borders or industries.

With these two questions clarified, I focused on completing my first degree. All thanks to God's grace and help, at the end of June 1999, I finished my program at the University of Lagos attaining a 2.1! What almost looked bleak even at the end of my third year became a reality in the fourth—and for that, I was immensely grateful to God.

Then the wait began to receive my call-up letter to know where I had been posted to complete the mandatory National Youth Service Corps (NYSC) year. The scheme, which was set up in 1973, aims to involve Nigerian graduates in nation-building and development activities. Hence, one often gets posted to a State outside of that of their origin, region, or where they studied to serve the people in a less familiar community with their skills—although, by my time, people had found ways to influence their posting. The posting was communicated to the Institution where one graduated, as they would have afforded the governing body the list of their graduates. Therefore, I had to wait back in Lagos so I could easily pick up my call-up letter from Uni once the posting list was published. Without much else to keep busy with, I occasionally went back to the department, where I was allowed free access to some of the computers and started to teach myself how to use Microsoft Office tools, especially Excel, Access, and PowerPoint.

It was during this waiting period, with a lot of time on my hands, that I made a dangerous discovery—one that would hold me bound for decades. I found out that the words of Proverbs 16:27–29 are very wise indeed—an idle mind becomes the devil's playground.

> **Reader alert!** The next few paragraphs may seem explicit, gross, or unholy to some, so please feel free to skip these. However, it's about time that individuals, parents, and the church feel comfortable discussing such topics. After all, it's about the human body. Plus the desire for sex catches up with all of us whether we are professed Christians, celibate, or otherwise. Keeping this aspect hush-hush in what should be the safest environments to learn about it, and inquisitive-minded persons like myself not having opportunities to openly discuss what is being experienced or explored, has quite a huge negative impact on individuals and societies in the long-term. Since a key aim of this book is to help others learn a thing or two from my mistakes, I consider this aspect of my experience to have had such a significant effect that it cannot be ignored. But please proceed as best as suits your personality.

Alright, let's talk about sex.

It was a really hot afternoon and there was no electricity as part of a load-shedding activity to help maintain the available power infrastructure. I started to burn up so much that I could feel my blood coming to a boil and my skin roasting. Unable to take the heat, I decided to take another shower just to get water on my body, although I knew that the water flowing through the taps would be equally hot having been pumped into an overhead steel tank that had also been exposed to the heat. As I stepped out of the shower and towel-dried, I burst into an uncontrollable sweat from my scalp to my toes due to the heat hitting me in full force. Since I was home alone and had nothing to do, I decided to lay on the bed naked, fanning myself with a paper fan just to keep my skin slightly cool. I'm not sure how long after I laid down that I fell asleep but was awoken by the cranking of the fan which had been stationed on me where I laid. There was also this burning sensation in my vagina which got me alarmed, and I jolted upright like one that had been stung by a thousand bees. I rushed to the foot of the bed where there was a stool for sitting in front of the dressing mirror. I remember spreading out my legs to help identify the source of this burning sensation; it was the first time I looked at myself in a mirror with such attention and certainly the first ever, I looked that closely down there.

Staring at the anatomy of my vagina in the mirror, I noticed the little 'cherry' at the top was red. For a split second, I thought I had developed a boil or abscess of some sort, so I made a move to touch it—my most regretted move to date—and a sharp but desirable pain went through my veins.

"What was that?" I thought.

Normally, a painful sensation in any other part of the body is uninviting, but this seemed to have wrapped a web around my mind that made me want nothing more than to touch it again and again until I was in a state of ecstasy. And just as quickly, it all stopped. I had never felt anything like it! Not even my mum, I thought, had told me anything about this in all of her various topical lectures, especially when we started seeing changes in my body. At that moment, I remember wondering out loud "What just happened?" Believe it or not, I had no idea what this was, and I set down the dangerous path of really understanding it by experimenting more. This was a terrible decision. But for those who are still as naïve about what happened as I was then, (spoiler alert!) I had just pleasured myself. *Masturbation*, it is called.

It might be strange for you to hear me describe my journey in this regard as an error against the backdrop of the highly sexualised society that we live in today. Yes, the need for sex might be a natural feeling, but should that negate the need for self-control? I found it addictive and also observed it to be the type of habit that flung the door wide open for all sorts of unwelcome demons (like other bad habits) to take root in my life. It did not take long after this started for my world to start crumbling, and it took decades before I could find my way to the road of restoration. These "side effects" are why I consider masturbation an error and misuse of God's intended purpose for sex—and beg to differ on what might be the popular take on it. Although we have become a more sexually aware society, the quality of individual and societal life, holistically, has been inversely correlated because knowledge is only truly beneficial when applied for the right purpose.

MORAL —

There is a God-hole in every human heart because it is His breath that is in our cells. Money, drugs, sex, fame, marriage, family, friends, or anything else—be it good or bad—cannot fill this hole because only He can. Ever wondered why people with vast possessions or achievements still feel empty? The desires of the human soul will be insatiable until you let God in. Trust me, I am saving you many years of pain and sleepless nights searching for fulfilment. Or, maybe now helping find the answer to your search for 'something' to complete you.

Sometime in November 1999; a few weeks after the discovery and awakening of my sexual desires (which I only thought of as a body-exploration activity then), Tosan came to visit me at my uncle's place—living in same area enabled us to stay in touch. I did more of the visits to his house as my uncle did not really like boys visiting the house. He knew of my uncle's preferences, which thankfully came in handy when he visited as my uncle was the first person to attend to his knock on the gate. Uncle gave him directions on how to get into the house and come upstairs to wait for me in the living room; then he informed me that I had a visitor. Realising who it was as Tosan was now almost at the top of the stairs, I froze, expecting to get into real trouble later. On seeing my uncle, Tosan greeted him prostrating fully in the traditional Yorùbá way a young person will greet an older one. My uncle was so impressed by this that he said nothing to me beyond the fact that he was on his way out for a meeting, which doubly shocked me. Not only did he seem comfortable with letting a boy into the house, but my uncle was also going out knowing fully well that it would mean we would be alone.

Once I got over the surprises and bid my uncle farewell, Tosan told me why he had come. Our NYSC postings had been published in school. When he checked for mine, he saw that I had been posted to Jigawa State.

I exclaimed "Jigawa! Where is Jigawa State?"

Tosan laughed, stating that he had reacted the same way at first. Then we started laughing at ourselves—"geography" graduates who knew much about North America (having done a course specifically on the region) but not a state in our own country. The irony of it all. While still speaking and laughing, Tosan leaned forward and gently pressed his lips against mine, mouthing the words "kiss me." Not knowing how to react as this was so unexpected, he came close and helped my hands around his waist as he carried on kissing me until my lips gave way to his. It was my first kiss.

I still cannot clearly describe how I felt in that moment. About 1996, I had somewhat formulated a plan in which I would get married at twenty-five (latest) and not have been with any man before my husband. So, whilst his kiss seemed passionate, I could hardly "live in the moment" because my brain was in an overdrive of thoughts—most of which were wondering what this really was.

I thought of our friendship and how that could be a basis for building a relationship. After all, I had heard married people say things like it is good to marry someone with whom you are friends. We had stood by each other through various difficult times. Although many in our class joked that we must have something going on to be that close, we never did whilst on campus. In fact, I played a role in him dating one of my roomies in our second year and equally supported his relationship when he started seeing someone else towards the end of our third year, despite her often aggressive behaviour towards me. To the best of my knowledge, they were still together, which in itself made me uncomfortable, as it was against my principles to be involved with a guy who was still involved with another woman. Hence, being in this situation where we were kissing was strange and uncomfortable on quite a few personal counts.

However, I also remembered the words of a lecturer in that moment. The lecturer was quite friendly and allowed easy access to his office should students and associate lecturers need a place to study or have some light refreshments (his fridge was often stocked). When he got to know me round about our year three, he often said to me, "Allow yourself to love and to be loved." I never quite paid attention to it, because I really didn't want to be part of all that flaky love that I had seen on campus, which had the potential of being dangerous if the wrong woman was in the mix. Now being out of Uni and put on the spot by what was happening right now, I thought to let it be and see what came out of it. I also thought that perhaps this was God starting to answer my prayers for my future husband and home. Therefore, I made no motion to stop it and came away wondering if this meant that Tosan, who was also a good friend, was to be the man for me. Hmmm…how naïve I was then!

Tosan's stay was not to be long, as according to him, he "only" came to inform me of my posting to Jigawa State so I could go to school to pick up my call-up letter. This was fine by me, as I needed some space to take in what had just happened. Moreover, I didn't know when my uncle would return and didn't want him to meet Tosan still at the house—his imagination was sure to run wild considering he had left us alone there, which might cause me to lose his trust that I had worked fairly hard to earn. I saw him off to the bus stop, about a five-minute walk from the house.

Just as I got back into my room, I heard my uncle's car horn at the gates; it was a little less than an hour since he had left the house. I thought, "Pphheewww, what a saving grace!" The housekeeper opened the gates, so I didn't need to go back downstairs. My uncle's first comment when he came upstairs was, "Your friend has left?"

I replied, "Yes," adding that he only came to inform me of my NYSC posting. While that was true and my uncle was satisfied, my heart pricked me deep within, knowing that it wasn't the whole truth of what had taken place in those few minutes, although I sure wasn't going to volunteer that additional information.

MORAL —

Here lies a potential lesson for parents and maybe spouses who are less trusting of one another. You really cannot watch anyone 24-7. The less you trust them to make the right decisions or stay faithful, the more likely you are to 'push' them to do that very thing you are acting like a hawk over. I think it is more helpful to create an atmosphere where kids or spouses can freely talk about what they are facing and be confident that they will get the necessary support that will help them out of the situation.

I was twenty, and had hormones flying all over the place without fully comprehending what was going on. Although my older female cousins still lived in the house at the time, they all had busy lives. Hence, I unconsciously developed the habit of keeping to myself and not sharing anything personal, which was unhelpful for my well-being. This period was probably the first time I felt the full weight of being away from my parents. So I decided that I would have to learn to figure some things out on my own, because I was never likely to be living under my parents' roof again.

This experience also formed one of the propellants of my desire to support young people. Most times, having a proper listening and solution-minded ear, non-judgemental or with pre-conceived notions, solves 50 percent of the problem being faced. It's only in recent years, when I completely opened my heart for God to expose any deep-seated pains, anger, and unhelpful behaviours, that I have started to understand where some of these habits began so I can work at undoing them. Layer by layer God is "peeling me back." Each year feels like He's stepping up the notch, but I have made up my mind to be committed to this journey because I am starting to see the benefits. It is not a comfortable process or easy thing to do, especially when you have been living like that for decades and have many life experiences that seem to justify those habits or responses to certain situations. But since being on this new journey, I have learnt that we need God's help to first accept the truth of what is exposed (rather than make excuses for it), acknowledge that we are the ones who need to change (not someone else), understand that there is no better time to change than now, and actively take those actions that will be required to keep making us better versions of ourselves. It is a constant process of taking deliberate actions. So far, I have come to appreciate God's intense love for me and immense grace over my life to break me out of bondage.

MORAL —

I have found that a good approach to breaking a bad habit or an addiction is to pay attention to what you watch, hear, and the company you keep. The information you expose yourself to greatly influences your thoughts, your thoughts influence your words, your words form your habits, and your habits shape your character. Therefore, it is important to pay attention to your information source and mount guard on what you let into your heart (Proverbs 4:23). Deliberately feed yourself with the right information—the ones that encourage you to reach your full potential and be a good member of your society. Indeed, some habits are more difficult to break but there is none yet that the Word of God cannot overcome. God's Word is the most powerful truth you can consume (Hebrews 4:12) so I encourage you to make a habit of 'feeding' on it daily.

A few days after Tosan told me of the posting, I went to school to pick up my posting letter. We were expected to resume camp in early December for three weeks, which meant that we would be returning home a few days before Christmas. So, I thought to stop by Tosan's house on my way home to let him know when I would be leaving for Jigawa and, of course, to know where I stood following that kiss—being conscious that he might still be with his girlfriend. The few days that had passed helped me to do a reality check and brought me back to my senses. Whilst I wouldn't have been opposed to us dating, I certainly was not going to get myself involved in a relationship if he was still with the other girl. So, I needed things to be cleared up, as I wasn't disposed to play games.

Not surprisingly, Tosan admitted to still being with his girlfriend, although they were having issues at the time. The kiss was merely a combo of his uneasiness with their issues and the realisation that I, one of his closest friends, was going away and we were not likely to see each other in that year-long period of my National Service. Tosan went on to say that he might have told his girlfriend what had happened. As someone who never liked me much, she retaliated by telling him a twisted version of an incident that occurred at Uni between me and another guy. This was most likely to debunk Tosan's "misplaced trust" in me, as he put it, so he was upset that I let him find out from her.

Here is the true story. One evening in our final year, I went over to Tosan's room to fetch him so that we could go to the classroom area for our regular study together. On arriving, I met his girlfriend there, who certainly was not going to let him go anywhere with anyone, let alone me. So, I decided to head out alone, when this guy, who was also in Tosan's room at the time, asked if he could come with me instead. "Sure," I said. Although I didn't know him much, I thought absolutely nothing of it.

On getting to Arts Block, we found the cartography classroom empty, so we went in and expected that more people would come in at some point in the evening. But not long after we sat down, it started to rain, so we ended up being alone in the classroom. Then he came over to where I was sitting, having initially sat a few seats away. I thought he wanted to ask a question when he leaned in, but he put his hands on my breasts and was kissing sloppily on me, which I found very disgusting.

With flashing images of what had happened in 1994 with that TV presenter, I pushed him away as I asked what possibly could have come over him or suggested that I had such interests. When he didn't seem to be backing down, I packed up my books and started to make my way out of the classroom when he finally apologised for his behaviour. I don't remember if I sat back down or still left, seeing as the rain had subsided, but I recall him walking me back to the hostel as it had become pretty late by this time. At the end of that day, I was of the mind that it was a mistake which he seemed to have regretted and I would forgive, not knowing that he had told someone else about it. And either he or Tosan's girlfriend had contorted what happened.

The version Tosan was told added that I had sex with him in the classroom!!! I was still trying to comprehend how the story morphed from him trying to grope me to us having sex (and how gross just thinking of it was for me), when Tosan asked, "If you wanted to have sex, why that person?" I was greatly offended by this question as it made me realise that the real intent was to damage my character, but I couldn't comprehend why anyone would do that. This was someone I wasn't friends with and one I chose to forgive his wrongdoing, thinking of it as a "moment of madness," but he had the audacity to broadcast it like it was something to be proud of. My mind flashed back to that evening, and I thought, "If I had only told some other boys I knew on campus what happened, they would have taught him a good lesson for such behaviour. Maybe then, he wouldn't have displayed this immaturity afterwards." But because I chose to let it go, there I was being shamed for something that I didn't even do. Again, this was happening all because of a boy!

Oh, I was livid. In my anger, I could barely speak or pay attention to any other thing Tosan was saying. I was in Uni when I learnt to control my anger reflex, which used to cause me to fling the nearest thing I could lay hands on. With God's help, I got rid of those tantrums. Then I realised that when I am really angry (not just upset) at something, I am still unable to clearly articulate how I feel in such moments, so I either fall silent while visibly shaking from the bottled anger or have uncontrollable tears stream down my face from the pain being felt inside without words to express it. At this point with Tosan, since the situation was an outright perversion of the truth, I had no tears to cry and so was angrily silent.

Watching Tosan go on and on, I noticed that he was also upset about this information, meaning that it wasn't a deliberate accusation from him but that he was confused about what to believe. Although I was partly upset because, as a close friend, I expected him to know me better than their story portrayed, I realised that he was torn between what he knew of my character or expected from me as a Christian and the trust he had in his girlfriend not to lay such accusations unless they were true. However misplaced I thought that trust to be, I understood the difficult position he was in so I decided to calm down. I also decided, again, to forgive all parties involved in this attempted defamation of my character—not because they asked or deserved it, but for my sanity.

My decision was based on an attempt to put things into proper perspective. I couldn't find any reason to hold on to this negative and painful experience when I might never see these people again to confront or discuss the wrongdoing, and perhaps get some understanding about why they did it. As pained as I was by what was said, I went with 'good reasoning' and chose that very day to forgive. This turned out to be a good choice—as forgiveness always is. Nowadays, I forgive just because I have been forgiven much myself. Plus, I have learnt over the years that God asking us to forgive others was more for our benefit than it is for others.

MORAL —

Unforgiveness leaves you with an ever-sore wound which only eats deeper and deeper into your soul, causing decay in your quality of life. When the very core of your being is unwell, you will no doubt start to manifest "foul" characteristics and experience deterioration in your physical health, especially when the person comes around or the same circumstances repeat themselves. Forgiveness is not a one-time action. Instead, it is a continuous and conscious daily action, and sometimes for the same person, until it resonates that "all slates are wiped clean."

Two practices I found helpful especially when someone's wrongdoing replays in my mind are:

> To say a word of blessing or prayer for the person the very moment they come to mind.
> To say aloud that "I, [insert your name], choose again today to forgive, or remind myself again today that I have forgiven ___________ for ___________, as I have myself enjoyed much forgiveness from God and others."

Once we were both past discussing the incident, Tosan and I agreed that our friendship was more important than having a complicated relationship. Then we went on to talk briefly about my upcoming trip to Jigawa State and what to expect knowing that we were not likely to see each other much in the coming year. On getting back home, much of the day replayed in my mind over and over again. I also couldn't help thinking, "What a shamble my first kiss turned out to be!" It was so not the sort of circumstance I thought it would happen in and certainly not how I ever thought I would feel about it. Unbeknownst to me, the lack of resolution in this area left open a Pandora's box that the following months were soon to reveal.

A TOUGH ROAD TO GROWTH

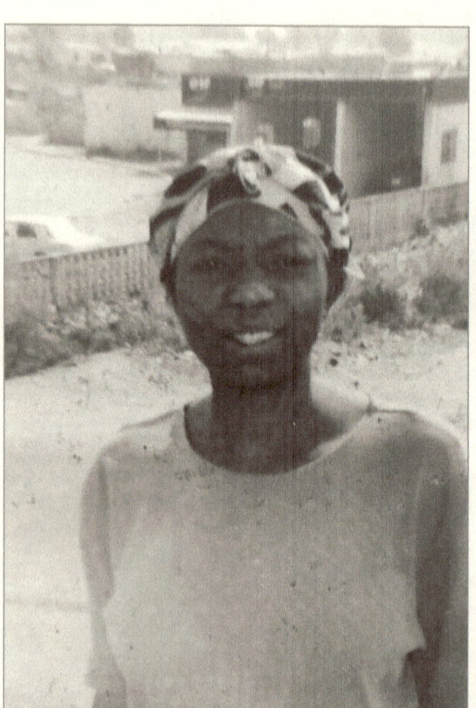

First arrival at Kano

In Corper uniform at Gumel NYSC camp

GOING NORTH

On November 30, 1999, I boarded the night coach from Lagos to Kano (Kano State) where I would board another transport to Gumel (Jigawa State), with the aim to arrive at the National Youth Service Corp Orientation Camp the next day, which was the stated resumption day. It was harmattan season, which was often dry and hot in the afternoons. This would be my very first time in the core Northern part of Nigeria, so I had no idea what to expect beyond the general knowledge that the North was often hot and dusty. I had packed only a small bag, not bigger than the size of a tennis bag, with a few T-shirts and shorts, and a scarf.

Arriving in Kano the next morning, I met other youth corpers from the South who were also resuming at the camp in Jigawa, so we boarded the same bus to Gumel together. Getting to know other people from other higher institutions across the country was a helpful distraction from the rather nervous feeling I had throughout the journey. I had done many travels, especially at secondary school, but never had I been in public transport where the driver was doing such an incredible amount of speed. To make things worse, the road was patchy with some areas eroded while other surfaces were scraped in preparation for repair works. The engine whined as the driver pressed down more on the accelerator. Using no brakes, he sped across the landscape the entire one-hour-plus journey, raising much red dust in his wake and bumping in and out of every pothole along the way. The dust was so much that we had to shut all of the windows and roast like a Christmas turkey in an oven, as the heat kept rising within the eighteen-passenger bus. Being predominantly Southerners and youth corpers for that matter, we knew not how to caution the driver and did nothing other than endure the journey by speaking to each other as best as we could. When we arrived safely at the gates of the Jigawa State College of Education in Gumel where the NYSC Camp was, I heaved a sigh of relief and thanked God that I got there in one piece. This was my first true induction into "living in the North."

Getting to camp, we were immediately directed to the locations for our registration. As I went from point to point, I noticed that some corpers were fully registered, as they were already about in their "day wear"—a pair of white T-shirts on white shorts, which was ironic considering the environmental condition of where we were. Then I noticed the presence of soldiers in the camp; some were walking around, and others seemed to be arriving just like us. I knew from history that the NYSC process involved some form of military training but did not realise that activities in the camp were wholly run by the Nigerian Army. With that realisation, I knew the next three weeks were going to be tough and I had better be mentally ready for whatever was going to come next.

Finished with registration and picking up all of my kit, I was pointed to the female accommodation up ahead and told we were expected to spend the day settling in, but that camp activities would be in full force from the next morning. When the bugle sounded the next morning, we were expected to be standing with our platoon on the Campgrounds, which was pointed out in the opposite direction. The Mammy Market, where we could get non-camp meals and other approved items, was on the way to the female hostels. Under no circumstance were we expected to leave camp without permission. A few other locations, like the kitchen and Camp offices, were pointed out, but it wasn't until I settled in that I fully understood what was going on or where to go for whatever I needed. I recollect looking at the stalls in the Mammy Market, all set up with sticks and thatched roofs, as I walked past in an attempt to identify what I could possibly get in each.

Arriving at the hostel, I walked into my allocated room, and there was my first pleasant surprise since beginning this journey. Sitting on the lower bunk was a distant relative. She attended the University of Ife, and we only saw each other at an annual wider family New Year's Day party. Family came from home and abroad, so it was always a good opportunity to see relatives. Anyone older was Uncle or Auntie, and those in the same age group simply referred to each other as "cousins", unless of course, they were our siblings. Anyway, right in the same room with me was Cousin Liz, and how happy I was to see her. Naturally, I took the top bunk; she was older and even already settled into the lower bunk. Just like me, she was not a foodie, so later that evening we settled for a meal of bread and eggs from a Mai Shai (tea brewer, the Northern Nigerian way) at the Mammy Market.

Unable to sleep much through the night as was usual for me when in a new place, I was up early to take a bath and was surprised at how cold it was. Thinking it was going to be a fairly warm temperature like the previous day, I hadn't boiled my bath water. So I had a cold bath and was shivering by the time I was done. I dashed to the room to get dressed, with the hope that I might be able to sleep a while before the morning call. Well, I was barely dressed when the bugle sounded—it was 5:00 a.m.! A few seconds later, soldiers were banging the hostel's main door with their sticks to get everyone out. Quickly getting into my white-on-white uniform specified for daily activities, I nudged Liz, who was also ready, and we started out of the hostel for the Campgrounds. Oh, what a sight it was! Some people were still half-asleep as they walked and some others were still in their pyjamas, as the crowd moved towards the Campgrounds.

The NYSC second batch was usually very light back then, so we were barely two hundred corpers standing on the massive expanse of bare land used for the camp, which was not helpful for heat generation. Falling into line in our platoons, we huddled together like farm animals trying to keep warm, strangers and friends alike. Liz and I were in Platoon 1, so we held on to each other until the sergeants came around to instruct us on how to line up and stand at attention. Then, we felt the cold wheezing through our ears and into our veins, as the harmattan winds coursed through the grounds. I was so cold that I thought I was going to die frozen like a stick in the ground!

Soon, our platoon commandants stood in front of their assigned platoons. As soon as the Camp Commandant got on the grounds, the call was made for us to sing the national anthem, followed by the NYSC anthem. Then, the Camp Commandant gave his address welcoming us, and of course, laid down the rules about dressing on Camp grounds. He wanted to see nothing but the white T-shirts on white shorts, and we were to be on the grounds within minutes of the bugle sound. Some people got clever later on with the outfits by wearing their PJs under the whites, which though frowned upon, the Commandant allowed after pleas about the morning cold. I soon got used to wearing just the whites knowing that once the "Assembly" was over, it was on to activities that caused us to sweat; notwithstanding the rising sun which gradually made the heat even worse. So, each day, we went from freezing cold to nearly unbearable heat and a dusty atmosphere—all before midday.

My platoon commandant was a very nice soldier. He was very approachable and helpful whenever we had questions, and as one who knew how to ask questions, we naturally became friends. Soon, I started to make friends, especially in my platoon, and didn't have much of an issue with the level of stamina required for the activities having previously been an athlete and involved in various sports.

By the end of the first week, I started to enjoy being in camp except for one thing, the food. I lived on biscuits mostly. Nearly every evening, I visited the same Mai Shai at the Mammy Market, ordering the same thing. I figured that this was only going to be for a few weeks, so I endured. Before this experience, I was not a fan of bread at all. So, NYSC Camp was where I learnt to eat bread, and not just the white bits inside, but I ate everything.

One day during the afternoon recess, while most people were heading towards the kitchen for their lunch, I was heading in the opposite direction—back to the hostel for a rest before evening activities began—when I overheard a conversation between two boys who were walking ahead of me. I did not understand a word of what they said, but it sure sounded pleasant to my ears. They sounded musical and seemed to be enjoying whatever the gist was about. Walking up a bit closer, I recognised the language as the Nigerian Pidgin. I became familiar with the language in Lagos but didn't understand it or know how to speak it. It had never interested me to learn it until I heard these two boys.

Slowing down my pace, I decided to follow them. Thankfully, they were going to the Mammy Market. They went into one of the other huts, and I followed in, choosing to sit a couple of rows behind them in what turned out to be a restaurant serving mainly meals from the Southern parts of Nigeria. Of course, I wasn't in to eat but had to order a fizzy drink to avoid having a weird conversation with the waiters that could blow my cover.

As the boys spoke on, I giggled at the sound coming from them—it was just too hilarious. I took note of their faces and that evening, found out the platoon they were in. Each afternoon thereafter, I purposefully waited for them to make their move, then tailed them wherever they chose to go. Since there weren't many places to go and not too many of us in camp, it wasn't long before my cover was blown. Plus, I got so comfortable laughing at their words that I was betrayed by my very own giggles.

I was sitting behind the boys at a restaurant in the Mammy Market when one of them got up and walked straight to the bench where I was. He said something in pidgin, and I looked up strangely at him in a manner that said, "I have no idea what you just said." Understanding my demeanour, he asked in plain English, "Why have you been following us?" I attempted to fake innocence, but he called me out. So I came clean, telling him that I just enjoyed hearing them both speak and apologised for turning them into my comic relief. I made it clear that I didn't understand them, so it was purely about sound. He laughed and asked me to join them at their table, which I did. Then he introduced himself and his friend. They had been friends since their Uni days in the very citadel of pidgin in Nigeria—Warri, in Delta State. It all made sense why they were so fluent and enjoyable, and their speech was quite different from that spoken in Lagos.

From that moment until the end of NYSC Camp, they took me under their wings and started to teach me pidgin, the Wafi way. However, they made it clear that in Warri, the slang changed so quickly that some words became outdated almost the day after they were introduced into the language. In less than two weeks of being with them, I learnt how to piece words together to get some idea of the conversation and how to make my tone sound like the pidgin twang, though my sentences might actually have been in proper English. What these boys taught me was foundational and has since been very helpful in my ability to converse more widely in Nigeria.

About two weeks into camp, we had the endurance trek and obstacle course, both of which lasted whole days when they were held…and both of which made me well-known at camp, especially the latter. I earned the "Iron Lady" camp title for being the first person (and lady) to complete all of the set obstacles, which included climbs of different shapes and forms, and walking tight ropes. After this unexpected popularity, I had nowhere to hide as everyone, including the Camp Commandant, knew my face. I did not know the import of this achievement until days later when Liz told me that they were serving yams and stew for dinner. Knowing that I loved yams, she encouraged me to eat the kitchen food at least once.

By the time I got down there, the kitchen ladies were tidying up. I asked if they wouldn't mind serving one more, to which a kitchen lady grudgingly obliged. My thought was that having walked the distance there, I might as well get the food, so I ignored her obviously displeased body language. When she started serving me, she was moaning and cursing under her breath, which made me speak out as I was uncomfortable being served in such a manner. Feeling upset that I told her to "Please take it easy," she dropped my plate of food on the floor saying, "If you like don't eat it." That upset me so I turned to walk away. Some other corpers, who had seen the whole thing play out, told me that it was unacceptable behaviour and should be reported to Camp Management; they referred to me as Iron Lady since they did not know my name. Another corper commented that the particular kitchen lady was always quite short with people and treated corpers like animals, when in fact, it was because of us being in camp that she was employed. On hearing that, I felt offended—not just by what she did to me but by the fact that several corpers around spoke up about her attitude. Some even said it loud enough for her to hear, and rather than apologise, she cursed even more. So, I decided to act by going to the Camp offices.

Thinking I would meet one of the administration staff to report the case, I bumped into the Camp Commandant in the corridors. He immediately asked, "Iron Lady, what troubles you?" as he probably saw the annoyance on my face. I went on to tell him what happened.

He responded, "What? She dropped the Iron Lady's food on the floor?" Then he motioned for me to turn around towards the kitchen as he was going to follow me there. That was unexpected and a surprise for me.

When we got to the kitchen, my food was still on the floor. The Commandant asked for the lady. It turned out that she was the Head Chef. The food on the floor and eye-witness accounts of the corpers around was enough evidence. The Commandant asked me what to do with her—suggesting if I wanted her fired, it would be done. Woah! I never expected to have her job at stake, I thought. Not to be the cause for someone losing their job, I asked for corpers to be allowed to cook our food until the end of camp, especially lunch and dinner, under the watch of the kitchen ladies. There had been talk among corpers that this happened elsewhere, plus the Government provided an adequate food supply for us. Yet most of the food was being syphoned by the ladies to our detriment, which was not right. This was where I got the idea, and all corpers on the scene supported the motion. The Camp Commandant sanctioned it to take effect immediately and asked the Head Chef to apologise to me for the treatment plus thank me for saving her job. She did so grudgingly, and I walked off with the Camp Commandant, leaving the food on the floor.

Subsequently, I started to eat from the kitchen because corpers were at the helm of affairs; good portions and tasty meals were served. Interestingly, the kitchen ladies still had meals to take away daily, so one wonders, "How much more they carted away all those days when we corpers were being short-changed?"

MORAL —

Some titles or positions may seem insignificant, but opportunity does present itself to check what you will do when you are in a position of influence. No matter how insignificant your position may seem, and wherever that may be—even within the family structure—do you use your influence to oppress others or to take actions that others reap the benefits of? It is a good practice to ask yourself this question and pay close attention to your ways in this regard. It's easy to point accusing fingers at those in obvious leadership positions, although each one of us has influence somewhere, yet we often look out for only "number 1" (ourselves) when truthfully considered. Sometimes taking that action or decision may not even be of any direct benefit to you, but if it will help others, have you ever asked "Why not?"

In the last week of camp, a football and volleyball competition was organised for the boys and girls, respectively, and my platoon won both games. I had never played volleyball until then but was roped into the team because my platoon barely had enough ladies to make up the six-per-side required. Having won the title of Iron Lady, I wasn't allowed to decline to take part. So, one of our platoon guys offered to give about three of us a crash course on the rules and how to play volleyball. With barely an hour before the games, we did the quick run-through. Somehow, to all of our surprise, my serve turned out to be the one hardly anyone on the opposing team was able to return, so I just kept serving—round after round. Finally, we won the competition that we had gone into thinking we would be out of in the first round.

This was the birth of my love for volleyball. Although I am not perfect in the game, but still play it for the fun. The lesson here for me, however, was to be open and never be afraid to try new things. Naturally, I am an outdoor sports person and do enjoy playing games for fun but will hardly ever step up to do something which I feel underqualified for, especially when it is a competition or the outcome impacts others besides myself. Prior to these experiences at camp, I often went with what was "safe" or familiar but discovered at camp that when "forced into a tight situation," I had reservoirs that could be drawn upon from within. And I believe this is true of every living being especially humans.

Today, with my work especially, I go from one client site to another helping to proffer solutions to business challenges so that they can deliver better quality services to their customers and keep being profitable. Do I always have the answers? You know the resounding response to that. However, I am not afraid to start from what I know and work together with the client as ONE TEAM to resolve the problems faced.

I wouldn't be surprised if, as you read through the obstacle or volleyball experience, you wondered if it was more of a "show off" than a learning experience (smiles). Well, the latter was why they had a mention. I realised some years back that every experience had contributed something to my person. Some circumstances were so grand that they completely shifted my perspective of life, whilst most had been subtle or trivial (like learning to play volleyball), because their occurrence seemed, at the time, like just one of those things life threw me. "It was just another day in life," one might say. But when I think deeply, I realise that the outcomes of the so-called negligible events did something in me that perhaps another subtle experience helped to build upon or a challenging situation helped to expose.

When I speak with people today and they say things like "My life isn't as exciting as yours," I caution against such thoughts. The Jet Age we live in makes us clamour for the spectacular so much that we ignore the "precept-upon-precept" building events that occur daily in our lives. These too matter; mundane as they may seem, most times they are the greatest influencers of who we are. Yet we seem programed to pay little or no attention to their effect on us.

By the way, when we pray to God, how do we think He answers the prayers most times? By pouring out manna from Heaven, or by allowing us to be in situations intended to help us lay hold of what we asked? Pause to think for a moment. In my experience, if we pray for patience then we are more likely to face situations that can tip us off the scale, with the hope that it helps us learn to be patient. Hardly (and might I say *Never*) does good character get deposited in one overnight; it is a process. The longer we take to recognise those daily opportunities presented, the greater the likelihood that it will be long before we see that prayer being answered. Like every good Father, God trains His children (all of us), and each one needs to value the path which they are on.

MORAL —

God gives you abundant grace to run your own race! Quit looking at another person's life or comparing yourself to others—you aren't them and just may not survive the journey were you to walk in their shoes from start to finish (not the point that they are at now). Therefore on your journey through life, count every blessing and see every challenge as an opportunity to become more resilient or to build character.

The days rolled by, and NYSC Camp came to an end, which also meant that Christmas was around the corner. The next task was to obtain details of our places of primary assignment and sort things out before returning to our various families. People were distributed across the various towns and villages in Jigawa State. Some had to get on public transport to find their postings, but I got a place in Gumel.

I was assigned to Lautai Science and Technology Secondary School which was just across the road from the Jigawa State College of Education (Campgrounds) to teach geography. Four of us were posted there, so we went over to the school together. The school was boys only and started from SSS-1 (year 10). They prided themselves in accepting only the best students, based on their JSS-3 results, from states within the region. On meeting the school principal, he "accepted" the placement of only two of us.

I pleaded with him to reject mine, as I had decided (with Liz) to request for redeployment when we returned to Lagos. Having no plans to return to Jigawa State, the "Rejection Letter" was to be one of my grounds for requesting the redeployment. But the principal refused my pleas, saying that the school needed a teacher for geography. This was the first blow to my plans, so I took the acceptance confirmation from him and started to ponder how else to get my redeployment. Liz, on the other hand, had health concerns which were good grounds for her redeployment, as she needed proximity to family and good healthcare.

With that, I got on the bus and returned to Lagos, using the same methods by which I came to Jigawa State. Throughout the journey, I reminisced about my NYSC Orientation Camp experience, thinking "Camp turned out to be fun but this is good-bye to Jigawa." Or so I thought.

START OF A NEW SOJOURN

Back in Lagos, I informed my auntie of the events at Jigawa and the need for her to help submit my redeployment request when she returned to work in Abuja in the New Year. Once the Christmas and New Year festivities were over, I had my twenty-first birthday party—organised with the help of my cousins and auntie—and awaited news of my redeployment application, being certain that it would be granted. A few days after my birthday, I heard the sad news that my redeployment request had not been granted. I was shattered and greatly disappointed. Thank God the update wasn't received before my birthday because that would have ruined my excitement about turning twenty-one.

My auntie informed me of an opportunity to appeal the decision but that it was best done in person to ensure a quicker decision, especially as we were approaching January end, by which time corpers were expected to have returned to their place of primary assignment. This meant that I needed to travel to Abuja, where the National NYSC Directorate Headquarters is located. So that week, I set out for Abuja with only a travelling bag and a handful of clothes—with the expectation that I would be back in Lagos in a few days with my Redeployment Letter and continue my service year somewhere in the South, at least.

At Abuja, I stayed at Uncle Julius's house because he and his family had moved there. After a day or two of shuttling the NYSC offices, I realised that getting my redeployment would not be straightforward. I was advised to return to Jigawa State and obtain a Rejection Letter from the school in Gumel or some sort of redeployment acceptance from the State's NYSC headquarters located in Dutse. Being adamant about pursuing redeployment as opposed to returning to Gumel, I decided to go to Dutse. To assist me in this pursuit, my uncle gave me the contact information of a senior person at the National Electric Power Authority (NEPA) office in Dutse as my starting point. He also called the man ahead to let him know that I was coming.

Setting out by road using public transport, we did not arrive in Kano until about 9:00 p.m., and there were no more buses from Kano to Dutse at the motor park. Thankfully, there was a corper on the same bus with whom I had chatted briefly during the journey. Seeing as I was stranded, he informed me that he attended the Nigerian Christian Corpers' Fellowship (NCCF) Kano Chapter and was sure that they would be able to accommodate me for the night. I had heard of NCCF while at NYSC Camp and attended some of the fellowship meetings they conducted there. Without any other choice, I hopped on the motorbike with him to the NCCF House. When we arrived, he explained my predicament, and I was very well received. For people who were meeting me for the first time, at about 10:00 p.m., they were very kind hosts. To this day, I cannot vividly recollect even one person's face because it was very dark when I arrived.

When I settled in a little, I noticed some of the housemates watching a video in one of the rooms, so I joined in. The film turned out to be a collection by Roberts Liardon which profiled the extraordinary achievements of men and women who dared to believe in God. I was so captivated by the collection, entitled *God's Generals*, particularly the stories about Smith Wigglesworth and Kathryn Kuhlman. Kathryn had such a renowned bond with the Holy Spirit which enlightened me on how to relate with God as a Person. She was said to have had a seat dedicated to the Holy Spirit, around which people could tangibly feel His presence. Hearing about these men and women who, despite their struggles, chose to believe and take God at

His Word changed my way of thinking. I ended up staying up to watch the series, falling asleep for only a few hours in the same chair.

Before long, it was dawn and time to continue on my journey to Dutse. Saying my "thank you's" and "goodbyes" to those awake at that time, I set out before daylight so I could get to Dutse in good time to sort the issue out at the NYSC offices and potentially return to Lagos that night. However, those few hours at the NCCF House in Kano had so impacted my life that I said the kind of prayer that I had never done before. I asked God to help me sort out the redeployment, but more importantly, that "His will be done." As someone who was used to planning everything to the smallest detail and pursuing my own goals, it had never occurred to me to "create a seat" for God in my life by going with His plans, not mine. So, as I journeyed to Dutse, I remembered Kathryn Kuhlman and asked God to not just "endorse" my plans but to direct my path in line with His will. This was the first time in my life that I actively sought for Him to drive the outcome of events that concern me.

At Dutse, I met with the NEPA official my uncle directed me to, and he was very helpful. However, we didn't have much luck at the NYSC Dutse office. I was told that it was too late to process redeployments from their office and that the only grounds that could be considered were critical medical conditions, being newlywed or pregnant, or being rejected by my place of assignment. One or two hinted that I could fake a medical report or marriage certificate. They could show me where to go if I wanted to, and by the next day, I could be on my way back to Lagos. Though an attractive offer, I told them that I would think about it.

Knowing now that NCCF were very accommodating of fellow corpers and that most *Okada* motorbike riders knew the location of the NCCF House in state capitals, I called for one to take me to the NCCF House in Dutse. Arriving there, I introduced myself and told them why I was in Dutse. Again, I was very well received and cared for. This gave me some mental space to plan my next actions.

That day, two things came up paramount in my mind. First, my prayer for God's will to be done. The only option for redeployment that did not involve me telling lies was to obtain a rejection letter from the school I was posted to. Having attempted that before, it did not really feel like an option. So, I could either go with forging the documents that would earn me an immediate redeployment to a state of my choosing or I could "go with the flow" and return to Gumel, where I was posted, trusting that God was now directing my steps. Second, I remembered my dad's admonishments to always do one's best to keep your ways or hands clean. Observing my drive to change things in society and plans to be in politics, I was about the age of ten or eleven when he gave me that advice. He said that when you lead or are in a position of power, there will be people who will make it their responsibility to dig into your past to find any dirt that can be used to bring you down. Therefore, "as much as you can, keep your hands clean," he advised.

My thoughts also went to the fact that I could produce my medical history of hospitalisation every three months since I was a child, and the fact that having access to a particular pill and good medical facilities—which were not likely to be available there—were the only ways I recovered from the illness. But then, I also remembered my battle with the sickness—using the name of Jesus to enforce my healing—and how I had been without any episode for years since then. I could not imagine claiming that sickness again (being conscious that it was a spiritual one) just because I wanted to avoid a single year of national service in a faraway land. I had realised by this time that my words and proclamations were powerful; after all, it was by such means that I had won the battle against the sickness. So, I wasn't about to put myself back into that bondage. I would rather be in health than strive for temporary gain using sickness as my cover, I thought.

My path in life so far had been one of travels and battles, one that wasn't like that of others nor could be described as commonplace—as my mum always reminded me. Therefore, I made up my mind that evening to return to Gumel. The next morning, I visited the Dutse NEPA office to inform the man of my decision so he could also help relay it to my uncle in Abuja. He gave me his card to contact him if I ever had need of anything during the service year and bade me farewell. I set out for Gumel, not knowing what to expect besides "the Lord's will be done!"

THINK ON THIS...

Keep God at the centre of all that you do—He knows all things, loves you deeply, and delights in seeing you succeed. Everything in your life has been orchestrated in such detail that it takes a wise heart to seek God's will and to walk in it fully. This is your choice to make if you want to take full advantage of what He has already prepared for you.

THE MANTLE OF LEADERSHIP

Early afternoon that day, I arrived in Gumel and went straight to the principal's office at the Lautai Science and Technology Secondary School—my place of primary assignment. The principal was surprised to see me, saying that they thought I had redeployed. I asked if he had changed his mind and would "reject me," but he said no. He, in fact, mentioned that my arrival was timely, as the teacher who had been helping to cover the geography class had resigned and would be leaving the school in about a month. So, my services were still highly needed.

"However," he continued, "because we were not expecting you back, your accommodation has not been prepared."

The principal then asked me to find a corper that I could stay with or find accommodation in town for a couple of weeks while they worked on my room. This was a shock to me because I presumed they would have expected my return in January and had an accommodation already prepared. Although I was grateful my space was still reserved, all I could think in that moment was the fact that I only had with me a small travelling bag and little cash following the unexpected journeys made since leaving Lagos. Therefore, renting in town was not an immediate option, meaning that I needed to find someone who could take me in pending when my accommodation in the school became ready. Not knowing where else to turn, I started walking across the road towards the college where the NYSC Camp had been held in December, with the hope of meeting at least one corper that would be kind enough to accommodate me—because out here, there was no NCCF House.

As I walked down, I remember thinking, "God, this is your plan so please sort this out." On entry into the college, I met a lady who looked like a Southerner, so I knew she was likely to be a corper. I stopped to ask her for directions to where I might find other corpers in the town, stating that I had just resumed duty but had nowhere to stay. She introduced herself as Títí and immediately invited me to stay at her place, which was a huge relief.

As we walked back to her room, Títí mentioned that she was a corper in Batch A, who started their service year in March 1999 and were finishing in February 2000. With most of her set members having left for their homes already, there were about three of them left—one other lady who was leaving in a few days and a guy who was currently leading the NCCF Gumel Chapter but needed to handover to the next person in my set (Batch B). She promised to introduce me to everyone around so I could quickly catch up, as she too was planning to leave in less than two weeks. But first, I needed a rest, having been on the road for several days, with little food eaten that day. Her room was one of two in that corpers' lodge, and it was close to an exit that led to the road dividing their school from mine, which would make my daily commute very easy.

I do not recall much of what happened the rest of that evening beyond being thankful for having a place to lay my head and accepting the fact that I was now in Gumel to stay. Everything felt very surreal, as I was still trying to wrap my head around the fact that I had started my journey about two weeks earlier, hoping to be back in Lagos with my family. But there I was in Gumel, having been taken care of mostly by strangers along the way, and with no means of communicating to my family where I was or that I would be staying back in Gumel for the service year. Yes, I believed that God had a reason for closing up every turn I made to finally lead me to this place; this most certainly was not my will, so I was going to have to trust each door that He opened or closed henceforth. And whilst there, I needed to give it my best despite the current overwhelming feeling of being lost!

The next morning, I resumed at the school. The principal took me to the staff room, showed me my designated desk which was right by the entrance into the room, introduced me to other teachers, and handed me over to the outgoing geography teacher so that he could start taking me through the curriculum for the year and what was left to be covered. I felt like I was being thrown into the deep end all too quickly. This was a boys-only school, in a place where their culture and religion (prevailing beliefs) were very different to mine, and I was saddled with the responsibility of teaching students in senior years (10 to 12) with absolutely no prior formal teachers' training to go on—besides the occasional lesson notes that I helped my mum write or the collation of her students' term results. "I will have to figure this out," I thought. I could draw on some of the things I had observed my mum do for her students, albeit at primary school level.

On returning to the room, TT (as I later started calling her) and her corper neighbour were kind to have cooked, so I had something good to eat. I knew that this was another thing I would need to figure out fairly quickly, considering I had close to zero skills in the kitchen department. At the NCCF fellowship meeting later that evening or the next, TT introduced me to the guy who was the Gumel coordinator.

The moment he heard my name, he exclaimed, "So, you are the person we have been waiting for!"

He broke into a dance and all manners of display of thanksgiving to God, all the while I stood wondering what he was on about. When he had collected himself a bit, he told of how they (at state level) had prayed to know who God wanted to lead the various chapters—Gumel being one of the key ones because it was the host town during the NYSC Orientation Camps. He mentioned that my name was chosen despite being the one with the least attendance record at Camp NCCF meetings. Furthermore, when other co-ordinators were handing over to their successors but I hadn't resumed, they prayed again, and God insisted that I was His choice. Apparently, God had assured them that I was coming back, so he had continued in prayer for God to bring this person. Normally, people chosen would have had some level of participation in the fellowship meetings during their NYSC Camp that made them known, but in my case, no one really knew who I was. The situation was further complicated by the fact that there was attendance from January by people in my set, and to not be able to handover to any of them seemed strange. But each time they prayed, God gave them my name, so the guy had no choice but to wait. Now in February, he had thought the options were either to extend his stay in Gumel pending my arrival or that God would change His mind, giving them the go-ahead to choose another person.

Right then, the level of excitement he displayed and the experiences I had leading me back to Gumel all made sense. Certainly God wanted me in that town—my redeployment request was denied, whereas Liz's was approved; my appeal at Abuja was refused; the stopover at Kano changed my mindset from pursuing "my plan" to having "God's will" prevail; I met nothing but blockers at Dutse with the options being to do things I wouldn't want to do as a Christian; and finally I ended up in Gumel. This young man had been praying for my return off the back of God's direct instructions to him, so it all made sense.

All that was good for him because his prayers were answered, but "How about me?" I thought. While he rejoiced, I suddenly felt a weight being put on my shoulders. My head was spinning with questions like:

- What does my young, little self know about leading people, let alone a whole Fellowship, and one that was at the very core of the State's activities?
- Why would God think that I am the person for this job? Why am I being thrown into the deep end without warning?
- I have only been back a few days, but wait, I am the one that the school has been waiting for, and a whole Fellowship already made up of people too?
- Why should they accept me as their leader, having not been part of this Fellowship or being the newest member to join?

Yes, it probably made logical sense why I finally ended up in Gumel, but it absolutely made no sense why I was chosen to bear this much responsibility—and that scared the life out of me. Whatever questions I had though, I knew it was not with this guy but with God. The poor guy must have been anxious, wondering if he was going to be able to return to his family with each passing day that I did not show up. So, he had full cause to rejoice.

We made plans to spend the next few days for his handover—of the fellowship accounts and other records, including bringing me up to speed with the sub-zones under Gumel (which was the largest NCCF Zone in the State). He also handed me the keys to the Evangelical Church of West Africa (ECWA; now known as Evangelical Church Winning All) building where the fellowship meetings were held. With these done, he left Gumel for good, while I was left to basically learn on the job.

Deep down within, I was angry at God for leading me this way; I wanted His will to be done but was not really prepared for it not going my way. (Isn't that how we are most times?) This anger, however, opened "a crack in my fenced life," which I was completely unaware of at the time. It gave room for the enemy of our souls to strike me beyond reasoning.

Sometime in March 2000, a few weeks after I arrived, TT also left Gumel for her home, being the last one in her set to leave the town. Shortly before her exit, she introduced me to Suzie, a white British lady who also taught in the college. Suzie had been given an apartment with two bedrooms by the college. Seeing as my accommodation in the secondary school was yet to be ready, TT thought Suzie might be able to accommodate me in her second room, knowing that the college would ask me to vacate the room once she left. Although they had become good friends, Suzie was unable to grant TT's request, so I became anxious.

My arrival and sudden leadership of NCCF Gumel hadn't been taken well by the people in my set that I met there, so I couldn't ask the other two girls in the fellowship for such a favour. The only alternative was to ask a male corper who wasn't in the fellowship but I knew him from Lagos, and had connected with him when I found out he had been posted to Gumel. Ayọ̀ had an accommodation provided by the organisation he was posted to and was okay with my request since it was only for a short period—till my accommodation became ready. However, he had to confirm first with his roommate. The boys had been initially placed on a room share until some of the other rooms in their quarters were made more habitable. A few days later, he confirmed that his roommate was cool with the idea of me sharing their room, though I would have to sleep on the floor. This was "better than nothing," as true to TT's suspicion, the college sent someone to me some days after she left, asking me to leave the quarters as I wasn't a corper that was serving with them—a fair and totally understandable point. However, with no other feasible alternative nor funds to get my own accommodation in town, I moved in with the boys, completely naive and oblivious to the dangers that lay ahead. Willy-nilly as it may seem, it was the only choice that seemed plausible at the time. My accommodation will be ready in a few weeks, I thought, plus one of the guys is well known to me and I'm used to being around boys, so all will be fine. Not once did I stop to think, What message will this send to onlookers as a leader of a Christian Fellowship for that matter?

Ayọ̀ and his roommate, Shawn, received me well and made me comfortable in the first few weeks of moving in with them. Shawn was the cook, and a good one at that, so this felt like "God's provision," making me more relaxed about the decision. He also had qualities that made me comfortable around him; he was quite personable, intelligent, spoke Yorùbá fluently though from another Nigerian tribe, and shared my love for music. Soon enough, Shawn and I became friends, so we hung out alone more—often about town or going to the market so I could learn how to do food shopping. In the evenings, we would walk together to Ike's provision store—the spot where Gumel corpers often met for a catch-up.

Ike, an Igbo guy, had been a resident in Gumel for so many years that he owned a shop in the centre of town. The locals generally did not give permission or land to businesses owned by "foreigners" (i.e., non-indigenes) or churches to be located in the centre of their town. Such are often found on the outskirts, so Ike's shop and the ECWA church were the anomalies. Being a young guy who spoke the Hausa and English languages fluently and ran a provisions store located on the main road from Kano into Gumel, and was close to the Gumel Motor Park, Ike was popular with the locals and youth corpers alike. Hence, it was a corper tradition to hang out at his shop, especially in the evenings, as a way of cooling off and keeping in touch with one another. Suzie also hung out with us occasionally, so we started getting to know each other better.

All seemed to be going well, and I gradually started settling into my new life in Gumel. The only things it seemed I had to worry about were understanding the Hausa culture and language, and coming up with ideas on how to get the geography subject across to my students so they could learn. To emphasise, my students comprised a wide demographic. There were the young and exuberant, mostly from families based in Kano. Also, there were those who were older than even I was, some much taller, a few were married, and a decent percentage had little command of the English language. So, when I say "getting across" to them required some thinking, I meant that I knew it was going to be a real challenge doing so. The greatest challenge of my service year in Gumel. Well, or so I thought.

LEARNING TO TEACH

At school, the principal and I did not always get along for a myriad of reasons. Although he was quite approachable, I mostly blamed him for being so nonchalant about providing me an accommodation. It had been a few weeks since I returned, yet he kept giving excuses as to why the place was not yet ready. Once he told of how bats lived in the room and they were finding it difficult to get them out. Hearing that alone made my skin crawl. Then, there was the unnecessary pressure he was putting on me to sit in the staff room all through school hours, even on days I either had no class to teach or only had say an hour of lessons on the timetable. This didn't make much sense to me. Thirdly, I found some of his mannerisms when conversing somewhat nauseating. Admittedly, I was easily irritated back then, which living in Gumel eventually forced me to learn how to manage, but I had expected a slightly more polished outlook from him as an educated man.

He was fond of chewing some local red nut that not only stained his entire mouth but also meant he cleared his throat often. It's no surprise to anyone who has lived in Northern Nigeria that the people often clear their throat, making a sound that can only be described as a cross between an itching throat, a bad moist cough, and a grunt of a pig. I found it disgusting, and it was so bad that sometimes I could barely eat the whole day. So, to be in close proximity with someone who ate something that caused him to make that sound like every other minute was mega uncomfortable for me.

I will never forget an occasion when he called me into his office for a chat. The previous geography teacher had just left, and he wanted to check that I was finishing up the lesson notes, etc. Right in the middle of a sentence, he cleared his throat and instinctively spat out the phlegm that landed on the wall of the office. I recoiled and was so irritated that I stood up, by reflex, and started to head for the door. All I could mutter was no more than "I will see you later." As I got outside his office, I let out my held breath, and vomit came pouring out. Thinking about it now still isn't pleasant. Anyway, to help me cope with all these, I limited my time on the school grounds to only the hours I had a class to teach and perhaps some time before or after that to mix up with other staff, plus attend to additional needs by my students or to sort anything school-related out.

Soon enough, I realised that I actually enjoyed impacting knowledge, which propelled me to understand the individual boys in my class and design my lessons in a manner that used more pictures than words. There weren't many classes with the boys in SSS-3 (year 12), because by this time, they were being prepared for their WAEC exams starting in May. Therefore, the principal asked me to focus on the boys in years 10 and 11. Whilst the year 10 boys were less of a hassle because they were the new ones to the school and probably glad to have gotten into one of the few prestigious secondary schools in the region, the year 11 boys were my biggest challenge—and later, biggest fans. The experience in between was as tough as it was enriching for me. The key issue at the beginning was that they didn't have much regard for me. I looked young, and for some, I was young enough to be their wife. It also didn't help that I was a Southerner who did not understand or speak the Hausa language. Yes, they did get away with making fun of me by speaking in Hausa, but they soon found out that I wasn't the type to be "toyed" with.

One of the defining moments was when I had had enough of them getting up and walking out of my class without any explanation. Initially, I thought it was because they couldn't easily express themselves in English but later found out, by their mockery, that it was a lack of regard for my presence or respect for me as a teacher. So that fateful day, as the first boy attempted to walk out, I stopped him and gently asked where he was going. Shocked, he started to laugh and turned around, still attempting to walk out. So, I pulled him back, only this time holding the cane (a stick) I had come armed with. Not my style, but the look on my face told him I was not going to hesitate to use it. Suddenly, the whole class fell silent, and he ran back to his seat. Realising the opportunity, I ceased the moment to issue a stern warning to the whole class.

"I want to teach, but I will not tolerate indiscipline. From now on, you put your hand up if you have anything to say or need to ask permission to use the toilet," I continued. "Attendance in class is part of assessment scores, so if anyone leaves to pee and does not return till class end, I will start deducting points. Should anyone not attend class at all without reason, they will be sure to lose one mark."

After speaking, I continued with my lesson. The same boy put his hand up and asked to be excused because he needed the toilet, which was all the evidence I needed that they got the message. Above all though, with deliberate actions, I subsequently showed them that I was committed to their success if they were interested in the same.

With time, I formed a bond with some of the boys who were comfortable communicating with the English language, using them to help their classmates learn. Four, in particular, were very intelligent and willing to learn, though they were actually the younger ones. The two I probably remember the most were from Kano, and I later found out that one was already an Arabic scholar. All of them became my "wing men," and actually, my inspiration. My goal during each lesson was to ensure that this group of boys, at least, understood the topic very well. Therefore, I often gave them an insight into upcoming topics and chapters to read in their textbooks ahead of the class, while I prepared pictures to help with explaining the topic to the rest of the class. That way, we maximised the hour we had for each lesson. Their job after classes, especially during the prep time, was to help the others better understand the topic by communicating it to them in Hausa (if need be). I also allowed for the class to answer my test questions using pictures and few words, which helped me gauge the extent to which the topic and subject were understood individually and by the class as a whole. Where there were gaps, I was happy to give the boys extra lessons or attend to their queries at any time, but that depended on each one's enthusiasm towards the topic.

With this breakthrough and memo of understanding (as it were), school became enjoyable and I actually wanted to be there. A few students took up my offer and would either stop me in the corridors or come to the staff room to ask their questions. One of the other teachers once asked me why I allowed the boys to meet me in the staff room. He said that they generally didn't encourage students coming to the staff room, as teaching should end in the classroom. My response was that one, I was not a professional teacher, so apologies if I missed the memo on that etiquette, and two, my desk was right next to the door, so I would happily step outside the (massive) room with the student if their query warranted more than a short response. But turning back a student when I had an opportunity to impact knowledge wasn't something I was prepared to do.

It wasn't long before I started to see improvements in the coursework done by the boys. Their improvement was much more than I could have imagined at the beginning, and certainly more than I could boast of in my personal life (outside of school activities) at the time. In a twist of fate, school hours became the best part of my day—a time when I was actually making a difference. It was a time during which I could forget the turmoil within and a personal cry for help that was so disguised no one could hear it.

THINK ON THIS...

Although not often celebrated in modern cultures, hard work, still pays off and more often than not, shortcuts still cut many lives and dreams short. As a principle of life, diligence produces phenomenal results both in your character and in whatever you apply it to. Life's true worth is not in how much wealth or degrees you amass but in the lives you improve. Stick to doing that which is good for humanity, and no matter how tough the road may seem right now, it will be rewarding if you remain diligent and disciplined in your approach. Remember also, there is dignity in every labour! Do not let other people's views taint your view or cause you to look down on your dream; they may not (and are not obligated to) understand it but as the carrier of that purpose, you have the onus to prove them wrong. Each one of us has something unique and good to contribute to our society; don't give up on yours— otherwise, we all will miss out on the value of you.

A WEATHER REPORT

Gumel had two main seasons—dry and wet (or rainy) seasons. Although in reality, they were not that simple. When seeking to be dramatic, I often compared the weather in Gumel to the plagues that came upon Egypt when they refused to set the Israelites free from slavery—according to the Bible accounts in the book of Exodus. It was so serious that I wore my NYSC boots nearly every day for the entire year I was there.

My first experience was the harmattan phase of the dry season, which was also on during the NYSC Camp in December. The nights and mornings were colder than anticipated for a far north region of Nigeria, though not as cold as Jos in Plateau State (visited during a Geographic Information Systems (GIS) course trip at Uni). The harmattan in Gumel felt dry, and visibility was often poor due to rising dust and fogs. Temperatures could drop as low as 12°Celsius (54°Fahrenheit) in the evening into early mornings. The dust-filled air made breathing slightly difficult, and the intense dryness started to crack my skin; not even the Pears Baby Cream, which I had used since childhood, could help. I wore the NYSC boots during this period to get some warmth whilst protecting my feet from the elements to reduce cracking. Little did I know that this was going to be the best weather that I would experience there.

About the end of February or early March, the temperature got warmer—I mean hot! This was by far the period with the most dramatic experiences. For example, I recall:

1. Shortly after my accommodation in the secondary school was ready, I stayed over so I could be on time for an early class. I was awoken by the sun rays, which was so intense that they shone through the little gap that was in my wooden window, hitting me straight in the face. I woke up in a panic, thinking I had overslept and was late for school. I must have had an 8:00 a.m. class to teach. Quickly, I picked up a bucket and rushed to the bathroom to have my shower.

    I was rushing out of the bathroom when my neighbour, Ṣọlá, a corper who served in Gumel many years before me and remained as an English teacher in my school, came out of her room to find out what the commotion was about. Seeing me in a towel and dripping with water, she asked where I was going to so early in the morning. I hurriedly told her that I had overslept and needed to get going. She motioned for me to calm down and asked if I had checked the time. I replied that my bedside clock must have broken because it was showing 5:00 a.m. when I looked. Then she let out a big laugh saying, "Welcome to Gumel. It is actually 5:00 a.m."

    I remember standing there completely bewildered as to how the sun can be so high and already this hot at 5:00 a.m. I went back into the room, sat on the bed, and could not get dressed. The water on my body had dried in that little time, and I was starting to feel the heat again. That was the moment I knew it was going to be a very interesting season. We prayed for warmth from the cold harmattan, and here it was, very full-on.

2. As temperatures could rise upwards of 40°Celsius during the day, there was often no electricity supply. It was explained that the transformers were shut down in a bid to keep them as cool as possible so they wouldn't explode. Unfortunately, the hours of sunshine were very long—from about 5:00 a.m. till after 8:00 p.m. at least—so we only had a few hours to get water chilled in any fridge. Even if

we did, it turned warm very quickly once the power was cut. It was then that I learnt the value of the clay water pots, often found in each home and in strategic places across town. They were the only things that kept water cool all through the day.

3. In the evenings, while I was still staying with the boys, people would come out of their rooms to sit outside as the temperature started to drop. While this was an opportunity to chat, it was more to enjoy the cooler breeze as the brick walls started to release some of the heat absorbed during the day, making the room too hot to endure. Similar to us, creatures that normally live burrowed in the ground also came out to the surface for some air because the ground was releasing heat too. Initially, it was scary to sit in the same open space where there were snakes, scorpions, lizards of all kinds, and scorpion-spiders, but soon there seemed to be a mutual understanding between us such that none troubled the other—we all just wanted to keep cool. The NYSC boots were therefore a necessity, as they provided protection should I mistakenly step on one of these in the dark or encounter one that got excited for a minute. It was still more important to be protected from a potentially deadly sting than the heat.

   Then at night, when electricity was usually restored, we went back into the room and somehow had to manage to get some sleep despite the heat. But I just couldn't. My skin often felt like it was on fire (explaining the serious burns I had, which were only realised upon my return to Lagos—as I had become so dark that I was unrecognisable to friends and family). To cope, we went with a tradition of pouring water into the mattress. Having it on the concrete floor allowed for us to pour one or two buckets of water into it (yep!) so that we could sleep coolly through the night, with the fan on if there was electricity. But as the days progressed and temperatures rose, we would often do a "refill" at least once or twice before morning. It was just unbearable.

4. Flies were another menace of the heat. Goodness! Never have I seen so many flies in one place. We learnt things like not to wear fragrances, as this attracted them, and to always have a stem of Dongoyaro (Neem) leaves to hand whenever we stepped out.

Thankfully, the body cream I used then didn't have any fragrance. Anyway, those flies put me off the use of perfumes and anything with fragrance for many years (not totally cured still).

On one occasion, I was walking to town and assumed that the man ahead was wearing a black T-shirt. It was not until he lifted his hand and swept the leaves across his back, and the flies lifted that I realised the T-shirt was actually white in colour. Immediately, I felt an uprising of vomit within and had to quickly look away, as I was incredibly irritated by the scene of hundreds of flies hovering all over him. The local people, however, were used to such. In fact, some would openly eat meals and be totally unperturbed by the flies perching on the food or their lips as they ate. That image still makes me shudder!

Whether wearing fragrance or not, I found that it was impossible to go from point A to B without at least one naughty fly settling on you. Thankfully, the Dongoyaro tree was planted everywhere, so there was always one to get some leaves from as we stepped out. The trick to ensuring the flies didn't follow us into the room was to stop at the door once we had unlocked it, do a quick sweep of our heads and backs with the leaves whilst shaking our bodies to stop any from resettling, and then take a dash into the room as we shut the door behind us. That was some amateur Ninja move right there!

A few months into the heat, I was desperately praying to God for some rain. One afternoon around April, I was walking back from town and stopped by Ike's shop to say hello but noticed that he had packed up the items for purchase normally displayed on the outside porch area of the store. Seeing me, he came outside, and without much explanation, dragged me into the shop and began closing the doors. I dropped the things in my hand and started to beat at him, shouting to be let out as I thought the worst—rape! Opening the doors slightly, he apologised for not properly explaining himself and asked me to please look up at the sky as he pointed in a specific direction.

I looked up to see the dark clouds and said in a loud voice, "Yes, I saw the rain clouds earlier; hence, I was heading back home. What about it?"

He responded, "Well, there is no way you will get home before that comes down, so I was protecting you by getting you into the shop." He went on to explain it was why he packed up the things and put them inside, pending when that cloud came down and it ended.

Ignorantly, I said that I had been praying for rain and wouldn't mind if I got caught in it. It would at least cool down my body temperature.

He laughed and said, "That is not rain."

By this time, we started to feel the effects of the cloud coming down as heavy winds began to approach. So, he asked if I was comfortable to stay in and allow him to secure the doors, as we were fast running out of time. I nodded in agreement, so he closed the doors and began bolting them from inside.

Barely had he done this when the heavy winds started to knock against the doors. Through the slight gap in them, he invited me to take a look at what was happening outside but to be careful not to press my face too close to the door as dust could get in between them. I peeped and was in utter shock at what I saw. The force of the wind was so strong it was carrying house roofs, cars were stopped dead on the road, and people with nowhere to hide were grabbing onto poles or trying to stay low, hoping not to be hit by any of the things that were being tossed by the wind. What was more shocking was that I saw something pouring down, but it was not rain. Ike just sat back in the shop laughing as I let out gasps of fright at the disaster that was unfolding right before my eyes. It went on for a good fifteen to twenty minutes (or more) before everywhere suddenly fell silent and calm like nothing had happened.

When Ike opened the doors, there was a heap of sand on the porch, and I couldn't believe my eyes. He said, "You have just experienced a sand storm," adding that a couple of these occurred each year before the actual rains. Apparently, it was often the cause of random blindness in the local communities. People who get caught in the storm could easily be blinded by the fine sand, and get killed or maimed because of the force. Looking around, there was not a single drop of water that fell—it was all just fine, reddish-brown desert sand. I thanked him for saving my life and went on my way—all the while thinking, How does sand fall from the skies like rain?

We had about two or three more sand storms, the latter containing a bit more precipitation, before the wet season fully kicked off around

May. The early rains also came with heavy winds. I recall praying on the first one that the roof wouldn't get carried away, which would have been disastrous because this was dead in the night. The good thing was that it brought lower temperatures during the day, hovering around 30°Celsius, and much cooler nights. I was able to sleep again.

The issue, however, was always the morning after a downpour. When I stepped outside the door, it looked like I was in a frog farm. Again, this left me dumbfounded the first time I saw it, because I couldn't believe the sheer amount of frogs that covered nearly every inch of the open space. I had to go back into the room and change into my NYSC boots; otherwise, I would not be able to make the walk to the school. By this time, my boots were starting to wear out, but we were not entitled to new ones after those supplied during the camp. If it was possible, I would have petitioned the NYSC Management to allocate additional pairs of boots to corpers serving in regions such as Gumel; they were invaluable to me.

Sometimes, I had to hop from spot to spot to avoid stepping on a frog until I got onto the tarred road. I wondered where all the frogs came from. Someone once said that the frogs buried their eggs deep in the sand, and the rains indicated that it was time to hatch. I don't know how true that was, but only that it wasn't a very pleasant sight at all, especially when they died after a few days having no water nearby to go into besides a few ponds. So much were the frogs across the State that we heard the then state governor brokered an agreement with another country to harvest them, as people of that nation ate them. Technically, it was a natural resource to Jigawa State, so it made sense to sell what we had (and didn't need) for funds that could be used to develop the State in areas that were needed.

The rain continued into August, dwindling as we got into September and the last quarter of the year. By the time I was leaving Gumel in early December 2000, there were no more rains, and the dry harmattan season was starting to get more of a grip on the region once again.

DRAWN FROM THE LION'S DEN

After a few weeks of staying with the boys, Shawn was allocated his own room which was much bigger than the one we shared. Since we had become closer friends, all three of us agreed that it was better if I moved with him. As Shawn and I spent more time together, our friendship morphed very quickly into a sexual relationship—a grave consequence of my naivety and carelessness. We went from what was simply a platonic friendship one day to being sexually involved the next. I didn't see it coming! This was so not my plan, and much to my dread, I was no longer in control. Thereafter, my daily life felt like I was both a guest watching it all unfold and an actor embodying a character that supposedly was me. Worst of all, I had no clue on how to get out of it. Basically, I was sleepwalking through my own life so much so that I became what can be described as a living corpse.

Of course, I lived in denial at first and blamed my school's principal for my woes with all the "if only he had…" statements. It wasn't long before I started to feel stifled, hapless, and hopeless. This did not help my ability to find a way out, so I ended up on a downward spiral mentally. Did Shawn treat me well? Yes, but that was only relevant if I set out to or wanted him as a boyfriend. I wasn't interested in being more than friends and certainly never planned to be sexually involved with someone I was not married to.

The latter was a dream and fundamental principle by which I had guided my life all through Uni days. So, it was no easy pill to swallow when I realised that all that effort seemed to have gone down the drain, and in a moment that I could not even vividly recall how I got there.

Thanks to my mum's detailed discussions about sex and the cultural repercussions were I to fall pregnant outside of marriage, I could muster the strength in the "heat of passion" to avoid and enforce having no intercourse. Her lesson was so deeply ingrained in my subconscious that it helped provide the only boundary I could set in this situation. So he settled for oral sex—yeah, he taught me the difference. This aspect was new to me, so I rationalised it as an experiment. No one had taught me there were other ways of deriving sexual pleasure outside of intercourse between a man and woman, nor did I ever have the need to read up about it. Since it was uncharted waters for me and we were both single, I convinced myself that it wasn't a sin. Yet, I struggled to shake the wrenching feeling that was deep down in my soul. Trust me when I say that the promise of whatever pleasure was derived was nothing compared to the devastating disappointment (in myself) that always followed.

This was not his fault; it was all mine! I was the Christian, a practicing one for that matter. Worst of all, I was leading the Christian Fellowship and should be the one showing others the example of how a godly woman should behave, but there I was, living worse than someone who doesn't even know God at all. Ah! I was filled with such unspeakable levels of shame and disappointment that I occasionally blamed God for bringing me to Gumel whilst regretting ever taking that first step of compromise of moving to the boys' accommodation. It was the easy way out—perhaps I could have slept in a classroom or even the staff room in my school after TT left and I was evicted from her room. Perhaps this, perhaps that, perhaps whatever—the point is that my dream of only ever sleeping with the man who is my husband was gone and could never be gotten back. This was the painful reality that I carried around. The pain ate me up from deep within, but it was buried so deep that no one saw it.

Soon enough, our unholy relationship became evident to other corpers and the few who attended the fellowship stopped coming. That made me feel even more lonely and devastated. Rather than speak to me or ask what was going on, they chose to avoid me and sometimes to publicly mock me. Of course, I didn't blame them for their actions but secretly wished someone would take a step to speak to me about it. What broke my heart the most, however, was the thought that God entrusted me with the fellowship, and rather than feed His sheep (John 21:15–17), I was scattering the flock by my actions. So not only had I disappointed myself, I was bringing disrepute even to God.

Well, at some point during this time, the principal told me that my room was ready, so I moved in thinking that it would break me free from this bondage. I don't think I lasted a week there, because night after night I heard crashing sounds against the window, which reminded me of the bat story that the principal told me. Fearful of them successfully breaking in one night, I went back to Shawn's. I certainly should not have, I knew, but my mind was too messed up to actually think clearly. On hindsight, I realise that the first step out of an unpleasant physical situation is to change your mental state. Not being able to do so helps explain why most victims keep going back to their abusers and can't seem to see or break away from the problem, even when it is destroying them. A mental reorientation and break-free are required first—this was what God did for me in His infinite mercies, graciousness, and unfailing love.

I had stopped going for the fellowship meetings since no one was attending. Besides, I couldn't face the shame of opening the doors to God's house every week when my lifestyle didn't show that I knew Him. The only practice I kept up, still reminding myself that I was a Christian, was attending Sunday services at the only other church in Gumel, which Ṣọlá had introduced me to. The church was situated on the outskirts of town; it was a very long walk through an expanse of white sandy land in the desert-like heat. It provided the only ounce of connection to God that I could feel, especially through the soul-lifting songs, and gave me a tiny glimpse of hope that I could still be saved—spiritually, mentally, and physically.

That hope held until one day, sitting alone in Shawn's room, I heard the familiar voice (in my heart) of Òránmọníṣéfàyàtí—the One that sends a child on an errand or mission and stands fully with them irrespective of the circumstance. It was a fellowship meeting day, and He asked me, "Why are you here and not in My house?" That question caught me a little by surprise for a few reasons, the main being that I thought it was obvious—I was unworthy.

"What will God want with a low-lifer and embarrassment to His name, like me?" I thought (and seemed to be responding to Him). He certainly would not want to be associated with me!

Right then, I had this overwhelming feeling that I was "keeping God waiting," while I wallowed in self-pity and dejection. Without much delay, I got myself up and started out for the meeting. Running late, I picked up the pace a little.

As I opened the doors to the ECWA church where the fellowship meeting was held, the deep sense of being welcomed by God was undeniable. I went in, sat on one of the benches, and broke down in tears. They were both tears of sadness and of joy—sadness for the lifestyle I had and not knowing how to get out of the quagmire, yet joy to feel that God still loved me in spite of it all. We speak of *grace*, but that day I realised that one would probably not understand the extent and depth of God's redeeming love until they had fallen so far from it that they knew their life would amount to absolutely nothing if lived only in satisfaction of their own desires. This was the point I was at, and to know that God the Father did not castigate or condemn me to my own woes (like others around me did) brought me so much joy and peace that cannot be put into words. I don't know how long I was there with my face bowed, but by the time I raised my head, I was a changed person. It still wasn't clear how I would leave Shawn, but I was filled with a resolve and certainty that I would come out of this.

From that day on, I started to sing again. I sang God's praise genuinely and sang of my freedom—spirit, soul, and body. To my frustration, I still couldn't leave Shawn immediately, but he probably got the sense that I was changing. For one, I stopped participating in the sexual acts by not giving it nor deriving any pleasure from it, and I had started to say "no" more often. That doesn't mean the situation was better than what was, from a Christian perspective, because sin is sin—so I am not trying to make light of the gravity of that fact! However, I had started to find myself and gradually spoke up about not wanting the relationship anymore.

Although I still lived in sin, my heart was in a different state. Once I had felt hopeless, but now I knew there was and daily sought the way out, knowing that God still loved me and was with me. Each day, like the Prodigal Son (Luke 15:11–32), I asked God's forgiveness and chose to run to Him rather than focus on what I was doing wrong. I realised that I was better off being disciplined by God, because He would do it in love and always aim it at bringing the best out of me, than staying in a state of hopelessness where the enemy—Satan—would do nothing but keep dragging me down with the sole aim of destroying me (John 10:10).

This might sound like "taking Grace for granted" to some, but it was the absolute opposite of what I felt, especially from God. To me, this was actually Grace (God) reaching out so lovingly to save me! I was already in a condemned state, so what "Good News" would there have been to me if condemned any further? Condemnation certainly didn't help me come out of that situation, but Grace did. Unlike what some may think or preach, sometimes the change is gradual and isn't always immediately evident. God's love was doing a work in me that no one yet saw on the outside. Contrary to what they would have thought, I knew my heart was changing because of the power of God's redeeming love. All that remained was the ability to completely walkaway from it all; whilst unclear about how or when it would be, I was certain that it was possible and that it would happen.

By the way, there was more to our relationship than sex, but I have emphasised the latter because it was the aspect that bothered me as a Christian. There is absolutely nothing wrong with two consenting and unmarried adults being in a loving relationship. In my case, I really wasn't looking for a relationship at the time and hadn't clearly set the boundaries when this came to be. This was why it morphed into an unhealthy and sinful relationship, and one that needed to end.

Having received renewed hope, I took time weekly to prepare a message for the fellowship meeting. Both the time of preparation and the time of delivering the message (yes, you read right!) were building my faith up. Each week thereafter, I never missed a meeting. I knew that it wasn't about the numbers but about the One I was going to meet, and because God always showed up. I was also always on time because of that tangible sense of God being there. Each time, it was just me, but I was never alone. The bizarre bit was that God got me running the meeting like there were many others in the service. So, I stood up to say a prayer to start the meeting, "lead" in songs of praise and worship, then stayed standing to "preach" the message, sang more songs as I gave my offering and prayed over it, and finally closed the meeting with a prayer. Whenever I sang, I clapped my hands. Then one day, I picked up the church's conga drums and played them—with no prior lesson or experience.

No one week was the same. Sometimes, I had an overwhelming pain, knowing what I was going back to when I left the meeting. To have had such an awesome time with God yet return to an undesirable situation became my new struggle; I never wanted to leave His presence nor an atmosphere where I felt deeply loved. It was during this period that I understood King David's statement in Psalm 84:10—where he said that he would rather be a doorkeeper in God's house than dwell with the wicked. I, too, would rather be considered the lowest of God's children and take whatever He gives me so long as I am in His presence.

MORAL –

Realising that you need God irrespective of how "strong" you think you are and that His grace welcomes you into His presence no matter where you are in life is humbling and lies at the heart of salvation—which, by the way, is not and should not be taken as a one-time nor a once-and-for-all experience.

One day, as I sang and danced during the fellowship meeting, a young man walked in. He introduced himself as Richie (Richard), a corper serving in one of the Southern States. He had been sent to support a project his company was undertaking in Gumel. Strolling through town, he heard my singing and decided to stop by. Plus, he didn't know anyone outside of work in the town and wanted to associate with other corpers. Oh, such a delight this was! At a time when no other corper was really speaking to me, God yet again showed me His love and care by bringing me respite in the form of another corper all the way from the South. To top it up, he was a Christian and spoke the Yorùbá language.

God surely knows what each one of us needs and will align things to work in our favour if we only seek His face.

As I started to know God's love in a new and deep way, God knew that I still needed encouragement to fully embrace the restoration that my soul desperately needed, and this young man was notably the trigger of that for me. Richie was such a fervent Christian yet had no air of arrogance around him. During the week, he organised for us to visit people in the hospital and prison to pray for them, though I was only able to join him on a few occasions to the former.

At the hospital, we split up into the different wards, as male and female patients were kept separate and there were strict rules about visits from an opposite sex that wasn't family—the *Baa Shiga* (Don't Enter) concept. There, I saw firsthand the pain that vesicovaginal fistula—popularly known as VVF—causes to young girls, the majority of which had it by reason of being married off early to much older men and having sex or giving birth at that young age. My heart broke for them because I couldn't imagine being in their shoes, especially when thinking how bad I felt for sleeping with someone my age even though I was more mature than they were; not to mention that the person was not forced on me and we weren't even having intercourse. The stench in the wards was overpowering, but one couldn't help but feel for these girls, so I went as often as possible.

Richie's passion for God was as infectious as it was a reminder that I needed to do more in giving back to the locality that I lived in as a Christian. The situation I was in had so clouded my judgement that I forgot that I had something to give. Muslim community as it was, God still loved the people and cared about them—just as He did me. In his spare time, aside from visits, Richie would often ask me what I would have him do; his life was absolutely about service. I saw Richie's presence in Gumel similar to that little rain-bearing cloud Elijah saw when he prayed earnestly for the famine to end (1 Kings 18:41-46)—the foretaste of answered prayer!

Feeling a bit more high-spirited (actually slightly more comfortable with asking God for anything, to be honest), I remembered a prayer I always said during my university days. Generally, people refer to employment or working as the "labour market." Call me pedantic or anal, but the word "labour" used to conjure a sense of travail and difficulty that just didn't sit right with me. Especially in a country like Nigeria where the ruling mindset was to take whatever you got against the backdrop of there being more graduates (or school leavers) than there were work opportunities. So, I knew my only edge and hope of getting exactly what I wanted was going to come by favour—of God and then of people. Hence, I started to refer to it and pray that I was going into the "favour market."

Slowly, I started to move my things out of Shawn's room and spend more nights at my own accommodation. My room was in the school's staff quarters, which was a fairly long walk from the school gate and Ike's shop. This meant that I was totally isolated whenever I spent the night there. I might see Ṣọlá on occasion, but it was mostly a very lonely experience. To make matters worse, I hadn't invested in anything that could be used for cooking, so I either went hungry or munched on bread sandwiched with balangu (freshly smoked slabs of beef) if I got the opportunity to buy these from town. Once at my place, I always needed to summon courage to walk through the paths that led back to the school's gate and main road, as they could be flooded or crawling with potentially dangerous creatures like snakes and scorpions. Therefore, I still found myself going back to Shawn's place more than I really wanted to. But thanks to God, Who did not give up on me!

Sometime towards the end of April or early May, I got a visit from the State NCCF Leaders—popularly known as the Papa and Mama. Owing to the state of my life, the guilt, embarrassment, and so on that I felt, I hadn't really been in touch or visited the State Headquarters in Dutse, as often as expected. With Gumel being the largest zone in the State and the location for NYSC Camp, the Gumel NCCF Leader—me—was in charge of all necessary preparations to have an NCCF stand and full representation on the Camp. I was technically responsible for hosting members across the State and welcoming the new ones. Of course, support was provided by other zones, but I had to take the lead. Again, I still couldn't understand why God positioned me in Gumel and gave me the responsibility of leading the most crucial NCCF zone in the State, knowing full well that I was going to mess up big time.

That is where God differs from us; He sees things that we cannot, beyond what we do or don't do, and orders our footsteps (as His children) in such a way that glorifies His name even when it doesn't seem so.

God doesn't lead us into sin because He created us to be "free agents" who always have a choice—including hard ones like to face death, for example, which most of us will never even consider an option when in tough situations. But as I study the Bible more and experience life daily, I realise that it is actually better to die in Christ than to succumb to the enticements of sin. When we reach that point of self-sacrifice like the three Hebrew boys before King Nebuchadnezzar (Daniel 3; note verses 16–18), God steps into the situation to work things out such that His Name is glorified above all. We, on the other hand, would have learnt a lesson or two that would lead to our maturity. So, in our everyday lives and in tough times when we might be discombobulated about what to do, we should learn to pause and ask, "Which action or choice will bring God glory?"

While the visit from Papa Raymond and Mama Ruth was embarrassing because they met me in Shawn's place, it was equally the cementing catalyst for the changes that I desperately needed. I had been alone in the room, and it was quiet in the boy's quarters as most people were at work. I didn't have any classes that day, likely due to a term break, so I was enjoying being alone when I heard the knock. It was a huge shock to see them both standing there.

The first thing they said was, "What are you doing here?"

I felt so ashamed and too dumbfounded to respond. Suddenly, whatever I had to say sounded so much like mere excuses that I could not voice them.

They sat at the doorstep, refusing to come in or even have a drink, despite the heat at that time and their long journey. After a momentary pause and glances, Papa Ray began to speak. He was often a jovial, gentle, soft-spoken but firm person, while Mama was always a calm and caring personality. Papa Ray told of how the news of my shenanigans got to the leadership in Dutse, their intentions to replace me as the leader, and how God insisted that I was still His choice for the role when they prayed about the actions to take. Therefore, they had taken a step back, deciding not to intervene even though they had known of the issues for some time. However, they felt God tell them that it was time to step in, hence the visit. And by "step in," God asked them to speak words of faith and encouragement to me rather than condemnation, which was exactly what they did. They made me feel so comfortable that, for the first time, I was able to start putting into words how I truly felt. All guards were down, and they listened. At the end, we discussed options and practical steps to take so that I was no longer reliant on Shawn, which would then remove my need to stay at his place or even continue the relationship. To me, the actions to take became clearer—my mind was no longer dillydallying.

It was only when that discussion ended that they mentioned the fact that the next NYSC Camp was going to be in June and quickly went over what was expected of me plus the preparations that needed to be made to host the event. Then they encouraged me to get my act together so I could focus on what God had called me to. This was the main reason for their visit, and they looked forward to hearing the good news. With that, they left me and returned to Dutse. Hence, what began as an awkward conversation ended with encouragement.

Somehow Shawn found out about the visit and was obviously not happy about it—sensing that I was definitely going to end things this time. I don't recall us having any discussions about details of the visit or even deciding to break up, so just as the relationship started—without formality—it also ended. In the morning. I woke up with a clear head, packed up whatever was left of my things, and made my way to my own accommodation. With every step, I felt a sense of shame for how I had lived and the disrepute brought to God's name by so doing. On getting to my accommodation, I shut myself in. The bats still knocked against my window at night, but they scared me no more because I was here to stay.

It must have been a few days of being there before I bumped into Ṣọlá in the corridor that adjoined both our rooms, in front of the bathroom. Surprised to see me, she asked when I came round. She must have noticed my emaciated state as well, because she asked if I could have lunch or dinner with her that day. She made *Tuwo Masara,* a traditional Hausa corn meal, which I had never had. I could still see and taste the maize shaft, so I didn't quite enjoy it, but I ate it anyway because I was starving. Over the next few days, she checked on me daily and often cooked for us both, which was another of God's provisions that helped me gradually start to pull myself together and adjust to living there.

My routine turned to room-class-room for a while, as I hardly left the school grounds. Hence, I didn't have to worry about bumping into anyone or answering undesirable questions. Richie was the only corper I saw much of because we met up on Fellowship days—not going for that was no longer an option following the lesson God already taught me about that. He wasn't the type to pry into personal affairs, which was good because I wasn't yet in that space where I could discuss my deep feelings with anyone. But having him around gave me the sense that I had a spiritually mature person to turn to if ever it was needed. One day after another, precept upon precept, and I started to go to other places like Ike's store and the market. Slowly, I started to live freely again.

The whole experience humbled me beyond words. Besides it dawning that no one, especially me, is truly beyond the grasp of sin so we cannot boast in our own works, I also realised the importance of staying in God's presence, no matter the circumstance. This experience taught me those in an undeniable way, which has helped my stance in other experiences in life. This is not to excuse remaining in sin, because we (especially those who lead) will be judged for our conduct, but it is to magnify the power of God's grace above anything that we can ever face.

MORAL –

Understanding God's grace involves the realisation that you can never earn it or be worthy of it, yet He's chosen to lavish it on you. Grace, most definitely, is not a license to sin but a force that shames sin, paling its power with so much love that it draws the recipient back into righteousness. By grace, God anchors your soul in Him until His glory is manifested and perfected in you. There is nothing in the world that can compare to God's grace towards us all, absolutely nothing! Take being alive—it is not a given, it is God's grace at work. So, we all need it each and every day and should always be grateful to God that in Christ Jesus, He made His grace abundantly available and accessible to everyone of us. No matter where you are in life or what others have said about you, you only need to turn to God today and ask Him to step into your situation. His Grace will definitely locate you!

As one who loves to observe nature and learn from it, I could point to a number of things that I suddenly started to see more clearly. Getting out of that relationship was like having the scales fall off my eyes. I had been missing a lot of what was going on around me because my being uncomfortable with the relationship somehow tainted my view of the world, and I stopped appreciating even the simple things of life.

A quick word for someone out there—if you are feeling this way about life or some aspects of it, take a step back to understand the root cause so you can make the necessary changes. Sometimes, because you are in the middle of a situation, you might not be able to decipher the problem even after taking a step back. Ask a family member, friend, or even a neighbour that you trust to tell you if they have observed any negatively impacting changes in you. Please don't care about how they phrase the response because that depends on each person's maturity level or personality. Stay focused on hearing what they have observed. They may phrase their response carefully or in less sensitive ways, but give them permission to tell you the absolute truth—whether it makes you feel good or not. It could save your life or stop you from going down unnecessary rabbit holes, as I did.

I only understood this after my return to Lagos at the end of the service year and had a chance to meet up with Ayọ̀. Conversations led to me asking him why, as someone who knew me from Uni days, he never made a move to stop me when he saw me behaving in a manner that was contrary to my natural person or Christian beliefs, which anyone close to me knows I hold very dear. The summary of his response was that I never reached out to him after moving in with Shawn, nor did I ask his opinion about anything. Apparently, he knew from the outset that Shawn liked me because they discussed it, hence his support for me to move with Shawn when he was given a separate room. However, Ayọ̀ suspected something was amiss when I stopped being my smiley self and often looked a shadow of myself whenever he saw me at the evening corper hangouts. Had I knocked on his door and visited with him in his room, Ayọ̀ might have had the chance to discuss with and advise me. But since our interactions were often when the group met, it was difficult to talk about things he might have suspected in Shawn's presence, so he decided to "mind his own business."

MORAL –

Again, please speak to those around you and who've known you before the current context, because it just might save you a lot of heartache down the road. And to all the relatives and friends out there, if something looks wrong with your friend or family member, you are probably right. Make attempts and don't give up trying to have a one-on-one discussion with the person. They might be deceived or simply cannot see the problem until someone cares enough to help them do so.

THINK ON THIS...

God is about people. He demonstrated the depth of His love by sending Jesus to die for us all (Romans 5:8) so that each one may have equal access to His forgiveness and adoption as His children (John 1:12). Therefore, no matter who you are or how far you may have fallen, salvation in Christ is freely yours. In Christ Jesus, there is no distinction between people—their backgrounds or sins—we are all bound by His love. To God, every life counts, even yours!

MY NEW OUTLOOK

Now firmly in May 2000, my students began their end-of-year examinations, so there wasn't much demand on my time. Therefore, I could focus on my mental health as well as get on with other things that needed doing. NYSC Camp, for example, was starting the following month, which meant I had a lot to do: corralling the other leaders within Gumel Zone, organising to secure the venue for the fellowship meetings on Camp, securing a space and constructing the NCCF tent in the Mammy Market section of camp, and so on. The camp was going to welcome the first batch of corpers for 2000, so we were expecting thousands of youth corpers posted from across the country, unlike the few hundred that were posted in second batches—like my set. Many of these would never have been to the North and would be in need of guidance around the NYSC Camp site, so this was a huge event that needed all hands on deck.

I also visited Dutse for the first time in a long while and felt greatly at ease being in the midst of fellow Christians who did not judge me—whether or not they had heard or knew the details of what had happened. My visit to Dutse included choir rehearsals in preparation for the upcoming camp; even being able to do that again was soul lifting. The other great benefit of this "freedom" was that I started to pay more attention to my environment. I had been in Gumel for several months and realised that I barely knew anything about Hausa people and their culture, nor could I say even the simplest sentences in their language. I was appalled at that realisation.

As I now often went into town alone, I started to get back into my curious self and explore my environment through questions. One of the fascinating things that I learnt was using donkeys to tell the time. Before, I only saw them wandering about town with loads, mostly farm produce, and without a human guide. But when I asked about the donkeys, I discovered the following characteristics of these beautiful creatures:

1. Donkeys are such lowly and meek animals—very unimposing in nature and with no impressive or majestic appearance, like say horses. Hence, they are easy to disregard. However, a donkey's meekness and obedience were virtues well explored by Gumel's inhabitants, as they used donkeys to support farm work and carry loads. Although some of it was visibly burdensome on the animals, one would never see them complain, throw tantrums, or cast off their loads. I never observed donkeys getting into a brawl with one another, other animals, or people. A donkey has too gentle of a soul. By the way, doesn't it say a lot about God's character and love that this was the animal Jesus chose to ride upon as King on what we now know as Palm Sunday? (Matthew 21:1–11; Mark 11:1–11; Luke 19:28–40; and John 12:12–19). Think about that for a moment.

2. Donkeys are very clever. Yes, they do not look it, but they are. For example, I was told that the reason most of them go about town with no human guide is because they know where they are going. Apparently, the owners will take them through the same route from house to farm, for example, twice or thrice. Subsequently, the donkey is able to make that journey alone, which can span several miles. Therefore, people are able to send harvested crops back home in several trips without physically leaving the farm themselves. The donkey takes the harvest home. When they have been off-loaded by someone there, they are sent back to the farm, and so on until the final return with a person in the evening.

3. Donkeys don't get easily distracted, hence demonstrating some form of loyalty to their purpose and the person that set them their task. Aside from one that doesn't yet know its way around or is with its recognised handlers, donkeys stick to the path that leads them to their destination unless they are physically moved. Be it a car or human being, a donkey would rather go through it than change its course. Hoot the car horn, scream loudly, push them, or do whatever, and the donkey will not react nor cave in—it just keeps going forward to its destination. Oh, that makes them seem foolish, right? On the contrary, I saw a lot of strength in that and wish that I could be that tenacious sometimes, especially when there is a God-given purpose to be achieved, and stay focused on the goal rather than pay attention to (and be distracted by) prevailing circumstances or challenges.

4. Lastly, they only make a sound at particular time intervals. Mind blowing? I know! I have seen mean people hit their donkeys unjustly, but never have I heard them make a sound unless at the appointed time. This characteristic makes them reliable time watches.

   Each donkey had a unique bray that it belted out at certain intervals. They were so loud that it echoed through the town. Some brayed every fifteen minutes, others did every thirty minutes, while another was every hour. A donkey didn't sway between intervals; it always stuck to its "programed" time—one needed to observe each to know what that interval was. So, I just familiarised myself with the unique brays and could tell you just by that sound what time it was. Often, I would check what time it was based on the first bray heard when I woke up in the morning. Thereafter, I knew the time in quarterly intervals at least, till my bedtime. It was without fail.

   Knowing things like this makes one appreciate God even more. For example, the timing of each bray is not genetic, so a foal can have a different time from that of the parents. I didn't quite find out if this manifested from birth or if it developed at a certain age in the animal, but the concept of it having a "program" and never deviating from it is one of those evidences in nature that makes it difficult to deny God's existence or His sheer magnificence. Also, with this knowledge, I would hope that you will read the Bible's account of Balaam and his donkey (Numbers 22:21–35) very differently—and perhaps better understand what transpired in that story.

Also, I learnt that the Hausa were not mean or difficult people to live with; you only needed to ask or show interest in a thing, and the people graciously explained. Often times, I found that their religious beliefs were the cause of the tensions that occurred in the community—and probably the biggest cause of the divide between the Northern and Southern parts of Nigeria. I do not aim to cast aspersions on Islam, as I do not know enough about it to authoritatively do so. However, having lived amongst the Hausa people to see that they are traditionally peace-loving and knowing that the only time we experienced tension in Gumel was due to a jihadist movement, which started in Kano and resulted in the killing of several Southerners—some of whom were also Muslims—makes it difficult to separate the religious beliefs from the disposition of violence or extremism. Although I acknowledge that nearly every religion has had some form of violent history, no cause—religious, political, cultural, or otherwise—should justify such acts against humanity, especially in today's society.

In Gumel, I recall how we prayed for God's intervention when we heard news of an impending jihad and started to feel the tension in the air. The only way out of Gumel, to the South, was via Kano, and with that in turmoil, we had to hide out in our rooms praying daily (I was still with Shawn then). That prayer was answered by the sudden return of the Emir, HRH Alh. Ahmed Mohammed Sani II, to town the night before the rumoured showdown. We heard he summoned the Imams that night and warned them against stirring up trouble in the town, so there was calm the next morning. One of the locals came round to the quarters to break the news that all jihad plans had been dismissed. My respect for the Emir went up again that day. When we were in camp, he had invited us (corpers) to his palace and provided a welcoming feast. Now, he'd taken a stand to maintain peace and protect the lives of all who lived in his town, no matter their ethnicity or religion. That is a good leader!

Oftentimes, the lines between culture and religion can be blurred, making it difficult to determine whether an individual's actions are driven by their local beliefs or a religious expectation. What became abundantly clear to me through the Emir's action is that each person has a choice and is fully responsible for what they do. There are actions that clearly do not demonstrate love for the person next to you or foster our collective progress. Hence, it is for the choices we make that each of us will stand accountable to God Almighty. That said, the role of leadership in the making of right choices cannot be underestimated. We need more and more leaders to put aside personal preferences—tribalism, racism, religious beliefs, political ambitions and affiliations, or many of such—to make decisions that are in the public interest and for the greater good of all humanity.

The Emir of Gumel demonstrated these through his actions that day, thereby helping people like me to also conclude that, naturally speaking, Hausas are peace-loving people. Following his intervention, life carried on as normal, like the tension never even arose, and we all lived peacefully for the rest of my time there.

The incident also highlighted how easy it is for the masses to be influenced by their leaders. It helped me better understand why people take to arms or get involved in jihadist movements and other terrorist activities; they simply are pawns in the hands of powerful people who gain from unrests and chaotic situations. The Emir, after all, is Muslim, yet he sought and insisted on the maintenance of peace. "What then are other leaders saying or doing?" I thought. Where the majority of the populace are uneducated, they often take advantage of and lead them astray under the guise of religion rather than seek to empower them. Such leaders, to my mind, are the real problem or major contributors to the problems in our societies today.

THINK ON THIS...

Leadership equals taking responsibility—it is not just some management or political position to be coveted. It requires a great sense of *humility* and *service* to others, and the ability to make often difficult decisions. In my view, a leader is one who is able to pave the way or create opportunities that allow others to reach their full potential while also role-modelling the qualities required to build a healthy society.

A NEW COMMUNITY OF BELIEVERS

In May 2000, as I began to prepare for the new NYSC Camp starting in June, I bumped into Suzie. She told me how the other room in her flat was now available and that she was happy for me to move in there at no cost if I still wanted it. Apparently, it had been available for some time, but she didn't think to mention it, as she thought I wouldn't need it being at Shawn's. Of course, I jumped at the offer because her flat was located on the college grounds where the NYSC Camp would take place, making it easier for me to attend to things as required. The flat also had a kitchen, which had the basic things that one needs to make a meal, like a stove, worktop, pans, and a fridge. Though my allocated room in my school remained mine and had the majority of my belongings, I spent most of my remaining time in Gumel living at her flat.

Suzie knew that the relationship with Shawn had gone sour but never asked or sought to know further details, which I was grateful for. However, she mentioned to me ahead of moving in an occasional practice where she hosted corpers at her flat and Shawn attended sometimes, so she asked if I was comfortable being around him. I said "yes" and actually made an effort to be in the house for the first one after the breakup. I used it as an opportunity to establish the fact that I was able to move on without despising Shawn or being uncomfortable when he was in the same space. The most difficult aspect was moving past the shame suffered at the hands of others, justified as it might have been, for the lifestyle lived despite being a Christian Fellowship Leader.

Moving in with Suzie was a blessing. I had a room that allowed me to stay alone when I needed to and another female to talk to if needing a companion, unlike my own place, which was quite isolated. There was much business done with God in that room; just facing the wall to pray or cry my heart out, and I began to grow stronger in my faith, little by little.

Another remarkable blessing during this period was the arrival of Ben. He stopped me in town one day to introduce himself; someone had pointed me out as the leader of the Corpers' Fellowship in Gumel. The timing of his arrival was perfect, because it wasn't long after that that Richie was recalled by his company to the original town of his NYSC posting. Richie had been such a great support in putting things in place for the new NYSC Camp. Having Ben around made the workload easier on us, as he didn't have much else to do in the hours Richie and I would normally be at work. He was even much more helpful when Richie left, building the NCCF tent and running around during the camp itself. God knew I really needed a right-hand man and brought him in time to support me, knowing that Richie was going to be recalled—so suddenly that it took even Richie by surprise.

Ben was a trustworthy and very reliable gentleman, and a breath of fresh air. I noticed though that we got uncomfortable stares whenever we were in town together, so I asked Ike one day when an instance occurred in his presence. Lightly, he responded that it might have been because Ben was the only Gumel indigene, at that point, to ever convert to Christianity and had recently returned to town, only to be associating with a female corper. I later asked Ben for the backstory so that I would know exactly what I was getting into.

Ben told me of how his mum was from Benin, a popular city in southwest Nigeria, but his dad was from Gumel. The family lived in the town when he was growing up but split up some years back when his parents' marriage broke down, and his mum returned to Benin City. Growing up, his mum went to church, but Ben was never allowed to do the same as an indigene with a Muslim father. In his teenage years, something happened (I don't remember what), and he decided to give his life to Christ. When his father and the people of the town found out that he was a Christian, they threatened to kill him. He fled to the South in search of his mum and had been in Benin since then.

Ben had attended seminary school in Benin City and felt that God was calling him back to his father's home, hence the return to Gumel. He was staying alone because he hadn't been well received by his family. It had been many years since he had run away; finding out that he was still a Christian meant that he still was not welcome. His dad was now old and needed looking after, so he was doing that, although the man barely interacted with him for fear of persecution from others. Hence, Ben was seeking to relate with other Christians in town as a way of helping him stay and grow in his faith while getting involved in more Christian activities—and felt drawn to me as a person of his age that he could easily talk to.

It then made sense why I increasingly got unkind stares from people in the town, but I chose not to push him away in fear of "my safety." I had recently been through a situation where there was no one but God to lean on, so I knew the value of having friends or someone to relate to in times of trouble. My thought was that he had made the choice to be a Christian long before I came to that town, and I couldn't find a justified reason not to relate with a brother-in-Christ just because his kinsmen didn't like him. Moreover, Ben came to me. Not to be ignorant of the potential for the situation to escalate, though, I always prayed for both our safety and his faith—that God would strengthen him and fully establish the purpose for bringing him back to Gumel. For the time being, I was happy to have a strong and faithful right-hand man, so we just carried on doing what needed doing. Thankfully, there was never a hostile action attempted or directed at either of us for as long as I remained in Gumel.

Come June 2000, the college grounds came alive with all sorts of activities, and the NYSC Camp was buzzing with human bodies moving all over the place. It was as expected—thousands of youth corpers from across the country. Being a large group, their camp was about three weeks long, and the weather was HOT!

For me, it was an extremely busy time having to juggle school activities (though reduced due to ongoing exams), attend to the needs of the new corpers as they visited the NCCF tent and fellowship meetings, as well as meet the demands of people from other NCCF Zones who came to support the State Fellowship's activities on Camp—all because I was the Gumel Fellowship Leader and the only resident corper that was involved in the Camp activities. With Richie gone, I went back to being the only corper that attended fellowship meetings, with occasional moral support from Ben prior to the start of camp. Things were so busy around the time for Camp that I barely had time to focus or even think of the past. There was a real and present need that required my attention, and that was what I gave.

Like all things that have a start, the June 2000 NYSC Camp came to an end, and we started to pack down. As was the custom, the corpers were given a few weeks' time off to return home and prepare for the continuation of their service year in their places of primary assignment. The NCCF Zones, on the other hand, were preparing for an influx of corpers into the various Fellowships. For someone like me who had been alone most of the time, I became anxious for several reasons—mainly my broken past and if I was truly cut out to lead. I knew the latter was going to be put to a real test, so I chose in the waiting period to pray for God's help, as He had done in times past.

When schools broke for the summer or long-term holidays, I decided to use the time to explore some of the neighbouring towns around Gumel. I regained contact with Harvey, a friend in my platoon, who was posted to Auyo. We rode on his power bike whenever he visited Gumel. I was enjoying not being cocooned, getting the opportunity to relate with more people, and actually experiencing the environment in which I lived. I began to see and embrace more of the good things about the people and learn the Hausa language, as well as wear more of the traditional attires—which were stunning. I wish I had started to learn the language earlier, as I might have become fluent by the time I left.

I also got to spend more time with Suzie, as the college too went on break and she had more time to spare when she wasn't visiting friends in Kano. She was fun-loving and more outgoing and would on occasion drag me out for a walk to town or around the college grounds, which were quite massive. It was through Suzie that I learnt that Gumel was a border town to the Republic of Niger, and we took a trip to the border together. It was less than an hour's drive from the house, and thanks to her, Niger became the first international soil upon which I set foot. We couldn't go into the country to explore though, because I didn't have a means of identification like an international passport. Therefore, the border guards allowed us to go only a few feet away from the border post—firmly within their sight and just to the end of the tarred road that marked the boundaries.

We spent only a few minutes on Niger soil, enough to take pictures of me outside the country. It was in those moments that I decided to get an international passport so I could explore more of the world, having travelled across and lived in all the major regions in Nigeria. I enquired and found out that I could have it done in Dutse without the hassles that come with doing it in an oversubscribed state like Lagos. So I did. I remember taking the passport photo wearing a borrowed T-shirt from a staff member at the passport office to cover my NYSC-branded T-shirt as I went there straight after the passing out parade in Dutse. A few days later, my international passport was ready for pickup, and so began the expansion of my horizon of places to explore—a desire that is still unfolding.

It wasn't long before the new corpers posted to Gumel started to arrive back in town, and the fellowship meeting began to fill up. Many had been introduced to NCCF during their NYSC Camp. Being committed Christians already, they didn't need any convincing about taking part in and, more importantly, taking up responsibilities within the fellowship. In a few weeks, we were all relating like people who had been friends for years. They were mature, jovial, loving, and just a joy to be with and lead—it was as if God had hand-picked the best of corpers to be posted to Gumel.

Some of the boys lived in the same boys' quarters with Shawn, so it wasn't long before they heard discussions or were told of my past, with the intention to damage whatever "good" this new group saw in me and make them comfortable being led by "someone like her." Interestingly, I was glad it came up quite early on, as I didn't want to appear to be a fraud if they found out months into being in the fellowship.

One of the new guys, Tony, invited me to his room for a discussion. By this time, I had taken full responsibility for everything that happened and made progress in the decision to move on, so I went knowing full well what was likely to be discussed. Tony told how Shawn bragged about sleeping with me, saying how unfit I was to be a leader of a Christian Fellowship, and so on. Then he paused and said that he just wanted to know my side of the story—a gesture that was testament to his maturity. I will never forget how comfortable he made me feel knowing that it was going to be difficult to talk about.

Yes, hearing all that was being said conjured up some of the past pain that I still felt, but having reconciled with God, the shame was gone, although I still carried the guilt. Looking directly at Tony and seeing that he would believe anything that I said, I decided to tell the truth—"Yes, I did it." At that point, to my mind, the accuracy of Shawn's account of the relationship was irrelevant, as were the circumstances that surrounded my getting in or out of it. At stake here was Tony's (and undoubtedly the other new corpers') assessment of me as their fellowship leader, or "Mama G," as I was fondly called. So I took full responsibility for my actions.

After a few more conversations, he thanked me for being forthright about the issue and was happy that I didn't turn it into an uncomfortable discussion. He also mentioned how he was a firm believer in God's ability to forgive our past actions and was not going to let this affect his commitment in the fellowship.

I also thanked Tony for choosing to discuss the matter with me rather than keeping quiet and making all sorts of assumptions about it. I asked him to please try not to defend me when they mocked me, as the best response I would appreciate was for him to walk away. There was nothing to gain from trying to engage with people who chose to highlight my past mistakes when they knew nothing about how it made me feel, where I currently was, or where I was going.

In retrospect, my mulling over the discussion with Tony that evening brings a few lessons to mind:

1. Rather than engage in gossip or backstabbing discussions, it is good practice to speak to the person or persons involved. In my experience, ***context is king!*** So to judge or conclude on a matter without understanding the context in which it occurred is unwise, just as

making decisions without hearing all sides of the story. While not discussing it with the person might keep them in the dark about what is being said of them, ask yourself if the quality of your life has been improved by that piece of information that you hold. Yes, the rumours might be true, but wouldn't you rather confirm with all parties involved before drawing conclusions that could lead to more detrimental behaviour on your part?

2. The fear of maintaining a certain reputation is one major cause of failure as a leader and the breakdown of societies around the world. There is the general assumption that a leader ought to be one who is perfect and without mistakes. This mentality is what compels most people to lead fake lives and tell lies laid upon lies just to cover up their perceived shortcomings or maintain an image of someone they are not. Yes, some actions have more grave implications than others, and the right punishment should be meted out for criminal offences. However, which human being is perfect? Knowing that no one, including Christians, is perfect will perhaps change our attitude towards others, make us more patient with one another, and give more room for discussions that help to identify ways for improvement rather than focus on what is wrong.

3. It is definitely important to look at the track record of anyone being chosen to lead. So, we all give a bit more careful thought to our choices, like my dad once advised me. However, we also need to broaden the conversation to include an understanding of what they have learnt from the past—good and bad experiences alike—and how they plan to use that knowledge to improve the future. The issue with stirring up the past occurs when it is not intended for the purpose of drawing out wisdom for the benefit of the individual, listeners, or wider society. Let us forget any history that bears only the fruit of agony and rather tell the stories that gift sagacity to all.

4. Dear elected leaders, you have done well by stepping up or accepting the nomination to perform a role that many would shy away from. However, stop circumventing an issue when the knowledge of it by others can destroy the very thing you are trying to

protect. Leadership is a service role, and the led should be given enough information to help them decide if they want to follow you or not. If their choice is not to follow, do not chastise them for it and be willing to step down from the role if need be. There is no joy in leading people who wish not to follow your leadership; you will achieve more when you have willing and loyal followers. Also, always remember that the respect accorded is mostly for the position and not you as a person. So, be a servant-leader. Stay humble; maintain your integrity even in the face of difficulty. Perhaps at the end you might leave with your head held high, confident that you did your best with the opportunity given.

Following that meet with Tony, I experienced nothing but pure love from him and the others. The air had been cleared, my anxiety was gone, and we had a lot of fun serving God and our town together. They were so seasoned and full of ideas that I barely had to think of anything. In fact, I don't recall doing much after that, as each one took up various responsibilities without needing much convincing. My role as coordinator was made abundantly easy by this godly bunch—I learnt a lot from them.

Sometimes when I look back, I think that God perhaps chose me as the leader of that fellowship because He knew I had the most growing to do—spiritually, socially, and mentally, at least. Of course, some of the lessons weren't immediately evident, but as I have journeyed through life, I have seen how the experiences in Gumel have given me a solid foundation to build upon.

One of those times of "rooting," as I call them, was during the Rural Rugged Evangelism (RRE) organised at both the zone and state levels. It was an NCCF outreach program aimed at demonstrating the love of Jesus through humanitarian services, using skills possessed by corpers. It was often directed at less-privileged communities and often hard-to-reach areas within the zone or state. At state level, we would take medical supplies to those communities, with the medical people amongst us tending to unique needs, as well as provide information on basic hygiene, including hair care, water filtering, clean ways to cook, and many more. They might not have spoken a word of English, but we communicated God's love for them by simply helping them with some chores. We would normally spend a few days in those communities, and for both the State and Zone RREs in my time, all we got were knitted mats to sleep on in open spaces under the moonlight.

Simple as all that may sound, there were spiritual forces to overcome. I saw creatures that words cannot even begin to describe, but equally saw (literally) the outworking of the authority that is in the name of Jesus, reminding me that there is undeniable power in both individual and corporate prayers. Those mission trips tuned up my spiritual antenna such that I became less driven by the things seen with my physical eyes.

MORAL —

There are unseen forces all around you; no location is exempt. Were God to open your eyes to see a little bit, your heart would either faint or you would cling more tightly to Jesus, knowing that your salvation (and protection) lay only in His name. As apostle Paul admonished in Ephesians 6:12–18, the real battles of life are not physical (flesh and blood) but against spiritual forces of evil. Therefore, we must never be weary of praying.

For the Gumel Zone RRE, we were linked with a Nigerian missionary who lived in a remote community and was happy to host us for some days to enable us to reach out to the people. This gave us a very soft landing with the villagers, as he was well known to them. They were known as the *Isawas*, meaning followers or disciples of Jesus (*Isa* in Arabic). The fascinating thing was that this group of people knew only of Jesus by reading the Qur'an. The realisation that there was a mention of Jesus, let alone several texts about His life, in the Qur'an was a major point of learning. This certainly was news to me and begged the question why this wasn't common knowledge, especially among Muslims. While there is a responsibility on each person to study the text for themselves, the fact that it was mostly printed only in the Arabic language meant that some responsibility was on the Imams to teach every aspect of the text contained within the Qur'an. The response given by the people provided further clarity to that thought—persecution.

The people told us how they became a nomad community scattered all over the desert plains. It was years ago, probably a century or more in fact, when an Imam in the city of Kano discovered the texts on Nabi (Prophet) Isa in the Qur'an. As a good teacher, he decided to teach his disciples every aspect of the holy book, emphasising the miracles that were cited that Isa (Jesus) did—which seemed to be the most recorded about any Prophet. The word about the imam's teachings obviously began to spread around the city. He was arrested for teaching heresy and was publicly tried. When he refused to renounce his belief in Nabi Isa on the testament of the texts contained in the Qur'an, he was found guilty and burned at the stake. Some of his disciples were also captured and brutally killed, which caused many to flee from Kano and go into hiding. Whatever settlements they found themselves in and however small their numbers, they maintained that Imam's teaching, passing it on from generation to generation and differentiating themselves as the Isawa, though reading the same Qur'an as the Muslims.

This historical account was told to us on the first night spent with the Isawa. On subsequent evenings, we sat with them in the little village square, mainly comparing scriptures—in both the Qur'an and the Bible—using the latter to expand their understanding of Jesus. It was really enlightening, for me, to find out that the Qur'an contained the majority of the text in the Old Testament part of the Bible. It contains instructions as were issued directly by God. In the Bible, there is the mention of Moses writing down God's laws and other instructions in the Book of Instructions, which the likes of Joshua added more to (Joshua 24:26), as did other prophets and law keepers in Israel. With my curiosity sparked, I tried once to purchase a Qur'an when I saw one in the English language, but a fellow corper ratted me out by shouting, "She's an infidel." Dressed in a Hausa outfit, the seller assumed I was a Northerner and Muslim too. I had no idea that it was "forbidden" for a non-Muslim to touch the Qur'an—at least so I was told. All I was after was knowledge, having become curious following the experience with the Isawa and wanting to do a personal study.

I still wonder to this day how much better Nigeria would be if more of these conversations, peace-orientated dialogues, and scripture-expounding sessions were openly encouraged across the nation—as well as in the other countries of the world with similar religious (and other fundamental diversity) issues. Open discussions would help to enlighten, reduce, or eliminate assumptions, and be highly likely to result in more unity than the constant issues being faced today because of religious wars (of whatever shape or size).

For example, if you met an Isawa on the street and saw them with a Qur'an, it would be assumed that they were Muslim. In fact, they had more in common with us Christians than the neighbouring village to them, which was predominantly Muslim—for understandable reasons of historical experiences. Although the two villages shared a water well that was located in the middle of both boundaries, they never approached the well at the same time. Usually, each villager looked at the other side to ensure no one was coming before they proceeded to the well to draw water. This was the treaty of peace both had, which we also had to respect.

I will always cherish the time spent with the Isawa. They didn't have many physical possessions but were peaceful, resilient, lovely-to-be-around, and simply wonderful people. It was difficult when we had to say goodbye.

I learnt from this experience not to judge people by their outlook or make assumptions about their faith or beliefs until I hear them speak. It is a good place to start. Perhaps we can do more of this and apply the principle to all areas of life.

MORAL —

Before jumping to conclusions, you will save both yourself and other parties much heartache if you just spoke to them first and listened effectively to their stance.

Another huge and more personal lesson which I took away from the RRE to the Isawa was the value of rising early to pray. On our final evening there, after sharing with the people, a few of us stayed up when we retired to the missionary's home. Sitting outside under the moonlight, he told us stories about his mission trips. Taking advantage of the opportunity to learn, I told him about the heaviness that I often felt when trying to pray, although I didn't think much of it. Then he asked what time I often prayed, to which I responded "random." The missionary then taught about a number of things and concluded that in his experience of being in environments such as this, it was best to rise up early to pray—before others did. One of the things he shared was the prevailing practice, in the region, of speaking to the sun, moon, and stars. To paraphrase his point, he said that when you have allowed others to tell the elements what the day should be like, then it is most likely that your day is going to take the shape of what they have decreed. It basically highlighted the power of the tongue, which the Bible talks about, and the need to set your day in course with God's plans rather than inherit or live under the proclamations of another.

So, on return to Gumel, I formed the habit of rising about 4:00 a.m. to pray—and oh, what a difference that made! The tiredness and heaviness that I used to have to push through even after a restful night was no longer an issue. Sometimes, I would get a full hour of prayer in and then go back to sleep, confident that I had put God in charge of my day and my experience was going to be one of joy. And so it was. Either it was a case of being disciplined to pray first thing in the morning or it was more spiritual, as he explained, I nevertheless saw a change in how things went around and for me. I have since endeavoured to keep up the practice, maybe not rising as early at 4:00 a.m. but remembering to make prayer (of thanksgiving especially) the first thing I do when I wake.

THINK ON THIS...

No one is an island of knowledge (Proverbs 4:5–9). Thus, the day you stop learning is the day you start dying, and the day you stop sharing your knowledge is the day you begin stagnating or become extinct. Embrace knowledge and get understanding so that your mind is always open to 'think' and not just to 'tick' through life. Sharing helpful knowledge, especially with the younger generation, not only impacts others positively, it also improves you.

MY FINAL ACTS
OF SERVICE YEAR

The rest of the summer holidays was fairly busy as I had to mark exam scripts—for my years 10 and 11 students and those of random year 12 students from various Northern schools who had undertaken the May/June WAEC exams. Apparently, there was a shortage of geography teachers in Jigawa State, so all schools had been notified to send theirs to Dutse to participate in the state-wide script-marking exercise. Corpers were also invited to participate in marking any subject for which they could demonstrate proficiency, which was mostly determined by the course studied at the university. Of course, people took up the offer as it was paid, depending on the number of scripts marked. However, I wasn't given much of a choice as a geography teacher. My school principal summoned me to his office to inform me that my name had already been passed to the coordinators of the exercise, so I only needed to present my ID card and the name of my school to be accepted as one of the markers.

During the induction, I could see why we were summoned because there weren't many of us certified to mark the WAEC papers submitted for geography. Therefore, the few of us were allocated a mountain of scripts with a set target of the minimum to complete daily, which we had to check in at the Coordinating Centre as a way of ensuring that the work was being done. It helped that a number of corpers were involved with this, as the

NCCF House in Dutse was our home for a number of weeks. It gave me the opportunity to mix with the new corpers from other zones, especially the new Papa and Mama.

Papa Raymond had left for his home in Rivers State upon the completion of his handover to Papa Paul, so I didn't get to see him again after the June NYSC Camp in Gumel. Papa Paul was more outspoken and firmer, but just as jovial as Papa Ray. On those nights that I (and a few others) stayed up all night marking scripts, sometimes with only lanterns as there was no electricity, he would come round checking on how we were doing and often tell jokes that helped us to see some bright side of the pain we were facing. His famous line, and the one which we started to greet him by, was "The Lord is your fire!" He enunciated the word *fire* in a low and deep rumble that caused one's head, at the least, to vibrate joyfully.

Sometimes in the evening, when there was a bright moon lighting up the skies, we would sit outside singing songs of praise. The Mama and other residents in the House were fabulous at ensuring that we always had food to eat. Although there were a number of us rattling through the house daily, it was a really happy time. When I was done marking the scripts and it was confirmed that all geography papers sent to the state had been marked, I returned to Gumel.

The first week back to school, I was again summoned to the principal's office. This time, a parent had laid a complaint that concerned me. The principal started by telling of how I had narrowly missed the boy's father, who came all the way from Kano to lay the complaint and had waited around for some time in a bid to speak directly to the teacher who had the temerity to fail his son. I was told that he was a powerful, educated, and wealthy man who took pride in the fact that his son had never failed a subject in his schooling days until now, the end of his year 11. As the man could not wait any longer, the principal assured him that the matter would be resolved and had taken steps to retrieve the boy's geography exam script, which I had handed in after marking it and recording the scores. He tossed me the paper and asked me to look at it again there and then.

I took the paper, and after about a minute of staring at it and being utterly confused about what I was expected to do with it, I looked up at him and said, "But I don't understand what the boy has written down." All I saw was a bunch of characters put together that made absolutely no sense, no matter how long I stared at it. I went on to explain that I had taught them to use pictures where they struggled with writing in English, but he had chosen to write several pages of gibberish. The only marks I could award were for the few diagrams he provided.

Standing and getting impatient, the principal took the paper from me and flipped through the pages. Puzzled, he looked back at me and questioned how I couldn't understand what the boy had written down because he could. Which further got me confused, because unless he was a Jedi of some sort, I didn't understand how he could make sense of the paper. Again, I took the paper from him, hoping to suddenly develop some psychic powers that allowed me to understand it. I even started to think in the little Hausa that I knew, in case that was the clue, yet I recognised no words. Therefore, I asked if he didn't mind re-marking it, since he somehow understood what had been written down.

The principal insisted that it was my responsibility to do that as the subject teacher—plus, it would be unprofessional of him to do so. Somewhere along the line, he started to lament about how such an intelligent boy, who was already an Arabic scholar, could fail a subject such as geography. It was right about when he mentioned that the boy was an Arabic scholar that the penny seemed to have dropped.

He exclaimed, "Oh, the boy writes from right to left."

Wondering whether that should mean anything to me, I asked, "What does that mean?"

Then the principal explained that the boy was schooled in Arabic from a young age. Therefore, he wrote English in the same way the former is written—right to left. With that in mind, he asked me to take a look at the paper again to see if I could make sense of it. Remembering how I used to do some mirror writing in my secondary school days, I began reading his paper with that mindset, and it all made perfect sense. All of the other teachers were aware of this about the boy, so they marked his papers without thinking much of it.

After reading a few lines in each question and realising that this boy was actually one of my favourites in the class, who had a very good command of spoken English, I decided to take a stance for his future—even if I was alone and would not be liked for it. So, I turned to the principal and told him, I would not be re-marking the paper, and the score issued was the best I could give. At the time of marking the paper, I had assumed that the boy was one of those who struggled with the English language, so I had been a little generous with my scores of the diagrams he had put down. Had I realised then that he was actually one of my brilliant bunch, I would have scored him even less.

Shocked by my response, the principal warned of the wrath we might incur from the boy's father if this was not resolved, and so on. Hence, I told him where to find me the next time the boy's father came to school, as I would also like to speak directly to him to explain my rationale. I told the principal that I was okay with him re-marking the paper and scoring the boy as he wished, but I was not going to be doing that. My view was that as an educator, I owed it to my students to ensure that they understood the subject and were prepared for what lay in their future—not just to pass them. I was not going to buy into the idea of massaging egos when such actions were detrimental to the boy himself.

I went on to explain to the principal that I had just been marking the WAEC exam papers of students from schools I had never even heard of. There was a marking script with the answers provided, and I had to mark about a hundred papers daily. I did not have the time to think that perhaps the incoherent words in front of me could have been English written from right to left, for example. Surely, part of learning the language and being good at writing it included knowing that it reads from left to right. With the new school year now starting, he was in year 12, and come May/June 2001, he would be sitting those same exams. My questions, therefore, were "Who knows the people that will get his exam papers and have to mark them?" and "Who will be there to explain to them that the boy wrote English from right to left?" Then I asked further, "Would he have passed Arabic, let alone become a scholar if he wrote it from left to right?"

To my mind, the system had let the boy down by never making him realise what he was doing wrong and being "understanding" of his predicament. I actually felt that being a brilliant boy who always strove for excellence, he was very capable of making that change had someone simply explained the principles to him.

Seeing as I wasn't backing down, the principal released me—and that was the last I heard of it from either him or the boy's father. I do not know whether or not the principal made a change to the scores. The boy, however, approached me later to ask what he did wrong, as he did not expect to fail the subject. I explained to him the same things I told the principal. He seemed to appreciate the feedback and revealed that no one had ever corrected him as such. That term, which was my last with them, he started to practice writing English from left to right—as I knew he would if only shown how.

THINK ON THIS...

"Say what you mean" and "mean what you say" are important rules for living with integrity. An integrous person is far more valuable than precious stones. Stand for what you believe in and do what you say you will do, no matter how long it may take to achieve it. Saying one thing and meaning another fools no one but oneself—in the long run, doing that causes people to distrust you and, worse of all, confuses your own spirit till you no longer know who you are or what you stand for.

A GRACIOUS FINISH

During the time lapse between graduating and getting my NYSC posting, while I self-trained in the use of computers and Office applications, I researched consulting firms in the country and made note of the addresses of the then top four—PricewaterhouseCoopers (PwC), KPMG, Deloitte, and Andersen Consulting (now Accenture)—and had it on me at all times. So, sometime in April 2000 (it was at least six months to the end of my service year), I put together my curriculum vitae (CV) and a cover letter stating my interest in consulting and the fact that I was in my service year at Jigawa State with completion in November 2000. As they were all headquartered in Lagos, where I would be returning, I provided my paternal uncle's address for correspondence purposes, half not expecting much of it.

The last few months of my time teaching rolled by very quickly. Then came November—the end of my service year—but I was having such a good time, I was not mentally prepared to leave. Since I had left home in Lagos earlier that year, I had not been back to the South. Unlike most people in my set who went with their luggage and went home from the passing out parade at Dutse, which officially marked the end of the service year, I returned to Gumel hoping to have fun a little while longer before returning home. Having handed over fellowship responsibilities to the new leader, I had no more formal obligations, so it felt like I was at the beginning of my time in the state again.

I started visiting corpers in other zones with whom I had made friends either during the State NCCF RRE or the Send-forth Conference held for us as outgoing corpers. I travelled to places like Sule Tankarkar "Sule-T," Gujungu, and Hadejia, where the main river running through Jigawa State gets its name. I climbed a mountain at Birnin Kudu but nearly died afterwards from food poisoning by the tinned mackerel in tomato sauce "Geisha," which I bought after the climb from an Aboki's roadside stall. I also went to Maigatari, where the famous meat market was.

Maigatari Market Days drew crowds from across the country, especially the South, because it was where you could get live cows, goats, and other meat animals at wholesale (meaning cheap) prices. Large amounts of cash changed hands, so it attracted way more thieves than the other market towns. There was hardly any Maigatari Market Day that we didn't hear of some bus that had been ambushed by armed bandits. The bizarre thing was that they were known to kill every single person on board, including children, before ransacking the luggage of the deceased for whatever they could find. So, I never visited the market, and my one time visit to Maigatari was not on a market day. When 9/11 occurred in America, my mind honestly flashed back to Maigatari, thinking what we put down as actions of bandits could actually have been the early indicator of the presence of terrorist activities in Nigeria. Fast-forward a few years, and that unimaginable thought is now a reality. If only action had been taken then to flush out the perpetrators, perhaps the whole country would have been spared the current battles of banditry, kidnapping, and all sorts of malicious attacks on the citizens.

Often times, I would travel from Gumel to the destination and return to Gumel before heading out again. Depending on the distance and who I knew there, it could either be a day trip or a few days. When in Gumel, I hung out with the lovely corpers. It was on one of those return trips to Gumel, about late November or early December that I got summoned again to the principal's office. "This is becoming a habit," I thought, and I wondered what was wrong this time. I went over to the school, not knowing what to expect. I was no longer teaching students, although I dropped by occasionally to check on them.

On seeing me, the principal excitedly told me how he had gotten a call from Lagos asking me to return immediately, as I had an interview with PwC. Let's say that the interview was on Wednesday, and this is now Monday. Then, I remembered the letters I sent out with my CV some months back and was elated that someone got it and actually kept it till it was the time I had mentioned my service year ended. "God is certainly in this," I thought. What a great favour this was—remembering my prayers since Uni days about going into "favour market."

I thanked the principal for the news and hurriedly made my way to the bank, which was only a few minutes' walk from the school, to withdraw all of the cash I had. Then, it was back to Suzie's place to pack anything I could. If I was going to get into Lagos in good time and get some rest before the interview, I needed to leave with the night coach from Kano that day. Thankfully Suzie was home, so I got the chance to say "good-bye" before heading to the Gumel Motor Park. And that was it.

As I walked on, I couldn't help but think how blessed I was. Imagine if I was still out of Gumel and didn't return till, say, Tuesday or after? I certainly would have missed the opportunity, so I was grateful that God ordered my steps to get back just in time. Moreover, the school's telephone lines were often down and not in use, so it was yet another "favour" that the call from Lagos came through. Although the principal said the line was bad, he was at least able to pick up the key aspect of the message. Plus, he could have dismissed the call or not even bothered sending an urgent word out for me. All in all, I was immensely grateful to God for aligning everything in my favour—though I really didn't deserve it.

Nervous as I was about the interview and not having time to prepare for it (not like I knew what was needed anyway), I knew God was using this to get me moving on to the next phase of life. I thought, "Well, the same way I came to Gumel not expecting to, I am also leaving not expecting to." But from what I have experienced, I knew that God is in control of it all. As the bus exited Gumel on the way to Kano, I remember thinking, "Phew! What a roller coaster and life-changing experience it has been." I went to Gumel a naïve, proud-in-my-achievements, stubborn, and generally confused young girl, but was leaving more aware, confident only in God, humbled, unassuming, better in understanding of grace and the power of God's salvation (being not just for non-believers), and generally more open to other cultures and backgrounds—with the scars of the battles that taught me those lessons being visible only on my heart. I was headed to Lagos to face whatever lay ahead, knowing without a shadow of doubt that I was not going to walk that path alone.

MY
ROCKY
LIFE

First year of work (post-NYSC)

At Lagos Bar beach celebrating end of training school

LABOUR IN THE "FAVOUR MARKET"

I arrived in Lagos the next morning, the day before my interview at PwC. My cousin, Tola, told of how they didn't open the letter when it first arrived in November thinking that I would return to Lagos immediately after the NYSC passing out parade. But when I didn't show up, she decided to open it and discovered that it was an invitation for an interview that was happening in December. Remembering the name of the school I was serving at, she searched for the school's contact details and kept trying the phone line but never got connected. Although getting nervous that the line might never go through or that I wouldn't get the message in time, she did not give up trying until that day when the call finally went through, and thankfully, my principal was there to pick it up.

My head was hurting from the long journey, but I couldn't afford to sleep until I figured out what to wear—certainly not from my Gumel luggage—and found out how to get to the PwC offices. I had no clue nor the time, anyway, to prepare for the interview itself. Then it was the next morning—my first work interview day!

Much of what I recall of the interview was being asked if I liked accounting and my rather instinctive response of "no," which came out more like an exclamation. Believe it or not, I didn't know then that PwC was mainly known as an accounting firm. At the time of researching where to apply for jobs post my service year, my search criteria was for consulting firms, and the name came up, so I noted down their postal address as did the others. I never again got the chance to look into them as an organisation. Hence, my response took the interviewers aback. I attempted to explain, saying something along the lines of "My issue isn't with the course, so to speak, but more about the stinginess of most accountants that I know." (I was digging my own grave more, but ignorance was certainly bliss on this occasion.) One of my interviewers then asked, "What would you like to talk about?" Pushing through the lingering headache, all that came to mind was a small research done while at Uni that looked at the erosion activities of the Bar Beach in Lagos State and the implications for the flooding of the Victoria Island environs. They indulged me, so I spoke about that (and this was well before the issue materialised), while they asked questions around it as I went on. And that was the end of the interview.

On getting home, I told my auntie about what I said at the interview, and she retorted, "Did you not know they are an accounting firm?" Then she tried to encourage me to look on the brighter side.

Realising my gaffe and the likelihood of not getting a call back, I went into the room and just fell asleep. Thereafter, I went visiting friends around the Gbàgádà axis, letting them know I was back. Without fail, each one mentioned how "black" my face had become. One even told me that he couldn't tell which was darker between me and their video player.

A week must have gone by when I received the letter of employment from PwC. I genuinely was not expecting it, having resolved that it at least had brought me back to Lagos and the interview had given me an idea of what to do for the next one. But there was no need for another, and my thought was that this was nothing short of God's favour!

On January 2, 2001, I started my three-week induction at PwC in their then Surulere offices, in the Mainland part of Lagos. There were about twenty of us. Almost from day one, I knew that I was in the company of intelligent people; "the best and brightest" was repeatedly drummed into us. It was the start of my professional career, and I counted myself highly favoured to have such a great organisation take me on. There was a lot to learn, and I was like a dry sponge, soaking it all up as much as I could. There, I met some of the best professionals I have known to date. As one who always had the focus of being a management consultant, I poured myself into the work with the goal of not just delivering high-quality service to my clients each time but also learning the guiding principles of the business world. Of course there were challenges, but I was determined to glean all I could.

I also gave the job my best because of a Bible principle about attitude to work, which I learnt whilst at Gumel and have cherished and put into practice to this day. Colossians 3: 22–25 (NIV) says

> *Slaves, obey your earthly masters in everything; and do it, not only when their eye is on you and to curry their favor, but with sincerity of heart and reverence for the Lord. Whatever you do, work at it with all your heart, as working for the Lord, not for human masters, since you know that you will receive an inheritance from the Lord as a reward. It is the Lord Christ you are serving. Anyone who does wrong will be repaid for their wrongs, and there is no favoritism.*

Bottom line, I understood this as working with integrity, knowing that I was accountable to God for whatever I did, even though there was also a human boss to report to or appraisals to measure my performance. What I have found through the years is that when you hold yourself accountable to God, you actually surpass human expectations, although sometimes that can attract various persecutions by people who just won't get you. Nonetheless, I would rather obey God because His Word and reward are of more eternal value than to follow people who are only here "temporarily."

A few months later, I took a few days off leading up to the weekend so I could return to Gumel. Knowing that the corpers would be finishing their service year about May, I wanted the chance to say a proper "goodbye" to them, having previously left in a hurry. It was such a joy to see them all and catch up on what had been happening with them, as well as tell them about my meagre experience of the professional world. I wanted to encourage them by showing that it was possible to get a job after one's service year in an organisation of one's desire, even if they didn't serve in that organisation or the state (a point of frequent worry amongst corpers).

Either that afternoon or the next day, I visited the school where I served. I was heading to the principal's office, of my own accord this time, to thank him again for taking the message for me on that day, when I got waylaid by some of my students. Excitedly, they were shouting "Mallama" (teacher) and gathered around me, all speaking at once. Although I could barely make out what they were saying, it made me really glad to see them. Above all of the excitement, I barely managed to tell them that I was now back in Lagos and just wanted to pop by to see them.

The principal must have heard the noise because he came out of his office and instructed them to go back to their classes. We exchanged pleasantries. I told him why I came and that it was a brief visit, so he motioned for us to go into his office. Then he explained that the students were excited to see me because they had recently participated in a state-wide geography competition, and the school won. He said they all knew it was a direct result of my efforts and dedication to ensuring the boys learnt the subject, and therefore were all very grateful to me.

Wow! I was elated and very proud of what the boys had achieved. I also believe God brought me back there to hear that feedback as an encouragement.

MORAL —

Choosing to do the right thing even when the situation may look bleak always yields the best results in the end.

I was still basking in the exciting news when the principal added that they were yet to find a replacement for me and asked if I wanted to take the job. Then, I broke the news to him that I got the job for which he took a call for me some months ago. Although he was happy for me, he proceeded to ask, "How much is PwC paying you? We will do more than that."

Thinking it was a joke and that there was no way a school could afford such, I told him. He replied, "We will double it."

Taken aback by his response, I said, "No."

He quickly added, "OK, name your price, and I will make it happen." Then, I realised that he wasn't joking and was desperate to get a geography teacher for the students. Understanding his plight, I told him a kinder "no," adding that the reasons I could not take the offer nor remain in Gumel were beyond money—and unfortunately, were things he could not control. By this, of course, I was referring to the weather conditions. We chatted a little more; I thanked him again and said a final "goodbye." It broke my heart that I couldn't help as I had come to really love teaching those boys, but I knew deep down that my time in Gumel was over.

Later that evening, I caught up with the corpers and wished everyone well, exchanging contact details. I have stayed in touch with some of them till today. They were God's answer to my prayers and played a major part in making my latter days in Gumel much more enjoyable than I could have hoped for—certainly a million times better than the former days.

Just a year after I joined, in 2002, the firm moved offices to Victoria Island, which prompted my move from the Mainland to the Island. Moving to Ìkòyí, my maternal uncle's home, made it easier to beat work traffic, as most of my clients were in the financial industry—the hub of which was on Victoria Island.

Despite working there for only two years, I was glad that I took advantage of the opportunities presented. I learnt how to seek out projects and put forward my interest early enough to get selected as part of the team. It also helped that I was never shy to ask questions, even the ones that may make me look silly. I remembered my dad's words, "Someone out there has the answer to your questions, and it is better to ask (and look foolish) than remain in ignorance (and stay foolish)." This helped me relate better and gain more from all of my project team leaders and managers (OK, except one!). I took advantage of the firm's culture, which allowed "juniors" to demand knowledge of the "seniors" and also provided me with a really good mentor who helped shape and stir my professional development.

Sometimes, you don't realise or even value how much experience there is to gain in such an organisation until you work in one where the thought of such ethos is akin to daydreaming—and I have experienced a fair share of such organisations. The most notable, probably, was when I worked with a financial institution. While the general culture in the consulting firm allowed for more open discussions amongst people of different grades, this organisation was more hierarchical, and focus was more on who you worked with than about the team goal to be achieved. Unfortunately for me, I didn't have one of the best managers, which made the overall experience pretty dreadful.

To be frank, I learnt more from managers outside of my department and indeed, could reason better with the Managing Director (MD)—to whom I had a dotted line of report—than I could with my direct line manager. She perceived spending the night in the office and working weekends as the only ways to show one's commitment to the company's goals, but would spend actual working hours chatting with others and brown nosing rather than doing the work at hand. So, we were very different in our approach to work and general ethos.

Admittedly, there was a lot to do, but my refusal to work overnight after working an already long day was deemed a rebellion. She tried to introduce this concept just a few days after I started work in the department, so I asked to understand the justification for it, as I couldn't see any. My aim was not to be rude, as she concluded, but simply that the task at hand was not about the length of time spent doing it and certainly not about working through the night, but about the quality of the output and ability to deliver within the stipulated timeframe (as much as possible). The other team members in the department, all men, were used to doing this and never challenged it, so she could not understand how a new joiner would take differently to the suggestion and still go home when others stayed back. Of course, I would resume early the next day, after a good night's rest, and always got the job done in good time to meet set timelines. Moreover, when they went home for a change of clothes, I had to hold down the fort, effectively doing three other people's jobs whilst still working to have our deliverables completed on time. Well, needless to say, she didn't like to have been proven wrong and thereafter determined to be my nemesis. In some ways, she succeeded, because I eventually resigned.

I mention this experience to emphasise the importance of a manager's role in any organisation. Many great employees have been frustrated and impeded from giving their best because of incompetent and one-size-fits-all management styles. Although the blame isn't always solely on managers because there are always a minimum of two sides to every story, my experiences and observations suggest the buck often stops with how the situation was managed.

When the MD heard of my sudden resignation, he requested a

one-on-one chat (which was more than my own manager did). He asked for the reason I was leaving, offered me an increase in pay, and was surprised when I turned that down. The thing is…money has never been my main motivation for work. Whilst getting decent pay for one's contributions is great, I gravitate more towards roles that have a fair amount of challenge and where I can absolutely add value, because that means I have the opportunity to learn even if it's just one new thing. As my parents put it, "Knowledge is the one thing that can never be taken away from you, and when the time is right, you can sell it for whatever price you want."

Anyway, not wanting to speak ill of the manager and perhaps cost her the job, I chose to tell the MD that I was tired of the job and could no longer give it my best—citing reasons such as the constant long working hours and having to work weekends, which were but only half the truth and certainly not the main reasons for my exit.

One good thing out of the experience was it strengthened my resolve to focus on value-adding activities (to the organisation and myself) and to cherish those work environments that foster growth. Challenges are inevitable in a workplace, but when well managed, they cultivate resilience and professionalism in business.

THINK ON THIS...

Packaged in life's favours is some form of labour, and with every seeming disappointment there is a disguised blessing. Therefore, we must learn to be patient and to seek out 'the best' in every situation. In the long run, the quality of life lived far surpasses the quantity thereof—lived without adding value to anyone or anything.

MON CHÉRI

During the summer of 2003, I decided to take French classes at the weekends to rekindle my love for the language as well as better position myself for potential job opportunities, including in French-speaking countries. The latter was driven by a past experience, when I lost out on being selected for a project in Togo simply because I couldn't speak French. What made it painful was the fact that I previously studied French during my Junior Secondary School (JSS) years. At that time, I was proficient enough to read and write comprehensions in French. Unfortunately, I lost the knowledge over the years, having not continued with it during my senior years nor spoken the language with anyone. The woman who made me fall in love with the language in my JSS days died in my third year (year 9) as a result of domestic abuse, and so did my desire for the language.

As a result of losing out on the project in Togo because of a language, and one that I once had love for, I had included learning French in my ten-year career plan, which was constantly being reviewed with my mentor at the time. Hence, late that summer, when I discovered an Alliance Française (AF) school near my home in Ìkòyí, I decided to enquire about taking weekend classes there. Thankfully, they had the Introduction to French Language course for professionals, which was run only on Saturdays in six parts (A1–A6), each lasting six weeks.

The Saturday that I went was actually the last they were willing to take new students into the beginners' (A1) class because it had started a week or so before I joined. They asked if I was willing to join the class that day or would rather wait some weeks to join the next set. I chose the former—thinking, "no better time than now." Upon completion of the registration process, they pointed out the classroom, but it was empty because the class was on lunch break. So, I took a seat right at the back to ensure I didn't mistakenly take a seat already in use by someone else. When people started to return from break, of course they were surprised to see a new face in the classroom, so I kept a friendly smile on my face and intermittently looked up.

On one of those occasional glances, I locked eyes with a certain young man, and he smiled back at me, which made my heart flutter. Like one that had been hypnotised, I kept staring at him until he took his seat in the front row. I just couldn't take my eyes off of this beautiful man.

The tutor's voice broke my stare as she was asking me to introduce myself to the class. "In French, please," she added.

I opened my mouth, but no words came out, so she must have assumed that I didn't know what to say. After all, it was French class, and I was there to learn.

She offered to help by saying, "You start with *Je m'appelle*," but my mind had drifted again, so I just stared back at her. Again she asked, "*Comment vous appelez-vous?*"

Catching myself, I replied, "*Je m'appelle Yétúndé.*"

The rest of the class was mostly a blur. I'm not sure how much of the lesson I actually took in. I left immediately after it ended to avoid speaking to anyone, especially him. I drove back home and sat back wondering what was happening to me. I had never been in love with anyone at first sight. Never! I am the type that grows in love, typically out of friendship. At Uni, I would joke (though serious) about the fact that "my love wears double-lens glasses," which was a way of saying that I get to know people and we will need to be friends first before I can progress to a love relationship. Moreover, since the Gumel experience, I had at least two really nice male friends show interest in me, but however much I tried to reciprocate their affection, I just couldn't get to the feeling of being in love with them. Therefore, it was baffling to me that I could be so captivated by someone I knew absolutely nothing about. Yet, I knew what I felt wasn't a desire to be just friends. This experience was a first (and has so far been the only) for me.

To ensure that I got my head straightened out, I decided on the "avoid strategy" for the remainder of the weeks—that is, get to class early to take my "advantage seat" at the back (which is out of character for me because I generally do not like "back benching"), avoid going out on lunch breaks, and leave immediately after classes so I wouldn't have to "mingle" that much with anyone. Doing this should help get him out of my mind and prove that whatever I felt was nothing but a fluke. Unfortunately, he always came in early but always sat in the same area at the front. Hence, we would often exchange glances and smiles, which only made my heart grow fonder of him, no matter how hard I tried to resist the feeling.

Then came the last weekend of the lessons in A1 class, and sign-up was being opened for A2. There was going to be a two-week break in between classes to give people time to decide and register if they wanted to progress. The thought of not seeing him again—should he decide not to continue at AF—scared me more than anything. So that day, I waited behind after classes. I thought the least I could do was find out his name. Although there was one challenge—I would need to do the approaching. I could tell that most of the class perceived me to be a snub of some sort, having hardly spoken to anyone in those weeks of classes.

Annoyingly, he was chatting to some other guys in the class, so when my wait (alone) started to look awkward, I left and went to wait in my car. I had observed where he parked and positioned mine in a way that gave me a good view of his so that I could see when he was heading home. He came downstairs after what seemed like forever. He got into his car and started the engine before I could get close enough to motion for him to wait. I could see the surprise on his face as I approached—perhaps that I was still around, or that I actually wanted to speak to him, or maybe both. With my business card in hand, I walked round to his side of the car and ended up stuttering rather than speaking as I thought to myself, *What am I doing?* To save the now awkward situation, he told me his name. We exchanged business cards. Mine had my personal mobile number at the back. We shook hands, and I started to walk back to my car as he drove out of the premises.

Getting to my car, I sat down and couldn't believe what I had just done. Bad as it seemed being the lady and having heard many stories about how the guy should approach first, I still felt rather happy that I got to speak to him.

MORAL –

Maybe it is best that the guy should be the first to make a move, but there is no harm in a lady doing so if, for example, the guy doesn't seem forthcoming and it's eating at her not knowing where she stands with him. The worst that can happen is that she gets rejected, but at least she won't waste time daydreaming or suffering in silence. This advice applies to men too. Many have missed a great opportunity for fear of rejection. And to those wishing to say "no," there is nothing wrong with doing so, but please do it in a manner that doesn't ruin the other person's ego, courage, or ability to take such risks in the future. That a person isn't right for you doesn't mean they aren't perfect for another. Be kind!

Anyway, I finally got myself together and headed home. I heard the notification of a text message as I pulled into the driveway. On retrieving the text, I immediately knew who the sender was. It was mostly incomprehensible because it was in French, so I rushed into the house and grabbed my French dictionary to help in interpreting the words I was not familiar with.

I don't recall much of the text message; besides that, it started with *Mon Chérie,* and the last sentence read *J'aime tu, Dylan.* I couldn't believe my eyes and was excited beyond words to think that he felt the same way as I did! He had not only used words of endearment to address me but had gone further to expressly say, "I love you." He certainly wasn't beating about the bush, which was very courageous of him. If my approaching him was a step-of-faith, his message would certainly classify as a leap-of-faith in my books, and that made me love him even more. I think I replied to his message with a text or call back, but that moment was the beginning of what turned out to be a beautiful romantic relationship. Of course, we later found out that the correct grammatical construction of those words in French was *Ma chérie* and *Je t'aime,* meaning "my darling" and "I love you," respectively. Though he corrected the former, we retained the latter because it was ours; *J'aime tu* became our unique way of telling and reminding each other of the captivating love we shared.

Dylan and I spoke nearly every day during the two-week break but never met up due to work schedules being difficult to align. He lived and worked on the Mainland, while I was on the Island. This was good in some ways because it tested our ability to communicate as we always had something to talk about and grew our emotional and mental connection such that our love transcended physical contact. Though he'd only known me a short while, I felt he was rather mature in how he related during our conversations, like knowing when to call or speak, how to sense my mood and what to say, and how to focus on the things that really matter rather than being petty—he just "got me."

Needless to say, I longed to see him, so I was really looking forward to the start of the A2 classes, both of us having registered. By the way, he discovered an AF school on the Mainland but chose to continue at the school in Ìkòyí because of me. While I looked forward to being with him in person, it bothered me sometimes that I was already in love with this guy before knowing much about him. Yes, we had a great connection—one that I have never felt with anyone else—but I still needed the assurance that we were genuinely in love with each other and it wasn't just an infatuation.

The week came when the A2 classes would start, and the weekend couldn't come fast enough. We hadn't spoken for about a day or two before the Saturday, so I was anticipating seeing him. That week, I had also developed a fever, which refused to pass by that Saturday, but I wasn't going to let that stop me from going to class…and it wasn't for the love of French. As was my practice, I was in class ahead of the start time, hoping to see Dylan—this time not as a weird admirer but as his girlfriend. I took a seat at the back, knowing that it would be the first area he would look for me, then waited.

One by one others came in, mostly the same group from the A1 class, but there was no Dylan. An hour into the lesson went by, and he still was nowhere to be found. Then it was two hours. Then it was lunch break, and my heart sank. I contemplated calling him but thought he would have told me if he wasn't going to make the first class, and perhaps I would not have bothered coming since I wasn't feeling too well.

I was thinking about what to do next, when I looked up. There he was at the door, looking at me with those charming eyes. He was explaining why he was late as he walked towards me, but that didn't matter anymore. I just sat still and kept my gaze firmly on him. When he came close, all I could say was "Would you like a lemon sweet?" which seemed odd. I had an unwrapped one in hand, so offering it to him was all I could think to say.

He politely said, "No."

I instinctively tossed it in my mouth, as if that would help calm my nerves. *Something about him makes me lose my cool*, I thought. I could not understand how I was still this speechless around him despite all the time spent during our phone conversations.

Then he said, "Can I have the sweet, please?"

I looked around my bag and said, "Unfortunately, that was the last one. Unless you want this one."

I stuck out my tongue to reveal "the one" I meant. I intended absolutely nothing seductive about that, so what he did next completely took me by surprise. He leaned forward, lifted my face with his left hand, and kissed me tenderly. It was a very welcomed surprise. The look in my eyes must have told him I wanted more, so he kissed me again, this time more passionately and playfully. Then gently stroking my face, he looked into my eyes and said, "I am sorry for being late, and I missed you too," and kissed me once again.

My world stopped; I was completely mesmerised. What could I say to that? I could feel the ground beneath my feet moving as I tried to take in the moment. This was our first kiss, and it was far better than I could ever have imagined; my lips most definitely loved his lips. Dylan just seemed to have this sixth sense that allowed him to know exactly what I was thinking or needed, and he was not afraid to respond to them, nor did his response fall short of being perfect. With this kiss and how his touch made me feel, I realised that I was totally and utterly in love with him and that the feeling was mutual. That day, all of my worries disappeared, such that I knew that I wanted to spend the rest of my life with him.

My routine prior to meeting Dylan was triangular—home, work, church—and I was happy with that life. But with Dylan in the picture, it was all the more exciting. We still didn't see each other on weekdays but spoke at least twice a day—first thing in the morning, and his voice was the last thing I heard before going to bed. Yet, there was never a dull moment in our interactions. When we saw each other on Saturdays, we often sat next to each other in the French class or had lunch together, and we always stayed back after classes just to talk and to enjoy each other's company as much as possible. We found comfort being in each other's arms so often that we would sit at the back of my car just talking. We both had tough jobs, which meant busy and long weeks, so most times being together and in a quiet place was far more relaxing and preferred than hanging out in busy places. Yeah, we were affectionate towards each other, but the few hours we had together were so precious, we spent them finding out more about each other. We had disagreements, like any other "serious" relationship, but we never left each other angry or upset. If a resolution couldn't be found, then we slept on it, but never did we end a conversation without saying "I love you" or the reassuring feeling that we were in this together.

There was nothing typical about our relationship. First (and personally), it was love at first sight. Then, we rarely hung out in the usual dating locations like restaurants, cinemas, etc. Most of our courtship was in the back seat of our cars—not because we were trying to be cheap, but because they were where we could easily sit and talk privately. Plus, we did not shy away from discussing often difficult subjects, such as the church to attend (he was Catholic), kids, work, career plans, and so on.

We were also real about our feelings. We both knew we were sexually attracted to each other. But as practicing Christians, we were mindful not to ask it of the other until we were married and were respectful enough never to push that button too far. He made sure to earn (and not demand) my trust in that area. On one occasion, early in our relationship, we went to the beach for a picnic. After a walk on the beachfront, we decided to get some rest and have a meal in the rented tent. We sat there talking and laughing, and at some point we started kissing. As I began to lean back and he seemed to be on top of me, my reflex kicked in, and I pushed him off. Shocked by what happened and realising my actions were a result of some trauma from my past, we both sat back to talk about it. In his gentle nature, Dylan listened as

I spoke rather briefly of the experiences that have made me overly suspicious of men's intentions and uncomfortable with one being on top of me.

"Let's do an exercise," he responded, and went on to explain.

Dylan very slowly guided me to lay on my back, repeatedly and very calmly saying, "Keep your eyes on me. I am not going to do anything 'funny' to you."

When I was fully lying on my back, Dylan moved his body to be on top of mine, such that our torsos were in parallel, but our bodies made no contact; all the while, our eyes remained locked on each other. We lay there holding both our positions for a short while—for as long as he could see that I had stopped fidgeting and had become calm.

Then he said, "I am never going to hurt you."

My heart melted at those words. Looking into his eyes, I could see that he meant every word of it. Then Dylan asked if he could kiss me, to which I nodded affirmatively. As he did, he still didn't lay skin-to-skin on me. Instead, Dylan was pulling back so that I started to sit upright. It was in that last gesture I realised how emotionally mature he was and knew that I could trust him. All through our relationship, never again did he have me on my back, nor did he ask to know more about what happened in the past.

Dylan had equally been vulnerable with me a number of times about his past, so it worked both ways. One that I recall well was the story of how he nearly got married to a girl he met at university. They were planning their wedding after completing their NYSC, when one day he received a mail—it was her wedding invitation to another man. To think that she and her family kept stringing him and his family along, and chose to announce her breakup with him by sending a wedding invitation in the middle of planning a wedding with him was just callous! He told me of how that experience broke and nearly destroyed him. I could not imagine how someone would do that to another human being, especially one that they professed to be in love with. But then again, people take advantage of gentle people and often take for granted what they have—so, it is also not surprising that some can act that way.

While we tried to understand each other's backgrounds and experiences, we focused more on helping each other move forward and creating our own experiences together. Since we didn't see each other frequently, like most couples in love do, the times we shared became very valuable as they helped us build our own experiences together. Focusing on the important stuff was good as it allowed us to know a lot about each other in a short time and develop mutual trust. Sometimes, we could sit in silence without uttering a word, yet we would have said a lot. I particularly enjoyed cuddling up in his arms and resting my head on his chest, because in that position I could feel every ounce of love he had for me and just bask in it. Once, he went overseas for about three weeks on a training course, so we didn't speak as often, mainly to allow him to focus on the course. However, to not be able to see him or hear his voice regularly was heart-wrenching for me; it felt like a piece of me had been cut away. Several nights, I went to bed longing just to hear his voice and to know that he was okay. It scared me on occasion when I thought of how quick it was for us to get to that level in our relationship.

Christmas came that year. As was my custom, I travelled to Àkúrẹ́ to spend the week (into the New Year) with my parents and siblings. Being there, I thought of him every day. Unfortunately, we could only speak once a day. My network provider didn't offer service in Àkúrẹ́ then, so he had to call my dad's mobile in order to speak with me. A few days in, I could hear my dad properly interrogating him—of course. By the time he handed me the phone, Dad was smiling and said to me, "I like the boy."

Curious what they had discussed, I asked Dylan how he felt, and he was laughing. He wasn't going to disclose but said, "I really enjoyed talking with your dad; he is very funny." Well, neither ever disclosed what they spoke about, but I was happy that the two most important men in my life got along well.

Family is very important to me, and I have a great deal of respect for parents—mine especially—so having my dad's approval was a very big deal. I didn't expressly tell my dad about Dylan because I wasn't sure how he would feel about me planning to marry someone from the south-south region of Nigeria. I was waiting for the right time to introduce them, but since he had to pick up the calls before handing me the phone and seeing as we spoke for hours, I'm sure he knew what was going on. Hence, when they spoke and both felt comfortable with the conversation, it made me really glad. When I returned to Lagos in the New Year (2004), Dylan still mentioned how much he liked my dad—often jokingly saying how much easier it was talking to him than to me (lol).

Early in the New Year, Dylan invited me to meet his parents. While I was nervous about this, I was equally excited that he asked, because it signalled progress in our desire to be married. The day finally came when we agreed for my visit, so I decided to fast with the plan to break at noon because I wanted the meet to go well. I have met several of my friends' parents—in fact, I make a point to do that as part of any friendship due to my upbringing to have high regard for family and respect for parents or the elderly—and I get along with them. But never had I needed to meet anyone's parents as someone who was in love with their son, so I didn't know what would be seen as good behaviour or how to approach conversations. This, however, was an important "rite of passage," so I had to do my best to calm my nerves.

That morning, I had a church meeting at Ikeja, Lagos Mainland, so the plan was for me to go from there to their house. I could barely concentrate all through the meeting, because each passing hour meant I was closer to the time when I would be meeting my future parents-in-law for the very first time. The plan was to be at Dylan's for midday, but the church meeting overran. I couldn't leave, having brought some friends from the Island with me, and I needed to hand them my car keys so they could have a ride back while I took a taxi. We had agreed to meet back at the car, not anticipating the meeting would run so late; hence, we were not sat together. On one hand, I wish it had occurred to one of us to give them the car keys when we parked, because I would have been able to leave in good time to make the next appointment. But on the other hand, I was thankful for the additional time to be calm—although being late was definitely not the way to make the good first impression that I had hoped and prayed for. Immediately after the session, I saw my friends as we were heading out of the church grounds, so I quickly handed them the car keys and caught a cab.

The house was fairly easy to find. As I alighted from the taxi, I took a deep breath and knocked on the gate. A lady approached the gate with a little girl in hand. As she did, she asked to know who I was looking for and started to beam with a huge smile when I said "Dylan." Her smile gave me some relief because it meant I was in the right place and, more importantly, I was welcomed. She opened the gate and introduced herself as Dylan's older sister, and the little girl was his niece. As we walked back towards the house, she spoke of how excited they were to have me, which was why she had to come by the house when their parents mentioned that her "baby" brother was bringing a girl home. She told of how he hadn't spoken of any girl nor brought one home in a very long time. They were starting to get worried if he would ever be in love again, let alone get married.

My mind flashed back to the story of his heartbreak, and I felt his pain again. *No pressure*, I thought, as we stepped into the house and she announced my arrival.

Dylan's mum was in the kitchen, so she was the first to come out to the living room where I was, while his sister went to fetch Dylan. His mum welcomed me with such a lovely smile and hug that I started to understand how important this visit was to them. I also realised how unprepared I was because there I was without a gift in hand! This was very unlike me, and I couldn't believe that I had completely forgotten about that all this while. I was embarrassed, but didn't think anyone took notice.

As Dylan and his sister emerged from the room, his mum told me she was cooking their traditional meal as a welcome gesture for their "special" guest, and asked if she could be excused to keep an eye on it. Dylan gave me a big hug. I so did not want to let go; I had missed him. By this time, I was no longer attending French classes due to work schedules, but Dylan carried on. Hence, our meet-up in person was even less frequent, mostly when he was able to drive to my place after classes for a catch-up. So, we were really happy to see each other. As we sat down, I apologised for coming late and explained why. Then, his sister, who had gone into the kitchen with their mum, came back out and said her goodbyes. She had only come round to see me and drop off her daughter to hang out with the family for some time. With that, we exchanged pleasantries again, and she left. Not too long after, his dad came out of the room and was very kind to me. He was all dressed up for a meeting that he had in their church, but was running late. He had delayed leaving so as to meet me, which made me feel sorry again for being late, and I apologised.

When Dylan's mum started serving the meal, I saw it was pounded yam (which I love), served with a native South-South Nigerian white soup (which I had never eaten), and shelled periwinkle snails (which I also love). Seeing the soup, I urged Dylan to tell her that we would eat together, as I didn't want to waste the food were I to be served a portion I could not finish, especially as I had only a little appetite owing to the excitement and nervousness of it all. Wasting food is a no-no in my mum's books, and she is fairly strict about it. We asked for only the quantity we could finish. She would rather we request more than not finish what was served. When Dylan told his mum my request, she asked me if I was being shy or just didn't like white soup—a name derived from the colour, as no red palm oil is used in the cooking process. Admitting that I had never eaten the soup before, I was willing to try it, but the main reason was my appetite. I had a taste of the meal but didn't quite take to the soup, so I whispered to Dylan that he would have to eat it all. Hence, we settled on having just the one plate, promising to ask for more if needed. Dylan made a start with eating, while I remained glued to his side, just enjoying watching him eat. Then the unthinkable happened.

We were sitting across from their family prayer altar, which had images of Mary and Jesus, the Holy Rosary, etc., so I was looking in that direction when the scene turned into a vivid and open vision. In it, I saw Dylan and me preparing for the Naming Ceremony or Dedication of our second child, in what seemed to have been about ten years of marriage. We were bickering over which church to go to. Our parents and immediate families were in our house and equally arguing, so we went into what was our bedroom to iron out the issues. He was upset, and so was I. The situation seemed to result from a strain in our marriage, although we still loved each other. Alone in the room, I started to explain to him how it was "unfair" that our first child was dedicated in the Catholic Church because his dad was a Knight there, yet he was planning to do the same with our second child. I thought that this would be the opportunity to honour my parents by doing it in the Anglican Church. The interesting bit was that we didn't attend either of these church groups, yet it seemed to be causing an issue because of our families, who looked like they were not on speaking terms. Then he looked at me and said this wasn't just about the church but about our cultural differences and family backgrounds. He expressed how he was no longer enjoying the marriage but wasn't looking to walk away because he still loved me. Listening to him, I saw the look of exhaustion on his face and realised that I was also tired of having to fight all of the time with the man I love. And just like that, the vision disappeared.

I was left wondering, *What just happened?* Then I realised that I had frozen and Dylan was trying to get my attention, as I had tightened my grip on his arm. He asked a question, but I remained speechless as I was trying to make sense of it all. Right there, I realised what had to be done, and it broke my heart.

The rest of the afternoon was a blur, trying to put on a smile or seem engaged in the conversation when deep within I was falling apart. Dylan sensed that something was wrong, so he made up an excuse to allow me to leave; hence, his dad and sister did not return to meet me in the house. He drove me to where I could get a cab, all the while trying to find out what was wrong. *How can anyone explain what I just saw?* I thought. We found a cab. I got in the front seat, as was my habit, and just stared into space while he had some brief conversation with the driver about making sure he drove carefully and looked after me. He asked me to call when home, as I always say to him too; kissed me; and bade farewell.

On getting home, I just wanted to be alone. I must have texted Dylan, so he didn't get worried or have to call me. Thereafter, I had a shower because it had been a long day, crawled under my bed sheet, and wept. I didn't remember my car, which was still at my friend's place, nor could I give attention to the rumblings of my hungry belly. I was feeling very miserable with no words to describe my pain, so all I could do was weep and weep some more. I cried till I no longer had the physical strength to make a sound; all through the night, my soul wept. As I cried, I wished for the love in my heart for Dylan to go away—perhaps it would help soothe the hurt and make the burden easier to bear—but the only thing that was ebbing away was my strength.

The next day, I pondered on the vision and still couldn't understand why this was happening to me. I had found someone who loved me as deeply as I loved him. We were having the time of our lives and wanted nothing more than to be together. Yet from this vision, I could deduce:

1. We were not enjoying each other in marriage because of cultural, family, and religious differences.
2. Our families were not getting along well.
3. We had spent what should be joyful moments in what looked like our first ten years of marriage bickering.

We had spoken about these differences in the past and seemed to have an agreement as to what we would do as a couple, so I didn't think they were going to be a problem. But clearly, according to the vision, life must have gotten in the way, and we were getting pulled apart. Familywise, we both occupied unique positions in our homes; hence, it was always important to us how we related with them on both sides. The thing was, Dylan was the only son and the last child. Therefore, culturally speaking, he was responsible for carrying on the family name and legacy. Myself, I am the only daughter and first child, hence somewhat responsible for coordinating the family and laying down the right examples. I was always aware of this family position dynamic but never thought much of it until that vision.

The biggest hurt I felt, however, came from the look of exhaustion on his face. I couldn't bear the thought that there would be a day or time when *Mon Chéri*, the love of my life, would be exhausted by being married to me. His exhaustion seemed to be coming from a dampened spirit, and that was certainly not what I ever dreamt for us or expected that our union would result in.

Of course, I know that marriage isn't a bed of roses, even though roses too have prickles, so expecting marriage to be devoid of any form of issues is not my idea of it—I don't live in movies! However, I don't expect it to be a bed of thorns either. It is a beautiful thing to be married and go through life with a companion. Therefore, I have always wanted to be that "good thing" the Bible speaks of in Proverbs 18:22—the one that attracts God's favour to her husband. I wanted to be the best thing that happened to him, such that he would always be thankful that he found me—especially after his previous experience—and be happy that he made the decision of being with me. I looked forward to going through life with us standing strong side by side to face whatever came our way, not for us to actually be each other's challenge. I dreamed of our families being in harmony, our marriage being an encouragement to many others, and Dylan and I being a blessing to those around us.

The vision was the stark opposite of that, so it shook me to my core. To me, he was perfect and the one I needed, but it made me realise that I wasn't perfect for him. It was that realisation that made me weep bitterly, because I knew it meant I had to let him go—my "happiness" had to be sacrificed for greater good. That was no easy pill to swallow.

As I pondered the whole thing further, I found that I genuinely loved Dylan, enough to put his happiness and the kind of person he deserved above my personal preferences. Letting go of him was definitely a very painful and heartbreaking thing that I never imagined I would have to do, but I also had to weigh the future consequences on us both, our children, and our families were I to ignore what I was privileged to see and plough ahead with the marriage in the name of being madly in love (which I was). This was not the answer nor the conclusion I had hoped for when I decided to fast and pray about our relationship, but the vision was too vivid to ignore. I had to trust that God sees the future way better than I can. Moreover, the repercussions of disobedience impacted more than just me, and I couldn't knowingly take an action that would jeopardise the excitement and joy that should be experienced when two families unite. My thought was, *What boldness will I have in the future to ask God for direction or resolution of an issue faced either as a couple going through life in general or with our marriage specifically, if I blatantly ignore the warnings?* My understanding of that vision wasn't that either of us was deceptive about our feelings or that our families were not good people. It was more that there were fundamental differences in our backgrounds that would cause the type of rifts capable of taking away from us the fun and joy of being together. Therefore, I had the choice to either go with the flow because we were all lovey-dovey or suffer pain so that we both (and our families) might be happier in the future.

I chose the latter; I would rather have long-term happiness than a short-lived gain. This is a principle that I try to live by and often weigh "big" decisions against. It is one of those ways I prize God's Word above my opinions and allow my trust in Him to trump my emotions, especially when God makes clear His thoughts about a thing. Having now resolved in myself what must be done, I needed to let Dylan know. Surely, it wouldn't make sense to him, nor anyone in fact. How do you explain breaking up with someone that you are still in love with and with whom you haven't had an issue or disagreement worthy of separation? Thinking of his reaction to the breakup news made me hurt even more, because I knew this was going to really hurt him, and I just never imagined that I would be the cause of pain to him—even though the decision was so he could have a more enjoyable future. It didn't make any sense, but I couldn't be comfortable pretending that all was well, so I called him.

Hearing Dylan's voice weakened my resolve and made me question again if I was making the right choice. But he could hear in my voice that something was wrong, so he started to ask how I felt about meeting his family. I had nothing bad to say, because they received me very well. I probably teased him about being the "baby of the house," in an attempt to disguise what was really bothering me. We joked about some other things until he asked me, "So, what is wrong?"

The tears started to stream down my face. I couldn't bring myself to tell him about the vision nor break up with him outright, so I told him that I needed some time apart to figure out what I wanted. Of course, he related it back to the visit with his family the day before and started to ask if he wasn't good enough for me, or if I didn't like his family, and so on. I knew he was simply shocked by the suggestion to be apart, so I kept trying to let him know that this had nothing to do with him or his family doing anything wrong—because they had been nothing but fantastic—and that I was still in love with him. But the more I tried to explain that this wasn't him but me, the more cliché I sounded and the little sense I made. Eventually, we settled on not communicating for a few days so we could both figure out what was next, although he made it abundantly clear that he was doing so because I asked and not that he understood why.

The next day felt very strange and uncomfortable. Since we met, we had not gone a day without texting each other at least, except for the time he was overseas on training. So, I couldn't stop thinking of him the whole day—what he must be going through trying to respect my request of no contact and the obvious longing I had to hear his voice. By the third day or so, I had become sick of having to suppress the constant urge to call him. Before I could do so, he sent me a text asking for us to meet up because he couldn't bear the silence any longer—that in itself was a relief. It didn't help that he still could read my mind, but I was glad to read something from him.

That weekend, he came to my house. Being in the evening, he parked outside the gate. I went out to meet him because we needed privacy. Seeing him, I ran into his open arms and held on tightly to him. Then we sat in the back seat, taking our favourite position in each other's arms.

As we kissed, tears rolled down my eyes because this moment reminded me of what I was going to give up by letting him go. I loved how he loved me and who I was around him. Oh, how I wish there was a way around it such that what we felt for each other would remain that way forever, and I didn't have to ever turn my back on him.

We remained cuddled and sat silent for a while. Then, ever so gently, he asked, "What is going on?"

I still couldn't tell him about what I saw but was doing the best I could to make the point that I wasn't the right person for him—a point that was difficult to understand when we both were clearly still in love. We talked for a very long time that evening, and with each word, I heard the pain in his voice, which just hurt me the more. Finally, he accepted our fate on the basis that "it is what I want," and he had to respect that. Though not entirely true, I settled for that conclusion because, from his perspective, it was the only thing that made logical sense in all of my explanations. Although neither of us had fallen out of love with the other, when we pulled away, we knew it was an agreement to move on. For one last time, we held each other tightly and kissed.

Dylan and I didn't communicate for about a week afterwards. I struggled with not speaking with him, but equally knew it would be unfair not to give him time to process what had happened and to decide how he wanted to relate with me going forward. Nearly two weeks later, he called to check on me. We spoke about how we were feeling. I felt really bad when he told me how he felt like he wasn't good enough for me. Indeed, my push for a breakup even when the reason didn't make sense and there was no obvious trigger for it could suggest that, but time had passed so that I didn't see a reason anymore to tell him what really happened. He had found a way to cope, hence no need to reopen the conversation. Well, so I thought.

Through the years, I have found that Dylan's conclusion is what still causes me the most pain. Each time my mind flashes back to what we had, I hurt because his last thought of it was more that he wasn't good enough, which suggests that I didn't want to be with him or found a fault in him—and that couldn't be any farther from the truth. Had I told him the whole truth, then perhaps he would have known that he meant the world to me, and my actions were actually a sacrifice made out of deep love for him and the desire for his long-term happiness.

Anyway, we kept reasonably in touch as we chose to remain friends. In subsequent conversations, I encouraged him to get a girlfriend, so "I could get over him." This was because I personally found it difficult to look elsewhere when I was still in love with Dylan, despite now knowing that I was not the right person for him. Therefore, the only way I could get over him was to know that he belonged to another. This is a form of restraint for me when interacting with men, as I don't covet or take what isn't mine no matter how I feel about the person. So, I focused on encouraging him to move on with another and would often suggest that he choose a Catholic and someone from a similar cultural background.

Then one day, Dylan visited me. I had just moved from my uncle's Ìkòyí residence to a little self-contained apartment on Victoria Island, so he came to visit. During his visit, Dylan mentioned that he had met someone and wanted to tell me that in person; the plus being that she had all the qualities discussed. I was elated for him, though sad for myself because he finally took the step to move on. I knew then that I would have to completely step back from his life so he could focus on and enjoy what lay ahead of him. Sad as I was, I took solace in the knowledge that he had found a good thing—that which was right for him—and if he was happy, then whatever pain I felt was not in vain. Not long afterwards, Dylan told me of their plans to get married. They have been ever since.

Personally, from the time I heard of her, I made it a point of duty to pray that they would be happy and that their union would result in the birth of a male child at least—one to carry on the family name—since this was one of the causes of the tension within the wider family in the vision I had. I chose to pray God's blessings upon them and didn't stop that prayer until years later, when he mentioned the birth of their son.

Although we don't keep in touch as much anymore, I will always fondly remember our time together. I look back on those times with gratitude to God for letting me experience a love so true, and at a time when I didn't think myself worthy of such.

The timing of Dylan's entry into my life seemed perfect in a number of ways:

1. Back when I planned life to the T, I intended to get married by age twenty-five. I met Dylan at twenty-four and had a beautiful relationship that was mutually loving and headed towards marriage—though I was no longer actively pursuing that plan.

2. It brought healing to deep pains I wasn't even conscious of. The concept of love had been tarnished by my past experiences, so I didn't think I would be able to love anyone anytime soon, especially when the relationships attempted afterwards didn't work. There was nothing wrong with the guys. We got along well as friends, but I couldn't emotionally connect with them, let alone receive or reciprocate their love, which was all the more frustrating.

   Then came Dylan, completely unexpected but absolutely what I needed to heal, making me believe that God orchestrated it to be so. God used Dylan to show me how I could be loved and that it was possible to have a strong loving relationship without sexual intimacy. More importantly, it showed me that I still had the capacity to love another romantically, as well as receive and enjoy the affection directed at me. I didn't fully realise how much pain was buried deep within, until one morning when as I woke up, I heard me telling me, as very distinct personalities and in clear words, "Yétúndé, I forgive you." Vocalising those words felt like cold water running from my head down my whole body, which brought me a sensation of refreshment. It dawned on me that day that though I had asked God for forgiveness and He had done that, I still blamed myself for my mishaps and hadn't actually forgiven myself for any part I had to play in the things that went wrong, so much so that it had tainted my view of myself. I realised in that moment that forgiveness is a key step towards healing (of any kind), and it isn't to be extended to other people alone.

MORAL –

Forgive yourself for mistakes made if you truly want to move forward. Sure, it is easier said than done; nonetheless, you need to make a practice of forgiving yourself as you do others who wrong you. Otherwise, you will just keep piling up this "dirt" inside you that increasingly makes it difficult for you to love others or appreciate anything around you—all because your sense of self-worth has been eroded and you genuinely cannot love yourself even if you go about with a façade that makes you think you do. If you really want to get on the road to healing, remember these words of William Shakespeare, "To thine own self be true" (Hamlet, Act 1, Scene 3, 78).

3. Being loved intensely by Dylan and the ability to love him back opened a new chapter in my life—one in which I could dream again of being in a beautiful relationship and a brighter future. My relationship barometer is definitely not yet perfect—still figuring things out. But he made me see that I deserve a good and loving relationship, and showed me how. If ever I am to describe a relationship that felt like being with a "soulmate," what Dylan and I shared is certainly number one (for now, at least). (PS: I'm of the view that you can have more than one soulmate, because that term describes anyone with whom you share a deep connection—which means you can have that with a parent, sibling, friend, and spouse, all at the same time.)

Of course, sometimes I wonder if I will ever find that type of love again, or if by letting Dylan go, I let go of my once-in-a-lifetime chance. But then, I also remember why I made the choice and realise that were I to go back into the mind of that twenty-something-year-old girl again, I would still make the same choice—even with all the retrospective knowledge. A forty-year-old me might choose differently because of my level of maturity, especially in handling differences, but the "young" me would still do nothing differently, mainly because I do not regret seeing him happy with a person who is right for him. Nor do I wish we had never met, because I gained an insight into how I want and deserve to be loved from that relationship. Therefore, however short our time together was, I still wouldn't trade that experience for any other.

Relationships are so crucial, especially those of choosing a life partner, that you need to learn how not to be carried away by emotions. Think about what future you want with that person when making that choice. The here and now is great, but is there longevity in it? Does "love" alone suffice in developing and maintaining a solid marriage? How much thought should you give to the backgrounds of each person? What should matter most when deciding who to spend the rest of your life with? These are some fundamental questions to ask, and each person needs to answer these for themselves.

THINK ON THIS...

Though 'love at first sight' is real, it should not equate to 'love is blind'. I encourage you to spend quality time getting to know the person you want to commit yourself to, asking yourselves potentially uncomfortable questions—including family plans and money—and providing honest answers to each other. If a person is unwilling to let you into their 'personal space' or makes you feel awkward when you ask questions that help you know them better, then it might be time for *your love to put on some glasses* so you can see clearly.

CHRISTENED BY GOD

Sometime in 2004, during a church service, the pastor sent one of the deaconesses to where I was sitting right at the back to give me an unusual message. The lady tapped me on the shoulder, as my eyes were closed during the prayers, and said, "Pastor said you should change your name."

"Why?" I asked.

"Don't know," she said. "You can see him after the service to ask."

I was so disturbed by the message, most especially because I was fairly new in that branch of the church and didn't know many people there. Moreover, a name is one's main identity and not one to be changed willy-nilly. *I don't have a problem with my name, so why should anyone else?* I thought.

When the service ended, I went up to the church office and asked to speak with the pastor. When I saw him, I informed him of his message received via the deaconess and enquired about why he did so. The pastor explained that as he ministered, the message came up strong in his spirit. So he felt it was from God and didn't want to forget to tell me, which was why he asked the deaconess to deliver it whilst he carried on ministering.

Then he asked, "What is your name?"

I replied, "Yétúndé."

"What does it mean?"

Knowing that he was Igbo, I said, "It means the same thing as *Nnenna*," adding that the literal meaning is "Mother has come back."

"Isn't that reflective of reincarnation?"

"Yes, but mine is simply because I am the first female grandchild to be born to my dad's family—where the grandmother is deceased."

"Maybe that is why God wants you to change it."

With that, the conversation ended. I left the pastor's office and went home, thinking *there is nothing wrong with my name, and I ain't changing it!*

I carried on not thinking about it, until one day, in the middle of something completely unrelated, I felt God say to me, "Speak to your parents about the circumstances surrounding your birth, and then you will know why you should change your name." It was then that I started to pray about it because I wasn't sure how to approach my parents about such. *What if there is nothing to tell?*, I thought, *this could amount to tomfoolery.* Yet, my conviction got stronger the more I prayed, so I finally settled in my mind that this was God's direction and subsequently called my parents to tell them what was going on. I assured them that this was what God was saying, not just something in my mind or that I was doing because a pastor said so. About a week later, they called me to share some details of their experiences during my birth, which I honestly wasn't really prepared for. I am certain my parents, Mum especially, would have prayed about it and been convinced that God was in this before they revealed the things told.

The summary of it all is that my mum (mostly) faced some challenges when she was pregnant with me that threatened both of our survivals and had several encounters—some classifiable as bizarre—before, during, and after my birth. The battle was so much bigger than her that she made a vow to God in the event that He kept her alive and brought me safely into this world—a vow she paid, by the way. When it came to my name, however, they didn't think much of it, so they simply went with tradition—especially as I already had two (default) names, of which one, *Yétúndé*, later stuck.

Talking through the circumstances of my birth helped us all understand why God had asked for my name to be changed. Suddenly, the Bible stories about the likes of Jacob and Saul, who had their names changed to Israel and

Paul, respectively, came alive. This was now my reality. It was during these conversations, which lasted a few weeks, that they mentioned my paternal granddad had given me a name, which declared the week as good because I was born on its first day (Sunday). But neither that nor the name my dad had intended to give me, to show his appreciation to God for my birth, were given because I already had "default names" by culture.

Through the discussions, what became clear to us was that I should have been given a name that reflected their gratitude to God for giving them victory despite all the challenges and life-threatening situations faced. However, God didn't say what the new name should be, as He did in the Bible examples. So, as a family, we decided to fast and pray for a set number of days. We summarised the backstory so my brothers could understand why and what we were praying about. They were no strangers to having joint family prayer and fasting activities, as my mum sometimes calls for these—on the premise that what affects one of us, affects us all!

On one of the days, I sat back in my little apartment and gave good thought to my life. I looked back on my journey through life so far to understand my own experiences. My parents had told of theirs, and it cumulated in gratitude. *But how will I summarise mine?*, I thought. As I retraced my steps, many incidences started to flood my mind, like the following:

- I left home in the West for boarding school in the East at ten years old, an age when many other children still had the privilege of being under their parents' care or were at least close enough to run to them for guidance when needed. Thank God for the principles and discipline with which I was already raised. I didn't see the need for cliques or to succumb to peer pressure. Otherwise, as one of the youngest in my set, I could very easily have been distracted and become wayward. When I started to go to the other extreme of being self-willed, God stepped in and turned my life around some weeks before I finished secondary school. Becoming a Christian (not by attending church or as a religion) was still the best thing that ever happened to me, which was all thanks to God. He came looking for me, even when I didn't realise that I needed saving.

- In the same Eastern part of Nigeria, I was kidnapped at age sixteen. The whole incident and how I came out practically unscathed is down to one Person only—God. The beauty of that experience was the many families who had their children back and the exposure of some real faces behind the crime.

- At the university in Lagos, I faced many challenges—to my education and health—and narrowly escaped several deadly cult activities, to mention a few. I recalled an incidence, amongst many, when I went looking for someone in one of the boy's hostels, but I had never been to his room before. In asking around for directions, I was taken to a room and was told to wait in there whilst they went to fetch him, not knowing that I was being lured into a den. Although I wondered why the lights were so dark in there, I sat down waiting, completely oblivious to the danger I was in. Suddenly, a guy walked in and literally started to drag me by the hand out of the room and the hostel. As he did, he kept saying, "Don't look back; just keep moving." When we got outside, he told me that he was standing in the corridor when he heard the guy ask me to go into the room, and something told him that I was an innocent girl. He therefore hung around the door, knowing that the boys in that room were notorious for gang rapes, and the boy that left was most likely going to fetch his gang, not the person I came looking for because the latter didn't stay in that room. Seeing the window of opportunity to get me out, as there was only one other guy in the room with me, he came in and dragged me out before that one could react. He then led me outside, because I wasn't safe being anywhere in the building. Mind you, this guy didn't know me but just felt the need to save me that evening. Who else could have prompted him to do so, if not God?!

- I went to the Northern region for my National Youth Service. The experience came with many troubles, not counting the reality of a jihad in a neighbouring town that threatened my very existence. It was a time of great loneliness and mental struggles—like I had never experienced before. I recalled a time shortly after leaving the unhealthy relationship, and while trying to make sense of my life, one of the female corpers started to befriend me. One day, she invited me to a birthday party at her boyfriend's place in town. I obliged and went with her, but realised what a huge mistake that was the millisecond we were ushered into the living area.

It was an afternoon party, but the curtains were all drawn such that only the dim lights from a few coloured bulbs and disco lights lit up the room. It was quite a spacious living room—there were people dancing at one end and another group sat around the TV at the other end. The host guided us to the sitting area, pointing out a specific space for me, while he called for drinks. Already feeling uncomfortable with the whole atmosphere, I made my way to the available space, taking note of the fact that everyone was sat in pairs except the guy beside whom I was asked to sit. Approaching him, I saw that he was a middle-aged man, as he introduced himself as Alhaji so-and-so. I sat down, turning to look at the TV, and nearly passed out from shock. They were watching a music video that had women dancing practically naked. Alhaji motioned that these were the "real Makossa dancers." Then it dawned on me what was really happening…this was an orgy! The people in pairs, including the lady that invited me, were hands and necks all over their partners. There were empty alcohol bottles everywhere, and cigarette smoke filled the air, making it even more difficult to see clearly. As the Alhaji made his move on me, I politely asked for the toilet, promising him a good time when I returned. He pointed the way. Weaving my way through the crowd and pretending to be dancing, I headed for the main door and ran as fast as I could the minute I stepped back into the broad daylight.

I saw the corper lady some days later and challenged why she would invite me to such a party. Her comeback?! Well, she thought if I could be sleeping with a broke corper, then she didn't think I would have a problem with a rich Alhaji. Then, she went on to say something about how I missed out on the US dollars that were given to the girls after that. Wow! Could I blame her? No, I blamed myself. If I hadn't acted in a way that was contrary to my beliefs as a Christian, she would never have made that assumption. Finding this out about her and some other girls in fact (I caught one with a well-known married man during a random early visit to her house), and realising that they enjoyed such shenanigans led me to keeping my distance from them, as I wanted to focus on getting my life back on track and living like a true Christian.

Again, I couldn't but give thanks to God for every single thing I went through and how He redeemed me. His light always shines the brightest in the darkest of nights, and I am a living testimony of that. I came out of Gumel still standing on my own two feet—a humble, better, and stronger person—not because of anything I did well, but because of God's grace alone.

Then, I thought of my work experience so far. My job came with all sorts of challenges, including life threats, many of which I had to confront because there was hardly any formal avenue for reporting such. I remembered an instance in Port Harcourt (south-south region), when the findings from an audit that I had performed did not sit well with the company's branch manager. He tried to bribe me by handing my teammate, who was less experienced at the time, brown envelopes full of bundles of brand-new notes of cash in exchange for our silence. He added a threat should we refuse the bribe or report the findings to the headquarters. God gave me the wisdom on how to handle that situation, considering that the branch manager was responsible for our entire itinerary during that visit. I told him to please help keep the cash in his office because we didn't have a safe place for it. Then, I told my colleague in private that we needed to leave town immediately. So, when he thought we were going on lunch break, we actually returned to the hotel to pack our bags and head straight to the airport.
Aside from things to do with the work itself, it was tough maintaining my decency as an unmarried young woman in a male-dominated industry. I had to deal with constant sneers for not wanting to sleep around and several unwarranted passes from the older men.

I started to wear clothes that were at least a size bigger, never had make-up on, and always avoided "dirty" talks so that conversations were focused on "the job"—all in the hope that it would take away the unnecessary attention, but these did little to help. So, I learnt to maintain a stone-face in order to get the message across on many occasions. But my real strength in the face of those challenges came from God. Following my past debacles and experience of God's love, I promised not to do such again. However, I recognised that the ability to keep that promise wasn't just in my resolve but in the help of the Holy Spirit, because many times I still took ignorant steps but He always found a way to snatch me out of the impending consequence.

■ Living in a metropolis like Lagos also came with numerous perils faced daily. I had been in several accidents—some only seconds away from being fatal. On two occasions, I had been held at gunpoint. Honestly, I cannot describe the feeling of having a potentially loaded gun pointed directly at you by someone you know isn't afraid to pull the trigger. It is a chilling experience.

The first for me was at the Nigeria National Petroleum Corporation (NNPC) fuel station's supermarket in Ìkòyí, just up the street from my uncle's house. I was on my way to the salon at Fálómọ. It was a nice sunny Saturday, so I decided to walk. On the way, I thought it a good idea to have a cool drink to hand for when I arrived at the salon. So, I stopped by the store to buy a ginger beer. It was about 10:00 a.m.; there were lots of people outside filling up their cars with fuel and attendants supporting them as required. How could I have known that there was a robbery going on in the store, which was only a few yards away from all that buzz? The door was open, and I walked in singing as is my habit. I was heading to the fridge when I saw a guy on the floor. I rushed to help him, thinking that he had collapsed. Then, I felt a gun pointed at my spine, and a voice said, "Lie down or I will shoot you." It was then that I realised the guy on the floor hadn't fainted but was obeying the armed robbers, as was everyone else in the aisles whom I started to see. They came for the cash in the vault and were with the manager inside, but chose to leave the doors open so as not to alert other people outside, knowing that most would not come into the store. I tried to lie down in the pathway where I stood so that it could serve as a warning to anyone else unknowingly waltzing in like I did. He shoved me with the gun, having realised what I was up to. Thankfully, as I began moving aside, the rest of the gang came out, and in a flash, they all took off.

The second incident occurred while I was stuck in one of those unexplainable gridlocks on Victoria Island. I was driving and had the windows down because it was terribly hot and it didn't make sense to keep running the car's engine when we had barely moved an inch in almost an hour. The next thing I felt was a gun pointed at my temple and a voice that said, "Give me your money." The conversation that ensued, in which I refused to give him anything and ended up preaching the gospel to that guy, could only have been God. I would never advise arguing with an armed person, so it was definitely not me. For some reason, in that moment, I felt no ounce of fear and could only think that the guy needed to know the love of Jesus. I told him the truth: I had just ₦500 (five hundred naira) on me, and I wasn't willing to give it to him. Then I added that the traffic jam had already got on my nerves, so he needed to stop pointing that gun at me, otherwise, I would get very cross with him. Perhaps it was out of shock or some other reason, but he obeyed me, which then gave me the opportunity to talk to him about Jesus. After that, he simply walked away. Now, I don't know the work God wanted to do in that young man's life, but I know that I was in no doubt afterwards that God just saved me from a situation that could have ended my life.

■ I also recalled an incident that was probably the singular, most devastating, and soul-destroying I had experienced. I was at a male friend's small apartment—not my first time there—and he prepared us a meal with okra, knowing that it was one of my favourites. It was a very enjoyable meal, but that was the last thing I remember doing that evening.

The next thing I recall was a searing pain in my vagina. It was so excruciating that it sent shockwaves to my brain, which jolted me from what seemed to be a very deep sleep in a faraway land. Half awake, I could feel a weight on me, so I pushed with every bit of strength I could muster—propelled by the sharp pain that was coursing up and down my entire body—and he went flying off. With my head a little foggy, I opened my eyes and noticed that it was dark all around and I was stark naked. Many thoughts started to flood through my head, but all I could ask was, "What is going on?" I could still feel the pain down below; my head was ringing loud, my mind was very puzzled, and for some reason, I couldn't stand up. He was quiet, so I lay still for a while trying to make sense of what was happening.

First, I thought, "Why am I naked?" because the last I remember I was fully clothed and sitting upright after the meal.

Second, "How am I on the bed with my body turned towards the ceiling?"

Third, I am a very light sleeper. "How tired could I have been that I didn't feel a thing when my clothes were being taken off or my body got laid out flat on the bed?"

Fourth, "Why in God's name can I not really move my body?"

Fifth, "What is that pain that I am still feeling?"

Then the penny dropped. I was experiencing an attempted rape. I let out a muffled scream! Turning on my left side, I spotted the shine of a knife and instinctively stretched my hand to grab it. My aim? To sever a vein so I could bleed to death.

In that moment, I could forgive him but not myself—blaming myself for putting me in this situation. Therefore, suicide was the only way out I could think of. To think that I went from not having sexual intercourse to being raped, and in a context where there seemed to be none but myself to blame, brought on far more soul-shattering pain than the physical one I was feeling. Hence, I thought it best to just end it all. With tears streaming down my face, I asked God to please forgive all of my actions so I could die "righteous." I also recall momentarily thinking of the pain this would cause my parents to lose yet another child, so I asked God to please console them. But as for me, I could no longer live with myself. In that thought, I turned back to face up and took the knife to my left wrist. *Believe me when I reiterate Jesus' message in John 10:10 that the enemy is only after your utter destruction—ceasing every opportunity to steal, kill, and ultimately destroy!*

As the blade touched my skin, the guy grabbed my right hand and knocked off the knife. He hadn't said anything or moved since I woke up. Now holding both my hands, he asked what I was trying to do. Sobbing uncontrollably, I begged him to let me die. Then he started crying too. He said things about how he loved me, was ashamed of what he had done, had never wanted to hurt me, and so on, but they were all ramblings to me. I felt nothing for him—not hatred, nor love. I just wanted to be away from the situation. I wished for it to be a nightmare that I could wake up from, but alas, my nakedness—now covered by a sheet—and the minor cut on my left wrist were reminders that it certainly wasn't a dream. Overwhelmed with tears, I gave up trying to reel out of his grip, as he continued to hold my hands down and just wept.

Once we both were calm and I regained some strength, I rose up from that bed with heavy eyes and a sombre heart, and had absolutely no further conversation with him, as we both knew that this was the end of any friendship we ever had. I put on my clothes and went straight home. My journey home and the next few days are forever gone into an oblivion. I cared very little for my countenance, appearance, or food. I was just in my room—not knowing what to think or how I was going to make it through this ordeal. I avoided all forms of public gatherings and did not breathe a word of the incident to anyone. The light that previously shined on my heart, helping me find my way through life, seemed gone. All I wanted to do was stay in the dark for as long as the pain remained.

Somehow, in that terribly dark place, God's grace and love reached out to me. I felt this unusual tug at my heart and an anchor that seemed to hold me in a still place, reminding me that God loved me and assuring me that I wasn't going to be ruined by this. Although I never quite doubted God's love for me, I wanted to hide from it because I felt He was being too generous and I didn't deserve it. *Why should One so pure, gentle, and kind continue to associate with or even care for someone like me?* I thought. But, no matter how hard I tried to ignore the tugging at my heart, He wasn't letting me go.

Through that experience, I realised how precious God is to me. He is the Anchor of my soul and the sole reason why I am still alive. Each time my mind goes back to that period, I see God's handiwork more clearly and how His saving power was at work. For example, He woke me up "just in time" and gave me the strength to push the guy off of me, because I don't think he intended for me to be awake during the ordeal. I have considered the possibility that the meal served could have been tampered with, which might explain the fogginess in my head and temporary paralysis felt as I was unable to effectively move my body for some time. I thought of a scenario where I might have woken up with absolutely no recollection of the incident, only to discover months later that I was pregnant and left wondering how. Believe it or not, I also see God's grace in letting the guy stop me from taking my own life that day. Yes, I still wish the incident never occurred, but I will forever treasure the overwhelming feeling of being loved by God that I experienced in the midst of the pain. Looking at the situation through this lens gives me cause to still give God thanks for loving me so and to want to share with others that they too might find courage to run to God—as quickly as possible—most especially in difficult times.

To anyone out there in a difficult place—please let God in! I make no excuses for sexual assault or assault of any kind on another human being, because they are NEVER warranted or deserved, nor should be condoned. But I am contending alongside God for your soul. In a dark and hopeless situation, it is easy to think that there will be no way out, but I can assure you that God is able to provide you with one and to wholly heal you—if you let Him.

Incident upon incident, and with each one recalled, I saw more clearly. Of course, they weren't all bad situations. There were many joyful moments along the way, too. In all, I realised that God had been faithful to me. The key thing that dawned on me that day was that my life had always seemed threatened since my conception (I still don't fully know why), and I had been fairly oblivious to it. At most, I thanked God at the end of each situation, if it occurred to me, but never had I given deep thought to "my ways" to identify a pattern or get an understanding that events were not as disconnected as I might have assumed. Beyond the stories my parents told, I realised that I personally had enough stories of my own to be immensely grateful to God, who kept His promise to keep me safe and be with me till the very end, even when I didn't recognise it or fully appreciate His protection. I was just in my mid-twenties but had gone through many things that even those twice my age would consider an "eventful life." Yet, I could not boast that the ability to pull through any of these incidences with my sanity intact (to some extent) is down to either my own strength or wisdom. It was all due to God and the grace He chose to lavish on me in spite of my shortcomings. A verse of that famous hymn, "Amazing Grace" by clergyman John Newton, perfectly sums up my life experiences:

> Through many dangers, toils and snares
> I have already come:
> 'tis grace has brought me safe thus far,
> and grace will lead me home.

Realising all these, I was humbled again and fell on my face to worship God. I also prayed for an end to the calamities, especially car accidents, which I seemed to be having a lot of then. As I prayed, tears poured out. *Who am I that He should be so mindful of me and want to keep me alive?* I thought. I had certainly done nothing to warrant His favour nor deserve to be a recipient of such intense love. That day, I gained a whole new perspective and absolutely understood why my name needed to be changed.

By the time we concluded the prayers as a family, two names were revealed, and the one chosen was *Modúpẹ́ooreolúwa*, which means "I give thanks for the goodness of God," with the emphasis on *Mo* (that is, I), because it is a constant reminder of all the things **I** have to be "thankful" for and how **I** must never stop giving God thanks. When the family agreed that it was to be my name henceforth, my parents prayed for me as one would a newborn child. From that day on, I can count on one hand the number of times they have made the mistake of calling me by the old name.

When I told the pastor of the name change, he decided to call me out during a zonal pastors' meeting, which he had often asked me to attend (though I was just the choir and the youth leader). The pastors in attendance prayed for me—in a fashion similar to that of a child's dedication or naming ceremony. The following Sunday, he called me out in front of the whole church and announced my name change. They also spoke blessings upon me. It was not commonplace in the church to make a fuss about things like that, so I saw all of the events that surrounded the name change as God's way of "singling" me out and letting me know that He was the One giving me a new name!

With my name change, I gained a new identity and consciousness— from one of complete chaos and confusion to one of thanksgiving. Through the process, I grew confident of God's Fatherhood and eternal love for me. By this time, we were firmly in 2005. Ever since, I have been more conscious of events that occur in my life and learnt to actively look out for what God is doing through each.

THINK ON THIS...

The church—as a place of worship—is a hospital for the human spirit. It is founded by God to provide a sanctuary and solace for our often weary souls. Therefore, one of our guiding principles must be to express the love of God revealed through Christ Jesus for all who come in. God does not seek for any of us to be perfect before partaking in His extravagant grace—only come with a repentant heart and a desire to be taught God's Word, which the Holy Spirit can use to help you mature in Christ. So let us be more accepting of one another and help each other grow in the knowledge of God, as the Holy Spirit does the perfecting work in each one (Proverbs 27:17, Ephesians 4:11–16).

LETTING GO.
LETTING GOD.

By my plans, I should have been married at twenty-five. But that dream was sabotaged by my self-inflicted heartbreak, albeit for the right reasons. With Dylan, I had learnt to love again. It was such a beautiful feeling that I didn't want to let go of it. So, inadvertently, my attention and affection somewhat got misdirected.

Tosan had recently moved to the Island making it easier for us to spend more time together, and I unknowingly started to extend all the love that was in me to him. At the time, he was my only long-time friend that was near enough for me to easily talk things through with. He was in the process of finding a new job and had started to attend my church, which was around the same area. Hence, we saw each other a fair bit every week. The regular contact and mutual support in what were "hard" times brought us even closer, blurring the lines of our friendship. However, we were so focused on current events that we didn't realise or formally acknowledge what was happening for a long time.

When Tosan moved into his own space in the Boy's Quarters (BQ), provided by friends from church, and was working in a telecommunications firm—which we had fasted and prayed together about—we both started to feel some respite from all of the challenges. Therefore, our attention started to turn back to our friendship, which was much stronger. Or, should I say, blooming relationship. By this time, I was hungry for some emotional stability and desire to be married, so the option didn't look any better than Tosan. We had been friends for about a decade by then. We talked about everything, including our future plans, and knew each other's movements at all times. I knew and was friendly with his family, though he didn't really know mine. We had always stood by each other through really difficult times since our Uni days. We communicated well, I thought, and shared many good laughs. Then, there was this growing chemistry. Both being single, I didn't see reason to look elsewhere, so I encouraged the possibility of us. All seemed to be going well. Until April 2006, when a storm came out of nowhere and caused things to go pear-shaped.

On April 3, 2006, I resumed work as normal in the Victoria Island offices of a client in the oil and gas industry. My car was due for servicing. Being located close to my mechanic's workshop, I called him to send someone to pick up the car so they could service it while I worked and return it before I closed for the day. It wasn't the first time I had done this, so I didn't think much of it. Some minutes later, the person sent called me that he was at the offices, so I hurried downstairs and handed him the car keys. The distance between my client's office and the workshop was no more than a ten-minute drive; they were connected by a straight road, and between them was only a roundabout and a T-junction that led directly into the workshop. It was shortly after 9:00 a.m. when he came to pick up the car, a time when most people would be settling into work, so traffic was fairly light, meaning it would take even less time for the guy to get back to the workshop. Therefore, about twenty minutes later when the mechanic, Yuletide, called me, I expected it to be an acknowledgement that the car had been received and to provide an estimated time for its return. Instead, it was a call that started a chain reaction of unpleasant events.

"There has been an accident," Yuletide said.

"What! Where?" I exclaimed.

"On Ajose Adeogun Street, opposite the bank," he said, adding that it was a head-on collision with a Danfo bus driver, who had been driving in the opposite direction. The other lane was closed for some road work, so cars were diverted to use the other side, which normally had two lanes. The bus driver, however, had carelessly swerved into the temporary lane and was at a speed that made it difficult to stop when he realised that he was heading for the oncoming vehicle—my car. The impact completely damaged the front of my car, one of the front wheels, and the windscreen. My immediate concern was for the guy that was driving my car, so I asked after him and was relieved to hear that he came out with only bruises to his forearm when the windscreen came shattering down on him. Had he died or sustained major injuries, things would have gotten very complicated, so I counted my blessings. Then I asked about the Danfo driver. Yuletide explained that the bus had some metal workings around the front panel, so it was practically unaffected by the collision, so the driver, his conductor, and everyone on board were fine. The only further bad news for me was that the Danfo bus was not insured! Yuletide then said that the police were at the scene taking the drivers' statements and wanted my confirmation that my car was being driven with permission. He passed the phone to the officers. After much conversation between us and the Danfo driver, the only way forward was to have the car towed to the mechanic's workshop. Unfortunately, the combination of no vehicle insurance, the Danfo driver not being the main bus owner, and the lack of strict regulations meant that the guy could only be fined the cost of towing my vehicle—and I was left to bear the cost of the damage. Thankfully, I had comprehensive insurance.

I told Yuletide to collect a copy of the police statement, as the insurance company would need details of what happened, having not been able to attend the scene before the police demanded to move the vehicles due to the standstill traffic the accident was causing. From that call, I rang the insurers to inform them of the incident and to book an appointment for their visit to the mechanic workshop in order to assess the damages and begin the claims process. Being on client site and with crucial meetings lined up, I had to calm my nerves and control my emotions as I went through the motions of that morning. I informed my project lead, Stanley, of the incident so we agreed that I could take the afternoon off to sort things out. From work, I went to the mechanic's workshop. When I saw the extent of damage to the front of the car, I knew that it was a miracle that the mechanic boy that was driving came out with barely any injury—it was a wreck. To me, it was a write-off, but Yuletide assured me that there were skilled car body repairers nearby who could restore the car, and I could trust them with all the internal workings. Still in shock, I left the workshop, hailed a taxi, and went home to sleep.

The next day, it felt strange to be going to work without my car. It was a red, 5-door, manual-geared Toyota Corolla hatchback—my very first car, purchased as a used vehicle. In the more than three years that I had the car, we formed a bond such that it moved effortlessly with every turn I made—sometimes weaving through the often dense Lagos traffic. I could tell the difference in how "she" felt and sounded after someone else had driven her. Though compact in size, the car had served me very well in many crucial moments, like when it sailed through the high floods caused by the Bar Beach overflowing its banks without the water getting into it and shed off the excess water when on dry ground as if nothing happened, whilst many other higher and more expensive cars failed their owners by packing up right in the middle of the floods. That car was to me almost what Herbie was to Paco (the little boy) in the 1980s movie *Herbie Goes Bananas*. I loved it, and it loved me back. So, losing it felt like losing a friend, and I missed it. Pending its return, I had to go back to hailing cabs or getting on the Danfo buses, and that was going to take some getting used to—having not done so in some years.

It was a few days before the insurance assessor visited the mechanic's workshop to view the damages, with myself and Yuletide present (to assist my knowledge). Prior to his visit, I had asked Yuletide to list the things to be fixed and provide a full repair estimate based on the actual cost of replacement parts. It also gave me a point of reference for what the claim assessor would report. Having ascertained everything that needed to be repaired, a list long enough to fill an A4 paper, the assessor reported that everything was covered by the insurance and that a restoration was going to be cheaper than replacing the vehicle; hence, they would go with the former. However, the bad news was that it could take months to process the claim and get the repairs done, and they could not give me a replacement car for more than a few days. Therefore, the assessor's recommendation was to go ahead with fixing the car, and they would refund my expenses when the claim had been approved.

"Also," he added, "we have our own rates for each part, which will be used in determining the claim amount."

Enquiring what that meant, the assessor explained that they obtained the estimated cost of vehicle parts from their trusted suppliers, which sometimes did not reflect the market rate. With my car not being a brand-new vehicle, the value would be further reduced to reflect second-hand costs. This was not the conclusion I expected. Realising that it was a strategy to cut their costs, I suggested that they take the car to any workshop of their choosing and return it whenever it was fixed. He refused to accept my suggestion as an option. After a few conversations going back and forth, with neither of us accepting the other's recommendation, he would send his report to the office, and someone would let me know the final decision—which I didn't need a soothsayer to let me know what it would be. I don't know about now, but the concept of insurance in Nigeria then was mostly a gimmick through which law-abiding citizens got taken advantage of by big corporations. Yes, insurers all over the world aim for reduced payouts, but there is often an enforceable law to prevent them from cheating the claimant outrightly, unlike in Nigeria. Anyway, all I could do was await the final decision.

A few days later, about a week after the incident, I receive a call from the insurance company. The caller proceeded to inform me of the decisions made. The verdict was that there was no availability in any of their certified workshops to fix my car, in the next few months at least, so I would have to use a workshop of my choosing to do so. A replacement vehicle would not be provided, nor would they cover any part of the cost of travel to and from work pending the car's repair. Then, the claim amount to be paid was a little over ₦50,000 (fifty thousand naira). I was livid. That barely covered the cost of a replacement engine, which was just one item on the list! Yuletide's estimate, which was based on actual market prices, was nearly four times higher than what would be paid out—the equivalent of my full month-and-half salary. This was excluding my daily transport fare to work alone, which was about ₦500 (five hundred naira), and would need to be covered in the estimated two to three months required to fix the car. Unfortunately, I didn't have much savings because of the high cost of living on the Island and other financial commitments. Taking a deep breath to take it all in, I realised that the next few months were going to be tough. But first, I needed to commission Yuletide to begin work on the car.

The next day, about midday, I went to the bank during my lunch break to withdraw half the funds required to purchase some of the parts needed to begin the repairs, which was nearly everything in my bank account—about ₦100,000 (one hundred thousand naira)—leaving just enough to cover my transport fare till the next pay day. All planned expenses that month would have to be cancelled or postponed, except that of the goods (a gift and cake) previously ordered as a surprise for Tosan's birthday later that month. When I called the lady to explain recent developments, she mentioned that the purchases had already been made but was willing for me to spread the repayment over two months because she knew I was good for it.

I went from the bank to the mechanic workshop, following confirmation with Yuletide that morning to provide the initial cash outlay that day, so he could purchase the parts from a famous spare parts market on the Mainland, where good-quality second-hand parts could be bought at discounted rates. This will enable the workshop to begin the repairs ASAP. The workshop was less than a twenty-minute walk from the bank. On getting there, I was told Yuletide had to close early due to a personal emergency but would be back in the next day. Unfortunately, he did not instruct any of the workers to receive such a huge amount of cash; hence, none of them was willing to do so. Therefore, I would have to come back with it in the morning. I left the workshop, went back to my client's office, and carried on with work for the rest of the day, completely forgetting about the cash in my bag.

As usual, things were busy at work, and it was about 10:00 p.m. before I could close for the day. Remembering the cash, I asked the few people left if they had drawers with keys where I could leave this—though at my own risk—but found none. So, I decided to take it home since I lived less than a fifteen-minute drive from the office. The office entrance was on an obscured street, which was surrounded by a one-way system. Hence, I had to walk some distance to the roundabout where I could find some form of transport to return home. I waited a while for a taxi but found none. A Danfo bus going via my route came round, but I got pushed out by the people-rush to get on board—as I wasn't used to the struggle required to fight for a seat when transport options become very limited.

It was about 11:00 p.m. when an okada (commercial motorcycle) came around, I hailed it and hopped on quickly, in a bid not to miss the opportunity and to avoid being alone at the bus stop. Having seen firsthand the recklessness of most "bike riders," I pleaded with him to ride carefully. As my destination was not far, he also didn't have the need for excessive speeding. When we were about a minute away from my stop, I could see the Dockyard outline in the dark—it was bordered by the Atlantic Ocean, which was now blended as one with the night sky and gave off the feeling of calmness as its gentle breeze refreshed the air. Suddenly, the night air was filled with the whirling noise of another okada behind us, indicating that it was approaching at top speed. Thinking they were going to ride past us, I was completely caught off guard when the passenger on that okada hit me from the back. Before I could comprehend what hit me, he snatched my handbag, shoving the okada I was on with his leg at the same time, and they sped off. The force of the unexpected kick to our okada sent it crashing, with both of us landing violently on the ground, narrowly missing the open gutter and concrete shootings on the right side of the road.

Almost the same instant as I landed on the ground, I sprang up, realising that my bag and everything in it—including the cash—were gone, just like that! The okada rider, a young Hausa man, got up too to rescue his motorcycle. Then he came up to me to ask if I was okay, but I couldn't grasp how to respond. I started to scream, the blood vessels in my head were tensing up, my whole body was vibrating uncontrollably, and my temperature started to rise. I was thinking of everything lost and the implications thereof. My brain felt like it was going to explode, and I could feel myself going insane. Seeing as I was gabbling, the okada rider pointed at a roadside pay phone trader just ahead, across the road from my house, who was still open should I need to call someone for help. He apologised for not being able to stay with me, then rode off.

Although I could hear him, I couldn't comprehend anything said in that moment, so I just carried on screaming and pacing. I couldn't help it; it was the only way to express the pain and tension building up in my veins.

I started feeling like I was slipping into an oblivion, when something else took over my consciousness. It was the Holy Spirit rescuing my soul, as I later realised. I heard myself speaking in tongues uncontrollably; the words rushing out of my mouth and fragile frame as if to snap me back into sensibility. In the teeny-weeny moment that I seemed to regain myself, I could feel that those words were a prayer, but I wasn't mentally engaged. Hence, I continued pacing with hands in the air, and my face lifted up to the dark heavens. My lungs were battling for air and my soul wailed for help! The agony went on for a while. Upon regaining consciousness, I still couldn't help the pacing up and down, as it seemed to help calm the vibrations felt in my entire body. I was still praying in tongues in a loud voice, only this time, it seemed to be more of a praise chant. My eyes were covered in tears, and my head was seriously hurting. Gradually, I started to calm down and tried to breathe normally. At that point, all I wanted was to lie down. Then, I realised where I was and remembered what had happened—my bag was stolen, and my keys were in there.

Covered in a mix of sweat, tears, and sand, I walked towards the pay phone lady, who was still there and with some guys. I asked her if I could call someone but explained that I had no money to pay immediately. I pointed out my house, which was opposite her stand. She said they heard someone screaming some meters away in the dark area but didn't want to approach as they thought it was an insane person.

"Well, that was me," I replied.

She handed me the phone, and I called the only number I knew by heart who could be of help. I called Tosan.

I had given Tosan my spare keys in the event that I lost mine—which had never happened. Also, it signalled that I was trusting him more with my heart, which I think he understood. Following that, I became more expressive about the desire for us to be more than just friends and wanted to know his thoughts. Well, that was shortly before my world seemed to fall apart and he started to seem distant. Anyway, when he answered the phone, I could barely speak, as I was physically drained and had a headache. All I could manage to say was that my bag had been stolen and I needed my spare keys. Tosan complained of it being late, almost midnight, and something else. So, I just begged for my keys because it was the best chance that I had to get into the room that night. There was no way I would be allowed to bring a non-resident into the senior naval officers' base at that time, even if I were to find a locksmith. He finally agreed to come, so I waited with the people at the payphone stand, my face drooping in my hands.

The incident played again and again in my mind. It made my head hurt just thinking, *Where do I start from?* It also dawned on me how easily I could have gone insane in those moments were it not for God's saving grace that showed up just in the nick of time—the prayer lasted close to an hour. I realised two things. One, not all cases of mental illness are triggered by the use of hard drugs or the abuse of substances, as believed then. Some could result from experiencing an overwhelming circumstance beyond the person's control. Two, Jesus is truly our Advocate, and the Holy Spirit is our "Ever-present Help in time of need." In my weakest of moments, when I couldn't do anything to help or save myself, He came to my rescue—and for that, I became grateful. Yes, the situation was bad, and I envisaged a long, painful road ahead. Yet I saw cause that night to give thanks, because only the person who is sane or alive has the opportunity to hope for a new day. Had I hit my head on the concrete slabs or fallen into the gutter when the bandit kicked the okada, I might not have survived at all. Then, to have the lady with the pay phone still out at that time of the night and willing to help, coupled with the fact that I had cut spare keys and given them to Tosan only a few weeks prior, were in themselves more reasons to be thankful. So, I remembered that "I am a child of thanksgiving"—the new identity reminded me that God had not forsaken me despite the calamities now befalling me.

Less than an hour after the call, Tosan appeared on an okada. Without so much as a "hello" or "how are you doing?" he dropped off the keys, and they drove off. I thanked the lady, who had told me not to bother paying for the call considering the circumstances, crossed the road into the Naval Dockyard, and went to my room. As the doors closed behind me, I dropped into my bed like a lifeless log and slept off.

When it was morning, I wished it was all a dream. But, alas, the loss was real. Whilst the headache was mostly gone, my eyes were very swollen and bloodshot, and I started to feel pains all over my body, likely from the fall and the bruises sustained. I got ready and went to work, using some emergency funds that I had hidden inside books on my bookshelf. Since a random discovery of money forgotten in one of my textbooks whilst in secondary school, I had formed the habit of placing a little cash in books—in times of plenty, for when I might need it. After many years, it finally came in handy.

I got into work fairly early so as not to attract unnecessary attention, although the few that saw me couldn't help asking why my eyes were so heavy and red. My response was simple: "I got robbed last night." With it being a client's office, I was mindful to still conduct myself in a professional manner, in spite of my personal woes. Stanley often came in early too, so I spoke to him privately, giving as much information about the incident as I could. Then, I requested the day off so I could focus on immediate tasks like informing my bank of the incident as my ATM card was in the bag, and filing a police report to cover everything else like my work IDs, drivers' license, and SIM card. I had already informed the client's reception to cancel the ID issued to me, so no one would be able to swipe it to gain access to their premises, and anyone who did so could be arrested immediately as it was definitely stolen. The next day was a weekend, so it was crucial to action everything that day, as there was no Saturday banking then and I couldn't afford the risk of the criminals misusing my identity or withdrawing the little funds I had left in the bank. Therefore, Stanley would have to cover any sessions for the day that I couldn't reschedule. This and the need to obtain his phone number and that of some other key colleagues were the main reasons I came into the office.

Once we concluded the work that he needed to handle on my behalf, Stanley gave me some cash to help with the running around. The bank was my first stop, but they wouldn't put a block on my account until I provided a police report, at least, since I had no form of identification on me. So, I went to the police station opposite my home—being the closest to the scene of the incident. Thankfully, the pay phone lady remembered me and proceeded to support me at the station, as the police were giving me a hard time about not reporting the incident immediately. She explained the state I was in when we met and how she had to give me a free phone call because I had no money. By leveraging her friendship with the officers, I was able to obtain the police report. In this also, I had cause to thank God. I wasn't sure how I would have coped with all of the trauma the interaction with the police was bringing on, especially when I had been trying all morning to keep my emotions under control. Mentally, I was still on the verge of insanity, so I was doing my best possible to get through the day and into the weekend when I could possibly have some brain capacity to reflect on all that had happened and to rest properly—before planning what to do next.

With the police report in hand, I went back to the bank. They cancelled the ATM and put a block on the account—I was not even allowed to take a dime out. From the bank, I met with Yuletide at his workshop. Hearing of the incident seemed to fill him with a sense of guilt since he had asked me to bring the cash. He explained that his wife had called about an issue with their child, so he had to leave immediately and forgot that I was expected in the workshop—a situation that seemed to have set off the chain reaction that resulted in me losing an entire month's salary, yet having no fixed car to show for it. Fixing the car was already going to set me back by about two months, cash flow speaking, so the loss just compounded things. I would need a loan to get started on the fix and cover my expenses that month—a salary advance or staff loan, which I had never asked for.

Thanks to the cash Stanley gave me, I was able to move around that weekend. I went to church and hoped to speak with Tosan, but he did not wait after the service. Normally, he would wait around with some of the other guys in his ushering department to pack up chairs, etc. whilst I was in the counting room—with other volunteers on the finance team—taking record of the cash received via offerings during service. The room was locked until counting was completed, all necessary documentation was signed by those present, and the total funds received were handed to the church secretary for safekeeping and subsequent payment into the church's bank account. It was usually a demanding few hours, taking cognisance of the fact that I would have been in church early to coordinate the choir and on occasion lead the prayers at the start of the service. So, it was always comforting to catch up with Tosan afterwards—we often discussed any and every thing.

On this Sunday, however, Tosan didn't wait behind, although I wished he had so we could talk through the incident. Also, the gift I ordered for his birthday was delivered as prearranged, while the cake was planned for the following Sunday—the day after his birthday—to enable him to share with his church team and other friends. I thought best to at least give Tosan the gift that Sunday and hoped that the gesture would let him know that I was still mindful of him despite all that was going on. Perhaps it would also serve as a peace offering for the midnight callout I made.

Since his sister's house was nearby, I walked there—fatigued though I was. My intention was to drop off the gift, knowing that she would definitely see him by his birthday, but I found him there. Seeing me, Tosan wasn't very receptive nor disposed to chatting, and didn't show any interest in knowing what had happened or how I was feeling. He had obviously told his sister of the incident because she offered her sympathies and some consolation, which was far more than my own friend did. He had simply collected the gift and walked away to play with his niece and nephews.

After a brief chat with his sister, I left. I went away fairly surprised by his attitude, because it was the first time that one of us would be going through a difficult time and the other was intentionally offering no support—emotionally, financially, spiritually, or whatever. While I tried to understand that the suddenness of the issues might have been a lot for him to handle, I struggled to understand how he could remain cold towards me and not even attempt to ask about my wellbeing. Though this hurt, I decided to put it aside as I didn't want to add any more stress—especially mental—to what was currently on my plate.

The week following the incident, I focused on securing a loan so that work could begin on my car and to enable me to cover ongoing expenses that could not be deferred. To minimise transportation costs, I took either a Danfo bus or hitched a ride. Though the latter was safer, it forced me to be reliant on other people's schedules and plans, which could change at short notice. So, getting my car back was tantamount to getting back my freedom of movement. In the meantime, my movements were restricted to work and church—Saturdays for choir rehearsals plus youth activities (if any), and Sundays for services. Any mid-week church activities and all other weekend events were firmly on hold. Also, that week, I was able to recover my SIM number but had no phone yet.

The company I worked with was a burgeoning start-up, so I had a close working relationship with the management team, who decided to provide me an equivalent of a month's salary as an interest-free loan rather than a salary advance. Repayments would be deducted at source over an agreed period—a huge blessing as it reduced the pressure that would have been on my finances. A check was issued since my bank account was still blocked, and I cashed it on the day I confirmed that Yuletide was at the workshop. *Once bitten…*, I thought.

Then came the Sunday after Tosan's birthday. The choir sitting area was at the front of the congregation, at the right-hand side of the pulpit. I was sitting in the front row that Sunday, when during service, I noticed the head usher wearing a shirt that had a notable semblance to the shirt I gave Tosan as his birthday gift. But I dismissed it, thinking he absolutely wouldn't do that. After the service, whilst in the locked room recording the finances, the cake was delivered to him because I couldn't be reached and it had his name on it. By the time we were done and came out, I caught the end of his celebration with others. I approached him, excitedly, to wish him a happy birthday, but again, Tosan's reception was cold. The most I got was a "thank you" for organising the cake, and he started to make his way out. I asked about the cake, hoping that he had saved some for me and his sister's family. Tosan replied that he had left it with the others to share as they deemed fit, because he wasn't interested in having any part of it and did not want to be carrying cake back to his sister's. Moreover, she was preparing a family meal for him and would likely have baked a cake too. Tosan's tone suggested that I wasn't invited for that. Not wanting to push any further because of the people there, I wished him well, and he left.

With the head usher, Mark, still around, I decided to ask about the shirt he was wearing.

"Brother Mark, that is a very nice shirt you have on."

"Thank you," he replied. Then he added, "Tosan gave it to me on Wednesday after service, saying it was given to him, but he didn't want it."

Mark carried on talking about the quality of the shirt and how he loved it, but my heart was breaking within me. I stilled my nerves and plastered a smile across my face, pretending to be interested or happy about Tosan's kind gesture to him. I left church broken-hearted. The most painful part was that I still owed a debt for the gifts, which was not my preferred choice, because of wanting to make this a special birthday for him. For the next two or so months, I would be paying for things that he did not use nor taste, and I didn't even get a piece of the cake for my troubles. Wow, I was hurt! *But now isn't the time to have the conversation with him*, I thought. I had more important things to focus on and was too emotionally unstable to have such a discussion. So, I kept quiet.

During the last week of April, things started to look up, as the mechanics began work on the car and were prioritising it, knowing all the pain surrounding it. Also, a friend gave me an old phone to use so I could at least make phone calls. It was one of those old models with the screen the size of a chewing gum packet; keypads designed for the true meaning of SMS (short message service), because my fingers were weary by the time I composed a simple text; and a ringtone that screeched like the house was on fire, so I just turned it to vibrate only. Still, I was grateful to have a means of being reached and reaching others. Somehow, taking one step at a time, I was starting to find ways to cope with my new reality.

Saturday, April 29 was a friend's birthday, and he was having a party at his house—near to where Tosan lived. One of my girlfriends picked me up and was going to drop me off back home, which allowed me to relax and enjoy the party. It was my first "timeout" since things started to unravel. Naturally, Tosan was at the party helping out and showed no signs of there being an issue, even though we didn't get the chance to interact.

When the party started to die down late evening, Tosan asked to speak with me outside, which I obliged. We decided to walk to his room so as to have some privacy. In the room, he sat on the floor, while I sat on the edge of his bed, looking around and commending the progress that he had made with redecorating the room. I knew the state of it when he first moved in and was there to help out with the cleaning plus fixing of a few things—I like DIY. Then, I asked what he wanted to speak about, vaguely expecting it to explain his recent behaviour but was absolutely unprepared for the things he decided to voice.

Tosan started by saying how unhappy he was that I rang him at midnight asking for my house keys. Then I bought him gifts, which made him feel pressured about me wanting us to be in a relationship. Without giving me much of a chance to speak, he went on to cite some other examples of when he felt pressured, like when I asked him to join me in meeting my mum who had come into Lagos with ladies from her church for a wedding and were returning to Àkúré the same day—which he declined, by the way.

On Tosan went, each word decking a deeper blow to my heart. I had to do all I could to maintain a facial expression that assured him that I was intently listening whilst fighting back the tears that had started to well up in my eyes—the pain being that my actions were misunderstood and this conversation could not be happening at a worse time. Then he said that he wasn't interested in being in a love relationship with me, nor was he ready to "settle down," although he still valued our friendship. Hearing him say "I am not yet ready" reminded me of my mum's words: a guy is only not ready for you because when he meets the person he is ready for, he will do whatever it takes to keep her. That realisation tore me apart deep within my soul.

The final daggers to my heart happened when Tosan asked, "Or have I ever asked you out?"

Ah, I have never felt so cheap in my life! I lifted up my eyes to the ceiling to avoid the tears rolling out of them, shook my head, and said, "No."

Nothing else he said afterwards was heard, because I started to feel a very sharp knife being plunged into my heart in repeated motions. My heart was palpitating with each thrust of the knife, and my body started to quiver, so I rocked back and forth to hide the pain and kept my face tilted upwards, as I was determined not to breakdown in tears in his presence. After Tosan was done speaking, I sat quietly for a few seconds to get the tears back into my eye sockets; that day, I realised the eyes are able to suck back tears because it all went back in. When I had managed to keep all emotions hidden away, I thanked him for letting me know where I stood with him and asked to take my leave.

Walking back to the main house where the party was, the tears began to flow, and I felt like the earth should open up to swallow me whole because I wasn't sure how I could live with the sharp pain now threatening to suffocate me. Approaching the house, I momentarily got myself together and went straight to the person giving me the ride back home to tell her that I needed to leave. Thankfully, she was ready too, so we left. When I got home, I wept.

The pain I felt was less about what was said but the who. I felt betrayed. But most of all, I felt rejected. I wept and I slept. Church was the next day. I half-hoped that the dawn of a new day would help take the pain away. I couldn't be more wrong.

Sunday, I went through the motions, performing my duties and focusing on the tasks at hand. I made all efforts to stop my brain from thinking about any of my woes, because I was starting to feel like one that had been cursed. After counting the offering and we had unlocked the door, a few of us girls were chatting with some other people, who had come from churches within our catchment area to meet with the church secretary; it was normal for the last Sunday of the month to provide a summary report of accounts, etc.

Standing in a semicircle, I was in the middle of a few people when Tosan came into the room. He started to greet everyone by shaking hands with them, starting with the person closest to the door. Putting on a smile and wanting to relate as "just friends," I put out my hand, but he skipped me and went on to the next person, as if I didn't exist. Then came the knife-thrust feeling in my heart again. Of course, people took notice, and I just kept my head down in shame to avoid contact with anyone else's eyes.

When the crowd dispersed, one of my girlfriends who had been at the party the day before asked me, "What is going on with you two?"

I replied, "Let's just say that I overstepped my boundaries."

I chose not to disclose anything more because it was my cross to bear, and I wasn't feeling like trusting anyone with my emotions at that point. I also thought that being the one who had been in the church the longest and already having friends there, it was better for me to take all of the blame and deal with any shame or mockery that came with it. Tosan was still getting to know people, and if I exposed details of what had happened, they were likely to look at him differently and could react in manners that would make him uncomfortable. No matter how bad he had made me feel, I didn't want that for him. Neither did I see how dishonouring him would make me feel any better, so why should we both "lose out." Although our friendship had begun to collapse, I chose to still protect his reputation for the sake of what we once were.

I also made a conscious decision to forgive Tosan for his actions, which made me feel like a nonentity, especially when he chose to publicly shame me. He may never have asked me out, but I knew I most certainly didn't deserve the treatment he dealt. I recalled that my feelings towards Tosan grew by reason of his actions, especially when he kissed me on the lips on a few occasions. Being both single and long-time friends, I took no action to stop him, thinking it could work out. Perhaps I should have asked what his intentions were right from the beginning. Though my longing to be married probably heightened my need for him, I knew that I would never have crossed the line of friendship had Tosan not previously acted in a manner that suggested we could be more. So, I felt really wronged to have been thrown under, and in a manner that robbed me of any form of the dignity that I had left. Therefore, the choice to forgive him was a deliberate and conscious decision. Doing so immediately was mainly because I am a Christian, remembering that I have also been forgiven much by God. Of course, some weeks later, when I was able to collect my thoughts, I told Tosan what happened from my point of view and how I felt about the manner in which he handled everything, stressing that I had already forgiven him—and he apologised. But forgiving him immediately after things went south helped me get on the road of healing and stopped me from becoming bitter, angry, or jealous about it all. Instead, I was able to turn my eyes to the right Person—Jesus—that could help me through what I was facing.

Imagine that in one month, I lost everything I had previously held dear, things that provided only a false sense of security, as I was now realising—money, car, love, human respect, trusted relationships, and so on. Things happened in such quick succession, I felt tried like Job in the Bible—though my losses were nothing compared to what he lost—taking consolation in the lesson that he still sought God. The pain of the losses was real, and I cannot overestimate the hurt that I endured for many months and years afterwards on the road to healing. But the events were an awakening that caused me to dig deep to understand where my hope truly lies. I decided to turn and fix my gaze on the only Person who wasn't leaving me and still held me close, even when I didn't have the strength to hold on to Him. His name is Jesus.

If you do not yet know Jesus or are going through such a tough time that you wonder where He is, let me take a moment to encourage you to call on His name because He is right near you. That emptiness in your soul can only be satisfied by Jesus, and only He can keep you through whatever phase you are in, to bring total healing and restoration of all that may have been lost. I pray that you find solace in Him today, as I did and still do.

In my pain, there were many times, especially on Saturday mornings when I didn't have work or church activities to focus on, that I just stared into space feeling dejected. Sometimes the feeling of a sharp knife being thrust into my heart would send shockwaves of pain via the same vein in my right palm through to my heart—having been triggered by listening to another's tale of their pain or watching a movie where someone is rejected or treated unfairly. Like a robot, I went through daily life, focusing on whatever was at hand without exposing the real turmoil within. At work, it was all about the client and project, while at church, my attention was on the teenagers during the Youth Fellowship or choir during our rehearsals and ministrations. I made efforts to be present with people if I needed to pray with them or provide counsel about something, because I still strongly believed in God and His Word, even though my personal life seemed to be in shambles. The Gumel experience had taught me that God remains God and His Word remains true irrespective of my personal circumstances. Therefore, if I needed a solution to anything, I was better off running to Him than staying away or wasting time blaming Him or anyone else. Though I was deeply hurting, I endeavoured to trust in God and keep serving others (through my work and in church), knowing that my healing would come someday.

Momentary consolation often came in a song, so whenever I was alone and drifting in thoughts that did nothing but put me down, I would sing songs that reminded me of God's greatness, faithfulness, and love for me. Then one Saturday morning, as I sang, I noticed a little bird land on my windowsill, hopping and turning around as if doing a dance. It was a colourful bird which caught my eye, so I stopped singing and moved near the window to look more closely at this beauty—with only the glass louvres and window net standing between us. As I moved closer, the bird didn't fly away, but it had stopped chirping and dancing. After admiring the beautiful creature up close, I moved back to sit on my bed facing the window and continued my singing, paying little attention to the bird. As I sang a few lines, the bird started chirping and dancing again. So, I stopped, and it stopped.

Then I realised what was going on—the bird seemed to be chirping along with my tune. *How can this be possible?* I wondered. To explore this further, I carried on singing, and the bird started to chirp and dance.

After a few hours of singing, about midday, I had to stop so as to get ready for choir rehearsals and the other activities of the day. When the bird realised that I had stopped for real this time, it flew away. I broke out in deep-hearted laughter at what just happened; it was my first cheer with a true emotional response to anything in a long time.

The next Saturday, I started to sing, as was my habit, and to my utter surprise, the same bird as the week before came by chirping and dancing on my windowsill. The same thing happened the week after, and the next, and the next. Then I noticed that the bird started to come at the same time each Saturday morning, even when I hadn't started singing. It just sat on the windowsill, as if waiting for something. When I saw it, I knew what it came for, so I would sing, and its response was the same as before. Somehow, I started to see God in this—that He would use even a bird to cheer me up at a time I felt so alone and dejected. It was an amazing feeling to know this side of God and to have His eternal love expressed towards me in this manner. Soon, my rendezvous with the bird became so personal that I often avoided any engagement that meant I wouldn't be home between the hours of 10:00 a.m. and 12:00 p.m. especially. I looked forward to our meet.

This went on till about October that year, when I travelled to the United States of America on holiday. On my return in November, the bird had stopped coming though I carried on the habit of singing. I guess it must have come a few times and found that I was away. However, I will never forget the experience or how it made me feel. Finding something to genuinely smile about, which made me think beyond myself or my woes at a point when the problems seemed overwhelming (about May), gave me hope in the midst of the storm and was the first glimmer of light that I saw, which further encouraged me to focus my attention on God. It reminded me that God was with me even in the troubles—using a seemingly "foolish" and simple thing of the world to bring me great joy.

MORAL —

Most times, God's help comes in ways and forms that we can never imagine. The key is to be open and receive His love response in the perfect way that He sends it. If we only look for His response in the way we want it or always expect the spectacular, we will miss the still, small-looking answers He sends in the course of everyday life, which often hold the actual solutions we need.

About the end of May or early June, the repair work on my car was finished. I was excited when I got the call to come pick up my old buddy. She had been fitted with a new engine, radiator, windscreen, brakes, bonnet, tyres, and air conditioning (AC), to name the biggest changes. Not only was she new on the inside, her outside look had also changed, as she now spotted a teal colour with a gloss finish in place of the original red colour. When I saw the car at the workshop, it was glowing. Though the changes may not have been to the *Pimp My Ride* standards, it definitely looked pimped. When I got into it to test drive, ensuring that the alignments had been correctly set before leaving the workshop, it felt so comfortable to drive, and the steering felt even smoother than before, like that of an auto car. I had the AC on full blast, and for the first time, it was actually blowing cool air such that I had to turn it down. Though the final cost of repair was over the original estimate, I felt like the job done was worth the wait and cost. I was happy that I chose not to cut corners but asked for it to be fitted with the best parts, since she was getting an overhaul by reason of the accident. "What is worth doing, is worth doing well," my mum always says. I was glad at the outcome. To me, this was a brand-new car!

Barely a week after getting the car back, I was cruising in it on my way back home—windows wound up, AC chilling, and music pumping—when I heard an audible voice say, "Give Me the car."

"Ehn! Car that I just got back!" I retorted.

After everything I suffered and the debts that were still being paid, I could not reason how this could be God. It sounded like some enemy that didn't want me to enjoy anything good, so I bound the devil very, very well.

On getting home a few minutes later, I heard the voice say again to my heart, "I want the car." This time, I recognised the gentleness of the voice, but more importantly, a peace that came with it. Of course, I wasn't happy about it, so I thought to discuss things with God—perhaps there was something else I could give. I sat down in the room, stilled myself, and began a dialogue with God, which contained more questions than anything else.

MORAL —

God is not afraid or weary of being asked questions. In fact, He would rather you express your thoughts so He can teach you His ways and show you His love, than you relate with Him out of an unfounded fear or, worse, arrogance.

I asked God several questions. "Why does it have to be the car? Why now that I have spent everything I had to restore it?" God answered each question. Bottom line, He wanted my heart. The car, at the time, encapsulated my material wealth, while my attitude towards it revealed the fact that I was still attached to or dependent on things that could be acquired. This was a surprise for me, because I didn't realise until then how much value I still placed in "things."

My mind flashed back to an encounter I had about 2002 or 2003, before meeting Dylan. I had returned home late from work and was so tired, I slept off on the sofa still in my work clothes. Then, in what seemed more like a trance than a dream, an angel came to me and said, "Come, I have been asked to show you something."

Standing up from the sofa, I realised that it was my spirit that got up, because I noticed that my body was still asleep and laid on the sofa with feet on the floor. Staring at my body and wondering why there was a fully conscious me standing while another me was fast asleep, the angel took me by the hand.

In a split second, we were standing at a gate. Looking to the left and right of the gate, there was no visible end. The most captivating thing was the strong light that emanated from the inside and covered the entire place— the warm glow radiated through the gate such that I couldn't see what was inside no matter how hard I tried to peer in.

Then, the angel said to me, "You are at Heaven's gates."

It was an incredibly beautiful sight. Excited to see what was inside, I told the angel to open the gates so we could go in.

The response—"No, this is as far as I have been asked to show you. If you go in, you will die on earth, and it is not yet your time."

Oh, I couldn't care less for earth. "Why would I want to go back to earth with all the suffering there?" I responded. "There is nothing on earth compared to this beauty, and I would rather stay here."

The angel replied, "It is not yet your time. Go back and remember what you have been shown."

With that, I was snapped back into my body on the sofa. I woke up with great clarity of what I saw and was disappointed to be back in a body that felt tired, with the thought that I would have to go into work the next morning to face another tough day. Aside from the vision I had seen, I had this overwhelming feeling that absolutely nothing here on earth was worth giving up Heaven for. There was nothing so precious that couldn't be left behind. After all, I came with nothing but God's gifts and would leave with nothing.

Thereafter, the concept of death no longer conjured fear in me, with the understanding that it was the "rite of passage" to that beautiful and glorious place that I saw. What mattered most was to use those gifts God put in me to make a difference on earth for the benefit of mankind. So, I started to make a conscious effort to do everything I got involved with in a manner that pleased God, while being aware that it wouldn't be the end of the world if I lost anything that could be acquired here.

Thinking that I was fully living with this consciousness, I was surprised when God pointed out to me that day in 2006 that I was still attached to material things. Meaning, I had lost focus on how I should really perceive things that can be acquired. I thought that I only saw them as necessities that improved the quality of life, but God who sees the heart revealed to me that I hadn't yet attained a mindset that wasn't controlled by my possessions. It dawned on me that this was a consciousness I would have to consciously remind myself of and use as a compass to regularly check the state of my heart.

God made me realise that though I said and thought that I was trusting Him, I was actually mostly working things out for myself and reliant on what I had to feel "comfortable." As He spoke, I fell silent, recognising that I had been approaching the whole issue wrong. Though God was okay with me fixing the car, enjoying it, and looking forward to the future with hope, it was not okay that my hope was hinged on the restoration of the car or on a time when I would have paid all debts and have some money to spend freely again. I realised that this wasn't about the car, but more that God was pruning me by cutting away things in my character that were not aligned to His will. In that moment of understanding, I surrendered the car! The pruning process is never comfortable, but one I have to yield to if I truly want to be God's child, allowing Him to teach and discipline me as necessary, like any good parent will. Right there, I decided that I was going to drive the car to church on Sunday and leave it there. Taking public transport and hitching rides might be my new reality for however long it took, but I would do so without grumbling or wishing that I had a car. I would choose to be happy, knowing that God was with me and was always looking out for me.

When Sunday came, I didn't take many things with me, knowing that I would be laying the car at the altar. On the way, I prayed and thanked God—with tears in my eyes—for the opportunity to be trained by Him, and to be able to give Him what was my best at the time. Please note, this was a sacrificial but freewill offering, and I knew exactly why I was giving it. So, though God specifically asked me to do this, I spent the days leading up to the Sunday ensuring that my heart was in the right place and I was joyful about having the car to give—God loves a cheerful giver. At church, I placed the keys into an offering envelope and blessed it—such that when the baskets came around during the service, I let it go.

THINK ON THIS...

Being able to rejoice and feel like you are missing nothing, even when you have little possessions, is an indication of where your hope and trust lie. Nothing that can be acquired should be able to control the quality of your thoughts and life. What is in vogue today will become archaic tomorrow—that's how the world rolls! So make it a regular habit to detox yourself of any attachments to *stuff*. Practice being open-handed, remembering that you came into the world with nothing and you will leave with absolutely nothing.

RETURN OF THE MIKE

Early in 2006, I booked a round-trip holiday to the US starting at the end of October—which I normally didn't do because work commitments could change my plans at short notice. When the issues arose in April, greatly impacting my cash flow for several months, I realised that it was a blessing in disguise to have planned the holiday and fully paid for the non-refundable tickets much in advance. Otherwise, I would never have been able to afford the travel costs, which would then mean I wouldn't get to use the two-year visitors' visa that was being issued for a second time and, more importantly, would have missed out on a much-needed holiday. Being that it would be my first time in the US, I had arranged to stay with Oma, a former secondary school mate living in Washington, DC, first, then go to New York to visit with Kenny, an ex-colleague and friend, before returning via the UK (which I had been to a few times before) to Lagos. With all the calamity that befell me, I actually forgot about the trip. I had just tried to live a day at a time, until the encounter with the bird, which was one of my early signs of hope and a reminder that I had something exciting to look forward to.

One day, I remembered that Mike, my childhood best friend, actually lived in the US. I didn't know exactly where, having lost touch for many years. Feeling excited at the possibility of seeing him again, I took to the internet to search for him, not knowing if it was even possible to find someone that way. Typing in his full name, a number of matches came up. At that time, people's phone numbers and month of birth were equally shown—the list had only one that matched is month of birth in May, so I jotted down the number. Later that evening, I called the number, half holding my breath and without a plan of what to say should it actually go through. Then it began to ring.

A man picked it up and said, "Hello."

I paused for a while wondering how to explain myself, until the voice came again saying, "Hellooo."

Lest they drop the phone, I quickly said, "Hello. Can I please speak to Mike?"

"Mike is at work," the man said.

Hearing that got me excited, because it meant I had the right number.

Then the man asked, "May I know who is speaking?"

"Yétúndé," I said, mindful to mention the name Mike would remember me by.

"Oh, Yétúndé. This is Mike's dad," he replied in a very familiar tone. Then he added, "Mike has just moved to his own apartment. Do you have his mobile number?"

I replied, "No, sir," completely surprised that his dad still remembered me.

Without wasting time, Mike's dad started to dictate the mobile number, so I quickly grabbed a pen to take it down. Once done, I heaved a sigh of relief and said, "Thank you, sir."

He said, "Take care of yourself," and dropped the call.

I paused for a moment so I could fully take in what had just happened. The last communication I had from Mike was in 1995, when he dropped off a card and gifts for my sixteenth birthday with my mum. Eleven years later, I almost couldn't believe that I was about to be reconnected with him. Without further ado, I punched in the digits and dialled the mobile number.

At the other end, Mike's voice came on the call. He said, "Hello," in a tone used when one doesn't know the caller and is unsure whether they have done the right thing by answering the call. For me, however, I was having a magical moment because I couldn't believe that what seemed like a simple thought to search for him had actually yielded positive results.

Now smiling at my end, I asked, "Do you know who is speaking?"

To which he replied, "No." He sounded cautious, as if not to annoy the other person by not knowing who they were when he was expected to.

To put him out of his misery, I said, "It's Yétúndé," adding, "People now call me Modúpẹ́."

"Modúpẹ́?" he asked, still wondering who it was.

I called my full name as he would have known it when we were in primary school. Instantly, Mike let out an excited scream. When he collected himself, he started to ask many questions in quick succession, so I just paused, knowing that he needed time for it all to sink in. It had been a very long time since we had heard each other's voices.

At some point, Mike asked how I got his number. So, I relayed the story, starting from how I decided to search for him on the internet down to the conversation with his dad.

Then Mike said, "Dad must have thought you were my cousin, Yétúndé," which totally explained why he had sounded very familiar with me.

It worked in my favour, I thought. Had he not felt comfortable, Mike's dad definitely wouldn't have given me Mike's mobile number, and I might never have had the opportunity to speak with him since he no longer lived with his parents. Everything came together, and I was just glad to be reconnected with my long-lost friend.

After a few moments of catching up, Mike mentioned that he was at work and would call me later that day to catch up properly. So, we dropped the call. It was about 11:00 p.m. that same day when Mike called back, as promised. After exchanging pleasantries, we started by catching up on the last decade of each other's lives—all the way from the university we went to, courses studied, what life was like, and ending in the present day. We spoke for hours that night, into the early hours of the morning for me. Though I was enjoying our catch-up, we had to call it a night because I had to be at work in a few hours and hadn't gotten any sleep. We promised to speak again later that day before saying "Goodnight." Oh, it was truly a good night for me, because I went to bed very happy.

Thereafter, Mike and I spoke every day for at least an hour. Somehow, we always had something to talk about. During our conversations, we touched on past relationships and realised that we both had recently gone through heartbreaks, and that we were both currently single. Since I already mentioned the fact that I would be visiting the US in October, we decided that it was worth meeting in person. Well, there was only one glitch—I was currently in debt because of my predicaments, which I had told him of, and would barely be recovering from that by the time of the holiday. So, any money I was able to pull together would likely be to cover my expenses and a little shopping during the trip. Thankfully, I would be staying with friends all through, so there was no accommodation cost added. Therefore, I was going to settle for just having phone calls with Mike while in the US, but he insisted on meeting face to face. He offered to pay for my flights from Washington, DC, to his state of residence and to New York thereafter, so as to keep within the roundtrip ins and outs that I already had. So, I obliged, and within a few days of discussing the dates that I could visit him, Mike sent me the electronic tickets. Receiving those tickets brought on a new level of anticipation and excitement because it solidified the plans to meet up, especially as we had discussed the option to wait until we met in person to decide if we still felt something for the other and would want to be in a love relationship. Suddenly, my plans to visit America went from being a simple opportunity to use my visa before it expired again, to a hope of finding love again. *Were things to work out between us*, I thought, *it would be an interesting story to tell in the future.* So eagerly, I started to look forward to October.

Before long, it was October, and the day of my holiday round trip finally came. I was going away for twenty working days. First stop was the UK for a few days, to celebrate the birthday of a friend from Uni and to meet her family, before heading out to the US. My journey to the US was not without drama, but the excitement of "Coming to America" overshadowed everything else. Finally, we touched down in Washington, DC, and I looked forward to the start of something new.

Oma and her cousin were at the airport to pick me up, which was very kind. They made me feel welcome right away—just as her mum did when we got to the house. I was going to be with Oma for about a week before heading to see Mike. They made it a really exciting time. Oma took me sightseeing as well as visiting some other former schoolmates that lived in the area, which made it all the more fun.

Using Oma's phone, since non-residents couldn't purchase a SIM card, I informed Mike of my arrival in the country and reminded him of my flight itinerary to his end. About a day or two before leaving Washington, DC, I called Mike to finalise the plan for him to pick me up at the airport, so I would know when to expect him. During the conversation, I sensed that he was distracted and asked if there was anyone with him.

"Yes, my girlfriend is here."

"You have a girlfriend?" His response absolutely caught me off guard. "I thought we agreed not to get into another relationship until we met in person to decide."

He replied, "Well, it just happened."

At that, I simply reiterated the pickup time discussed and dropped the call. My heart sunk. I clutched my chest in an attempt to hide the intensity of the pain from Oma as the sensation of a knife being thrust in and out of my heart had returned. Oma asked what happened. Like one who was now getting used to being let down in love, I answered, "He has a girlfriend."

Clearly hearing the disappointment in my voice, Oma asked if I still wanted to go, as she was prepared to host me for the period we originally planned. I told her that I would go, if only just to visit with an old friend. She reiterated a concern she had once expressed about me going alone to a different state to meet with someone that I knew as a boy and hadn't been in touch with for over a decade, because, as she explained, "People change, and lots of people in America can be wildly unpredictable." However, I allayed her fears, saying that despite the disappointment, he still seemed to be the same boy at heart. Going by our conversations in the past few months, I wasn't worried at all about being safe around him. Well, she had his phone number, because I used her phone to call him. If she didn't hear from me when I was there, then she could call the police. We laughed about it, but deep inside I was hurting.

The day came, and I bade goodbye to Oma and her family. Unlike how I felt when coming to America and the previous few days, the excitement had dissipated. I didn't know what to expect anymore. As the flight drew closer to the final destination, I wondered if I had made the right decision by leaving Washington, DC. The flight landed behind schedule, so I hurriedly cleared security, picked up my baggage, went outside in the cold, and voila, there was no Mike. Thinking he might be somewhere within the premises, I went back into the arrival area to find a pay phone. On calling him, he was still at his girlfriend's place and had lost track of time. So, I told him where to find me and began the wait.

By the time he showed up, well over an hour later, I was extremely tired, hungry, and generally irritable. Thankfully, he brought me something to eat, so I had that on the way to his house. While I was glad to finally see him, the events leading up to that moment had stolen every bit of excitement that I had imagined would be the case when we saw each other again after over a decade.

A few minutes after we got in and I sat down, his girlfriend came in. I quickly realised that it was to "mark her territory" rather than a visit to make me welcome. It was the first and last time she saw me throughout my ten-day visit. She obviously must have heard of my friendship with her boyfriend and made sure I was clear about whose he was—like, ensuring that he slept at her house most of the nights, even though I was in the guest room, and that he spent the days he was off duty with her rather than with me. But for his brother and sister-in-law, who frequently checked on me and took me out, it might have been an overall miserable visit. I spent most of the days indoors, as there wasn't a good public transport system to allow me to get about on my own, and was mostly alone in the apartment. Although he made sure I was comfortable in the house and had whatever was needed, I didn't see much of him, which was slightly disappointing because the last remaining reason for flying out all that way was to spend time with a long-lost friend. The few quality times we had were on the day he took me around town and drove to the river that marked the state's border with Canada, and the night before I left.

On the Saturday before Thanksgiving, the night before I left, we reminisced about primary school and our time in Àkúré. It reminded me of why I always enjoyed his company and how we became friends in the first place. We chatted for a few good hours and well into the night; singing and laughing at various childhood memories—it was as if the night should never end. Like little kids who never want to be apart from their friends, we decided to spend the night in the same room. He fell asleep almost immediately after getting into the bed, but I couldn't sleep. I watched him as he slept, and silent tears streamed down my face. How I wish we had spent more time together, even if it was just to enjoy his friendship. Alas, it had taken up to my last night of the holiday for us to have some quality time. So, I started to miss him. I also realised that I was falling in love with him again. Although everything in me wanted to snuggle up with him, I constrained myself because he had a girlfriend. As a matter of personal principle, which I had so far maintained, I did not "touch" or covet what was not mine and I did not fight over men. So, I would have to "suck up" my feelings and move on, no matter how hard that weighed on me. It was the last thought on my mind by the time I finally fell asleep, in the early hours of Sunday morning.

When the morning came, we discussed the potential of moving my flight by a day so we could spend more time together that Sunday, as he was off duty. However, I concluded that it wasn't worth it. To my mind, one more day together was not going to make him mine. I had gone through a process of accepting "my fate" during the night and couldn't go through that again. It certainly was a game I wasn't willing to play with my heart, nor his, or that of his girlfriend for that matter. It would have been better if he never went into that relationship before I came, so we could freely explore the possibilities. That morning, he had been exceptionally kind, generous, and helpful with me getting ready, so I could tell that he was missing me too. So while my heart wanted to be with him, my common sense advised otherwise. Therefore, I still left for New York that day. Saying goodbye at the airport was really difficult for me, but I did all I could not to show it by keeping up a rather jovial appearance. Once I had checked in and he left, I was overtaken by sadness, disappointment, and a deep sense of loss. I could barely eat on the flight; I just stared out the window aimlessly. As I reminisced on our time together, I knew that we could never again be anything more than friends, which was somewhat heartbreaking. Nevertheless, I will always treasure the memories shared and time spent together.

MORAL —

"Common sense" is relative—shaped by cultures, experiences, and ways of thinking each individual has been exposed to or cultivated. Were it truly common, we would all think and act alike. Hence, before judging or advising the actions of others, be curious and patient enough to understand the thought process that led them to that point. In there will likely be the lie to unplug or the lesson to encourage.

It was late evening by the time we landed in New York, and to make matters worse, one of my bags didn't arrive. Being told that the next few flights departing from the same airport could bring the luggage, I waited for several hours to no avail. So, I decided to keep the other bags in overnight storage to go find Kenny's place. That wait meant that I could only spend a few hours catching up with my friend, Kenny, as I arrived at his place much later than planned. I had lost my way trying to find Wall Street, which shockingly, people (including a policeman) couldn't provide directions to. I mean, this was supposed to be the famous Wall Street! I couldn't sleep much that night, this time wondering about my missing luggage and flight back to London. Early in the morning, before it became busy, Kenny saw me off to the subway and bade me farewell.

Back at the airport, I got the disappointing news that none of the flights that landed during the night brought in my luggage, so it was now being considered as lost. This got me very worried because there were a lot of valuable items in the bag and no lock on it, in compliance with the prevailing airport security policy. As I needed to board my flight to London, I was asked to provide a statement describing the key items in my luggage and my forwarding addresses both in the UK and Nigeria, adding that I had only two days in the UK before returning to Lagos. Thankfully, the bag was delivered intact to the UK, the day before my return to Nigeria.

At the end of the trip, I had this overwhelmingly sad feeling of unfulfillment, largely due to the build-up of expectations. I had started out very hopeful and thinking it was going to be a very exciting holiday, but unfortunately had way more low moments than exciting ones. The one big question now rampaging my mind was if I would ever find love again. Although all hope seemed lost, I wasn't ready yet to give up on love—all because it was in my plan to be married, though the initial target age of twenty-five was now long gone. The more I pondered, the farther back my mind went in recalling my experiences. I recalled the calamities of April that brought about the feelings of dejection, and other events since then that had led to that very moment of feeling unfulfilled. In that place, I also remembered the lesson not to be attached to "things"—*perhaps people should be added to the list*, I thought.

I concluded on two things—as the Bible teaches. One, it is natural for human beings to fail us or not meet up to our expectations; hence, our trust should ultimately be in God (Jeremiah 17:5–8). Whilst I wouldn't give up on love, I realised that it wouldn't come the way I had previously imagined nor at the time I planned for it to happen, so I needed to start trusting God in this area too. (Though I still wrongly believed that finding the love of a man was the way to heal that pain of rejection which I tangibly felt in my heart, not realising that it was pushing me to desperation, which never augurs well.) Two, the "things" of life are all temporal, and when critically appraised, are "Utterly meaningless! Everything is meaningless" (Ecclesiastes 1:2 NIV). Therefore, one truly needs to learn the act of letting go. It feels better and more fulfilling when you do the giving away than to have them taken from you. But, to do the former successfully, you have to constantly remind yourself that God is the Source and the One who gives good gifts in the first place—that they may be a blessing to you and those around you, not to become our masters nor instruments of pride or oppression of other people.

TIME TO MOVE

Turning my attention to what was at hand—to pack my bags because I had been assigned to work on a national transformation program based in Abuja and was resuming there on Monday. I got the call a little over a week before my return from holiday, informing me that the team had been constituted and work had begun in earnest. They were willing to hold my position till I returned from holiday, on the condition that I resumed immediately after. Of course, I embraced it wholeheartedly; it was a huge opportunity involving international organisations and teams from various technical and cultural backgrounds. I had a significant role to play, so there was value to be added by me and to me. Plus, the timing was right to have a change in environment to help me refocus on my plans going forward. And refocus I did, but not in ways I had thought.

The program was an incredibly challenging experience in all ramifications, mainly because a number of workstreams were dependent on my deliverables, making them core to the achievement of the program objectives—with little room for mistakes. With this came the (bad) habit of working late into the night just to meet the rather tight timelines. The most stressful was one occasion when the client gave a press release that contained timelines for completion of certain activities across the country, without prior consultation with the team. This resulted in a number of us whose workstreams were impacted having to work three straight days, getting barely an hour's sleep each day, to ensure the requisites to meet the publicised timelines were in place. Tough days!

Though entitled to one weekend trip in every two, I barely got the chance to return to Lagos once a month. But besides the program and how busy things were, that one-year-plus period of working and living in Abuja hotels was instrumental to the opening of a new chapter in my life. Unknown to me then, everything that had been happening was actually preparing me for and getting me to the mental space that allowed me to be open-minded for what God wanted to do with me next. God used that time of being isolated from my "normal" circle and environment to teach me certain things that developed me in a different but more mature way of thinking and approaching life. My personal plans were cumulating in "settling," which He not only exposed but made me realise that His plans were far greater, and I was just about to begin living with purpose.

God started to address and show me that He was interested in building my personality—that is, the combination of all those characteristics and qualities that make me a unique individual—the core things that define my character as an individual. So much that I knew about me were things like my strengths and weaknesses, interests, and plans for various aspects of life, but never had I peeled or even known to peel layers that address things like attitude, perception of life, how I reason and respond to challenges, and the "why" of the things I do. My parents raised me to know that I am a unique person—just as everyone else is—with certain abilities that help me contribute "my bit" to society in a way that only I can. So, I generally focused on being better in my area of strengths and how I applied them, but never did quite realise that there was more that went on in the background—the combination of which constituted "who I am." God was very interested in that "whole" me.

One of the big things that I realised was how emotionally unstable I had become. Being alone in Abuja, living in hotels, and working long hours initially provided a good mask for the underlying problem. In my continued pursuit of finding love, which wasn't scarce as a single lady working in a male-dominated environment, I had a few dates—with guys my age, younger (though unknowingly), and older. I made a few "compromises" just to make it easier for them—as people advised to not have "high" standards—yet, I was still struggling to have a real connection with any and I couldn't understand why. Instead of being in love, the harder I tried, the more frustrated I became. Of course, I passed the frustration on to whoever was in my life at the time. Finally, I decided to take a step back to understand what was wrong by speaking to God about my problems. More like, I prayed, I cried, I shouted, I begged, and I constantly asked God, "What is wrong with me? Why can't I feel a thing for anyone?" But I didn't seem to get an answer. That was until I caught a Joyce Meyer message on the cable channel. She spoke of her battle, having been sexually abused by her dad and subsequently transferring that brokenness to others around her. It was an eyeopener, because I hadn't heard anyone on TV, especially a pastor, openly discuss past hurts and make the connection to how it could impact those around us if we don't take time to heal. That message, and others that I started to ardently listen to, were my answered prayers! Surely, God answers our prayers, although His "how" is often very different from ours.

Listening to Joyce, I realised that I was still driving myself by a goal I set (not God), and when things didn't happen to plan, I was frustrated. Magnified by the losses and hurts of 2006, I had become a walking emotional wreck who used the busyness of work and other activities to drown the aches in my heart. Being able to admit my brokenness to myself and knowing that I didn't know where to begin the fix allowed God to begin the work of healing that I so desperately needed. Therefore, I made the conscious decision to stop dating so as to put an end to the vicious cycle of hurts (being hurt, I was only hurting others) till I tangibly felt relief in my heart and mind. Though it took a few good years for that peculiar knife-thrusting pain to completely heal, the journey began with this conscious decision in 2007. By removing my attention from getting married by a certain age or time period, or the need to be in a relationship, I could focus on what God was doing in me to make me whole—a complete human being in Christ Jesus.

God exposed the things I had unconsciously put on hold simply because I wanted to meet the man first so we could define what we wanted together (good as that may be). He also showed me how I had allowed my desire for a partner to define who I was rather than Christ and His Word. He made me understand that I am complete in Christ and so also should be the person that I get with. We are not two halves trying to make a whole, as is sometimes taught about unions of two people in love. Each one ought to be separately whole. When each party walks in God's purpose for their lives, our unions could have a far greater impact and be a blessing to others. God started to help me see that I could remain confident in Him and His purposes for me, with or without anyone else in the picture—providing a solid foundation for the what and the why of the relationships that I would get into.

MORAL —

Personalities can and should improve over time, having been founded on core principles that enable us to maintain a stable, and more importantly, a fulfilled life. However, it doesn't often get the attention needed because it is so deep in our core that it takes a conscious effort to lift the lid to reveal what is buried within. And sometimes, we are so scared of what we might find or what might be exposed to others that we blatantly carry on through life without ever attaining a real sense of fulfilment. God is the most delicate and trusted Person to allow into this space. It's certainly not comfortable letting Him confront beliefs about who we are at the core (how we conduct life and in what we find purpose) or our prejudices (the lens with which we perceive, interpret, and interact with our environment). Having Him help us constantly rebuild our thoughts based on the principles of His Word is the only way to find a true and sure sense of identity, no matter the challenges that life hurls at us. God is keen on all of us having the right sense of our identities. It is only God, in whose image that we are made, that can help each one of us see that clearly. So, ask Him today to help you.

Armed with this knowledge, I started again on the process of letting go of the reins in various areas of my life. Gradually, I created room for God to take the lead so He could give the right definition to them, while I learnt to go with His plans—not mine. This saw me doing less of the detailed "planning for the future" based on my desires and looking more to God to ask, "What is the plan?" Hear me right, this isn't propagating living aimlessly but to develop a habit of setting your goals based on God's directions. This point may apply more to people who are goal driven or, detail orientated, or have the tendency to plan or be in control of everything about their lives. For such, like me, it can be difficult to accept and to have the mindset that the plans we make should not be set in stone unless they are aligned to what God has communicated as His plan for us. In addition to allowing Him to direct you on how to execute those plans—trusting that He is a sure foundation to build upon, and that His ways are inexhaustible and much better than ours. It took me years of practice to learn that, and I still remind myself of this often (even at the time He mentioned the writing of this book) because life presents differently at various stages.

Returning from work one evening, after I had started to pray and listen to God about His plans for me, I had barely dropped my bags when I heard a resounding voice in my mind saying, "It's time to leave." I was in no doubt that it was God because I wasn't in the frame of mind for "thinking" at that moment. The words thundered in my chest in a way that I knew it wasn't a random thought, though it was also not in a manner I had been previously used to God voicing things to me. Being unclear what the statement was about, I sat down and had a chat out loud with God.

My first question, "Leave what?"

God's answer, "Leave the Country."

Absolutely shocked and taken aback, I responded, "What? Why? To where?"

My mind was in overdrive! Here I was just trying to get the pieces of my life together, on a job that I was enjoying (never mind the challenging nature), in a nation where I had easy access to my family for support, and being asked to leave it all. Why would I want to leave the stability I had become accustomed to for somewhere else and have to start life over again? I was firing many questions and almost started to accuse God of taking pleasure in destabilising my life—considering even just the events of 2006 and the lessons I was still learning about myself.

"Why, why, why?" I cried, not wanting to ask any more details. Does that sound familiar? Like a child's tantrums when they haven't even fully heard what you, as a parent, are trying to communicate—enough to know that it is for their own good. Lol.

The great thing is that God is love, is patient, knows where we are, and certainly knows how to get us to where we need to be (if we let Him).

Anyway, I finally calmed down and asked God, "Where am I leaving to?"

He replied, "To the United Kingdom."

Again, I went, "What?"

By this time, I had visited the UK a few times on holiday and had family there. However, I had never had the inclination of being resident there, largely because of my perceptions of the culture. My general observation, especially of London, was that it was a madhouse just like Lagos, sporting all the menaces of a metropolitan city—people weren't polite nor tolerant of tourists, especially on the Underground; homes were rather small in size; roads were quite narrow; it had a stiff economy; and so on. Certainly, living in the UK was never a dream of mine, so this was a difficult plan for me to accept.

Since this was "God's plan," I succumbed, but added the conditions upon which I would make the move—all of which would require God to accomplish and thereby demonstrate to me that this was truly His plan. My conditions were that God would make the visa application process easy for me, especially in getting my company directors to support the idea. God would ensure that I get a job in the UK because I didn't want to leave a "good job" in Nigeria to go live in a tight economy with none; I would not have to live in London; and finally, God would need to make possible the completion of my master of business administration (MBA), which was the last major milestone on the ten-year career plan I had been running with. Those conditions made me feel some sort of control over the new plan, which in hindsight showed my level of immaturity in Christ then. I certainly was no Abraham! Thank God for being gracious in holding me firmly in His hands through every stage of life.

For the first time in my life, about mid-2007, I was building my future on a dream that was not originally mine—nor had even remotely considered. Leaving my country for another, not knowing what I would find there, was no mean feat and mega scary for me. It was not a visit, but a relocation! When I found out about the Highly Skilled Migrant Programme (HSMP), a points-based system to attain residency, and started to put my documents together, there were many times I went back to God to check, "Are You serious about this?" or "Should I stop now?" I was genuinely nervous about what lay ahead.

A short while after discussing this new plan with God, one of my company directors visited the program team in Abuja. So, I decided to let them know formally that I was making plans to relocate. I was expecting a reaction to stop or scare me from pursuing this path, but that wasn't what I got. Instead, the director said things along the lines of, "You are a really good staff, and we will hate to lose you. But we will be fully supportive of your plans and will be willing to provide you any information or reference required to help the application." In fact, she later told the other director, who apparently once lived in the UK, so the latter would occasionally check on me to know the progress of the application. In October 2007, I was granted the work permit without any hassles. When I let the company know, they still chose to keep me on staff till I was ready to move. The support I received from them all through the process completely blew my mind—not often what you get from employers—which started to give me confidence in the fact that God was taking care of it all.

There was also the tough hurdle of getting a job in the UK, which having a busy schedule didn't do much to help with—though I didn't even know where to begin, nor was I in a hurry to apply anywhere. One day, one of the consultants on the program came to the offices where I was based to request something of me. Normally, she would have spoken to my bosses, but the need was "urgent" such that she came personally to find the person responsible—and that was me. Not knowing who she was and finding her not very forthcoming with the intended use of the requested documentation, I chose not to release it since it was still a work in progress. I took a stand in not releasing it prematurely nor rushing the completion to produce a shoddy output because my name and the company logo were going to be on it. We discussed and agreed on options that removed the "urgency" tag and allowed me to release the documentation through the formal channels that made them accessible to all relevant parties on the program.

Some days later, after the release, she returned to commend me for the work done, mentioning the importance of my stance not to compromise on standards. In the course of our chats, I found out that she was based in the UK. So, I casually mentioned that I had a UK work permit but wasn't planning to relocate till I was able to secure a job. To my surprise, she took an interest in supporting me—eventually resulting in a UK job offer. The deal included the company's sponsorship of my MBA—which they never did, but it achieved the aim of motivating me to relocate at least. The beauty of it was that the company was based outside London, which ticked another box on my list. Suddenly, God's plan to relocate me was becoming a reality! *He is orchestrating things to make sure I have no excuse or reason to delay the move further*, I thought.

As the program started to wrap up the first phase, I handed over my responsibilities to another team member and returned to Lagos towards the end of 2007 to begin my relocation preparations. To further make things easy, an administrator in the UK company decided to help with finding me an accommodation ahead so that I had a place to live in once I arrived. As an added totally unexpected bonus from God, when the news of my departure became known in my local church in Lagos, a couple with whom I was friends decided to cover my flight cost while some other people gave me cash gifts! Things were happening very fast, with one blessing on the heel of another—all very surreal. I no longer doubted this was God's plan and started to develop the trust that He was more than able to take care of me, as a Father, when in the UK.

In less than six months from the time God told me of the plan, everything that I needed to start this new journey was in place. It was going to be an adventure like none other for me. Though I was convinced it was where God wanted me to be, the only other information He gave was the overall purpose for the move. Hence, I had absolutely no idea what needed to be done next or what lay in-between. Two things, however, were certain—one, God had just flipped open a new chapter in my life; two, I had to totally trust Him to unfold the full or next picture as He wills.

THINK ON THIS...

God knows how to use all of your experiences—the good, the bad, and the not-so-pretty. He is an expert in making beauty out of ashes, so quit discounting yourself. All you need to do is give it all up to Him because He knows and accepts you as a full package, and He is sure to make something beautiful out of you. I can attest to this.

CHRIST, MY FIRM FOUNDATION

A London photoshoot experience

MBA graduation – Durham University Business School

JEHOVAH RAAH
Lord My Shepherd

In February 2008, I relocated to the UK, spending a few days in London before moving to my new home in Cambridge. At this point, I knew I had to develop absolute trust in God's ability to sustain me in a foreign land, especially since He had more than proven Himself all through the relocation process. Though I had left home from a young age and was used to travelling, having my parents within reasonable reach provided some sense of "safety" for me. Being thousands of miles away from my family, God became the only "near-by" parent figure I had, which created in me a sense of dependency on Him that was more than I had previously.

To add to that, I had no clear-cut plans or goals of my own to enable me to know exactly what my next pursuits should be whilst living here. Besides going to work and the plan to do my MBA, which I had applied to selected schools for in the early months of my arrival, I didn't have much understanding of what to expect out of life in the UK. Normally, I had clarity on my focal purpose for being in a place, accompanied by a plan of what to achieve and by when, which then drove the step-by-step actions that I took. Back in Nigeria, I was involved at work in helping my clients improve their businesses and profitability, while my activities in church gave me a sense of purpose in life. For example, I often came early to help set up the church venue; used my voice in the choir to minister words of encouragement to others and sing praises to God; joined and later led the youth group as a way of demonstrating my passion for impacting knowledge to others and love for young people; and utilised my professional knowledge to help with church finance record keeping. So, the totality of my life felt "useful," but here in Cambridge, I was in a new and uncomfortable territory—I felt lost.

I lived on a close, which had a few houses and neighbours that were still curious about me—peeking through windows whenever I walked past. A few weeks after I moved there, I went knocking on my neighbours' doors to introduce myself so as to allay any concerns they might have had about "this unknown person." Only one family opened their doors to me and invited me in for tea; others either spoke through their windows (not that I blame them) or did not entertain any interaction. My bedsit was at the end of the close; the property had recently been renovated, and the main house, which was a shared accommodation, was not yet occupied, so I didn't have anyone to relate with on a regular basis. God became my Lord, Father, Brother, and Friend—He was every family member I could easily reach.

These early experiences set the stage for two things that quickly became my reality. One, I started to learn not to plan things to death but to put one foot in front of the other and go at the pace which God led or chose to reveal His plans—seeing as they always turned out better and more holistic than I could ever envisage. Two, the consciousness of God's presence with me grew stronger the more time I spent talking with Him, mostly about every-day things, including what I would wear, as one would a friend or sibling. I often spoke out loud, repeating what He said or was dropping on my mind. This newfound way of relating to God gave me a deeper sense of Him being a Person and One that can be related to. He became to me as the Bible describes in Proverbs 18:24 (NIV)—"*a friend who sticks closer than a brother.*"

After some time, I found the Christ Embassy Church in Cambridge, which helped me engage with more people outside of work as well as to get involved in church life. As often said, keep doing what you know to do until God tells you otherwise. I started to get back some sense of normalcy and being in control. But trust life to never stop changing—the global financial crisis of 2008 struck and started to hit hard on the economy about late summer. In response, the company initially changed employment terms to contract hours instead of full-time to manage its cash flow. Whilst better than being laid off, it resulted in a major dip in income for me. I was barely able to cover my rent and other basic household costs. Soon, the company started to owe payment for those hours worked. After a few months of the issue persisting, I decided to move in with a relative in London and search for other job opportunities, which were generally very scarce across the country, and worse off for consulting-type roles. A couple from the Cambridge church kindly offered their garage space to allow me to store most of my belongings, pending when I was resettled in London and could return to pick them up. With only a few bags left to move, a former classmate from Uni drove from London to help me do the move with ease. All of these things, in themselves, were huge blessings to me.

Prior to leaving Cambridge, I had been offered an admission to start my Executive MBA at Durham University in January 2009 and got £5,000 (five thousand pounds) in scholarship funds towards the fees, having not been granted the full scholarship applied for. This was enough to encourage me not to defer the course despite the financial crisis, as I saw the fund as that "little hand of provision" from God, which gave me enough light to stay on the right path while I trusted Him to make a way through the dark night. Also, in December 2008, I was able to secure a contract role based in Reading, which further gave me the courage to start the MBA. Interestingly, I later asked the hiring manager why I was offered the job, realising that I wasn't the most qualified candidate and having made a request to be off for three days every six weeks in order to attend my MBA lectures in Durham.

Her response was, "Because you were the only candidate that smiled during the interview. This place is full of difficult and unhappy people, so we need someone whose joy is not dependent on their environment and can help infuse some of that into this place." By that someone, she was referring to me, saying that she could feel the joy in me during the interview.

Well, I know that it was purely God's favour that gave me the job! For when the agency called about the role, I was in Nigeria attending both a church conference towards the end of November and a friend's traditional wedding in early December, having booked my tickets earlier in the year and choosing to still travel despite the global financial crisis that later happened. I told them of my return to the UK about mid-December, as I didn't have the funds to change the ticket. For some reason, the hiring manager extended the interview period to accommodate me and eventually gave me the job. That could only have been God's favour. Getting that job turned out to be crucial to my continued stay in the UK because the income earned was the sole evidence of earnings that I needed for my HSMP visa renewal in October 2009—something that was absolutely not on the forefront of my mind, having been overtaken by the crisis and busyness of life when I started my MBA in January 2009. But God never misses a beat!

JEHOVAH SHAMMAH
The Lord is There

In January 2009, I moved into a rented flat, which meant a daily commute between London and Reading for work. Also, that January was the MBA Induction Week, which happened to be the same week as my thirtieth birthday. I spent that birthday with classmates who were no more than strangers at the time. It was a rewarding week overall. From that week, I realised what a great opportunity it was to have started the program that year. I was grateful that I had listened to Stanley's advice to wait till I had about ten years of work experience before going on an MBA program. He said doing such courses too early would make the experience no different from an undergraduate program, where concepts taught are more theoretical, whereas attending a master's program should be more about the application of those theories in the business world. And his advice was so true. For the Executive MBA, the minimum work experience requirement was five years. Thankfully, most of my classmates had close to ten years and more. Also, the twenty or so of us were from diverse industries, which made class discussions very engaging and impactful. It was like striking gold for a management consultant like me.

Thereafter, my schedule became extremely busy, and it wasn't until about late August that I realised my HSMP visa was due for renewal soon. To earn points in the income section, one had to provide evidence of earnings based on the past twelve months. Checking on the requirements, I realised that new standards had been introduced in February, which were binding on the renewal application I would be sending in. Thankfully, the income from the contract in Reading was enough for me to earn the minimum total points required for the renewal. A few days into October 2009, I put all of my documentation together and sent my renewal application to the Home Office, suspecting nothing could ever go wrong.

Not long afterwards, in November, my application came back denied on the grounds that the documents submitted in support of income earned were not original copies; hence, no points were awarded in that section, which led to my total points being inadequate to meet the minimum required points for a visa renewal. I was devastated by the news on many grounds. *Being in the UK is supposed to be God's plan, so why isn't it working?* I thought. I couldn't understand how this could be happening when God had said to come here. I was also counting on getting the visa renewed for three years per the process, which at least would have given me one less thing to worry about during job interviews and increased my prospects of securing a new role—as having the right work permit had become a major consideration in the recruitment process. In addition, I needed to be able to remain in the UK until January 2010, when I would sit the exams that concluded the first year of the two-year Executive MBA program. That way, I could defer the second year without losing the efforts (time and money) that had already been invested in the first year. Anyway, thinking that the originality of the documents demonstrating my income were the only things in question, I contacted the organisations I had worked with to resend my payslips, which were all in electronic format. On receipt, I submitted an appeal of the decision with the documents to evidence the income earned.

During a church service in December, I was praying about the situation at hand when I felt strongly in my spirit that God was asking me to literally give Him "my gold." By this time, I knew it was not the devil speaking to me and didn't resist the prompting, like I did when He asked for my car. Nonetheless, it was an equally weighty ask for me. I didn't have much jewellery, but at the time my little gold collection was my most valuable possession—both in monetary and health value. The latter sounds strange, right? My skin reacts to plated metals, causing rashes or skin peel after a few hours of wearing. Therefore, the real difficulty I experienced in letting go of them had to do with my health.

When I returned home from church service, I burst into tears. Yet again, God was asking a very costly seed from me, but based on my previous experience, I knew that such requests from Him were for reasons beyond the value of the thing. If God was asking me to release something precious, then the real work He wanted to do was in my heart and not in the possessed item because that could always be replaced. In that moment, I remembered the words from Alvin Slaughter's song, "That's When," which encouraged me. With eyes full of tears, I gathered each gold piece and the sets, putting them one by one into a bag—the pangs of a hefty sacrifice felt as each went in. It had to be done that very moment to give no room to doubt. Once I did that, in my mind, the jewellery no longer belonged to me. At the next church service, which was mid-week, I put them in the offering bag.

On January 5, 2010, the appeal response came back rejected—this time for totally new reasons. I couldn't be awarded points for income earned because I didn't meet the criteria set out in the new requirements that came into effect on October 1, 2009. These were applied to my application because the first submission was received by the Home Office around October 3, hence the rules on October 1 were binding. I became irritated because this new decision completely ignored the fact that I was claiming points based on twelve months up to September 2009. Plus, for a process that required evidence over a twelve-month period, it was unreasonable to expect a change in rules some days before an application was received to apply to someone in my circumstance. Being given only a few days to respond, I appealed the decision a second time, providing a cover letter that attempted to explain the circumstances and queries raised against my earnings. I also requested an oral hearing so that I could answer any queries in person and, hopefully, help whoever was making the decision come to the right conclusion. *Not a great start to a new year*, I thought, *but I have to stay focused on my upcoming exams.*

At the beginning of that year, God had asked me to fast and pray, and take the communion every day in the month of January—something I had never done before. I had thought it meant that things were going to be smooth sailing that year. Little did I know that it was God's way of preparing me for the long battle that lay ahead!

With the appeal coming back rejected so early in the year, I started to get discouraged and took two immediate and practical actions:

1. I requested a meeting with my landlord to inform him of developments, as it was now clear that I wouldn't be able to pay my rent from that month-end. Thankfully, the payments were done in advance, meaning that what was paid in December covered me till the end of January. I wanted to formally notify him of my intention to move out by month-end. I was pleasantly surprised by his response, however. He told me that he had always perceived me to be a focused person and was happy about how I cared for his property. Therefore, if I got to the point where I could no longer pay the rent, he didn't want me to worry, because he would not put me out and was confident that I would secure another job someday. This was mind-blowing for me because it was very rare to have a landlord, who had a family to cater for, willingly decide to accommodate someone without the likelihood of a rent income. This was my biggest concern, and just like that, God took away that worry.

2. I started to contact old colleagues and previous employers back in Nigeria to inform them of my likely return and ask about job opportunities, as the financial crisis had also hit businesses there. Assuring as my landlord's offer was, I wasn't one to take advantage of people. So, if I had other options where he didn't have to lose rent income and I didn't have to struggle with finances, I intended to take them. Such was my thinking. About two of my contacts confirmed that they had positions that I could fill, so we started to discuss the opportunities, with a potential start date in March.

As I prepared for my exams, I also started packing my bags to relocate back to Nigeria. Frankly, I was no longer interested in remaining in the UK at that point, because I wasn't sure how I was going to survive without any money if

I remained. Interpreting the events so far to mean that God no longer wanted me in the UK (though I didn't quite ask Him the question), I decided to draw up "my own plan," which had the pursuit of my career development at the forefront. The plan, in a nutshell, was to sit the MBA exams at the end of January, defer the second year of the program, return to work in Nigeria and earn some income, and then complete the program's second year by distance learning—which was an option. *No one gets hurt, and I don't have to live impoverished when I have access to much elsewhere*, I thought.

That Sunday, I shared the plan with my choir leader, who was the only person I had kept in the know of my circumstances. I had recently joined the church and choir, following the move to London. She wasn't happy that I had decided to leave the country, though she understood my reasons. Then, she asked if we could speak to the pastor, which I agreed to do. After praying with me, our pastor told me that she felt God saying my purpose in the UK wasn't done and asked me to talk to God about what actions He wanted me to take. Then, in what was a kind gesture, she gave me £100 (one hundred pounds) to cover my travel costs to Durham as her show of support.

As part of managing my cash flow, I had secured a free accommodation space in the hostels for master's students. I met the lady who offered me her room during one of the electives that we had together with students on another MBA program. She was going home to the United States for a break during the same week we were having exams, while her Malaysian roommate graciously decided to stay with a friend of hers for the week in order to allow me to study and focus on my exams without distractions. That whole arrangement came out of a random conversation and turned out to be a huge blessing. So, when my pastor gave me cash to cover the transport cost, it was a double blessing because it meant that I only needed to cover my food expenses. I felt God was working these out for my good, knowing how much I needed the cash flow, but I just didn't think He was still in the plans for me to remain a resident in the UK.

At Durham, I focused my attention on the exams and tried to put aside the immigration issues, though I was convinced that I would be relocating back to Nigeria shortly after. Then one morning, during the exam week, I had an encounter with God, which changed my perspective of the situation and life as a whole. It is the most intense interaction of all the visions, dreams, and so on that God had shown or spoken to me about until then. I have never shared it until now. Trust God with His perfect timing because that day I didn't have a paper to write in the morning so was fairly relaxed about when I was going to get out of bed and start studying.

I was awoken that morning by the sense of a presence in the room. But at the very moment I tried waking up, I fell into a vision (for lack of another word to describe it). I had slept with my head adjacent to the only window in the room, so as my eyes opened, I could see it was daybreak outside. Then, I saw this dark-coloured smoke rising from outside and gliding towards me. It appeared to be formless, yet with a closer look, I could about make out a human-like form. I saw neither face nor hands and feet, which unnerved me.

As it came closer, I heard a voice emanating from the form, which I recognised. Almost in the same breath, I realised this was God Himself in the room! I knew with certainty that it was not an angel and that I wasn't asleep or dreaming. (Remember, God had told me to fast that whole month of January, so that might have helped my sensitivity to Him. Nonetheless, I was too perplexed by this to make any move.) He spoke peace to me as He came closer. I immediately was no longer frightened, although my body still quivered with every word He said.

God told me how He had heard my prayers. He reiterated that it was still His plan that I remain in the UK but that the road ahead was not going to be easy. Therefore, He had raised up people at that very moment to pray for me. Then God asked me to look in a hand-like motion that seemed to point towards the window. As I looked in that direction, the window and wall area opened up such that I could see into the car park, which was physically a few floors down. Through the opening, I saw about six or seven people gathered in a circle, their hands held to form a chain, and I was kneeling in the middle of that circle with my head bowed as if receiving the blessings of their prayers—each one was praying in tongues. I leaned forward to get a closer look and realised that I didn't know any of them; they were people from different nations. I saw the face of a guy that looked uniquely Asian, which made me realise that there was no way that they were physically co-located. Then God began speaking again from this dark smoke next to me. As if to explain what was happening, He said each one was praying in other tongues—a language given them by the Holy Spirit—at that very moment in different parts of the world where they were physically based. They did not realise that the Holy Spirit was praying through them for me or that the prayers were united in purpose, hence the linking of their hands in the realm of the Spirit to show agreement.

"The prayer," God said, "is to give you strength and courage for the journey My plan will lead you on, but you have a choice. You asked to know My plan and desire for you. My plan is that you remain in the UK. However, you can choose to return to Nigeria, and I will be with you as I promised in times past, but that isn't My perfect will for you at this point in time. So, the choice is yours."

With those last words, the whole thing ended, and I found myself sitting upright in the bed, wide awake, shivering from chills brought on by hearing God speak while still breaking out with and totally covered in sweat.

As I gazed at the window, still dazed by what had just happened, I thought, *The Creator of all things and the King of all kings was here!* I remembered how in the Bible Moses spoke of not seeing God's face and how God always showed up in various forms—speaking from a burning bush that was not consumed by the fire (Exodus 3), for example. *Such magnificent stories of God Himself showing up in Person and speaking to a human being mostly occurred in Bible times, but here I am experiencing the same in the modern day. I could never have imagined (nor deserved) that,* I thought.

I was so caught up in the whole experience that I spent the next few hours just pondering what had happened. Every aspect of the encounter was humbling and defining at the same time. To think that God cared enough about me, imperfect as I was, to raise people up to pray for me made me utterly speechless.

Then my mind flashed to some years earlier, about 2006, when I worked in Abuja. I was awoken in the wee hours of the morning with a strong urge to pray, but I didn't know what about. As I opened my mouth, these tongues began to pour out of me. I kept praying until I got a relief in my spirit and could then go back to sleep. When it was morning, my mum sent a text message saying to praise God for saving my dad, who had nearly died in the middle of the night because he suddenly was unable to breathe and his inhaler wasn't working. Knowing what had happened to me that night, I called her to ask about what time the incident occurred. It turned out to be the exact time I got woken up to pray—so I had a firsthand experience that helped me understand the power of praying in tongues, especially when there was specificity in one's spirit to do so, and how it could save a life miles away from where I was.

I became emotional to think that God knew the road ahead of me and my frail ability to pull through, and He cared enough to raise people up from other countries and tribes, people who did not know me and whom I was likely never going to meet this side of Heaven, to pray for me. God is such a good, good Father—even now, that thought still brings tears to my eyes. Those people who heeded the Holy Spirit's nudge to pray for me in that very moment will never know why or what they prayed for, but I am certain that they will be blessed for allowing Him to fulfil His divine purpose through them.

MORAL —

If you think God isn't hearing your prayers or doesn't care about you, please let this be an encouragement to you to know that He absolutely cares! Perhaps you have felt the need to pray but are unsure of what to pray about. Please yield your tongue and words to the Holy Spirit. He just might be nudging you to do so for the sake of a family member or someone you may never know who is likely in a dire need. I believe that God doesn't intervene in anything on earth without the prayers of at least one person. He gave us the Earth, including everything in and about it (Genesis 1:26–30), as our place of dominion. So sovereign as He is, God doesn't trample that authority given to us. Therefore, when you feel the urge to pray or just a thought crosses your mind, why not just pray into it? Praying in tongues is great, but if you do not yet have that gift, pray anyway. He who gives utterance in a language you do not understand equally can give you the right words to pray in the language you understand. The beautiful thing about prayer is that it isn't the prerogative of Christians or any religious group alone. God hears the prayers of EVERY living thing that He has made, especially humans who have been made in His image and have the primary responsibility for this planet.

Sitting in the bed, still pondering, I revisited my plans to leave the country. I certainly wasn't going to have it any other way after that! My thoughts were simply, *I choose to be where God wants me.* Going back to Nigeria didn't mean that God would forsake me, and I probably would still be successful in my career pursuits if I did. However, I asked myself, *Do you want to live life in pursuit of your own plans and career? Or, do you want to live a life of purpose that is aligned to God's will?* I thought, *How can the all-knowing Creator of all present me with a choice, having made clear His perfect will, and I choose otherwise?*

The foolishness of my attitude towards this plan since that first time God said He wanted me to move to the UK dawned on me that morning. God had given me an overall purpose for that move, yet I behaved like a sulking child who just never saw anything good in what the parent offered simply because I wasn't given the exact thing I wanted. Oh! How foolish I was (and often am), but for the grace and mercies of God.

Right there, I made the choice to remain in the UK. The biggest shift was in my mindset. What I saw as God's plan, which I simply "tagged along" with, became my personal plan. I realised that all the while I never quite accepted or owned His plan, which explained my fickleness whenever opposition arose and defaulted to my "familiar." But that day, I fully embraced God's direction as the only way forward. I considered no other options, deciding that I would rather go hungry while being in God's will than to live comfortably in a place that wasn't aligned to His perfect plan for my life.

From that point on, I started to form the habit of speaking to God first about what I should do, including the job I should take, so that I could be where He wanted me to be and learn what He wanted me to learn. If it seemed like I was getting no answer or not sure about what I was hearing, I kept asking for clarity and carried on doing the last thing He made clear to me—mostly simple everyday things but often with the common factor of serving others. It also deepened the lesson not to plan for the future in excessive detail, removing the irritation that occurred when things didn't go according to "my plan," whilst fully giving God the permission to interrupt my plans so as to bring to bear His perfect will. My perception of the future stopped being about what I wanted or where I wanted to be and became more about what God might be positioning me to learn so that I could be better equipped for where He wanted to take me. From serving the church, my employers, colleagues, the community, etc., I found that every inter-action I had, job undertaken, place lived, and so on, culminated in character shaping and impacted some form of knowledge that always turned out to be what I needed in the next place that I found myself. I learnt to always ask the question, "What do I need to learn?"

JEHOVAH JIREH
The Lord Will Provide

After my exams, I made arrangements to have the second year of the MBA deferred by one year so I could focus on resolving the immigration issues and hopefully start working to save enough funds for the fees before the academic year in 2011. Thereafter, I returned to my home in London—a changed person, fully convinced that my home was in the UK. To my mind, the only way I would leave the UK was if God showed up again to tell me to move elsewhere or the immigration case ended in the government asking me to leave (hence in obedience to the law). Therefore, I was not going to quit the fight and would do all that was legally (and humanly) possible to obtain my visa renewal, especially when I had the clear conscience that I satisfied the stipulated requirements to be granted the work permit extension.

Although I was very resolute about my decision to stay, I didn't fully grasp how tough the journey was going to be. For some reason, I assumed that since God Himself reassured me that staying in the UK was His perfect will for me, then things would ease up from then on. I couldn't be more wrong (and the Holy Spirit was certainly right about praying ahead for me).

I didn't share details of the encounter with anyone or provide any reason for my unwillingness to entertain other options besides that God told me to remain in the UK. Of course, many judged my reasoning as laughable, while some others thought I was foolish to pursue a "lost cause" and choose a path leading to penury rather than return to Nigeria, where I had opportunities to "progress." So, I was losing friends very fast, especially when the challenges that I was facing grew in intensity. But I wasn't too perturbed by these, as I constantly reminded myself that it wasn't them God met with, nor was it their cross to bear. Equally, I didn't owe anyone an explanation or the justification for my choices. I had an audience of One, and His validation alone was what I needed.

MORAL —

This isn't suggesting that you shouldn't seek advice from other people or blatantly ignore them because God can use people to provide direction for you. However, when God has made His plans clear to you in an undeniable way, then do not allow yourself to be swayed by a million other voices or distracted by the physical circumstances around you. You will surely face opposition to God's directions, but it's up to you to choose to trust wholeheartedly in God. God's Word (written and revealed) is true, and He watches over His Word to bring it to pass (Psalm 138:2, Jeremiah 1:12, Matthew 24:35), so you can stake your life on His Words without giving room to doubt.

Soon, I ran out of money and had no recourse to public funds. Yet, I was at peace because I was where God wanted me to be. I cut back meals to once a day or not at all just to manage my food supplies, but they soon ran out too. One day, when I did not have a single grain in the house, I put a little salt in a cup of water and blessed it, because that was all I had left for food. After "eating" it, I was walking around the house singing praises to God when I heard the letterbox sound and thought it was a response from the Home Office. On getting there, it was a Tesco voucher of £5 (five pounds) to spend on anything in store. I was elated because I couldn't remember the last time that I shopped in Tesco to deserve the voucher, so I knew it was God's miraculous provision. I immediately went to the store and bought food stuff to cook a meal that ended up lasting a long time.

Every week, I still showed up on time in church for services, choir rehearsals, and youth programs, without most people knowing what was really going on. It took an hour to walk from the house in Lewisham to church on Old Kent Road, and I always did it singing and dancing, till the hour felt like a few minutes' walk. Despite all of these, my resolve and faith in God were unshaken, because being where God wanted me was to be aligned to my eternal purpose, and that had far more weight of value to me than any luxury life could ever present. Though I was going through this, I wasn't mistaken to think that suffering always equated to being in God's purpose or that having an abundance meant being outside of it. God wants us well and prospers us, but prosperity is more than monetary wealth.

It was during this period that I began to understand the "peace" of God and why the apostle Paul in Philippians 4:7 described it as something that surpasses all understanding when we put our trust in God. There is a protection over one's mind that God's peace brings, even in the middle of a storm, which cannot be put into words. I started to learn how to let that peace guide my decisions and reassure me of God's influence in every area of my life.

One of the things God told me during the encounter at Durham that greatly helped me stay focused on His words and purpose throughout the trial was to fast and to take the communion at least once a week. Fasting would help my attentiveness to His voice, while taking the communion was to remind me of the covenant that we have in Christ Jesus and the power that now works in me. Prior to this, I had never taken the communion by myself. Hearing God say that was both a deep insight into what was available to us as Christians and a reminder of the power in the blood of Jesus. I started doing it even if all I had was water and a biscuit. I have kept up the practice ever since, often declaring upon myself the Bible verses in Colossians 2:11–15 (NKJV):

In Him you were also circumcised with the circumcision made without hands, by putting off the body of the sins of the flesh, by the circumcision of Christ, buried with Him in baptism, in which you also were raised with Him through faith in the working of God, who raised Him from the dead. And you, being dead in your trespasses and the uncircumcision of your flesh, He has made alive together with Him, having forgiven you all trespasses, having wiped out the handwriting of requirements that was against us, which was contrary to us. And He has taken it out of the way, having nailed it to the cross. Having disarmed principalities and powers, He made a public spectacle of them, triumphing over them in it.

During that period, I knew God's provision in numerous ways through several people, most of whom I either didn't know or had little relationship with at the time. I cannot count the number of times that people offered to pay for my groceries; that a complete stranger randomly gave me a train ticket whilst I was standing at a bus stop, knowing that I only had cash to take a bus but needed to be somewhere such that using the Tube (London Underground) would be a better option; or that I was given cash by someone who just felt God asked them to do so. Then, there was a friend's wife who decided to pay a certain amount into my account on a monthly basis when she found out about the situation. She did so even though we weren't really close at the time, without ever being asked, and without fail at least till the end of 2010. There was also the accommodation, which my landlord allowed me to stay in without paying rent. He never did once come by to "check on me," which could have made me nervous about him changing his mind. Yes, I couldn't spend as I wanted, but I still counted myself greatly blessed because, through it all, God sustained me.

One day, in about June of that year, I became overwhelmed by emotions whilst praying as I recalled the kindness upon kindness that I had received. I was just in awe of God, thanking Him for all of the favours and people used to be a blessing to me. God told me that I was reaping the fruit of the kindness my parents had shown to many others—how they had helped feed many neighbours and strangers because our doors were always open for people to come in, provided accommodation for others, paid school fees for struggling students, mentored many young people, and always treated everyone fairly irrespective of their social status. He also reminded me of times past when He had put it on my mind to give to friends and total strangers alike, and I had done so with respect for the basic human dignity. At one time, I gave a monthly allowance to at least two friends who hadn't gotten work while I had the opportunity of getting a good job immediately after my National Service year. They never asked. It was something that felt right to do then, but I didn't know that God was behind the "feeling" to do so. God told me those were seeds being sown in the time of "harvest" and were now being reaped in my time of "famine."

MORAL —

The great thing about God though is that He repays you a million-fold more than you could ever give—with good health (which no amount of money can buy), peace of mind and general well-being (again, which money cannot buy), favour wherever you go, success in your endeavours, and material gifts, to name a few. It is important to live a life of giving—be it in time, money, knowledge, giftings, or anything else you have to invest in others. God will always repay whatever you do for humanity, not just to you, but your children and their generations too will reap the fruit thereof. So, do you want to leave a truly lasting legacy? Be a giver!

A few days into February 2010, I received the response to my second appeal, and it was…DENIED! I decided to appeal the decision again because it was the only option I had. I thought to use an immigration lawyer in case they would be able to help structure my appeal using language understood by the tribunal and to advise me on the best approach to preparing the appeal. The challenges, however, were that I had no money and there were only five calendar days or so to send in an appeal. Therefore, I needed to move fast. Consequently, I called my friend, Mya, a classmate in secondary school that I knew had studied law, to help point me in the direction of a lawyer, as there was no time to start searching for one. She advised that she wasn't practicing but, thankfully, knew someone who was and referred me. Fred, the lawyer, advised me of the options available, which were not cheap. He was willing to give me a deal because of Mya. Though a very good price, I still couldn't afford it, hence resorted to putting the appeal together myself.

Later that afternoon, Mya called to check on me. I told her more about my circumstances and the main reason for deciding to do it myself. Her response was surprising. She felt it was definitely worth using a lawyer and decided to help with the fees by sending Fred £100 (one hundred pounds), so he could at least start reviewing my documents. She would also guarantee me so he could allow me to pay the balance in instalments. Some minutes after she dropped, I received a call from the lawyer. Fred spoke of how she was a long-time friend of his, so he couldn't say no and was happy to offer a further reduced price on the basis that he would review the case and advise me on points to highlight, but I would do the work of preparing it. Still unsure of how I would pay the balance, and seeing his willingness to support me, I agreed to the deal. My task was now to scan all of the documents and send them to him. I immediately got ready and set out to look for an internet café. Little did I know that Mya didn't stop there.

I was on the way when another friend, Trina, called me. She mentioned a phone discussion she just had with one of our mutual friends in Nigeria, Janet, asking if she knew anything about my needing to raise funds to get a lawyer with regards to my visa renewal, which of course she didn't. She proceeded to literally scold me for not updating her when I decided to remain in the UK, having previously mentioned that I would be returning to Nigeria. Hence, it was embarrassing to hear that I was "begging" for money and didn't think to tell any of my "close friends" and that they had to find out from someone who called Janet, and so on. I tried to explain, but as she went on, I decided to keep quiet and keep my focus on the task at hand—to scan my documents to the lawyer.

Shortly after Trina dropped the call, I received another call from a UK number that I didn't know and answered it. The lady introduced herself as a former classmate in secondary school and asked for my bank account details. I had barely finished that conversation when another call came in asking for the same information. So it was, call after call and multiple text messages asking for my account details. By the time I had scanned the documents and returned home, I had received enough money to fully pay the legal fees and have some left. I broke down in tears.

Of course, by the second call that afternoon, I realised that Mya must have contacted Janet and our 1994 set of girls residing in the UK to inform them of the urgent need to support a "sister"—as we call ourselves. That was how the word got out. Rather than being angry or feeling embarrassed, I was in total awe of God and grateful to Mya that she took my problem so personally as to go the extra mile to contact others for support. Prior to this, I had only attended the set reunion once, and it was while I lived in Cambridge, so I didn't know most of the girls and vice versa. Yet, when they received the call to support an old classmate, they didn't ask questions but just gave whatever they could.

My friends, on the other hand, decided to make mockery of my decision to stay. Although they heard of my need, they did absolutely nothing to support me—not even an encouraging phone call was put through. I later found out that Mya also called Janet because she knew we were friends. I had introduced them some years back as both were into the same line of business and felt they could profit by doing business together, so she had Janet's phone number to hand. To think that Mya put the same call to two groups of women who knew me somehow—my current friends and my classmates from secondary school—and I got two very different responses. Neither was what I would have expected from either group, but in the long run, God's purpose was fulfilled.

MORAL —

When it comes to God, always expect the unexpected, never fix your mind on what anyone "should do," and trust that God always works the outcome for your good (Romans 8:28–34).

That evening, I called Mya and expressed my deep gratitude for what she had done. I would never have thought of doing such a thing in a million years, but the experience showed me the power of alumni and the impact that can be made when a group of people are united in purpose. I decided from that day to interact more with my classmates and stand for the togetherness of the group. Personally, it takes a lot of efforts to really connect with women—not my natural gifting—but due to that singular experience, I often step out of my comfort zone to ensure we keep in touch with one another, look out for the welfare of individuals as much as they are willing to share, and more widely, to befriend a lady. Women are often stereotyped as jealous, spiteful, and weak, but my eyes were opened that day to how much a group of women can achieve when united. Women are a force to reckon with. Throughout history, there was no revolution or positive change that happened in any society or civilisation that didn't have a woman actively driving or campaigning for it. I may not yet fully know what it means to be a woman, but I am for sure no longer ignorant of the power we possess to bring about change for individuals and our societies.

The other big lesson I learnt from that situation was to rely on no one besides God. Human love is fickle by its very nature, so we are bound to fail one another. Again, rely on no one except God! The dictionary says to *rely* is to depend on someone or something with full trust or confidence. Now, in whom would you rather put your full trust? (Pause to think before responding). Think first of what characteristics the person who is deserving of that level of trust needs to have. Ask yourself, Is there any one person that can possess such characteristics, including yourself? Like me, your conclusion might be "no," because one of those characteristics is consistency, no matter the weather. This change of perspective was crucial to my ability to forgive the friends who abandoned me to my woes, paid no attention to my circumstance, or mocked me when they heard me say, "God told me to stay in the UK, and so I will," because the physical situation they could see showed no evidence that God had a hand in that decision.

I know that God uses people to help people, but I have learnt not to fixate on who He decides to use. Staying focused on and fully trusting in God, and looking out for the resolution He brings are what I have learnt to concern myself with. The "how" and "when" of that resolution are God's. I am now conditioned, by reason of experiences in 2010, to trust and know that He always works all things together, including myself, to get the best outcome. As Solomon advised in Proverbs 3:5–6, and I love how *The Living Bible* (TLB) puts it:

> *If you want favor with both God and man, and a reputation for good judgement and common sense, then trust the Lord completely; don't ever trust yourself. In everything you do, put God first, and he will direct you and crown your efforts with success.*

Lastly, from that experience, I learnt the humility of asking and receiving help. I am a fairly private person by nature—only ever allowing myself to be vulnerable with family and, at most, very close friends whom I consider family. At the start of this issue, the only people that were aware of the developments were my nuclear family; the choir and Youth Fellowship leaders; my then church pastor; my prayer partner, whom I met whilst volunteering in the church's books and tapes department; and one or two close friends. Hence, the circle I could personally ask for help, if I was ever going to, was limited. That day, I recognised that God used Mya to show me that it takes humility to ask for help. My close friends would never have dared to do what she did because they knew the "private me," so God introduced someone with whom I once shared a network in secondary school and who had the ability to do what I wouldn't have thought of doing myself but absolutely needed. On getting home that day and seeing how a single message from her raised hundreds of pounds sterling in a few hours for someone they all had little contact with during the past decade, genuinely provoked humility in me. I just couldn't be angry about the fact that she put "my business" out there. All I saw was God's grace at work and Him using Mya to show me an area of weakness that I had.

With the money I had received, I made a transfer of the remaining fees to Fred, who had already commenced a review of my documents. With his help, I was able to put the third appeal together and send for next-day delivery (thanks to the additional funds received) to meet the restricted window allowed for the appeal. Once done, I could breathe again—though not for long.

THINK ON THIS...

Know when to ask for help. When that help comes, receive it with humility and gratitude. When you start trusting God fully, you will learn that how God often answers prayers isn't always how you imagine. Therefore, be humble enough to pray and equally humble enough to receive the answered prayer in whatever package He brings it. Many have lost out on the answers to their prayers because they were looking out for the spectacularly miraculous, when the answer was clothed in a messy, despised, prejudiced, or undesirable exterior. God cares more about what you need than your fantasy or greed, and often seeks ways to grow us, through humility, into mature people in Christ Jesus.

JEHOVAH SHALOM

The Lord is Peace

During my waiting period, I took intentional steps to guard my mind and invest in my spiritual growth by listening to faith-filled music and Bible teachings from various church pastors, especially those of my then global church leader. I took seriously the Scripture that says God's Word is *"living and active"* (Hebrews 4:12 ESV) and has the power to read you as you study it, getting deep into one's spirit and renewing the mind so as to bring about a change in your life that then becomes visible on the outward for others to see. I read stories of how God worked out the seeming impossible in the lives of people such as Abraham, Isaac, Moses, Joseph, King David, Esther, Hezekiah, and the three Hebrew boys—Shadrach, Meshach, and Abednego. I also meditated on Scriptures, often declaring aloud those that stirred up my faith and assurance that God was in this with me. Second Corinthians 4:8–9 (NIV) declares

We are hard pressed on every side, but not crushed; perplexed, but not in despair; persecuted, but not abandoned; struck down, but not destroyed.

Each time I prayed, I checked back with God to ensure that staying in the UK was still the plan, like King David often did before he went out to battle. It was not out of doubt but more from a growing conviction and realisation that the most important thing to me was to be where God wanted me. The fact of it being in the UK or not gradually stopped mattering that much to me. I was starting to see from God's perspective that this journey wasn't really about the visa—because God had and could sort that out in a matter of moments— but the condition of my heart and alignment of my life and purposes to God's will. The more I looked into God's Word rather than at the circumstance (2 Corinthians 4:16–18), the more convinced I became that God was the greatest possession I could have, and to Him only did I want to cling. I could afford to lose anything else, but not God. These habits helped me to stay the course despite the seeming hopelessness of the diverse hardships that came with this issue, and to focus instead on the improvements being made in my person and see the value in using that time to become more spiritually minded.

A few days into April, I received the response to my third appeal, which was dated March 30. It was again denied. I was also denied the opportunity of an oral hearing, despite it having been requested since my second appeal. This news got to me as I started to wonder, *Why are things not aligning to what God told me?* I had clearly met all of the requirements. Since the first appeal, I had annotated and cross-referenced every figure in the submitted documents to make all of the documentation easier to understand and the numbers so glaring that even a child could add them up. Yet for some reason, the people handling the case just didn't seem to be "getting it." Not being given the opportunity to explain it all in person was equally upsetting, add- ing to the frustration I started to feel. Though I knew beyond all reasonable doubt what God's plans were, I truly couldn't comprehend why it was so difficult to attain despite doing everything I knew to do. So, I started to ask God, "Why am I being subjected to so much pain and difficulty?"

At this point, I had already learnt what I thought there was to learn from Him taking me through this process—accepting and aligning my plans to His, knowing how to stay faithful to Him and His Word even in adversity, being humble to know that my abilities or education or whatever I could attain on my own wasn't the source of my promotion because it is Him uplifting me (Psalm 75:6–7), and so on. *What more does God want from me? Has He become oblivious to my plight?* I wondered.

I was becoming mentally exhausted by the constant battles and the daily odds I had to fight. The news of my third appeal being denied decked a blow that got me frustrated to the depths of my soul. However, I knew I couldn't afford to stay in that mental space and had to encourage myself to try again, because the one thing I could not doubt and upon which I was resolute was God's plan for me to remain in the UK. Truth be told, a part of me wanted God to change His mind so I could leave the country and end the suffering, for His word was the only thing that mattered to me. But until He said otherwise, I encouraged myself—like King David often did when he faced opposition or fell into dire situations, such as in Psalm 42:11 (NIV):

> *Why, my soul, are you downcast?*
> *Why so disturbed within me?*
> *Put your hope in God,*
> *for I will yet praise him,*
> *my Savior and my God.*

Some months later, I realised that the very mindset that caused my frustrations was one of the reasons the situation persisted. God had to get me to a place where I wasn't trying to earn His favour by being committed to His work or always doing things right. He also had to get me to where I could trust Him with a reckless abandon—such that I could hold on to every word He has spoken and know, like the three Hebrew boys, that even if He didn't rescue me like I thought or completely changed His mind, I would still serve Him because He remains a good God all the same (Daniel 3:16–20). That turning point happened for me about June that year. But in April, I did the only thing that could be done to obtain my work permit, which was to appeal the decision again. Without the funds to secure a lawyer's services and not wanting to trouble anyone for funds, I prepared the fourth appeal and sent it to the Upper Tribunal where the case was being treated.

About two weeks later, I was surprised to receive a letter from the tribunal, because previous ones often took about a month before the appeal responses were received. On opening the envelope, I read one of the most traumatic lines of a letter that I have ever experienced. The letter, dated April 22, began by saying that the appeal could not be heard because the right of appeal on the previous notice was done in error; hence, I had exhausted all the appeals that were allowed. My jaw dropped, and my heart started racing at a thousand miles per hour!

I hadn't read the details of the last letter to notice it had mentioned that I had exhausted my appeal options within the UK court system for immigration cases. All that I had read were the first few paragraphs, covering about half of page one, which stated that the appeal was denied, followed by a long list of reasons, most of which I had become accustomed to by this time. Hence, I couldn't be bothered to read all of the other paragraphs that occupied the remaining page and a half or more. My position was that I had no more documentation to submit and there was no more explanation or commentary I could add to clarify the fact that I had earned the money for which points were being claimed, so I would just keep appealing (rather naively) until it was approved or I was invited for an oral hearing, or worst case, I was formally told to leave the country. Therefore, when I read the lines that said the appeal options had been exhausted and the fourth one sent could not be heard, I stopped to read every single paragraph in the letter.

Despite not being heard, this letter proceeded to restate the reasons for denying the visa renewal, which was slowly getting me into a frenzy. At the back of my mind was the realisation that I couldn't appeal any of those statements even though I didn't agree with them. The feeling of being denied a voice or a right is certainly not a comfortable one for someone like me who inherently abhors injustice. So when I read the last paragraph, which said something along the lines of "even if this case were to be heard again, it will not see the light of day," I was so enraged that I blurted out similar words to those of the young David when he heard Goliath curse Israel's army, "*Who is this uncircumcised Philistine that he should defy the armies of the living God?*" (1 Samuel 17:26b NIV). Going through my head was the thought that questioned the audacity of any human being to make such a statement when I knew with every fibre of my being that it was contrary to what God, the Creator of all things and the Giver of the breath in every human blood cell, had said. In that moment, I felt every ounce of anger that David must have felt that caused him to charge forward towards Goliath despite the physical odds being against him, because this was a challenge to God and not me.

I picked up the letter, stormed out of the house, and headed to church, completely forgetting that it was an hour's walk away and the shutters might not be open because it wasn't a meeting day. Onwards I marched with one purpose in mind—to take this challenge to God's doorstep. Mouthing Scriptures as I walked, I took strides like that of one competing for an Olympic gold title and was in the church premises in no time. On getting in, I noticed that everything was quiet. One of the shutters to the church hall was halfway open, so I went straight in, placed the letter on the altar, and kneeled down to pray.

First, I read the letter's conclusion out to God. Then, with tears streaming down my face and a rather angry tone, I began to remind God of everything He told me and how He had just been challenged by this senior judge. As I prayed, the venom in my veins began to dissipate, and I prayed more calmly until the burden was lifted from my soul. Then I was able to hear God's response clearly, and my perspective on the whole situation changed. I began thanking God for His Word, which assured me of His presence and directed my path. As I prayed, I made proclamations that reminded me that situations like this, where man proclaims there is no way forward, are actually the best settings to experience God's power. I shouldn't have been telling God how "big" a problem it was because that is inconsequential. What mattered most was what God had said. With God, there is absolutely nothing that is impossible (Luke 1:37). If He can call light out of darkness (2 Corinthians 4:6), then He was surely going to bring to pass what He had spoken about me. My part to play was to believe and have faith.

Then, I felt God respond, saying that the reason He told me His plans ahead was because He knew the physical circumstances would not align but to be assured that it was only for a while (2 Corinthians 4:18). Hence, I should not let my heart be troubled but hold on to what He had told me and start seeing things the way He sees them so I could speak in agreement with Him rather than give voice to the current and temporal contrary situation. He reminded me that He specialises in calling into existence the things that previously were not (Romans 4:17), so I needed to start doing the same, and that He is well able to make a way where humans physically can see none (Isaiah 43:16, 19). At those words, a peace came upon me, and I could smile again.

Just as I rose up to leave, one of the church staff came into the hall and was surprised to see me, because he didn't expect that anyone was there. It was approaching the end of the working day, so he came downstairs to lock up the hall.

"How come the shutters were left open?" I asked.

He replied that the industrial cleaners had come that day to do some deep cleaning, especially of the marble flooring, and asked for them to be left open for some hours to properly ventilate the hall.

"Well, it was good timing, because I really needed to do business with God," I said and made my way out.

That in itself was a miracle for me, because I had come carrying a heavy burden and was not sure it would have had the same impact (for me and at that moment) if I had not been able to access the altar. Again, I realised that God worked even that out for my good. Thus, in my walk back home, I had spring in my step—full of joy; singing and dancing, not caring much for whoever was watching.

Back at home, I read the letter again. Whilst I still did not agree with the statements made nor with being denied the opportunity of an oral hearing, I felt no more anger, because laying the burden at the altar and hearing God's response to it assured me that He had it all covered and would carry me through the storm. The senior judge made that statement based on what they knew, which was understandable. However, as the one privileged to know how the matter will end—having heard God's perspective clearly—I needed to act in accordance with what I knew and not what I was experiencing. The Bible teaches that Jesus endured the shame and pain of crucifixion on the cross because of the joy that was to follow (Hebrews 12:2). Therefore, I needed to keep my gaze firmly on God and the eternal purpose He promised—being in the UK was just one of the elements in that plan.

As the letter ended without stating what the next action should be, I called Fred to inform him of the latest development and ask his advice. He had kindly offered to give me free consultations out of hours, so long as it was only to advise a course of action that I could implement myself. He advised that the options were either to request a judicial review, since I wasn't satisfied with the way the case was handled, or I could appeal the decision at the European Court, adding that neither option was going to be an easy process.

Then, the penny dropped. Although God was using the trials to train and help me develop spiritual resilience, the journey's end would not be anytime soon. With that realisation also came the decision to find another accommodation, because I didn't feel comfortable continuing to stay in the flat without paying rent, even though my landlord had said it was okay. I considered that he was a family man. Although he had a day job, that flat could be the source of income that helped him really make ends meet. I couldn't justify continuing to take advantage of his kindness, especially as I was uncertain about when it was going to end. That Sunday, I spoke to my choir leader and pastor about the need, gradually learning to be vulnerable to asking for help and choosing rather to be a squatter than live rent-free in a comfortable flat that could be denying a whole family some things. Some people may think this was unwise, but there was an unrest in my spirit about it, which grew the longer I stayed there—and I was starting to learn to be guided by an inner peace from God.

A few days later, my pastor asked me to speak to a lady who was also in the choir and might be able to accommodate me, pending when I was able to start contributing to the rent, as her landlady was also a member of our church. This was great news because the lady, Abíọlá or Aby, and I had attended the same branch in Lagos some years ago. After the church service, I approached Aby about the need, and she confirmed that it was okay but wanted to get her landlady's agreement as well. I accompanied her to speak to the landlady, who confirmed that our pastor had spoken to her. She had no problems with me being there, adding that when I got back into work we could discuss again to agree on rent. I thanked them both and settled the date to move in. Thankfully, most of my possessions were still packed from early January, when I had thought that I would be moving back to Nigeria.

That week, I requested an audience with my landlord to provide him an update and reason for my decision to move out. His response was the same as before—he was happy for me to stay there as long as was needed but respected my views on not taking advantage of his kindness, although he didn't feel that was the case. He wished me well for the future, and I expressed my deepest gratitude to him for everything, promising to pay back some of that rent when I was able to—which I fulfilled some years later, because a promise is a promise! Consequently, at the end of April 2010, I moved to Essex, which opened up a whole new chapter of experiences.

JEHOVAH NISSI
The Lord is My Banner

I considered Fred's advice on the legal routes available and decided to request a judicial review. Appealing to the European Court didn't seem appropriate due to the considerably longer time it took to conclude cases, not to mention it was more expensive. A prolonged case was tantamount to a longer period before I could be gainfully employed.

Up to that point in time, I had gone for a number of interviews, and the story was the same. It all fell apart when the evidence of my right to work was requested and I had to explain that my passport was with the Home Office. To further complicate the situation, new immigration rules were released in February 2010, which were even more stringent. Hence, most organisations erred on the side of caution when considering the risk of inadvertently employing an illegal resident. On one occasion, I had been offered the job before my documentation was requested. When I gave the normal spiel that they were with the Home Office pending renewal, the hiring manager called me to apologise profusely, saying that they would unfortunately have to offer it to the next best candidate. It was a crushing feeling! Yet, all of my attempts to get the Home Office to at least give me a cover letter clarifying that I could be employed while my case was still being processed—as they always told me on the phone—were in vain.

Therefore, I was left in this limbo of not wanting to do anything illegal and constantly being denied good job opportunities while I waited for God's plan to become a physical reality.

This was why I decided on the option with the shortest lead time—requesting a judicial review to the Home Office. While trying to put my statements together, the Holy Spirit asked me to take time to carefully read through and compare the paragraphs in the tribunal's responses to my third and fourth appeals, dated March 30 and April 22, respectively. I hadn't quite read the letters in detail when they were originally received and only kept them for their occasional use during my prayers. So, it was a huge eye-opener when I noticed quite significant differences and sometimes discrepancies in the reasons provided for refusing the appeal. This was despite the letter dated April 22 stating that the appeal was not heard and suggesting that the paragraphs contained therein were a mere repetition of those in the letter dated March 30. It was even more surprising when I saw that the April letter had actually been signed and dated March 30!

Right there, I heard the Holy Spirit say to me, "That is your way out!" Hence, after laying out my arguments on how I met the criteria to warrant the work permit being renewed, I added some fairly direct statements that expressed my deep disappointment in how my case had been handled. Rather than sending the judicial review request to only the Home Office, the Holy Spirit nudged me to send a copy to the Upper Tribunal too, which I did.

In late May, I received a response from the Home Office effectively turning down my request for a judicial review on the basis of concerns that had been raised way back in their January refusals, which I had adequately addressed in subsequent appeals. However, it offered no response to the discrepancies. All of this suggested that no one was really taking their time in reviewing the case, nor would they be interested in doing so no matter how many times I appealed or requested a review. Since I had decided that I didn't want to take the case outside the UK's borders and this judicial review was the last known option available for me to challenge the visa refusal, I turned to God in prayer as before.

Although the situation seemed hopeless, I chose to trust that if God said it, then He would bring it to pass, so long as I didn't give up (just as the Bible said of Abraham in Romans 4:17–21). Singing songs of praise as I prayed, I professed Scriptures such as those that reminded me that Jesus was wounded for my transgressions and the chastisement for my peace had already been laid on Him (Isaiah 53:5), that He had nailed to the cross every handwriting of requirements against me (Colossians 2:14), and that God is able TO DO (Ephesians 3:20)! Therefore, I wasn't going to let this situation steal my peace. I would wholeheartedly trust God, come what may. Asking God to direct me on what to do next, I got a very clear response from Him, though certainly not what I was expecting.

In very clear words, God said to me, "Be still."

Huh! "God, what does that mean?" I asked.

He replied, "Do nothing."

Trusting that He always knows the best path through a desert and can create a way in deep seas, I obeyed that instruction and spent the days-in-waiting thanking Him for who He is. Certainly, there were days I felt uneasy with His silence and to just wait on Him to get further direction. It also didn't help that the Home Office's response didn't provide any statement on what they now expected, knowing that I had exhausted all appeal opportunities. A minor point of comfort for me came from the fact that they had returned my passport, which had a five-year visitor's visa from 2005 that would run out about August 2010. It gave me a sense of "legal" standing to be in the country, at least, pending when it was clear what actions God wanted me to take towards securing my work permit.

Two weeks went by and still no fresh response from God, so I kept on waiting. In fact, the more I sang His praise, the more I started to notice a shift in my mindset and view of the whole situation. I was starting to see all that was going on with the eyes and heart of gratitude. The situation itself became least important in my desires as my heart started to take in the extent of God's relentless and reckless love for me in a whole new way. It was a mindset shift that saw me completely dissociating my service to and love for God from the things He does to simply loving Him because He first loved me (1 John 4:19). I knew that He chose to love me right from my mother's womb (Isaiah 44:24; Jeremiah 1:5), all through when I didn't know Him

(Romans 5:8), till that moment in time, and would for all eternity (Jeremiah 31:3). The only way to describe what this realisation felt like is with the prayer of the apostle Paul in Ephesians 3:17–19 (NIV):

And I pray that you, being rooted and established in love, may have power, together with all the Lord's holy people, to grasp how wide and long and high and deep is the love of Christ, and to know this love that surpasses knowledge—that you may be filled to the measure of all the fullness of God.

Deepening my understanding of God's love for me in this way helped me develop a more joyful, rather than a striving, attitude. I woke up each day with either a song of praise already on my spirit or a heart full of gratitude for yet another day to enjoy His mercies afresh (Lamentations 3:20–25).

About the second week into June, which was nearly a month into following God's instruction to be still and do nothing, I received a letter from the tribunal. It acknowledged receipt of the judicial letter, which prompted them to review my case. They admitted that there were errors in the judgements of March 30 and April 22, so those decisions would be annulled! I was going to get back my third appeal opportunity, and there would be an oral hearing as I had requested. I was asked to resend all of my documents to the tribunal in preparation for a hearing date.

My jaw nearly hit the floor reading those words! What I felt was more than the feeling of winning a huge lottery jackpot. I was filled with overwhelming joy and utter awe of God, but I couldn't find the words to fully express myself in English. I screamed and danced and praised God on and on in my mother tongue till I could speak no more. The way God did this was nothing short of a mighty, strong hand that paved a way where all hope seemed lost; He truly is the Extraordinary Strategist. I recalled the words of Isaiah 40:28–31 (NIV).

Do you not know?
Have you not heard?
The LORD is the everlasting God,

the Creator of the ends of the earth.
He will not grow tired or weary,
and his understanding no one can fathom.
He gives strength to the weary
and increases the power of the weak.
Even youths grow tired and weary,
and young men stumble and fall;
but those who hope in the Lord
will renew their strength.
They will soar on wings like eagles;
they will run and not grow weary,
they will walk and not be faint.

MORAL –

Is God asking you to wait about something? Have you been praying and waiting on God for something so long that all hope seems lost? Or you just don't think that God has heard your prayers or thinks about you? No matter where you are, how you are feeling, what circumstances you are in, what people are telling you, or what you've done—God loves you unconditionally. All that God does is motivated by and anchored in L.O.V.E. You cannot do anything more or less to earn His love; Jesus made that possible. All you need is to accept His love that has been poured out for you. The challenges you might be facing do not determine your identity, nor should they define you; Christ does. Seek to know Him as a Person and trust in Him wholeheartedly, not for just His works but for the Person that He is. You will find that you can still have joy and peace right in the middle of the storm.

Get into the Bible and study it. The stories in it show examples of how God relates with people. More importantly, the Bible reveals His Person, principles, and heart regarding a matter. The Scriptures are the ammunition you need to fight life's battles (Ephesians 6:10–18). By being familiar with them, you will be able to hear God clearer because He never contradicts His written word.

I put all requested documents in an envelope and sent them to the Upper Tribunal. In July, I received a notice setting the hearing date for August 10,

2010 at 10 a.m. The Sunday before the hearing date, I was filled with a heart of gratitude for all that God had brought me through, how He had helped me rise above the challenges faced, the lessons He was teaching me through those challenges that were helping to build my character, and how He had proven His Word time and time again to me. Remembering the precious seed of my gold jewellery that was given, I could now see how laying down my most valuable possessions at the time had helped me to look to Jesus for my sustenance and to hold on—just one more day sometimes—to His promises. Though I didn't have much cash on me that Sunday, I gave what I had as a Thanksgiving offering—not for a specific outcome but just to say "Thank You" to God for everything. During his preaching, the new local church pastor encouraged us to declare the verses in Psalm 121 upon ourselves throughout that week, which resonated in my spirit. I took it as a personal word from God to me.

The night before the hearing, I listened to faith-inspiring messages and prayed all through the night. The two main things that I asked God for were: first, that He would go with me as my Advocate (John 14:26, 1 John 2:1) to give me the right words to speak, as I didn't have legal representation and the most I had ever seen of a courtroom was in the movies; and second, that I would return with a definite decision so I could move on with life—whatever shape that turned out to be. I got ready fairly early so as to be at the court, which was in Central London, in good time to avoid potential train delays. Hence, I was on the premises by about 9:00 a.m. During a brief chat with the receptionist, she mentioned that there was a prayer room in the building, which was empty, thankfully, by the time I found it. Seeing as it was now about thirty minutes before the start of the hearing, I locked the door behind me and prayed in other tongues to remind myself of who was with me and calm the nerves rising up in my veins, as well as declare the verses of Psalm 121 (NIV).

> *I lift up my eyes to the mountains—*
> *where does my help come from?*
> *My help comes from the LORD,*
> *the Maker of heaven and earth.*
> *He will not let your foot slip—*
> *he who watches over you will not slumber;*

indeed, he who watches over Israel
will neither slumber nor sleep.
The LORD watches over you—
the LORD is your shade at your right hand;
the sun will not harm you by day,
nor the moon by night.
The LORD will keep you from all harm—
he will watch over your life;
the LORD will watch over your coming and going
both now and forevermore.

After praying, I made my way to the designated courtroom, having about five minutes to spare and meeting the end of the case that was before mine. I had heard stories about how the Home Office representatives did not turn up sometimes, or when they did, they attended with a clear decision on their mind, making the session really quick. Well, mine turned up. In less than five minutes into the case, it became evident that he came with one decision in mind—to deny me the visa renewal.

After about forty-five minutes of questioning from the Home Office representative, the judge moved to adjourn the case, stating that these cases were never more than fifteen minutes, yet, after nearly an hour, this one didn't seem to be going anywhere. The judge then mentioned my judicial review letter, stating that she had allowed ample time for me to prove my earnings to the Home Office representative, which was the remaining bone of contention, to ensure that I got fair treatment this time. The representative wanted to see specific documents with statements that were endorsed by my company accountants, which was obviously a new request. Hence she was adjourning the case to give time to obtain those documents. Then, she asked the representative to call out the requirements as she made note of them and repeated the same for me to make note of.

Just as I was taking the notes, I heard an audible voice to my right that said, "You mean you want to go and come back?"

Immediately, I recognised who it was and felt like God was sitting in the chair next to me where my legal representative would have sat if I had one. In a split second, it dawned on me that He was repeating the words I had said in prayer that morning. Having been carried away by everything that was happening, I had completely lost sight of what I had asked for, but God did not. My Advocate was tangibly in the room to help me out. In that same minutiae of a second, I felt my right hand go up. Before my brain could fully catch up with what was happening, I heard the judge say, "Yes, what would you like to say?"

Realising my hands were up and being unsure of what to say, I turned to my right side and asked the Holy Spirit, "Why are my hands up?" I could hear the judge repeat her question, so I turned back to face her. Just as I opened my mouth to speak, the Holy Spirit filled it with the right words.

"Well, I don't think I want to go and come back."

She replied, "But you don't have the necessary documentation to satisfy the Home Office representative that you earned the income amount required to be awarded the points being claimed."

I responded with the same line, stressing that I needed a definite decision that day, as I did not want my life remaining in limbo any longer.

She replied that she was willing to give me her direct contact details such that when I had the documents being requested, I could send them directly to her office, and she would ensure that I got an immediate court hearing date so that it wouldn't drag longer than necessary. Thankful as I was for the offer, I insisted on having a decision there and there.

Then the judge said, "Without being able to satisfy the representative's requirements, I will have to refuse your visa renewal. This means you will have to leave the country immediately."

I shrugged and said, "If that is the case, then it will be fine by me, because then I will have a decision made today."

"OK," the judge said. Then she started to write the judgement. Some seconds into writing, she suddenly stopped and said, "I could also adjourn the case for later today if the Home Office representative is willing to look through the accounts with you, as I need to take a break."

At that, she turned to the representative to ask. He said that he had to go because of some other appointment, which he would be late for having not planned for this case to last as long. But as he uttered those words, we started to hear the thundering sound of rain, with huge strokes that beat against the court window. Instinctively, we all looked out and saw that it was a heavy downpour—on a day that I recall the weather forecast being for on/ off light showers (because I checked). With that, I knew exactly what was happening—God had just changed the game!

With that alone, and in that very moment, I was blown away yet again by God's incredible mercies towards me. I recalled the story of when Joshua asked for the sun to stand still so that the army of Israel could win a battle, and it did for a full day (Joshua 10:12–15), effectively making two calendar days seem like a single day, all because God was on their side. I realised that just as God allowed the sun to stay still for Joshua, He was using the rain to fight for me so that His Word was fulfilled! Really and truly, I had stopped caring as much about the outcome but more about following God's plans. To see Him choose to fight for me by using the elements was absolutely humbling, and my eyes welled up with tears.

That day and moment have remained one of the most incredible and life-changing moments of my life till date—and trust me, I have seen God do many mind-blowing things. That moment confirmed to me that God always watches over His Words to accomplish it (Jeremiah 1:12)—not because I am special or do anything to earn His favour, but because of His name and promises. He had chosen to lavish me with favour, and that day, I learnt to embrace it without feeling guilty for any part of it. God has more than enough for everyone, so I choose to relish mine.

On seeing the heavy downpour, the Home Office representative, who was sitting backing the window, turned to the judge to say, "Well, there is no way I will be going anywhere in that because I didn't come with an umbrella, as such heavy rain was not forecast." Plus, an umbrella will not even be able to protect from that. I will be happy to wait and look through the documentation with her."

This made me smile, because I knew that if God went this far to change the game—starting first with me, then the judge, and now the Home Office representative—and with such a demonstration of His power, then I knew that the outcome was going to align to His purpose. Therefore, I focused my mind on being on the Lord's side.

Once the representative confirmed that he was going to stay behind to look through the documentation again with me, the judge turned to me to say that when he made a decision, the court officer would come get her, and whatever the representative decided would be her judgement. By doing this, she explained, I was losing the right to provide any more evidence or to argue against anything he decided. I answered in the affirmative. Then the judge informed us that there was no other case that day, so we could use the same courtroom, and she would stay back in her office till we were ready for her. At that, she left the room.

I got up from my side and went over to the representative's side. We laid out all of the documents previously submitted, and he began to interrogate me like we had just started the case. My mind was on what an incredible favour this was and that I was not going to give up on the opportunity God had created. Therefore, when he wasn't asking me a question, I would turn to face the window and pray in other tongues, my voice a little above a whisper. A few times of doing this, and I noticed the court officer was looking at me strangely, perhaps wondering what I was doing or muttering, but I didn't let that discourage me. This was no time to be embarrassed, but one to be seized.

After about twenty minutes of doing this, he requested a document which turned out to be one of those the Holy Spirit had nudged me to take along that day. Though it wasn't a previously requested document, it became the final piece of evidence that the representative seemed to want. I retrieved the document from my bag and handed it over to him to look through, following my brief explanation of the numbers. As before, I had turned to face the window when the representative suddenly said, "I am satisfied now."

The court officer, obviously tired of this session now running into two hours total, immediately left the room to get the judge without asking us to confirm whether we were ready or not. Turning to face the representative, I was still asking him if he meant that he was satisfied with the document provided, when the call to stand was made to usher the judge back into the room. True to her word, the judge turned to the representative to ask his decision without so much as looking in my direction. Then, I heard the Home Office representative say the golden words, "I am satisfied that she fulfils all of the requirements to have her visa renewed."

At that, the judge turned to me and said, "It certainly was worth the wait, right?"

I replied, "Yes, it definitely was."

She then read out her judgement, which was that my appeal had been successful and my work permit visa would be granted without the need to provide further documentation. And that was it!

I remained a few minutes after everyone left, thinking back on all that had just happened in that courtroom. It kept blowing my mind the more I thought—and still does till this very day. I was overjoyed but couldn't fully express it, so I decided to make my way back home without saying a word to anyone. Stepping outside the court building, I noticed that the rain had completely stopped with barely any trace of that heavy downpour we saw through the courtroom windows left on the ground. The sun shone bright as if attesting to it being a new day. I took in a deep breath, which felt like taking in an "air of freedom." In a huge sigh of relief, I released it all at once, as one might feel having fought a long, wearying battle, but in what seems like a blink of an eye, finally comes out victorious!

JEHOVAH SABAOTH
Lord of Hosts

On the train back, I was quiet. Still amazed by how events had transpired in that courtroom, I kept my mind from reminiscing till I got to a comfortable place, which happened as I stepped into the flat. In an act of worship and full gratitude, I laid prostrate before God to praise His holy name. I was completely caught up in gratitude and adoration for God—He chose for me to physically observe and appreciate the workings of His mighty power, using both living and non-living things to demonstrate His Lordship over all. It was a lot for my mind to fully comprehend. That day, I fell even more in love with God.

So far, I had known God's deep love for me and learnt to love Him. However, that day, His Person became very real to me, having felt Him in the same room—not by dream or vision, but by His tangible presence. Then, that He would show up for me the way He did, giving me the strength to stay focused on His purpose and providing the right words when in the presence of a judge, which would normally have been nerve-wracking, made His Person come alive to me. I saw Him as being a dependable Person and One that would never ever leave me in a time of trouble—and I was in love with a Person of such qualities. I have heard it said of God, and that day it became my reality that He is the Personality of my deepest affection. It changed the way I relate to Him, which is improving with each passing day and year. I am truly loving being in love with the Person of God. It was in that place of adoration for Him that I gave Him my all. Yes, I had given my life to Jesus Christ as a teenager, confessing Him as my personal Lord and Saviour, but I had not totally surrendered my life to Him. Through the years, I have learnt to hear His voice (though I still make mistakes as I grow in my walk with Him), but that day in 2010 was when I made a conscious no-turning-back decision to follow Christ. I was fully persuaded that the entirety of what makes up my person would be better guided and useful in His hands.

As part of that surrender, I handed over my emotions (which is an area He has since delicately and gradually helped me understand and to improve) and also decided that as long as I was unmarried, I would be celibate and date rightly. Choosing to be celibate wasn't because I "played" around. It was because I always seemed to end up in an undefined or confused relationship of some sort, like the one I had ongoing at the time. It was borne out of my need for emotional support during the immigration saga and meeting up with an old friend who equally needed emotional support as he was going through a difficult period. Noting my past pitfalls and experiences in the love department but refusing to let go of my dream of being married and building a loving family where all members thrive, things always felt like I was exerting so much effort in pursuit of making that dream a reality yet never quite "seeing the results" as one would expect it. Of course, I never ceased to pray about it through the years, but things still weren't working out as I planned. Therefore, with my new found understanding of how God could make "big" of my little efforts and cause things to turn out much better than I could ever imagine IF it was aligned to His plans and I went according to His timing, this decision was my way of surrendering my life in the area of love relationships to God and choosing not to get involved with anyone until I was sure that it was what He wanted for me and that I could do it His way.

My relationship with God and dependence on Him had grown during the immigration challenge such that I could lean solely on Him, including when I needed a "real shoulder to cry on." He knows me better than I know myself and has the safest arms that I could ever be in. I knew that I could trust Him to lead me to the right relationship just as He had done all through the immigration issues. In my full surrender to God, I asked Him to help me "live right" no matter what life might bring my way. He has been doing it ever since. God has been my absolute rock, and truly the One that is still helping me keep the celibacy promise. It's said that "old habits die hard," but I can assure you that they can die easily with God's help; therefore, be encouraged.

MORAL –

Let Christ into every area of your life so He can bring out that beauty which He knows has been deposited in you, to the glory of His name. It certainly won't happen overnight, but when you really let God in, then He will reveal to you things you didn't even know about yourself and will graciously help you overcome or mature in such areas, depending on what you need at each point in time in order for you to be fully equipped for the work He calls you to.

It was after that prayer, both of gratitude for the victory won and the surrender of my life to Him, that I was able to pick up the phone to give my parents the great news and tell other friends what a great and marvellous thing God had done. Whilst I have spoken a lot on what I did during the period to stay my eyes on Jesus, I do not have the misconception that I overcame this by my prayers alone—absolutely not! My parents and siblings also played a key role in helping me through this phase of life. Since the time I informed them of the decision to stay back in the UK, they had sent me funds—converting naira to pounds sterling, which cost them a lot—and importantly, never ceasing to pray for and with me. My mum taught us that no matter where we are as siblings, one person's problem is all of our problem. Therefore, she often called for joint prayer and fasting days to address any matter at hand. Then, there were ladies in the church and my pastor then who not only prayed for me but often encouraged me with words and with their material possessions too.

Sure, there were those that didn't think I was making the right decision and made it clear in their actions to have nothing to do with me, but God helped me understand that they could not be judged for their actions because it wasn't to them that He gave the vision. Using an analogy of the story of a man of God in 1 Kings 13, God taught me that where He gives a clear direction regarding His plans, He will equally speak to me if those plans change. Therefore, whatever anyone else expresses is their opinion based on what they observe with their physical eyes, which isn't bad in itself but isn't how He works. That lesson was crucial in helping me to forgive and overlook what was a painful feeling of being let down by those I considered close friends.

MORAL —

Perhaps you need to forgive someone too. You should choose to forgive wrongs, not because of the recipient, but for yourself. It is primarily for your own good, plus it is a way of extending to others the same blessing that God has shown to you.

As 2010 drew to a close, I reflected again and again on all that had transpired, and though I was still in awe of God (likely to be the case for the rest of my life), one thing still eluded me. Besides the dozens of lessons that I learnt during the period and my gratitude for how God revealed Himself to me and assured me of His presence with me, I still couldn't understand why this was the way God chose to teach me those things. It just never felt right or fair, especially when I had met the stipulated criteria and submitted all necessary documentation to evidence it—the very same documents that were used to exonerate me in court. Knowing now that every move of God, including the simple or random-looking action, has purpose in it, I asked this question to Him, "Why was my work permit visa renewal ever denied?" but I got no response from Him. Again and again, I asked, but again and again, He gave me no response. Sometime in 2011, I asked one last time, telling Him that I wouldn't ask again, but He still wouldn't budge. So, I never asked again.

One day in 2012, I was probably on my way to work, commuting to Reading from London again, when God decided to start having this conversation out of the blue. He came at me with a question that was so random, I recognised that it was Him putting the words in my mind. The minute I engaged, it became a clear conversation, which probably made those who were around me think I was out of my mind either for talking to myself or seeming to be discussing with someone they couldn't see. I couldn't see Him either, but His presence was so tangible I could relate as if speaking to a person.

God said, "When did you come into the UK?"

Once I collected myself, though not knowing where this was going, I said, "February 2008."

Then He asked, "When did you get the original HSMP visa?"

"October 2007," I replied.

"How many years do you need to be able to apply for indefinite leave to remain (ILR)?"

"Five years continuous stay."

As I said that, the penny dropped. God was responding to the question I asked more than a year ago to explain why my visa renewal application in 2009 had to be denied. The initial HSMP visa was granted for two years. If the conditions are satisfied, it is renewed for three years, thereby allowing the recipient to apply for an ILR after a total of five years of residency in the UK. Well in my case, because of my reluctance to move to the UK and the conditions set—all of which God met—I effectively lost about four months off the visa before relocating. Therefore, had my application for renewal in October 2009 gone smoothly, then my visa would have expired in October 2012, which definitely would not have given me the five years of continuous stay required for an ILR.

To complicate matters, the self-sponsored HSMP visas were stopped at the end of 2010, and even more stringent rules for residency were introduced. If God hadn't done what He did then, I would have struggled very much more to find an option that would have allowed me to recover those four months in order to apply for an ILR. In fact, I might have had to leave the country, which would have jeopardised God's plans. But, to cover my error and the shortsightedness of being human, the God who knows ALL things and watches over His Word to establish it made a way for His plans to come to pass, although I was completely oblivious to it. By having my visa denied in October 2009 and the court decision not being affected until October 2010, God bought me an additional year—in place of four months—as the visa was renewed till October 2013. That realisation yet again left me utterly speechless and in total awe of God! Hence, in February 2013, when I attained the five-year residency criteria, I was relaxed about going through the ILR process, still having months left on my visa.

One could look at the events of 2010 and focus on the negative repercussions—like being broke and unemployed, losing my home and independence, and the many emotional stresses that came with them. When I look at the totality of it, costs versus dividends, I have found that the benefits by far outweigh the costs. The reason being that it helped me to see clearly the things that God had in mind for me. That picture has only gotten clearer with the passing of years. The experiences of the year and subsequent victory upon victory seen solidified the foundation of my faith as a Christian and provided the building blocks upon which my maturity in Christ has been developed ever since.

THINK ON THESE...

1. Seek God's face or opinion first regarding every matter so that you can hear His views and plans on them, and have the Holy Spirit direct you step by step on what to do. Once God has given you a word, irrespective of the challenges faced thereafter, including any contrary opinions, hold on tight to what God told you and do that which He asks of you. In doing so, you demonstrate your faith in Him (James 2:26); your faith moves God to move mountains. God is bound by His Word thus, ensure that His voice is louder than anyone else, including that of your mind (1 John 5:9).

2. Be patient and prayerful as you learn to wait for things to happen in God's timing—when He works it all out beautifully (Ecclesiastes 3:11). Be confident that with God, you can never be disadvantaged or disappointed. In His time, He will make a way out for you, and neither will the situation overwhelm you when you put your trust wholly in Him (1 Corinthians 10:13).

3. Surround yourself with the right people, that is, those who encourage you to keep pursuing the path God has laid out for

you—whether they understand it or not. Although it is "your race" and not theirs, we all need encouraging words as we go along the way (Proverbs 27:17).

4. Maintain your confession, which should be aligned to God's Word and plans for you. God's Word never fails; if you stick to it, you will surely return with a testimony (Psalm 126:5–6). A former pastor of mine used to say, "It is better to keep quiet than to say the wrong things," and I found it to be so true.

5. Resist the urge to take shortcuts! Avoiding the situation or seeking shortcuts (no matter who suggests it) will only create more problems for you in the future. No matter how long the right way seems to be taking, keep your gaze on Jesus, Who is the Author and Finisher of your faith (Hebrews 12:2).

6. Seek information from professionals, as appropriate, but be careful not to consume what will make you fearful or doubtful of what God has told you. Once you glean information from others, double check with God by praying about it and listening for His directions before taking any final decisions.

EL ROI
The God Who Sees Me

Early in 2011, I had to leave the accommodation in Essex at very short notice as a result of a misunderstanding with Aby, which spiralled out of control. To avoid becoming a leech, being mindful that I wasn't contributing to the rent, I would often eat separately as well as use very little gas and electricity, as these were often the next big costs in running a home after the rent. Often times, I stayed with friends based in London for the weekend whenever I went over on Saturdays for choir rehearsals and youth meetings so I could be close enough to be in church early on Sunday, as well as to reduce my travel costs. These friends, usually two separate families, knew of the immigration battle and the challenges that it had brought on, so they would often give me cooked meals to take back—which to my mind helped me be less of a burden on Aby. I didn't realise that she saw it differently and was unhappy about it, although she didn't mention these concerns to me. A mutual friend told me of it after I had moved in a bid to hear my side of the story (of an issue I didn't even know existed). Perhaps being focused on getting through the immigration challenge caused me to miss this and some other incidences the friend mentioned were discussed in their clique.

Apparently, Aby's decision to ask me to leave was triggered by a misunderstanding of my question about the rent amount—bearing in mind the initial discussions that I would contribute to it when I started working, following the success of the court appeal. When she didn't answer the question, I naively asked it to the landlady, since we were in the same church and my paying part of the rent was also discussed with her at the outset. Of course, they discussed it and somehow reached the conclusion that I was trying to take over the lease agreement from Aby—which, if that was the case, would anger anyone. My intentions were purely to help me plan for that eventuality of paying rent, yet I was not asked about it until the problem festered, escalated, and became this concoction of they-said-you-said-which-means situation that completely blindsided me.

On the day of the incident, Aby called me about lunchtime from work, saying that she needed the space so I should find somewhere else to go. The suddenness of it and my trying to better understand the reason for it, plus how long I should plan for, since I would need to ask someone else to accommodate me in that period, resulted in an argument that concluded with her advising that I leave that very day and not make plans to return. You can imagine my shock and disorientation when she dropped the call. There was no way I could move all of my things that day, so my initial thought was to find a place to go first, and I would return at a later date to pick up my things. But where would I go? I could think of no other options besides the two families that had previously welcomed me to spend weekends in their homes, so I called them. One was out of town; the other, Deborah or Debbie, had her phone switched off. The rest of that afternoon, I kept trying Debbie's line, but it wouldn't go through, leaving me in a panic state and thinking, *"This couldn't have happened on a worse day."*

When it was getting to about 7:00 p.m., I was still unable to reach Debbie and knew that Aby did not want to meet me in the house. I packed a few items, having decided to just go into London. I had hoped to get through to Debbie before arriving so as to check if the family would be able to accommodate me for an unknown time period at short notice, though this was not the kind of relationship we had at that time.

It was late by the time I got to Limehouse Station in London, and still I had no contact with Debbie. At that point I became very nervous and wondered if I just might not have a place to sleep that night (at least). Throughout the challenges faced, I had never imagined that I could become homeless until that point, and the thought scared me very much. I looked up to the dark sky on what was a cold, wet day and thought to God, *Are You still in charge of this situation?*

Having not heard from Debbie and giving up trying any further, I decided to head towards Central London, where I knew there were lots of big and busy stations, which should give me a secure space to spend the night. As I made my way there, mostly lost in thoughts, my mind went to homeless people, as it dawned on me that not everyone in that situation is a miscreant as they are often painted. Some are likely victims of circumstances, just like me—accepting this would be my fate that night.

At some point, I was on one of those old bendy London buses that had three entrances—front, middle, and rear—and I was sitting near the middle door. I kept a straight face, trying not to think too much about what had transpired that day and attempting to keep my faith. I knew that no matter what happened, God would see me through that dark night, and the morning would soon come! I was lost in thoughts when a lady tapped my left shoulder from the back. Thinking she wanted to get into the seat next to me, I made a motion to move, but she gestured for me not to.

Instead, the lady said rather gently, "Please, I hope you wouldn't mind what I want to say."

I thought, *Well, what do you want to say?* but only managed a shoulder shrug.

The woman introduced herself as a pastor at a church on Old Kent Road. We were a few stops away from her church, where she was headed for a meeting.

At this point, I maintained my straight face, still wondering what she wanted from me, and partially preparing myself to answer that I already attended a church also located on Old Kent Road (which I realised we had now come to).

She then asked, in a very polite manner, "Are you a Christian?"

"Yes, I am," I answered.

The lady explained that she had come in through the rear door and sat at the back of the bus when God nudged her to give me a message. I properly turned my head towards her to pay attention to what she had to say, randomly expecting it to be some "preach." But it was not. She said God told her to let me know that He was with me and asked her to pray for me.

As she said those words, I couldn't hold back the tears. All through the day, I had been perplexed without the ability to pray or even hear God, yet He found a way to reassure me that I was not alone—that is what broke me. Seeing my tears, the woman told how she had to double check with God when He gave her those words. It was an unusual message to approach a stranger with, but I was glad that she did, seeing that the message meant a lot to me. She was right. Simple as those words were, it meant more than a tonne to me. With her stop fast approaching, she prayed with me and bade me well. When she got off the bus, I wiped away my tears in new-found confidence that although I might have to sleep at a station that night, God was with me—and that was all I needed to know.

It was barely ten minutes after, as the bus was coming up to the Elephant and Castle station, when Debbie called me. She mentioned seeing my many missed calls when she got some charge into her phone, but it wasn't until that moment, around 10:00 p.m., that she remembered to give me a call back. When I told her of my need and plans to spend the night at a station, she demanded that I come to their house and we could sort out sleeping arrangements later. That was how God saved me a night, at least, out in the cold, but equally opened my eyes to the realities of homelessness. Subsequently, God opened up another accommodation for me, and I moved to Hounslow.

By the end of 2011, I not only had one home where I was welcome anytime, but there were two others, including Debbie's place, where I was welcome as part of the family. Fast forward six years, and I had my own home—bought when I never even premeditated doing so nor knew that I could. The whole process of that, which began in 2016, had God's handwriting all over it. Therefore, I named it "The Lord's House."

Since that bus moment in 2011, I never saw a homeless person the same way again—even when I have met them drinking or doing things that one would otherwise attribute to being the reason they have remained in that situation. I remember not to judge because that person could have been me. With all of my education and abilities, one wrong circumstance could have very easily put me in that same situation. What I see now is the person, not their condition or addiction. Although I know that isn't a ministry I am called into specifically, the least I offer is to get the person a warm drink and meal.

The good news for anyone in a similar or other difficult situation is that God sees and cares for you. Ask Him for the help you need, and He will make a way for you.

THINK ON THIS...

Independence is not the ability to stand alone such that you don't need anyone, but the ability not to solely rely on a particular person. We are social beings and are created with various abilities that cannot reach their full potential in isolation. Therefore, we need one another. In your strive for independence, remember that God has deposited an ability in someone else around you that you would need to help attain the desired height—most times, they won't look like or be presented in the form that you might have imagined.

JEHOVAH EZER
Lord Our Help

I was due to return to Durham University for the second year of my MBA in January 2011. As the immigration issue dragged on and I didn't get my renewal documents until October 2010, I hadn't been able to secure employment that afforded me the opportunity to save up for the school fees. I decided to contact the university administration to request a deferment till 2012, but their initial response was that being a two-year MBA program, one could not defer for more than a year. Therefore, they could only offer me a postgraduate diploma since I had successfully completed the first year. That broke my heart, because after everything I had been through, completing the MBA was the one dream I had left on my personal pursuit. But with what I now knew, I decided to ask God for direction and prayed that He would at least let me finish what I had started. I don't recall God giving me a specific word about it, but I suddenly had the same resolve I felt in that courtroom when He moved me to demand a decision that day. That was enough to let me understand that God would not want me to give up on that desire. I called the Uni back and refused the postgraduate diploma offer, stating that I came in for an MBA and I would finish with an MBA.

After a few back-and-forth conversations, all the while I kept praying and taking Communion, they agreed to let me defer by another year and also to pay the same course fees that were quoted when I started the program in 2009—testimonials of God's mighty hand working all things out in my favour. My ability to pay the outstanding fees was also nothing short of a miracle. A former boss sent me some money to support payment of the fees, which was enough to cover the minimum deposit requested for my registration. Later on, my local church pastor helped pay the balance. All were given as gifts rather than loans, which meant that I owed nothing when I started the second year. A-ma-zing!!! In 2016, by God's grace alone, I was able to fully pay off the loan taken to complete the first year. I could have done none of it—returning on the program and fully paying the fees—without the support of people and the church whom God used just at the right time to favour me.

In autumn 2012, when I started the second year of my MBA program, I was also working a full-time job based in Reading and commuting from the hinterlands of London's Thamesmead. Combining both was an enormous undertaking, which was so incredibly demanding that I almost gave up sometime in 2013. My daily weekday routine looked something like this: out of bed about 4:30 a.m., shower and get dressed to leave home at 5:20 a.m., catch the 5:30 a.m. bus to Woolwich Arsenal, take the DLR to Canning Town, change for the Jubilee line (now going Underground) to Waterloo, then change to the Bakerloo line to Paddington, and finally take a surface train to Reading, which got me into the office about 7:30 a.m., if there were no delays in any of those legs in the journey. Plus, it was a 99 percent chance that I would be on my feet most of that journey, as the only guarantee of getting a seat was on the 5:30 a.m. bus. Therefore, I always had a research paper or article on me to read whilst standing or as I manoeuvred my way through the crowd at the stations. At work, I was involved in at least two projects at any one time, which had team members in disparate time zones, so there was no headspace to think about anything outside of work during those hours. As a matter of strict discipline, I stopped work at 5:30 p.m. to pick up MBA activities, which were mostly writing up an assignment and later my dissertation.

Thankfully, I had told the organisation during my job interview that I was looking to go back to finish my MBA, hence I was taking a role that I was "too qualified for" (their words) so I could have the stability required to devise a rhythm that would help me through the MBA year whilst working full-time. When the time came to resume the program, they supported my cause by allowing me to print articles at the office and gave me a copy of the office keys, as I was often the first to arrive and the last to leave. Typically, I left the office at 10:00 p.m. and made the journey back to London in reverse order, getting home about midnight. By the time I showered and settled in, it was at least 1:00 a.m. the next day. For one whole year, that was my routine—getting barely four hours sleep each day.

The weekends were equally busy with writing assignments plus my service commitments at church, especially my work with the teenagers and young adults, which I did not let slip. It was an incredibly busy time, but having found that rhythm, I couldn't dare to break it. Otherwise, I could lose control of a day or, worse, end up breaking down and be unable to complete the program. My daily prayers to God were simple—to give me strength for each day and to help me successfully cross the finish line on my MBA.

Sometime in January 2013, God gave me an idea to print a calendar and place it on the wall close to my pillow. Each morning when I arose, I struck off another day in a countdown to the finish. This was so helpful because it renewed my hope as I started to see the "finish line" being closer than the days already completed.

For my dissertation, I chose an area that had long been of interest to me from a young age—brands. During my early years in secondary school, I recalled a brand advertisement having a direct but negative influence on my family's purchasing choice, which I found fascinating. Hence, I was excited at the opportunity to delve deeper into understanding the approaches for developing brands and how an organisation can change how it is perceived by rebranding. It was very tough research because there was hardly any extant literature, specifically in the area of visual identity rebranding, which I focused on. But that childish passion, as it were, kept up my enthusiasm in the research. It was also a blessing to find someone to supervise what turned out to be novel academic work. The organisations used as case studies were incredibly supportive. One of them not only handed me a dossier of materials that detailed over a century of their history in managing the global brand, but also introduced me to their brand agencies, requesting that I be given all the support required whenever I needed it.

To speak truth, staying with that research took every ounce of blood and sweat that I had in me such that I knew that my daily ability to rise up and go was on God's energy. Each day, God gave me strength of spirit, mind, and body, until the very end when I submitted my dissertation. What was more fulfilling was knowing that I genuinely contributed to the body of knowledge with the rebranding model developed at the end of the research—some good work for the next person researching that area to improve upon.

I left work early on the day my dissertation was submitted, as there was nothing to study for! On the train, I looked through the windows and saw that there was still some daylight. It was a strange beauty, because that was the first time in a year that I was looking up whilst in transit and to properly behold daylight. On getting home, the evening felt very long because I didn't have anything to read or write up, and I couldn't get myself to sleep early. The weekend equally felt strange, because it suddenly felt like I had more than twenty-four hours in the day. The interesting thing was that I felt a smidge of guilt for not having anything to do. As I gradually readjusted to the human world, I realised how immeasurable and sustaining the grace of God that I experienced during that period was.

The big surprise came in January 2014, when the university sent me a note saying that I had been awarded a merit for the program. I thought, *What!* I was ecstatic and humbled at the same time, because I knew that only God could have crowned all my efforts with such achievement—counting also the successes with my work projects. I had a flashback to 2011 when I was offered a postgraduate diploma, which would have been an achievement considering the prevailing circumstances, but God wouldn't let me "settle." At that time, all I had to go on was the desire to finish what I had started, but God took that little light and turned it into sunshine. Never in a million years during those trying times could I think of more than just being able to graduate with an MBA, but God did.

MORAL —

Trust in God. Let Him define your path, not your circumstances. Situations change, as life here on earth is inherently temporal. Therefore, allow your life to be led by One who was before time and will be even when that is no more.

I could give one example after another of how God started to redeem everything that seemed lost by reason of the immigration issue in 2010. It may have taken years, and it isn't over yet, but I am already far better off than I would have been had God not allowed that situation to happen. In counting my blessings, the most important gain of all is my consciousness of the Person of God, which has shaped my desire to know Him more and how I relate with the Scriptures. Through the years, my knowledge of God has also helped me to see people the way God sees us—loved, forgiven, able, and uniquely packaged—rather than by their circumstances, profession, possessions, physical looks, or any of such lenses that human society restricts our minds to see people by.

With the passing of time also, I have started to grasp why God chose to bring me to the UK in order to learn these things. For the logical-reasoning minds, I submit that it is because of the extremely diverse mix of people that the UK—especially London and other major cities—brings together. God is about people. Being an international and multi-cultural society, God has used being in the UK to work on my prejudices—many of which I didn't even know were there—to bring me to a place of understanding how to separate a person from their actions, and to be able to love them or extend a hand of grace to them at least. I have only just begun to scratch the surface of this understanding, but I am much more aware of it now and of letting God search deep within me to unearth those things that do not help me justly represent and reflect His Person (a prayer my mind got enlightened to and I started praying since 2016).

Be careful what you ask for, though, because God knows how to make gold out of you, but it ain't gonna be a comfortable process.

I have come to understand and accept that there will always be room for growth in Christ. I love the result of every growth experience but the journey to becoming a better person is never comfortable. The ability to accept that and be open to learning in this manner is in itself a mark of personal growth for me.

If, by this point, you are thinking that these types of experiences that demonstrate God's favour and magnificence aren't meant for "people like you,"—whatever the reason—permit me to let you in on one secret: I did nothing to earn any of it (in case you haven't figured that out already).

MORAL —

Please know that God's favour cannot be earned, and thankfully, He gives it freely to all. Take a step of faith today and take that which you need (Hebrews 4:16). You can put all of your eggs in God's basket! Seek first to know Him for who He is (not just His acts) because He is a Person, and choose to do things His Way. Most times, we make plans and ask God's blessings upon them. While that isn't a bad thing, the question is, How much better do you think it would be if you aligned your plans to God's plans for you and then asked Him for the grace to accomplish it?

Each time I think back on the events of 2010 and see the victories still being won today because I chose to stake my all on God's plans, I am filled with an enormous sense of gratitude that God gave me the insights He did and still helps me daily to stay focused on His direction. In 2010, I literally lived and overcame by holding on to every word that proceeded out of God—there was no other trick to it. Seeing how having that conviction has helped me for several years, I have since made efforts to keep with the principle of finding out God's thoughts on a matter before I take an action, especially when it comes to decisions around family, finance, and career. Sometimes, what He asks to do may seem absurd, but I have learnt not to try rationalising God's Word. Anytime I have ventured outside of this structure, the end of the matter hasn't always been pleasant, which reminds me to run back to God for help.

What a great amount of heartache and stress you would save if you only asked God first. For when it is God's plan or timing that you are following, you will be less stressed or perturbed by circumstances because of the certainty that He will work all things out to fulfil His purpose.

Herein lies my conclusion, one that I remind myself of all the time: all that I have and all that I am have not been achieved by my power, nor by my might, nor by my skills, nor by my experience, and not even by my nationality, but by the Spirit of the Lord (Zechariah 4:6). Selah!

ALÈWÍLÈ̩E
The God Who Speaks and Does

After completing my MBA program, towards the end of 2013, I moved to a new town to be closer to work. It was a better commute, but I hadn't appreciated how empty I would feel to suddenly be cut off from the supportive and social circles that I had back in London, and not being actively involved in both the choir and what had become the Youth Church, which are two of my greatest passions. I was now in a new town, attending a new local church and having to make new friends. Not being remotely involved in anything music-related (I didn't listen to much either) or actively investing in the development of young minds left me feeling stifled and empty. The totality of my life felt relegated to just work and the attendance of church services without an opportunity to express the gifts in me, which was unfulfilling for me. I was desperate for a change.

My desperation led me to pray for "a change in the status quo, whatever it takes," which God used to start charting a new course for my life. Understanding better how God works with me and being mindful not to fall into old habits where I did the planning of things to accomplish (great as that is), I prayed instead to know God's plans so I could align my actions to them. Equally, I prayed for God to "search my heart and deep within my soul to unearth anything that is not of You," so that I could, with His help, let go of habits or beliefs that could hinder me from fulfilling His purposes for my life. I also prayed for Him "to break my heart for whatever breaks Yours" so that I could be moved with compassion for people, just as the Bible often said of Jesus.

Well, I didn't really understand the gravity of what I was asking for until God started to answer the prayers. My life got turned inside out and upside down. God showed me the things He wanted to improve in my life, one after another, which left me feeling exposed, although in a good way, because I would rather be taught by God. He also revealed several (and sometimes unspeakable) things that happened around the world, which broke His heart. I had the most poignant dreams that I had ever had, up to that point in 2016, so much so that it became difficult to live "normally," as many gave me sleepless nights—not out of fear but from heartbreak that human beings committed such atrocities against one another and ultimately, against God. I spent many nights on my knees and in tears praying for God's intervention as well as salvation for people of all nations—fully persuaded that only the knowledge of Jesus Christ could truly liberate a person.

During the day, I was constantly travelling for work and relating with business-minded people in complex operational environments, whilst by night, God stirred me into offering intercessory prayers for the state of humanity and various situations around the world. Over several months, God revealed His heart and message for the church, people, and nations (collections of people).

By reason of the revelations and conversations that I had with God during this period, I came to understand two things about Him very deeply:

1. God is the definition of love. Everything He is and does stems from and is driven by love.
2. God is about and cares for people—specifically, the one individual.

It was also in the place of intercession and worship that He began to give me songs to write—psalms and choruses—which gave me a whole new understanding of worship and restored my passion for music. During this period, God also helped me to clearly understand that every phase of my life and experiences was for a purpose—one that wasn't just for me to learn from but to share with others and ultimately designed to be for His glory. By the end of that year, He gave me the direction to write this book—a concept with which I struggled for about a year after considering how personal some of the experiences were (as you would have read by now). The struggle was never a question of "if" but of "when," because I had already resolved that where God led, I would do all that I could to follow.

My personal conviction, by this time, was that (my) life has no meaning and will be unfulfilled unless it is lived for the purposes for which God designed and has continuously spared it. I am not suggesting that this is an easy path to stick with, but having concluded as such, I focus on how to align myself to His plans rather than spending time fighting or disobeying it outright. My mantra ever since has been "to do God's Will, God's Way, and by God's Word."

A MESSAGE TO THE CHURCH

In 2016, I had my third vision of the events that surround the rapture or second coming of Jesus, but it was the first time that it concluded with a message. The message was for the church. One thing that is consistent in all three visions is that those who are waiting for His return will get a sense of the rapture occurring some moments before it actually does. What I have always seen, however, is that we (people) are so occupied with everyday life that many miss the opportunity to repent in those final moments when salvation is still possible by accepting the price that Jesus paid for all, according to Romans 10:9, 10.

The same preoccupation with activities was happening in this vision, when the night sky became even darker to reveal chariots, angels, and other heavenly hosts poised for the angel that had the trumpet to blow the final sound, although that angel too was waiting on God's instruction for the exact moment to do so. It was against this backdrop in the sky, while looking up in realisation of what was about to happen, that I saw Jesus, and He said to me, "Tell My church, My bride, this message" (which I now write, but not verbatim).

The first thing Jesus spoke about is how the church has been distracted from doing what He has chosen her to be—a light in a world of darkness and pain and an expression of His Person in every place (Ephesians 3:10). Rather than set the example by teaching what we have been taught in His Word, we have conformed more to the way things work in our societies and allowed those practices to dictate the standard by which we live. "This ought not to be so," Jesus said. Pointing to a congregation that was supposed to be in a church service but had people sleeping, loitering, gossiping, bickering, and generally distracted, He continued to say, "Tell My church, My bride, to rise up and take her rightful place."

Jesus reminded me that we are the ones through whom God has chosen to propagate the good news of His kingdom and the living examples of His wisdom, power, beauty, and Person to the world. Therefore, we must be united in Spirit and in purpose, demonstrating His love, which is in our hearts by the Holy Spirit, in order to be effective in our purpose, which is to help the world see God clearly such that they too will be reconciled to Him. "The time is near," Jesus said. "Tell My church to arise and be alert." With that, the whole scene faded.

Since then, I have prayed that God enlightens my heart and helps me to see the church and the world through His eyes. Not only for myself do I pray this, but also for my brothers and sisters in the church all around the world. Something in Jesus' eyes as He spoke those words revealed His deep love for people and the sadness to see anyone perish, yet it is God's sovereign plan that we (the church) be the means by which He fully communicates that. In sending a mortal that has been transformed by the Holy Spirit to another mortal, God is able to demonstrate His love for all. There is a divine purpose for the church; it is more than a gathering of people or place where we meet with God. The church is Christ personified. However, it will be unable to fully express what that means until its people are first united in love. Through that (timeless) message, I started to understand this. I pray that we all do too, as we grow in unity and love for one another. It is as much a prayer for myself as it is for the body of Christ around the world.

A MESSAGE FOR YOU, THE INDIVIDUAL

God showed me in various dreams some of the pain that people around the world are going through. Sometimes, I woke up crying, but with a consciousness that the tears weren't mine. They were an expression of how the Holy Spirit felt about those issues. Through those dreams and expressions, I saw God in a whole new way. The dreams ranged from children in agony due to hunger, sickness, being orphaned without help, and so on; to young girls and boys being traded as sex slaves; mothers and fathers being subjected to watch their kids being tortured or afflicted and unable to do anything about it; the elderly being ill-treated; and so many situations of helplessness. Recalling some of the scenes I saw, my eyes well up even now, having known how much these break God's heart. The further cause of heartbreak is that we humans are doing this to one another. God made me understand that He has given "gifts" to each person to enable them to live a good life here on earth, contributing their own part to society at whatever scale. "Each person has a purpose and relevance," He said, "yet the wickedness and greed of some have caused an imbalance through the ages such that so many are in agony and unable to help themselves." Oh, how these displease God.

To those who are in these situations of helplessness and dire need, and think no one knows or seems to care about your plight, God would like you to know that He does. He sees you, hears you and feels your pain. Can I encourage you to look to Him as your Source, Deliverer, Redeemer, and Restorer? Sadly, not all things can be made perfect with our world because of the fundamental brokenness of sin, but we can put our hope in God, knowing that one day He will restore balance on the earth. I pray that you will know God's presence, peace, and provision for whatever that situation is. In Jesus' name, Amen.

Often times, when God shows me things, He will ask me to pray about them—which I do, having known that there is no barrier in the Spirit and being a recipient of such blessings myself. On one occasion when I was in the scene of the dream, a plane crash occurred that took the lives of the hundreds of people onboard, so I had started praying from the dream till I woke up. About three or four days later, I saw the exact same aircraft being reported as having crash-landed but saved by the pilot's skills—I smiled. Most important to God was that those human lives were not destroyed. It is unlikely that I was the only one in the whole world God would have shown that event, so we could pray to stop it from happening. The key is to pray when you get such promptings. Another example was while I was on the road and an ambulance was passing by. I felt the strong urge to pray for whoever was inside, and I did. God used that to give me an insight into ways to pray into the pains of others around me, so I made it a habit to say a word of prayer whenever I came across an emergency vehicle or situation. Well, that habit seemed silly until around 2019 on my way to work listening to Premier Christian Radio station. A lady phoned in to testify of how she was in an ambulance when God met with her to heal her body and save her soul. God wanted me to hear that so as to be encouraged to keep doing it.

"How about other plane crashes or sick people who die?" you might ask.

"Well, how about all of the wars and pains that seem to have overtaken our world today?" I would add.

Some things will remain mysteries, but we know that God gave us dominion and authority over the earth. Although sovereign, He will do nothing without at least one human being asking Him to intervene. This, therefore, is a call to action for the church—each and every one of us. Our world needs our prayers and our actions—just as Jesus responded to the needs around Him when He walked this earth. Ever since, I developed a "hunger" to see more of the demonstration of God's power in today's world, as Jesus told us in John 14:12 (NIV),

Very truly I tell you, whoever believes in me will do the works I have been doing, and they will do even greater things than these, because I am going to the Father.

To be a Christian is more than ticking boxes on a form or survey; it is to be Christ-like (Acts 11:19–30) in what we do and how we meet the needs around us by the power of the Holy Spirit already deposited in our spirits. It is the, dare I say, only adjective with which you should be most comfortable describing yourself if you are a follower of Jesus. We can help the world encounter God's presence by being there for them and to know God's heart by showing everyone His love. God cares about each and every living being, and so must we. Apostle Paul brilliantly describes who we are and what God calls us to in Romans 8—Creation is groaning in pain waiting with eager expectation for our manifestation (vv. 18–22). God is saying that now is the time for the church to rise up to the calling upon us. He is not looking for perfect people, because that is the work the Holy Spirit does in us, but He seeks those who are available.

A MESSAGE FOR NATIONS AND ORGANISATIONAL GROUPS

Some of the things God showed me in this regard are unspeakable. But to you who lead people at whatever level in society, and to those who "make" leaders, often unseen or unknown to many, God says (and I quote), "I see you." He said you will know what that means and that you have the opportunity to repent now.

To give brief pointers of things seen, as sensibly as I can describe them: on several occasions, I saw the rituals involved in the "making" of leaders across continents, especially the Western and Arab nations. In others, I saw how unsuspecting victims were lured to join cults (some made up of women only) through birthday and house parties, funded by political figures who stayed in the shadows, ensuring that the activities of such organisations could never be traced to them. The majority of the revelations in this regard were so clandestine that it took only those who were involved to know they actually happened. God also showed me how some people wanted to get out of these groups but were fearful of the oaths taken (often in blood) and destruction that could be meted out to them and their families.

Here's what God says to you (and this may sound blunt)—you have two options to choose from:

1. Remain there to continue enjoying whatever fame or benefits there are to it. But remember, even if they last a hundred years, they will surely end because you are bound to die one day, and you will lose out on an eternity of peace.

2. Take the bold step to leave and come under the wings of Jesus that He may save your soul. There is no obligation to expose the activities of that organisation (God will direct you appropriately), but you must cut all ties, including funding, with that organisation. Now, there is no guarantee that you will not lose your life when they come after you, but you are sure of truly resting in peace if that is the case. In Jesus, you will have eternal life, so He is giving you the opportunity to repent today. The choice is yours.

To those people who are funding the activities of these clandestine groups, the message to you is the same: Repent! God says that you can see for yourself that the impact of these organisations isn't for the prosperity of all citizens, nor do they promulgate peace and unity amongst people. God cares for people and will hold you accountable for every life lost or society destabilised by reason of these activities, for you are as culpable as those who do the execution.

To those who execute these activities, whatever the name or cause in which you are involved, anything predicated on violence for personal gain or that of a certain group is not of God. Therefore, understand a cause before you sign up for it. Sign up to nothing involving violence, no matter how lofty the cause is said to be. While you have a right to protect your home or national borders, you do not have any right to trample on or destabilise that which belongs to another person. And please, quit trying to defend God or instigate violence in His name—that dispensation is long, long, long, long gone!

To all involved in such activities as have been mentioned, God sees you and does not approve—be it on a one-on-one-neighbour scale or national level. The message to you is to repent today. God's arms of love are open and ready to receive you into His family. Jesus is knocking at the door of your heart—will you let Him in?

THINK ON THIS...

I have this mind—I live to die, but when I die, I will live again (because of Christ), and at that time, I will be truly free of being subject ever again to death. The life you have today is a gift, can only be lived once, and will imminently end someday. Therefore, it matters how you live it! In Christ Jesus, you are invited to live life unafraid of physical death, knowing that it is merely a rite of passage to a life eternal—free of the pain, sickness, war, disappointment, and all manner of shortcomings that human life is subjected to.

MY
PSALMS

Grateful me at 40

Celebrating 40 years of God's faithfulness

SOVEREIGN LORD

A psalm exalting and magnifying the Lord God above all else. Written by me in 2020.

Sovereign Lord, how great You are!
Lord of lords, there is none like You.
You have done many great things.
And Your wonders, my mind continually ponders.
Who am I, to deserve Your favour?
What have I done, to earn your deep affection?
Through the ages, You have kept Your promises.
Oh! Sovereign Lord, You alone are God.

THE FATHER

A poem of gratitude introducing the One who really needs no introduction, the very Essence of my being, the Pillar that has held my life in place, the Charter of my course, the perfect Completer, and the Sustainer of everything and everyone. Written by me in 2017.

Let me tell you a little bit about my Father.
He is the very source of all life; my very breath comes from Him!
He is full of joy and laughter; He is always laughing by the way.
A blast from His nostrils parts the seas,
His cough causes the mountains to quake, and
The sound of His voice is the soothe for raging storms.

Oh please, permit me to tell you who my Father really is.
He sits in Heaven and the earth is His footstool; He has the
longest legs ever!
His arms span the very breadth of the earth; they are longer actually.
A word from His lips brings light out of darkness,
His touch is far better than that of gold, and
The beat of His heart is the summation of love.

Spare me a moment to tell you of God, the Father.
He is the Beginning and End of all there is; we really

cannot do without Him!
He makes the sun shine on all that exist; He really
doesn't discriminate.
A visit from Him changes you forever,
His audience is the only one that truly matters, and
The thoughts of His mind is the cradle of creativity.

Please give me this chance to tell you of the one true Father.
He loves all without prejudice; it's why He gave His life for us all!
His desires are made of pure good; they are the purest actually.
A proceed from His loins is perfect peace,
His reign is far more enjoyable than man's best inventions, and
The knowledge of His Person is the key to finding yourself.

OK, allow me to make just one more boast of my loving Father.
He hears everyone and everything effectively; that is the coolest
immeasurable skill ever!
His character is too vast to put into words; there really isn't enough room
to describe Him.
A gentle Lamb and majestic Lion mashed in one entity that He is,
His salvation is embodied in a name most powerful—that is Jesus, and
The grace He bestows is the echo that draws us all back to this very thread
of my being—God the Father.

GOOD TO ME

A song of praise. Written by me in 2016.

Lord I will worship You
I will worship You
For You are good, so good to me
And I will honour You
Adore Your Holy Name
For You are good, so good to me

AFTERWORD

Through toils, turmoil, and victories alike, I have learnt of God and keep growing fond of His Person. My desire above all else is to know Him more, show Him more, and live a life that honours Him in every way—even when my days on earth draw near to an end, I still want to be singing His praise with excitement of the joy to finally see Him face to face. Oh, I dream of that moment and anticipate it more than anything else the world can ever offer. I dream that at the end of my life, I will be able to declare with all confidence that I have ran my race, that I have completed my cause, that I have laid hold and fulfilled every purpose for which Christ Jesus saved me, and that awaiting me is an eternity of peace in His presence (2 Timothy 4:7) where I shall no longer be subject to sin, strongholds, sicknesses, and the many wiles of Satan.

For our world, I dream of that day when children born no longer have to face the struggles of racism nor wake up to a day of war, hunger, and inequality of any kind. I look forward to a time when we seek more to identify what unites us as human beings, not the things that create divides. I pray for that day when the church will awaken to its full identity—putting aside the squabbles of denomination to work together for the singular purpose of reconciling people to God, and radiating the love of God everywhere per the examples Jesus laid down for us, rather than following after the prevailing culture. Yes, I do dream also of when government and leadership positions are not used as tools of oppression, self-aggrandisement, or to rob generations of a good future, but rather, they are seen as opportunities and privileges to serve a community and to pave ways for the next generation so they can attain greater heights than those before them. I eagerly look forward to that day when people will stop killing people for whatever reason or differences that we may have, but will choose to dialogue as the intelligent beings that we are and find common grounds for peaceful coexistence. A time when children can play freely in the streets again, neighbours laugh with neighbours no matter the diversity of their backgrounds, and everyone looks out for the good of the other. If the God who created us does not lord His ways upon us, then why do we oppress one another? Today presents an opportunity to make a different choice. Let us—individually and collectively—choose the way of love.

You have read part of my life story (hopefully learnt a thing or two from my experiences too) to know that I am still a work-in-progress. To summarise—I am tenacious by nature; was self-righteous and judgemental; faced many battles, diverse storms, and beat to the floor; stumbled on innumerable occasions; once lived life without clarity of purpose; and a recipient of God's lavish grace. Jesus found me in my brokenness and dirt, saved me, cleaned me up, gave me a purpose to live for, and keeps holding my hand so that even when I fall, I can easily find my way back to Him each time. God, in His infinite mercies, has bestowed on me the grace to have my life be used to demonstrate to the world a pinch of His all-encompassing love, the comfort of His peace, the joy of His salvation, and the beauty of His Person. Believe me when I say that I am nobody and could never in a million lifetimes earn or deserve the lavish love that God pours out upon me each day—not trying to be humble, just stating the truth. This is why I am convinced beyond any shadow of doubt that God is for you and is willing to do wonders with your life IF you let Him into your heart.

God is not seeking for you to be perfect because that is the work He does in you, through the Holy Spirit. He wants you to see and know that He loves you individually and unconditionally, and has made full provisions for you to be able to possess eternal life and live a purposeful life. He can show you the purpose for which you were born and lead you daily into the fullness of that purpose. My journey in Christ has been characterised by God's grace and an intense love, which increases the more conscious (and grateful) of it I become. This can be your story too.

Perhaps you would like to take a decision to invite Christ into your life or renew your faith in Him? Can I encourage you to take that step of faith and say a prayer, as the Scriptures teach in Romans 10:9–10. He will hear you and come to live in you. Should you not know what prayer to say first, why not use this simple one to get you started;

> *Father, I thank You for sending Jesus to die for my sins. Today, I repent of my sins and ask for Your forgiveness. I believe in my heart that Christ is my Saviour, and I boldly confess that Jesus is Lord. Today, I commit my life to You and invite You into my life as my personal Lord and Saviour. I receive the forgiveness of my sins in accordance with Your Word, and I pray that You give me Your Holy Spirit so that I may learn each day to walk with You and live a life that is well pleasing to You, fulfilling the very purpose for which You have called me in Christ Jesus. This Lord, I pray, with faith in Your Name Jesus. Amen.*

If you said that prayer or any other, confessing your sins and inviting Jesus into your life, believe that you are saved! To help you grow and know Him more, ask Him to teach you as you study the Bible for yourself. Find a church where the Bible is taught and the name of Jesus is exalted above all else, because in Him alone is salvation made possible for all.

Finally, my dear brothers and sisters, whatever your race, mother tongue, upbringing, experience, social status, or giftings, I encourage you to put God first in all that you do. For I am persuaded that when you start seeing Him for Who He is, you will see how much you are loved by Him and will also be excited to tell the world all about it. May the Lord keep you in perfect peace as you journey with and in Him daily in Jesus Name. Amen.

Now, to the Lord God Almighty, the One to Whom the sun, moon, and stars give their report, Who knows the storehouse of the rain, the One that is able TO DO and to Whom I will give account, the Father of all spirits, the Blesser of men, my Father and my God, my Provider and Sustainer, the Rock and Pillar that keeps my feet from falling, my Salvation and my Expectation, the Lover of my soul, Protector of my inheritance, the Glory and Lifter of my head, the most extraordinary Personality, the only One that I intensely adore, the King Eternal, Immortal, Invisible, and only Wise God, to You alone be praise in all generations, throughout all nations, and in Your church, both now and forevermore. Amen.

PLACES
REFERENCED
IN NIGERIA

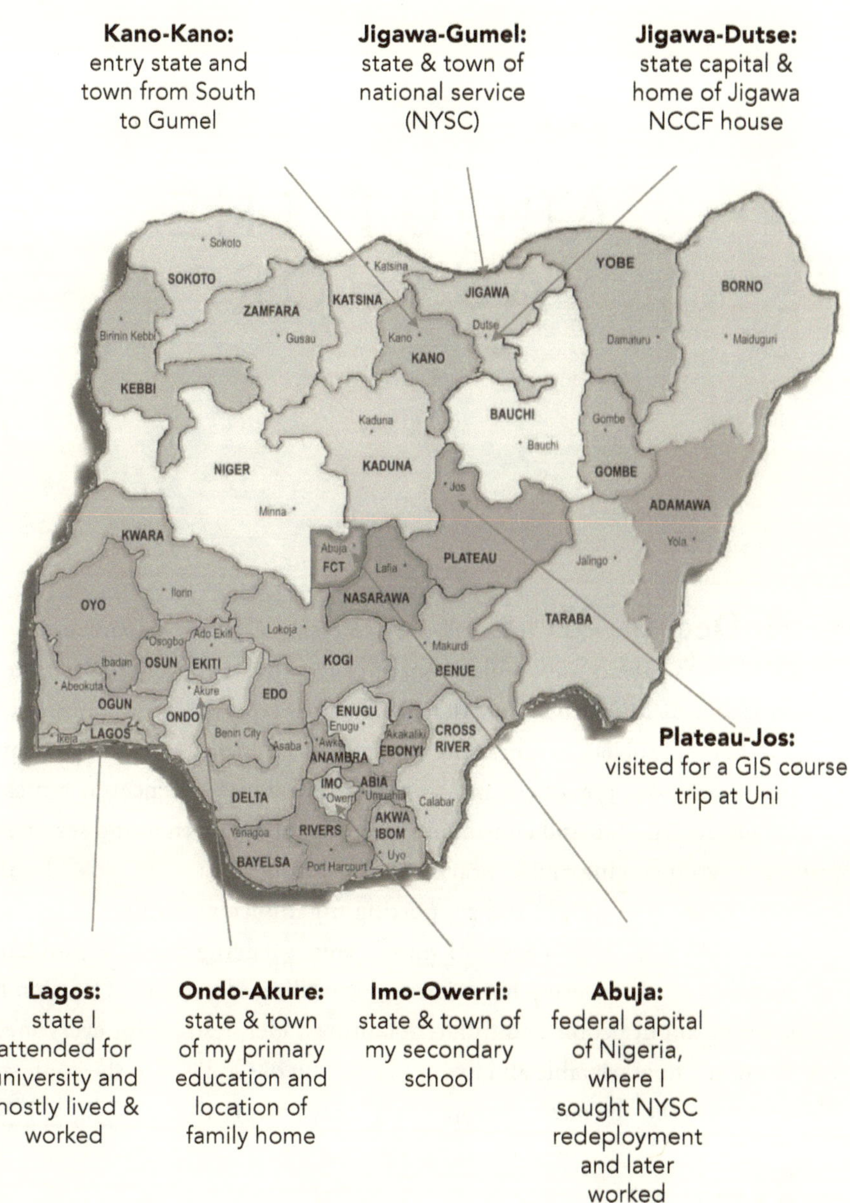

Map of Nigeria, showing the 36 States and their Capitals

ABOUT THE AUTHOR

MoDee (Mo) is a Christian and professional who is passionate about using one's talents and skills to serve others. She believes that no one is an island of knowledge and that by sharing experiences, we enrich one another and society at large. The first of four children, Mo grew up learning to look out for others and to reflect on own experiences as a means for self-instruction and continuous learning. She is often found serving in capacities involving music, prayer, teen or young adults, and kids. She also enjoys coaching people and supporting organisations into realising their goals. Mo is an ardent lover of music, enjoys solving business problems, storytelling, discovering histories, and travelling as part of her passion for learning about people and different cultures. Her desire is for everyone to know just how relatable and loving the person of God is—to the confessed Christian and the one still wondering what Jesus is all about.

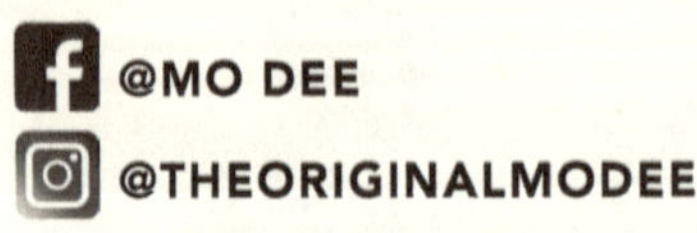

www.ingramcontent.com/pod-product-compliance
Lightning Source LLC
Chambersburg PA
CBHW031606060726
47600CB00007B/56/J